The District Controller's View
THE KENT COAST
LONDON - CHATHAM - CANTERBURY - DOVER/RAMSGATE

Although it was quite possible for boat trains to run to Dover Marine via Chatham and Faversham, under normal circumstances the basic service of five daily boats trains ran over ex-LCDR metals only for the first twelve miles of their journey, leaving the route at Bickley Junction where they transferred to the South Eastern main line. However, at the height of the summer when the number of boat trains could triple it was by no means unusual to find some of the additional trains being run via Faversham. The heaviest workings were the Night Ferry and the 09.00 and 10.00 expresses from Victoria; the last two being booked to Merchant Navy Pacifics while the Night Ferry was double-headed by a light Pacific and an L1 4-4-0. The two afternoon trains were light enough to warrant class 7 haulage and of these, the 13.30 Victoria to Dover 'Golden Arrow' is seen leaving Victoria behind Britannia Pacific 70014 'Iron Duke'.

In spite of having been merged into the South Eastern & Chatham Railway in 1899, the Southern Railway in 1923 and British Railways in 1948, eighty years after the first of these fusions the London, Chatham and Dover continued to remain operationally independent and even in the 1980's retained its own working timetables and self-contained train service while its stations and staff continued to be officially distinguished from those of the Southern Eastern; traffic circulars being prepared separately for the South Eastern and the Chatham.

The title of the main line, however, had changed over time and while the organisation continued to be known as the 'Chatham', the route was referred to as the 'Kent Coast'; a description that reflected the shift of focus from Dover - adequately served by the South Eastern - to Margate and Ramsgate.

The change of emphasis from Dover to Thanet dated back to the early years of the grouping when the Southern Railway had worked closely with house builders and estate agencies in order to persuade London office workers to migrate to coastal towns such as Herne Bay and Whitstable and thereby enjoy the dual benefits of working in London whilst living by the sea. The success of the scheme resulted in a frequent series of early-morning business expresses between Ramsgate and Cannon Street, several running non-stop from Whitstable with, until 1939, catering facilities being provided

in Pullman cars. In the evening the flow of traffic reversed with the army of season-ticket holders returning to the Kent Coast in a series of express departures that left London at roughly half-hourly intervals.

Between the morning and evening peak service, the backbone of the Kent Coast service was provided by a series of London-based workings which ran between Victoria and Ramsgate.

Other than the loss of some Pullman cars and the replacement of King Arthur 4-6-0's by a more modern locomotives, the service changed but little under British Railways and the last great change to effect the line prior to 1959 was that of 1938 when the third-rail was extended from Bickley Junction to Gillingham.

West of the Medway the electrification transformed services quite dramatically as multiple units replaced large numbers of 0-4-4T suburban locomotives, most of which were sent to replace older engines in the non-electrified areas. The extent to which one regarded electrification as an improvement depended very largely upon whether one was a passenger or a spectator.

Long distance services - which on the Chatham meant any train that ran for more than about 35 miles - continued to be worked in the traditional manner and no attempt was made to emulate the Metropolitan system by providing electric haulage over the London - Gillingham

section. These workings were divided between Ramsgate shed, which worked the Cannon Street business trains, and Stewarts Lane; responsible for most of the Victoria to Ramsgate off-peak expresses. Interesting as these workings were, they were as nothing compared to the secondary trains that ran in connection,worked as they were by the most variegated collection of motive power to be found anywhere in the country during the mid-fifties. Full details can be found on the pages following

Lest it be thought that these curiosities were confined to the rural areas of the district, the 16.32 and 17.21 expresses from Cannon Street to the coast were diagrammed to an L1 4-4-0 and a U1 2-6-0 respectively whilst the Sittingbourne section of the Pacific-hauled 17.45 ex Cannon Street flew merrily down the main line behind a class C 0-6-0 goods engine.

The volume of goods traffic was not insignificant although it was less noticeable than on lines north of the Thames. The main London yard was at Herne Hill whilst other flows centred on Hither Green, Bricklayers Arms and Hoo Junction. Tilmanstone and Snowdown collieries between Canterbury East and Dover provided work for quite a number of 2-6-0's whilst the much of the remainder of the goods timetable remained in the hands of efficient if venerable C class 0-6-0's right up until electrification. All in all, it was the railway of the connoisseur!

WORKING TIMETABLE : VICTORIA to RAMSGATE (1955)

m.ch	Engine	l in	22.46				00.15		23.42	00.56	22.00		23.40	00.56	00.56	01.00	01.20
From			CX				H. Via		CX	Q'boro	H. Gn		H. Hill	Q'boro	Q'boro	BLA	H. Via
Class			LE	Pass	Goods	Goods	Pass	Pass	Pass	Goods	Goods	Goods	Goods	Goods	Goods	Goods	Pass
Engine		l in:	2-6-2T	EMU	N 2-6-0	C 0-6-0	EMU	EMU	EMU	C 0-6-0	N 2-6-0	C 0-6-0	C 0-6-0	C 0-6-0	C 0-6-0	N 2-6-0	EMU
0.00	**VICTORIA**								00.25								
3.14	Brixton	567							00.31								
3.76	**Herne Hill**	176				23.40			00.35								01.35
5.02	W. Dulwich	129							00.38								01.37
5.57	Sydenham Hill	101							00.40								
7.15	Penge East	-268							00.44								01.42
7.66	Kent House	-116							00.46								01.44
8.53	Beckenham Jcn	213				00/05			00.48								01.48
						Main	Main										Local
10.03	Shortlands	1545					00.43										01.51
10.71	**BROMLEY SOUTH**	106					00.45										01.52
10.71	**BROMLEY SOUTH**					00/15	00.46										01.53
11.76	Bickley	95				00/22	00.49										01.56
12.24	Bickley Jcn	380					00/50										01.57
13.17	St Mary Cray Jcn	380				00/26										01/39	
14.57	St Mary Cray	-517				00/31											
17.31	**SWANLEY**	413				00/39										01/49	
20.41	Farningham Road	-139				00.49							01.17				
23.30	Fawkham	206															
25.76	Meopham	165															
26.71	Sole Street	220											01.35			02/11	
30.72	Cuxton Road	-122															
33.01	Rochester Bge Jcn	-191	00/05						00/57							02/23	
33.41	**Chatham Goods**										01.00	01.25	01.55			02.28	
33.61	Rochester	-191	00.06														
33.61	Rochester		00.07						00/58		01/03	-1/27					
34.25	**CHATHAM**	147	00.09						00.59			01.30					
34.25	**CHATHAM**		00.10						01.00		01/08	01.40					
35.75	**GILLINGHAM**	168	00.13						01.03		01.14	01.50					
35.75	**GILLINGHAM**										01.28						
38.74	Rainham	-1454															
41.44	Newington	1128															
43.68	Western Jcn	-309															
44.19	Eastern Jcn	-309								01/37							
44.59	**SITTINGBOURNE**	-309								01.40	01.52						
44.59	**SITTINGBOURNE**				23.55						02.11			02.26			
45.40	Murston Sdgs	-1258												02.31	02.55		
47.74	Teynham	-1258															
51.77	**FAVERSHAM**	586			00.10						02.27				03.10		
51.77	**FAVERSHAM**				00.30						02.48						
54.77	Graveney Sdgs	-528															
59.06	Whitstable	7119															
60.45	Chestfield	463															
62.58	**HERNE BAY**	1719															
62.58	**HERNE BAY**																
70.56	Birchington	2942															
72.35	Westgate	-1609															
73.69	**MARGATE**	-688															
73.69	**MARGATE**		00.10														
77.09	Broadstairs	147															
78.26	Dumpton Park	-208															
79.21	**RAMSGATE**	247	00.25														
	Destination		Loco		S'well		Orp				Dover						Orp

WORKING TIMETABLE : FAVERSHAM to DOVER (1955)

m.ch	Engine	l in	23.55	23.55	22.00	22.00	22.00
Train			S'bn	S'bn	H. Gn	H. Gn	H. Gn
Class			Goods	Goods	Light	Goods	Goods
Engine		l in:	N 2-6-0	N 2-6-0	N 2-6-0	N 2-6-0	N 2-6-0
51.77	**FAVERSHAM**		00.30			02.48	
55.18	Selling	126					
61.65	**CANTERBURY E.**	-273					
61.65	**CANTERBURY E.**		01/05			03/23	
64.58	Bekesbourne	236					
67.60	Adisham	349					
68.66	Aylesham	115					
69.60	Snowdown	164	01.35	01.50		03.48	04.25
71.60	Shepherdswell	412		01.58	02.15	04.35	04.55
75.09	Kearsney	-133					
77.23	**DOVER PRIORY**	-107			02/35		05/15
	Destination				Loco		Town

WORKING TIMETABLE : SHEERNESS to SITTINGBOURNE (1955)

m.ch	Engine			00.56
Train				Q'boro
Class		Light	Goods	Goods
Engine			C 0-6-0	C 0-6-0
0.00	**SHEERNESS**	00.30		
1.79	Queenborough	00.36	00.56	
3.76	Swale			
4.33	Redham Dock		01.03	01.25
5.75	Kemsley			
7.08	Middle Jcn			01/35
7.30	Eastern Jcn			01/37
7.70	**SITTINGBOURNE**			01.40
	Destination			Fav

WORKING TIMETABLE : RAMSGATE to VICTORIA (1955)

m.ch	Engine	1 in:	Goods	Pass	23.55 Gill Goods	20.00 Dover Goods	17.20 A'ford Goods	19.35 S'cliffe Goods	Goods	23.55 Gill Goods	23.55 Gill Goods	01.05 S'brn Goods	18.50 Dover Goods	Goods	Goods	18.50 Dover Goods
			C 0-6-0	EMU	C 0-6-0	N 2-6-0	C 0-6-0	N 2-6-0	2-6-2T	C 0-6-0	C 0-6-0	EI 4-4-0	N 2-6-0	2MT & C	N 2-6-0	N 2-6-0
0.00	**RAMSGATE**															
0.75	Dumpton Park	-247														
2.12	Broadstairs	208														
5.32	**MARGATE**	-147														
5.32	**MARGATE**															
6.66	Westgate	688														
8.45	Birchington	1609														
17.43	**HERNE BAY**	-2942														
17.45	**HERNE BAY**															
18.56	Chestfield	-1719														
20.15	Whitstable	-463														
24.24	Graveney	-7119														
26.44	British Fruit	528														
27.24	**FAVERSHAM**	528						00.50								
27.24	**FAVERSHAM**					23.50							01.15	02.00	02.30	
31.27	Teynham	-586													02.42	
33.42	**SITTINGBOURNE**	1258												02.20		
33.42	**SITTINGBOURNE**					00/10		01.05					01/35	02.50		
34.02	Eastern Jcn	309														
34.26	Western Jcn	309														
37.57	Newington	309														
40.27	Rainham	-1128														
43.26	**GILLINGHAM**	1454				00.35		01.28					02L02			
43.26	**GILLINGHAM**		23.55			00.55						01.42	02L15			
44.76	**CHATHAM**	-168														
44.76	**CHATHAM**		00/00			01/00						01/50	02/18			
45.40	Rochester	-147														
45.40	Rochester		00/04			01/05						01/55	02/21			
	Chatham Goods		00.06		00.35								02.23			03.05
46.20	Rochester Bge Jcn	191			00/40	01/08						02/00				03/08
48.29	Cuxton Road	191														
52.30	Sole Street	122			01/10							02/27				
53.25	Meopham	-220														
54.54	Longfield Sdg	-165														
55.71	Fawkham	-165														
58.60	Farningham Road	-206			01.22					01.43						
61.70	**SWANLEY**	139					01.25			01/57		02/46				
64.42	St Mary Cray	-413					01/32			02.05	02.25	02.52				
66.04	St Mary Cray Jcn	517					01/35			02/29						
				Local						Main						
66.76	Bickley Jcn	-380		00/22												
67.25	Bickley	-380														
68.30	**BROMLEY SOUTH**	-95		00.25												
68.30	**BROMLEY SOUTH**			00.26						02/35						
69.18	Shortlands	-106		00/28												
70.48	Beckenham Jcn	-1545		00.31						02/42						
71.35	Kent House	-213														
72.06	Penge East	116		00.34												
73.44	Sydenham Hill	268														
74.19	W. Dulwich	-101														
75.25	**Herne Hill**	-129		00/39						03.05						
76.07	Brixton	-176														
79.21	**VICTORIA**	-567														
	Destination			H. Via		H. Grn	H. Grn							S'ness		H. Jcn

WORKING TIMETABLE : DOVER - FAVERSHAM (1955)

m.ch	Engine	1 in:	19.35 S'cliffe Goods N 2-6-0	Light N 2-6-0
1.06	**DOVER PRIORY**			02/37
1.53	Dover Gas	107		
3.21	Kearsney	107		
6.53	Shepherdswell	133		02.49
8.52	Snowdown	-412	00.00	
9.44	Aylesham	-164		
10.49	Adisham	-115		
13.34	Bekesbourne	-349		
16.46	**CANTERBURY E.**	-236		
16.46	**CANTERBURY E.**		00/20	
23.12	Selling	273		
26.33	**FAVERSHAM**	-126	00.50	
	Destination			

WORKING TIMETABLE : SITTINGBOURNE - SHEERNESS (1955)

m.ch	Engine		02.00 Fav Goods C & 2MTT	02.00 Fav Goods C & 2MTT
0.00	**SITTINGBOURNE**		02.50	
0.40	Eastern Jcn			
0.62	Middle Jcn			
1.75	Kemsley			
3.37	Redham Dock		03.02	03.25
3.74	Swale			
5.71	Queenborough			03.40
7.70	**SHEERNESS**			
	Destination			

WORKING TIMETABLE : VICTORIA to RAMSGATE (1955)

Train	00.40	00.40	01.10	01.10		01.51		02.20	01.50	03.10	01.00					03.00	03.00
From	Snodl'd	Snodl'd	BLA	BLA		H. Via		B'friars	H. Hill	H. Grn	BLA					H. Via	H. Via
Class	Goods	Goods	Goods	Goods	Goods	Pass	Goods	Pass	Goods	Goods	Goods	Goods	Goods	Pass	Pass	Pass	Pass
Engine	2-6-4T	2-6-4T	N 2-6-0	UI 2-6-0	N 2-6-0	EMU	N 2-6-0	EMU	N 2-6-0	C 0-6-0	C 0-6-0	C 0-6-0	N 2-6-0	L 4-4-0	2-6-4T	EI 4-4-0	UI 2-6-0
VICTORIA																	
Brixton																	
Herne Hill					01.35	01.50		02.30		02.50							
W. Dulwich								02.33									
Sydenham Hill																	
Penge East								02.38		03.10							
Kent House								02.40									
Beckenham Jcn					01/57		02/12	02.42									
(line)					Main	Local	Main	Main									
Shortlands					02.03	02.19	02/18	02.46									
BROMLEY SOUTH						02.21											
BROMLEY SOUTH					02.07	02.23	02/22	02.48									
Bickley					02/14	02.26	02/29	02.51									
Bickley Jcn						02.28		02.52									
St Mary Cray Jcn			01/54		02/17		02/32			03/31							
St Mary Cray			01/58		02/21		02.37		02.57	03/34							
SWANLEY			02/06		02/29				03.07	03/44							
Farningham Road																	
Fawkham																	
Meopham																	
Sole Street			02/29		02.54												
Cuxton Road																	
Rochester Bge Jcn	02.35															04/17	
Chatham Goods												03.45	03.58				
Rochester																04.18	
Rochester	02/40		02/43		03/16						03/47	04/01				04.19	
CHATHAM		02.48		03w19													04.21
CHATHAM	02/45		02.53		03w24						03/50	04/05				04.25	
GILLINGHAM			03.03		03.32												04.29
GILLINGHAM	02/50		03.25		03.44						03/58	04/10				04.30	
Rainham	02.57	03.07									04/05	04.20					
Newington											04/11						
Western Jcn											04/14						
Eastern Jcn																	
SITTINGBOURNE					04.06											04.42	
SITTINGBOURNE		03.25	03/45		04.30											04.45	
Murston Sdgs																	
Teynham																	
FAVERSHAM		03.40	03.59		04.45											04.56	
FAVERSHAM		03.50		04.20												04.59	05.05
Graveney Sdgs																	
Whitstable																05.12	
Chestfield																	
HERNE BAY																05.19	
HERNE BAY				04/41												05.23	
Birchington																05.35	
Westgate																05.41	
MARGATE				05.10												05.47	
MARGATE														05.12	05.30	05.54	
Broadstairs														05.22	05.37	06.00	
Dumpton Park														05.26	05.41	06.07	
RAMSGATE														05.29	05.44	06.10	
Destination		S'down				Orp		Orp		A'ford	Q'boro			C'bury	Ashford		Dover

WORKING TIMETABLE : FAVERSHAM to DOVER (1955)

Train	02.18	
From	Snod	
Class	Goods	Pass
Engine	2-6-4T	UI 2-6-0
FAVERSHAM	03.50	05.05
Selling		
CANTERBURY E.		05.20
CANTERBURY E.	04.30	05.26
Bekesbourne		
Adisham		05.36
Aylesham		
Snowdown	04.50	05.42
Shepherdswell		05.47
Kearsney		05.55
DOVER PRIORY		06.00
Destination		

WORKING TIMETABLE : SHEERNESS to SITTINGBOURNE (1955)

Train	
From	
Class	
Engine	
SHEERNESS	
Queenborough	
Swale	
Redham Dock	
Kemsley	
Middle Jcn	
Eastern Jcn	
SITTINGBOURNE	
Destination	

WORKING TIMETABLE : RAMSGATE to VICTORIA (1955)

Train	01.05	21.35	01.05	03.30	02.30				04.02	03.40	02.30		03.25	02.30	05.00			05.07
From	S'brn	Dover	S'brn	Orp	Fav				Orp	Sutton	Fav		S'oaks	Ashford	Orp		Loco	Orp
Class	Goods	Goods	Goods	ECS	Goods	Goods	Pass	Pass	Pass	Pass	Goods	P&P	Goods	Pass	Pass	Pass	LE	Pass
Engine	E1 4-4-0	N15	E1 4-4-0	EMU	N 2-6-0	N 2-6-0	EMU	EMU	EMU	EMU	N 2-6-0	H 0-4-4T	N 2-6-0	L 4-4-0	EMU	EMU	L 4-4-0	EMU
RAMSGATE														03.31			04.15	
Dumpton Park																		
Broadstairs																		
MARGATE														03.40			04.32	
MARGATE																		
Westgate																		
Birchington																		
HERNE BAY																		
HERNE BAY																		
Chestfield																		
Whitstable																		
Graveney																		
British Fruit																		
FAVERSHAM																		
FAVERSHAM																		
Teynham					02.55													
SITTINGBOURNE					03.05													
SITTINGBOURNE					03.20													
Eastern Jcn																		
Western Jcn																		
Newington																		
Rainham					03.35						03.57							
GILLINGHAM											04.05							
GILLINGHAM							04.00			04.30	04.41							
CHATHAM							04.03				04.45							
CHATHAM							04.04			04/35	04.46							
Rochester							04.05				04.48							
Rochester							04.06			04/40	04.49							
Chatham Goods										04.45								
Rochester Bge Jcn							04/07				04/50							
Cuxton Road																		
Sole Street																		
Meopham																		
Longfield																		
Fawkham																		
Farningham Road																		
SWANLEY		03/25							03.59									
St Mary Cray	03.05	03/21				03.45			04.04									
St Mary Cray Jcn	03/09	03/35				03/49			04/06									
	Main	Local							Main	Local					Local			Local
Bickley Jcn		03/35							04/07	04/07					05/05			05/12
Bickley	03.14	03.35	<u>03.37</u>						04.08	04.09			04.40		05.06			05.13
BROMLEY SOUTH									04.11	04.12					05.08			05.15
BROMLEY SOUTH			03/40						04.12	04.18			04/45		05.09			05.16
Shortlands									04.15	04.20					05.12			05.19
Beckenham Jcn			03/46							04.23					05.15			05.22
Kent House										04.25					05.17			05.24
Penge East										04.27					05.19			05.26
Sydenham Hill										04.30					05.22			05.29
W. Dulwich										04.32					05.24			05.31
Herne Hill			04.08							04.35	04.35		05.15		05.26	05.30		05.33
Brixton										04.38						05.33		
VICTORIA										04.45						05.38		
Destination		H. Grn			H. Grn		CX	H. Via	H. Via		G'end				H. Via			Bfs

WORKING TIMETABLE : DOVER - FAVERSHAM (1955)

Train	
From	
Class	
Engine	
DOVER PRIORY	
Dover Gas	
Kearsney	
Shepherdswell	
Snowdown	
Aylesham	
Adisham	
Bekesbourne	
CANTERBURY E.	
CANTERBURY E.	
Selling	
FAVERSHAM	
Destination	

WORKING TIMETABLE : SITTINGBOURNE - SHEERNESS (1955)

Train	01.00
From	BLA
Class	Goods
Engine	C 0-6-0
SITTINGBOURNE	
Eastern Jcn	
Middle Jcn	04/16
Kemsley	
Redham Dock	
Swale	
Queenborough	04.35
SHEERNESS	
Destination	

WORKING TIMETABLE : VICTORIA to RAMSGATE (1955)

Train	04.21	03.58	01.10		03.15		02.50	04.05		04.05	04.05		04.50	04.05	03.58	05.00	05.31
From	Strood	Chatham	BLA		H. Via		H. Hill	H. Grn		H. Grn	H. Grn		H. Via	H. Grn	Chatham	H. Via	S'ness
Class	News	Goods	Goods	XP	Pass	Pcls	Goods	Goods	Pass	Goods	Goods	Goods	Pass	Goods	Goods	Pass	Pass
Engine	H 0-4-4T	N 2-6-0	U1 2-6-0	V 4-4-0	EMU	BR5 4-6-0	C 0-6-0	C 0-6-0	EMU	C 0-6-0	C 0-6-0	C 0-6-0	EMU	C 0-6-0	N 2-6-0	EMU	2-6-2T
VICTORIA						03.30			04.52								
Brixton									04.58								
Herne Hill					03.28	03/40			05.00				05.03				
W. Dulwich					03.30								05.05				
Sydenham Hill													05.08				
Penge East					03.35		04.08						05.11				
Kent House					03.37								05.13				
Beckenham Jcn					03.39	03/50	04/15						05.17				
					Local	Main	Main						Main			Local	
Shortlands					03.42		04/20						05.21				
BROMLEY SOUTH					03.44		04/25						05.24				
BROMLEY SOUTH					03.45								05.26				05.32
Bickley					03.48								05.29				05.35
Bickley Jcn					03/50	03/58							05/31				05/37
St Mary Cray Jcn						03/59		04/34									
St Mary Cray							04.38			04.55							05.40
SWANLEY						04/05				05.03	05.05						05.45
Farningham Road												05.15		05.33			
Fawkham																	
Meopham																	
Sole Street						04/22											
Cuxton Road						04/27											
Rochester Bge Jcn	04/23					04/31											
Chatham Goods																	
Rochester	04.24					04.33											
Rochester	04.27					04.46											
CHATHAM	04.29					04.50											
CHATHAM	04.35					04.54											
GILLINGHAM	04.39					04.58											
GILLINGHAM						05.03						05.20					
Rainham		04.50										05.26					
Newington		04/56															
Western Jcn																	
Eastern Jcn																	05/53
SITTINGBOURNE		05.05				05.16											05.54
SITTINGBOURNE						05.20									05.40		
Murston Sdgs																	
Teynham															05/46		
FAVERSHAM						05.31									05.55		
FAVERSHAM						05.36											
Graveney Sdgs																	
Whitstable						05.46											
Chestfield																	
HERNE BAY						06.03											
HERNE BAY						06.13											
Birchington						06.25											
Westgate						06.34											
MARGATE						06.43											
MARGATE			06.50	07.03		07.10											
Broadstairs				07.09		07.17											
Dumpton Park				07.14													
RAMSGATE			07.00	07.17		07.31											
Destination				C. St		Orp							Orp	G'end		S'oaks	

WORKING TIMETABLE : FAVERSHAM to DOVER (1955)

	Pass
Train	
From	
Class	Pass
Engine	2-6-4T
FAVERSHAM	
Selling	
CANTERBURY E.	
CANTERBURY E.	06.20
Bekesbourne	06.26
Adisham	06.32
Aylesham	06.36
Snowdown	06.40
Shepherdswell	06.46
Kearsney	06.53
DOVER PRIORY	06.58
Destination	Folk

WORKING TIMETABLE : SHEERNESS to SITTINGBOURNE (1955)

	Pass
Train	
From	
Class	Pass
Engine	2-6-2T
SHEERNESS	05.31
Queenborough	05.37
Swale	05.43
Redham Dock	
Kemsley	05.47
Middle Jcn	05/51
Eastern Jcn	05/53
SITTINGBOURNE	05.54
Destination	

WORKING TIMETABLE : RAMSGATE to VICTORIA (1955)

			ECS	04.40		02.30	03.30	05.22			Loco		04.42	05.42				
From				F'sham		Fav	S'well	Orp					Dover	Orp				
Class	Pass	Pass	P&P	Pass	Pass	Goods	Goods	Pass	Goods	Pass	Light	Pass	Pass	Pass	Pass	Pass	Pass	Motor
Engine	2-6-2T	EMU	H 0-4-4T	2-6-2T	EMU	N 2-6-0	C 0-6-0	EMU	C 0-6-0	L 4-4-0	2-6-4T	EMU	2-6-4T	EMU	EMU	EMU	2-6-2T	H 0-4-4T
RAMSGATE										04.34	04.38							
Dumpton Park										04.38								
Broadstairs										04.42								
MARGATE										04.48	04.57							
MARGATE										(04.57)								
Westgate																		
Birchington																		
HERNE BAY																		
HERNE BAY																		
Chestfield																		
Whitstable																		
Graveney																		
British Fruit																		
FAVERSHAM							05L00						05.34					
FAVERSHAM	04.40						05L10											
Teynham	04.47																	
SITTINGBOURNE	04.55						05.30											
SITTINGBOURNE	(05.05)				05.05												05.51	
Eastern Jcn					05/06												05/52	
Western Jcn																		
Newington																		
Rainham																		05.52
GILLINGHAM																		05.57
GILLINGHAM			05.05		05.15					05.28	05.40		05.52					
CHATHAM			05.09		05.18					05.31	05.43		05.55					
CHATHAM				05.19						05.33	05.45		05.57					
Rochester				05.20						05.34	05.46		05.58					
Rochester				05.21						05.35	05.47		05.59					
Chatham Goods						05.25												
Rochester Bge Jcn				05/22		05/27				05/36	05/48		06/00					
Cuxton Road																		
Sole Street																		
Meopham																		
Longfield																		
Fawkham																		
Farningham Road																		
SWANLEY	05.07															05.45		
St Mary Cray	05.12															05.50		
St Mary Cray Jcn	05/14															05/52		
	Main							Local						Local	Mail			
Bickley Jcn	05/15							05/27						05/47	05/53			
Bickley	05.16							05.29						05.49	05.54			
BROMLEY SOUTH	05.18							05.31						05.51	05.56			
BROMLEY SOUTH	05.19							05.32	05.35					05.52	05.57			
Shortlands	05.22							05.34						05.55	06.00			
Beckenham Jcn								05.37						05.58				
Kent House								05.39						06.00				
Penge East								05.41						06.02				
Sydenham Hill								05.45						06.05				
W. Dulwich								05.46						06.07				
Herne Hill								05.49						06.09				
Brixton								05.51										
VICTORIA								05.56										
Destination			Bfs	S'ness	Strood	H Jcn			B'ham	C. St	S'ness		Strood	H. Via	H. Via	C. St		

WORKING TIMETABLE : DOVER - FAVERSHAM (1955)

	03.30		
From	S'well		
Class	Goods		Pass
Engine	N 2-6-0	N 2-6-0	2-6-4T
DOVER PRIORY			04.42
Dover Gas			
Kearsney			04.49
Shepherdswell	03.30		04.56
Snowdown	03.45	04.05	05.01
Aylesham			
Adisham			05.07
Bekesbourne			
CANTERBURY E.			05.16
CANTERBURY E.		04/30	05.18
Selling			
FAVERSHAM		05.00	05.34
Destination		Sbn	Fav

WORKING TIMETABLE : SITTINGBOURNE - SHEERNESS (1955)

	04.40	02.00	
From	Fav	Fav	
Class	Pass	Goods	Pass
Engine	2-6-2T	C & 2MTT	2-6-2T
SITTINGBOURNE	05.05		05.51
Eastern Jcn	05/06		05/52
Middle Jcn	05/07		05/53
Kemsley			05.56
Redham Dock			
Swale			06.02
Queenborough	05.16	05.45	06.06
SHEERNESS	05.23	05.53	06.15
Destination			

7

WORKING TIMETABLE : VICTORIA to RAMSGATE (1955)

Station	ECS (N 2-6-0)	06.35 S'ness — Motor Pass (H 0-4-4T)	05.27 Strood — Pass (2-6-2T)	Pass — EMU	XP (WC)	Pass (L 4-4-0)	Pass (2-6-2T)	05.30 H. Jcn — Goods (C 0-6-0)	05.20 Gill — Goods (C 0-6-0)	06.10 Strood — Pass (EMU)	Goods (N 2-6-0)	05.45 Chatham — Pass (2 × 2-6-2T)	Goods (N 2-6-0)	Pass (2-6-4T)	05.00 CX — Pass (EMU)	Pass (BR5 4-6-0)	Pass (EMU)
VICTORIA															05.10		
Brixton																	
Herne Hill															05.22		
W. Dulwich																	
Sydenham Hill																	
Penge East																	
Kent House																	
Beckenham Jcn															05/31 Main		05.37 Main
Shortlands															05/33		05/41
BROMLEY SOUTH															05.35		05.43
BROMLEY SOUTH															05.40		05.52
Bickley																	05.55
Bickley Jcn															05/45		05/57
St Mary Cray Jcn																	
St Mary Cray																	
SWANLEY															05.55		
Farningham Road																	
Fawkham																	
Meopham																	
Sole Street															06.18		
Cuxton Road															06.23		
Rochester Bge Jcn			05/29					05/47		06/12				06/23	06/27		
Chatham Goods								05.50									
Rochester			05.30							06.13				06.24	06.28		
Rochester			05.31							06.14				06.25	06.31		
CHATHAM			05.32							06.16				06.28	06.33		
CHATHAM			05.34				05.45			06.18				06.30	06.38		
GILLINGHAM			05.37				05.49			06.21				06.33	06.42		
GILLINGHAM		05.35					05.50								06.44		
Rainham		05.40					05.56		06.15						06.51		
Newington							06.02		06.23						06.57		
Western Jcn																	
Eastern Jcn			06/54														
SITTINGBOURNE			06.55				06.08								07.03		
SITTINGBOURNE	06.14						(06.16)					06.16			07.06		
Murston Sdgs																	
Teynham												06.23			07.13		
FAVERSHAM												06.31			07.21		
FAVERSHAM											06.25		06.40		07.29		
Graveney Sdgs																	
Whitstable															07.39		
Chestfield															07.47		
HERNE BAY															07.52		
HERNE BAY															07.55		
Birchington															08.07		
Westgate															08.13		
MARGATE															08.19		
MARGATE					07.36	07.58								08.10	08.24		
Broadstairs					07.43	08.05								08.17	08.32		
Dumpton Park					07.47	08.09								08.21	08.39		
RAMSGATE					07.50	08.12								08.24	08.42		
Destination	Dover				C. Cross	Hastings					S'down		Dover	Ashford			Orp

WORKING TIMETABLE : FAVERSHAM to DOVER (1955)

Station	Pass (N 2-6-0)	Goods (N 2-6-0)	Goods (N 2-6-0)	06.40 Fav — Goods (N 2-6-0)
FAVERSHAM	06.14	06.25	06.40	
Selling	06.21		06.56	07.20
CANTERBURY E.	06.32			07.37
CANTERBURY E.	06.38	07/00		(08.45)
Bekesbourne	06.45			
Adisham	06.52			
Aylesham	06.56			
Snowdown	07.00	07.25		
Shepherdswell	07.06			
Kearsney	07.15			
DOVER PRIORY	07.20			
Destination				

WORKING TIMETABLE : SHEERNESS to SITTINGBOURNE (1955)

Station	Pass (2-6-2T)
SHEERNESS	06.35
Queenborough	06.41
Swale	06.46
Redham Dock	
Kemsley	06.50
Middle Jcn	06.53
Eastern Jcn	06/54
SITTINGBOURNE	06.55
Destination	

WORKING TIMETABLE : RAMSGATE to VICTORIA (1955)

Train			ECS	04.40		02.30	03.30	05.22					04.42		05.42				
From				F'sham		Fav	S'well	Orp			Loco		Dover		Orp				
Class	Pass	Pass	P&P	Pass	Pass	Goods	Goods	Pass	Goods	Pass	Light	Pass	Pass	Pass	Pass	Pass	Pass	Pass	Motor
Engine	2-6-2T	EMU	H 0-4-4T	2-6-2T	EMU	N 2-6-0	C 0-6-0	EMU	C 0-6-0	L 4-4-0	2-6-4T	EMU	2-6-4T	EMU	EMU	EMU	EMU	2-6-2T	H 0-4-4T
RAMSGATE										04.34	04.38								
Dumpton Park										04.38									
Broadstairs										04.42									
MARGATE										04.48	04.57								
MARGATE											(04.57)								
Westgate																			
Birchington																			
HERNE BAY																			
HERNE BAY																			
Chestfield																			
Whitstable																			
Graveney																			
British Fruit																			
FAVERSHAM							05L00						05.34						
FAVERSHAM	04.40						05L10												
Teynham	04.47																		
SITTINGBOURNE	04.55						05.30												
SITTINGBOURNE	(05.05)			05.05														05.51	
Eastern Jcn				05/06														05/52	
Western Jcn																			
Newington																			
Rainham																			05.52
GILLINGHAM																			05.57
GILLINGHAM			05.05	05.15								05.28	05.40		05.52				
CHATHAM			05.09	05.18								05.31	05.43		05.55				
CHATHAM				05.19								05.33	05.45		05.57				
Rochester				05.20								05.34	05.46		05.58				
Rochester				05.21								05.35	05.47		05.59				
Chatham Goods						05.25													
Rochester Bge Jcn				05/22		05/27						05/36	05/48		06/00				
Cuxton Road																			
Sole Street																			
Meopham																			
Longfield																			
Fawkham																			
Farningham Road																			
SWANLEY		05.07												05.45					
St Mary Cray		05.12												05.50					
St Mary Cray Jcn		05/14												05/52					
		Main						Local						Local	Mail				
Bickley Jcn		05/15						05/27						05/47	05/53				
Bickley		05.16						05.29						05.49	05.54				
BROMLEY SOUTH		05.18						05.31						05.51	05.56				
BROMLEY SOUTH		05.19						05.32	05.35					05.52	05.57				
Shortlands		05.22						05.34						05.55	06.00				
Beckenham Jcn								05.37						05.58					
Kent House								05.39						06.00					
Penge East								05.41						06.02					
Sydenham Hill								05.45						06.05					
W. Dulwich								05.46						06.07					
Herne Hill								05.49						06.09					
Brixton								05.51											
VICTORIA								05.56											
Destination		Bfs		S'ness	Strood		H Jcn		B'ham			C. St	S'ness	Strood	H. Via	H. Via	C. St		

WORKING TIMETABLE : DOVER - FAVERSHAM (1955)

Train		03.30	
From		S'well	
Class		Goods	Pass
Engine	N 2-6-0	N 2-6-0	2-6-4T
DOVER PRIORY			04.42
Dover Gas			
Kearsney			04.49
Shepherdswell	03.30		04.56
Snowdown	03.45	04.05	05.01
Aylesham			
Adisham			05.07
Bekesbourne			
CANTERBURY E.			05.16
CANTERBURY E.		04/30	05.18
Selling			
FAVERSHAM		05.00	05.34
Destination		Sbn	Fav

WORKING TIMETABLE : SITTINGBOURNE - SHEERNESS (1955)

Train	04.40	02.00	
From	Fav	Fav	
Class	Pass	Goods	Pass
Engine	2-6-2T	C & 2MTT	2-6-2T
SITTINGBOURNE	05.05		05.51
Eastern Jcn	05/06		05/52
Middle Jcn	05/07		05/53
Kemsley			05.56
Redham Dock			
Swale			06.02
Queenborough	05.16	05.45	06.06
SHEERNESS	05.23	05.53	06.15
Destination			

WORKING TIMETABLE : VICTORIA to RAMSGATE (1955)

	Goods N 2-6-0	EBV C 0-6-0	05.51 H. Via Pass EMU	06.00 H. Via Pass EMU	05.24 CX Pass EMU	Pass EMU	Goods C 0-6-0	ECS EMU	06.11 H. Via Pass EMU	05.20 Gill Goods C 0-6-0	2-6-4T	06.25 H. Via Pass EMU	Pass EMU	07.22 S'ness Pass 2-2-2T	05.37 C. St Pass EMU	03.58 Chatham Goods N 2-6-0	05.50 C. St Pass E1 4-4-0	05.30 H. Jcn Goods C 0-6-0	L 4-4-0
VICTORIA			05.44									06.24							
Brixton			05.50									06.30							
Herne Hill	05.23		05.52		06/12							06.32	06.37						
W. Dulwich			05.55									06.35	06.39						
Sydenham Hill			05.57									06.37	06.41						
Penge East			06.00									06.40	06.44						
Kent House			06.02									06.42	06.46						
Beckenham Jcn	05/45	05.50	06.04		06.22							06.44	06.48						
	Main	Local	Main	Main	Main				Local			Main	Main						
Shortlands	05/50		06.07	06.20					06.39			06.47	06.51						
BROMLEY SOUTH		06.00	06.08	06.21	06.26				06.41			06.48	06.53						
BROMLEY SOUTH	05/55		06.09	06.22	06.28				06.42			06.49	06.54						
Bickley			06.12	06.25					06.45			06.52	06.57						
Bickley Jcn			06/14	06/27	06/31				06/47			06.54	06.59						
St Mary Cray Jcn	06/05		06/15		06/32				06/48										
St Mary Cray	06/09		06.17						06.50										
SWANLEY	06/17		06.22		06.37			06.51	06.55										
Farningham Road						06.50		06.56											
Fawkham						07.00													
Meopham																			
Sole Street	06.42																		
Cuxton Road																			
Rochester Bge Jcn						06/39									06/59		07/09		
Chatham Goods																		07.16	
Rochester						06.40									07.00		07.10	07/20	
Rochester						06.41									07.01		07.11		
CHATHAM						06.43									07.03		07.13		
CHATHAM						06.45									07.05		07.19	07/24	
GILLINGHAM						06.48									07.08		07.23	07/32	
GILLINGHAM																	07.25		
Rainham																	07.31		
Newington										07.05							07.37		
Western Jcn																			
Eastern Jcn														07/38					
SITTINGBOURNE										07.15				07.39			07.43		
SITTINGBOURNE										07.25							07.46		
Murston Sdgs																			
Teynham										07.35							07.54		
FAVERSHAM																	08.02		
FAVERSHAM											07.37					07.40	08.13		08.08
Graveney Sdgs																			
Whitstable																			08.18
Chestfield																			08.24
HERNE BAY																			08.29
HERNE BAY																08/00			08.30
Birchington																08/25			08.42
Westgate																08/39			08.48
MARGATE																			08.54
MARGATE																08/44			
Broadstairs																			
Dumpton Park																			
RAMSGATE																09/05			
Destination			S'oaks	Orp	M'stone				S'oaks	Dover		Orp	Orp			Deal	Dover		

WORKING TIMETABLE : FAVERSHAM to DOVER (1955)

	Pass 2-6-4T	05.50 C, St Pass E1 4-4-0	06.40 Fav Goods N 2-6-0
FAVERSHAM	07.37	08.13	
Selling	07.44	08.20	
CANTERBURY E.	07.55	08.31	
CANTERBURY E.	08.09	08.34	08.45
Bekesbourne	08.15	08.40	08.55
Adisham	08.21	08.46	
Aylesham	08.25	08.50	
Snowdown	08.29	08.54	
Shepherdswell	08.35	08.59	
Kearsney	08.42	09.06	
DOVER PRIORY	08.47	09.11	
Destination			

WORKING TIMETABLE : SHEERNESS to SITTINGBOURNE (1955)

	Pass 2-6-2T
SHEERNESS	07.22
Queenborough	07.28
Swale	
Redham Dock	
Kemsley	07/34
Middle Jcn	07/37
Eastern Jcn	07/38
SITTINGBOURNE	07.39
Destination	

WORKING TIMETABLE : RAMSGATE to VICTORIA (1955)

			07.00	06.41		07.16	07.21		07.26		07.42	07.47	07.22	07.51					06.10		08.00	
From			Orp	S'oaks		Orp	Orp		Orp		Orp	Orp	S'oaks	Orp					Dover		Orp	
Class	Pass	Pass	Pass	Pass	Pass	Pass	Pass	Pass	Pass	Pass	Pass	Pass	Pass	Pass	Pass	Pass	Pass	Pass	Pass	Pass	Pass	XP
Engine	EMU	EMU	EMU	EMU	EMU	EMU	EMU	EMU	EMU	EMU	EMU	EMU	EMU	EMU	EMU	EMU	2-6-2T	2-6-2T	D1 4-4-0	EMU	EMU	WC
RAMSGATE																						06.06
Dumpton Park																						06.10
Broadstairs																						06.15
MARGATE																						06.21
MARGATE																						06.23
Westgate																						06.28
Birchington																						06.33
HERNE BAY																						06.46
HERNE BAY																						06.48
Chestfield																						06.54
Whitstable																						06.59
Graveney																						
British Fruit																						
FAVERSHAM																			07.07			07.09
FAVERSHAM																	06.44		(07.16)			07.11
Teynham																	06.53					
SITTINGBOURNE																	06.59					
SITTINGBOURNE																	07.01	07.10				07/22
Eastern Jcn																		07/11				
Western Jcn																						
Newington																	07.08					
Rainham																	07.15					
GILLINGHAM																	07.20					
GILLINGHAM	06.58	07.08													07.13	07.18	07.22			07.27		07/34
CHATHAM	07.01	07.11													07.16	07.21	07.26			07.30		07.36
CHATHAM	07.03	07.13													07.19	07.23	07.28			07.32		07.38
Rochester	07.04	07.14													07.21	07.24	07.30			07.33		
Rochester	07.05	07.15													07.22	07.25				07.34		07/40
Chatham Goods																						
Rochester Bge Jcn	07/06	07/16													07/24	07/26				07/36		07/41
Cuxton Road																						
Sole Street																	07.34					07/53
Meopham																	07.36					
Longfield																						
Fawkham																	07.41					
Farningham Road							07.06										07.46					
SWANLEY				07.04			07.17				07.45						07.56					08/03
St Mary Cray				07.09			07.22				07.50						08.01					
St Mary Cray Jcn				07/11			07/25				07/52						08.04					08/08
			Local	Main	Local	Local	Local	Main	Local	Main	Local	Local	Main	Local	Main						Local	
Bickley Jcn			07/05	07/12	07/15	07/21	07/26	07/26	07/31		07/47	07/52	07/53	07/56			08/05				08/05	
Bickley			07.08	07.14	07.17	07.23	07.28	07.27	07.33	07.34	07.48	07.54	07.54	07.58							08.08	
BROMLEY SOUTH			07.10	07.16	07.19	07.25	07.30	07.31	07.35	07.36	07.50	07.55	07.56	08.00			08.07				08.09	
BROMLEY SOUTH			07.11	07.17	07.20	07.26	07.31	07.32	07.36	07.37	07.51	07.56	07.57	08.01			08.08				08.10	
Shortlands			07.14	07.20	07.23	07.28	07.33	07.34	07.38	07.40	07.54	07.59	08.00	08.03			08.11				08.13	
Beckenham Jcn			07.17		07.25	07.31	07.36		07.42		07.57	08.02		08.06			08/13				08.16	
Kent House			07.19		07.27	07.33	07.38		07.44		07.59	08.04		08.08							08.18	
Penge East			07.21		07.30	07.35	07.40		07.46		08.01	08.06		08.10							08.20	
Sydenham Hill			07.24		07.32	07.38	07.43		07.49		08.04	08.09		08.13							08.23	
W. Dulwich			07.26		07.35	07.40	07.45		07.51		08.06	08.11		08.15							08.26	
Herne Hill			07.29			07.44	07.48		07.53		08.08	08.13		08.18			08/22				08.28	
Brixton			07.31				07.50				08.11			08.20			08/23				08.30	
VICTORIA			07.36				07.56				08.16			08.25			08.28				08.36	
Destination	C. St	CX		H. Via	H. Via	H. Via		H. Via	H. Via	H. Via		H. Via	H. Via			CX	S'ness		C. St			C. St

WORKING TIMETABLE : DOVER - FAVERSHAM (1955)

	Pass
Train	
From	
Class	
Engine	D1 4-4-0
DOVER PRIORY	06.10
Dover Gas	
Kearsney	06.16
Shepherdswell	06.25
Snowdown	06.30
Aylesham	06.33
Adisham	06.36
Bekesbourne	06.42
CANTERBURY E.	06.47
CANTERBURY E.	06.48
Selling	07.01
FAVERSHAM	07.07
Destination	

WORKING TIMETABLE : SITTINGBOURNE - SHEERNESS (1955)

	Pass
Train	
From	
Class	
Engine	2-6-2T
SITTINGBOURNE	07.10
Eastern Jcn	07/11
Middle Jcn	07/12
Kemsley	07.15
Redham Dock	
Swale	07.21
Queenborough	07.25
SHEERNESS	07.33
Destination	

There was no lack of modern motive power on the Chatham section but it was the inside cylinder 4-4-0's that were the focus of the greatest attention and to the relief many observers - not to mention railwaymen baffled by the vagaries of unrebuilt Pacifics - many of them remained hard at work until the end of steam in 1959. The D1 4-4-0's were a modified version of the D class of 1901 and in the mid-1950's were allocated to Bricklayers Arms (2), Dover (3), Faversham (5), Gillingham (2), Redhill (1), Stewarts Lane (3) and Tonbridge (1). Their survival owed much to their ability to work over the heavily restricted lines around Holborn Viaduct but one could generally be found on daily passenger duties between Dover, Faversham and Chatham. The class was also heavily used on summer seasonal work and 31743 of Stewarts Lane is seen passing Gillingham with a Victoria - Ramsgate holiday special in August 1958. (L.G. Marshall)

The E1 4-4-0's were a 1919 rebuild of the E class of 1905 and although the last of the older engines was taken out of traffic in 1955, seven E1's - divided between Stewarts Lane (4) and Bricklayers Arms (3) - were retained chiefly for the early morning parcels and newspaper trains that ran from London to the Coast via Dartford. On 1950's Summer Saturdays one of the Stewarts Lane engines was diagrammed to the seven coach 11.50 Victoria - Dover/Margate express which ran to timings very similar to those of the regular expresses. 31067 prepares to leave Stewarts Lane MPD in May 1957. (L.G. Marshall)

There were not many instances of British locomotives being built overseas but to expedite delivery ten of the twenty-two L class 4-4-0's were constructed by Borsig & Co of Berlin, the engines being received only two months before the outbreak of war in 1914. Initially the class was confined to the South Eastern section where much of their best work was performed on the Charing Cross - Hastings service and they did not gravitate to the Chatham section until 1930 when the last of the restrictions in Thanet were lifted. The class survived intact until 1956 and were distributed between Ashford (6), Faversham (4), Ramsgate (5) and Tonbridge (7); the absence of London allocations being due to their being prohibited between Herne Hill and Holborn Viaduct. One of the German engines, 31780 of Ramsgate, leaves Gillingham with a relief express from London to the Kent Coast in June 1959. (L.G. Marshall)

One of the English 'Germans', 31766 waits to back onto a Ramsgate train at Faversham on 13 June 1959. Four L 4-4-0's came to Faversham from Tonbridge and St Leonards in late 1955 to work a two-day cycle which took the engines on a circuitous route to Hastings via Ramsgate, Ashford, Tonbridge and Edenbridge. The return working was made the following day with the 16.12 Tonbridge to Faversham via Ashford and Ramsgate - one of the few instances of a train running through between the SER and LCDR. The L 4-4-0's were widely employed between Chatham and Ramsgate during the 1950's although care had to be taken to ensure that they did not stray onto the Sittingbourne - Sheerness branch over which the class was prohibited. (L.G. Marshall)

WORKING TIMETABLE : VICTORIA to RAMSGATE (1955)

		06.09				06.40	06.31		06.46	05.23	06.36	07.55		08.22	06.51						07.04
Train																					
From		C. St				Vic	H. Via		H. Via	H. Hill	C'St	S'ness		S'ness	H. Via						H. Via
Class	ECS	Pass	Pass	Pass	Pass	Pass	Pass	Goods	Pass	Pass	Pass	Pass	Pass	Pass	ECS	Pass	LE	XP	Pass		
Engine	H 0-4-4T	EMU	EMU	H 0-4-4T	EMU	EMU	EMU	N 2-6-0	EMU	C 0-6-0	C 0-6-0	2-6-2T	EMU	L 4-4-0	EMU	EMU	V 4-0	WC	EMU		
VICTORIA		06.40			06.44											07.04					
Brixton		06/45			06.50											07.09					
Herne Hill		06.48				06.52	06.57									07.12				07.16	
W. Dulwich						06.54	07.00									07.14				07.18	
Sydenham Hill						06.56	07.02									07.16				07.20	
Penge East						07.00	07.05									07.20				07.23	
Kent House						07.02	07.07									07.22				07.25	
Beckenham Jcn		06/55				07.04	07.09									07.24					
		Main				Local	Main	Main						Local		Local	Main				
Shortlands		06/57				06.59	07.06	07.12						07.20		07.27					
BROMLEY SOUTH		07.00				07.01	07.08	07.14						07.21		07.28					
BROMLEY SOUTH		07.01				07.02	07.09	07.15						07.22		07.29					
Bickley						07.05	07.12	07.18						07.25	07.30	07.33					
Bickley Jcn			07/04			07/07	07/14	07/19						07/26	07/32	07/34					
St Mary Cray Jcn			07/05			07/08								07/27							
St Mary Cray						07.10								07/30							
SWANLEY			07.10			07.15								07.35							
Farningham Road			07.15																		
Fawkham			07.20																		
Meopham			07.24																		
Sole Street			07.27					07.40													
Cuxton Road			07/32																		
Rochester Bge Jcn		07/30	07/35					07/50	07/52												
Chatham Goods								08.00													
Rochester		07.31	07.36						07.53												
Rochester	07.26	07.32	07.37						07.54												
CHATHAM	07.28	07.34	07.39						07.56												
CHATHAM		07.36		07.40		07.50			07.58												
GILLINGHAM		07.39		07.44		07.53			08.01												
GILLINGHAM				07.46																	
Rainham				07.52																	
Newington				07.58																	
Western Jcn																					
Eastern Jcn										08/14		08/41									
SITTINGBOURNE				08.04						08.15		08.42									
SITTINGBOURNE											08.27										
Murston Sdgs																					
Teynham											08.34										
FAVERSHAM											08.42										
FAVERSHAM																					
Graveney Sdgs																					
Whitstable																					
Chestfield																					
HERNE BAY																					
HERNE BAY																					
Birchington																					
Westgate																					
MARGATE																					
MARGATE														09.18		09.25	09.40				
Broadstairs														09.27			09.50				
Dumpton Park														09.31			09.54				
RAMSGATE														09.34	09.40		09.57				
Destination			S'oaks			Orp	Orp							S'oaks	Ashford	Orp	Orp	Loco		C. Cross	

WORKING TIMETABLE : FAVERSHAM to DOVER (1955)

	06.40
Train	
From	Fav
Class	Goods
Engine	N 2-6-0
FAVERSHAM	
Selling	
CANTERBURY E.	
CANTERBURY E.	
Bekesbourne	09.15
Adisham	09.25
Aylesham	
Snowdown	
Shepherdswell	
Kearsney	
DOVER PRIORY	
Destination	

WORKING TIMETABLE : SHEERNESS to SITTINGBOURNE (1955)

Train		
From		
Class	Pass	Pass
Engine	C 0-6-0	2-6-2T
SHEERNESS	07.55	08.22
Queenborough	08.02	08.27
Swale	08.06	08.33
Redham Dock		
Kemsley	08.10	08.37
Middle Jcn	08/13	08/40
Eastern Jcn	08/14	08/41
SITTINGBOURNE	08.15	08.42
Destination		

WORKING TIMETABLE : RAMSGATE to VICTORIA (1955)

	08.07	07.42	07.40		08.20			06.10	08.33	08.01		08.31					07.20	07.54	08.43			
Train																						
From	Orp	S'oaks	M'stone		Orp			Dover	Orp	S'oaks		Orp					Dover	M'stone	Orp	Loco		
Class	Pass	Pass	Pass	Pass	Pass	Pass	Pass	Pass	Pass	Pass	XP	Pass	Pass	Pass	Pass	Pass	Boat	Pass	Pass	Light	Pass	ECS
Engine	EMU	EMU	EMU	EMU	EMU	EMU	EMU	D1 4-4-0	EMU	EMU	WC	EMU	EMU	EMU	EMU	2-6-2T	WC&L1	EMU	EMU	WC	EMU	V 4-4-0
RAMSGATE											06.29									06.40		06.53
Dumpton Park											06.33											
Broadstairs											06.37											
MARGATE											06.43									06.56		
MARGATE											06.46											07.07
Westgate											06.51											
Birchington											06.56											
HERNE BAY											07.07											07.27
HERNE BAY											07.10											(08.20)
Chestfield											07.16											
Whitstable											07.21											
Graveney																						
British Fruit																						
FAVERSHAM											07.31											
FAVERSHAM								07.16			07.33											
Teynham								07.25														
SITTINGBOURNE								07.31			07.44											
SITTINGBOURNE								07.33			07.45					07.48						
Eastern Jcn																07/49						
Western Jcn																						
Newington								07.41														
Rainham								07.48														
GILLINGHAM								07.53			07.58											
GILLINGHAM						07.43	07.50				07.59		08.11									
CHATHAM						07.46	07.53				08.03		08.14									
CHATHAM						07.48	07.56				08.06		08.15									
Rochester						07.49	07.57						08.16									
Rochester						07.50	07.58				08.08		08.17									
Chatham Goods																						
Rochester Bge Jcn						07/52	07/59				08/09		08/18									
Cuxton Road																						
Sole Street						08.02					08/21											
Meopham						08.05																
Longfield																						
Fawkham						08.09																
Farningham Road						08.14																
SWANLEY		08.04	08.16			08.20			08.24		08/31							08.39				
St Mary Cray		08.09	08.21						08.29									08.44				
St Mary Cray Jcn		08/11	08/23			08/26			08/31			08/36						08/47				
	Local	Main	Main	Local	Local	Main			Local	Main		Local					Local	Main	Local		Local	
Bickley Jcn	08/12	08/12	08/24		08/25	08/27			08/32			08/36					08/44	08/48				
Bickley	08.13	08.14		08.23	08.27				08.33	08.34		08.38							08.49		08.53	
BROMLEY SOUTH	08.15	08.16		08.25	08.30	08.30			08.35	08.36		08.40						08.51	08.51		08.55	
BROMLEY SOUTH	08.16	08.17	08/25	08.26	08.31	08.31			08.36	08.37		08.41					08/47	08.53	08.52		08.56	
Shortlands	08.19	08.20	08/27	08.29	08.34	08.34			08.38	08.40		08.43						08.55	08.55		08.59	
Beckenham Jcn	08.22		08/29	08.32	08.37				08.41			08.46					08/52	(Via	08.58		09.02	
Kent House	08.24			08.34	08.39				08.43			08.48						Cat-	09.00		09.04	
Penge East	08.26			08.36	08.41				08.45			08.50						ford)	09.02		09.06	
Sydenham Hill	08.29			08.39	08.44				08.48			08.53							09.05			
W. Dulwich	08.31			08.41	08.46				08.50			08.55							09.07		09.10	
Herne Hill	08.33		08.38	08.46	08.49				08.53			08.58	08.59				09.03		09.11		09.13	
Brixton			08/40		08.51							09.01	09.04				09/04	09/08	09.14			
VICTORIA			08.46		08.56							09.06	09.10				09.06	09.10	09.14		09.20	
Destination	H. Via	H. Via	H. Via		CX				H. Via	Bfs	C. St	H. Via				CX	S'ness				H. Via	

WORKING TIMETABLE : DOVER - FAVERSHAM (1955)

	06.15	06.15
Train		
From	Town	Town
Class	Goods	Goods
Engine	01 0-6-0	01 0-6-0
DOVER PRIORY	06/25	
Dover Gas	06.27	06.45
Kearsney		06/55
Shepherdswell		07.05
Snowdown		
Aylesham		
Adisham		
Bekesbourne		
CANTERBURY E.		
CANTERBURY E.		
Selling		
FAVERSHAM		
Destination		

WORKING TIMETABLE : SITTINGBOURNE - SHEERNESS (1955)

Train	
From	
Class	Pass
Engine	2-6-2T
SITTINGBOURNE	07.48
Eastern Jcn	07/49
Middle Jcn	07/50
Kemsley	
Redham Dock	
Swale	
Queenborough	07.59
SHEERNESS	08.09
Destination	

Train	07.04	07.00	07.11			06.50		07.31		07.44	07.49	07.10	07.51	07.42		06.50	05.23	08.40	
From	H. Via	C. St	H. Via			F. Rd		H. Via		H. Via	H. Via	CX	H. Via	CX		F. Rd	H. Hill	H. Jcn	
Class	Pass	Pass	Pass	Pass	Pass	Pass	Goods	Pass	Pass	Pass	Pass	Pass	Pass	Pass	Pass	Goods	Goods	Goods	Pass
Engine	EMU	EMU	N 2-6-0	EMU	DI 4-4-0	EMU	C 0-6-0	EMU	EMU	EMU	EMU	EMU	EMU	EMU	EMU	C 0-6-0	N 2-6-0	C 0-6-0	L 4-4-0
VICTORIA	07.18					07.24		07.40		07.44					08.04				
Brixton	07/23					07.29		07.45		07.49					08.09				
Herne Hill	07/25					07.32		07.48		07.52	08.00				08.12				
W. Dulwich						07.34				07.54					08.14				
Sydenham Hill						07.36				07.56	08.04				08.16				
Penge East						07.39				07.59	08.07				08.19				
Kent House		07.32				07.41				08.01	08.09				08.21				
Beckenham Jcn	07/31	07.35				07.43		07.55		08.03	08.11				08.23				
	Main	Main	Local			Main		Main	Local	Main	Local	Local	Main		Main				
Shortlands	07/33	07.38	07.40			07.46		07/58	07.59	08.06	08.14		08.21		08.26				
BROMLEY SOUTH	07.34	07.39	07.41			07.49		08.00	08.01	08.08	08.10	08.16	08.22		08.28				
BROMLEY SOUTH	07.35	07.40	07.42			07.51		08.01	08.02	08.09	08.11	08.17	08.23		08.29				
Bickley	07.36	07.43	07.45			07.54		08.04	08.05	08.13	08.14	08.20	08.26		08.32				
Bickley Jcn	07/38	07/45	07/47			07/55		08/06	08/06	08/14			08/28		08/34				
St Mary Cray Jcn	07/39		07/48					08/07					08/29						
St Mary Cray			07.50					08.10					08.31						
SWANLEY	07.47		07.55					08.15					08.36						
Farningham Road	07.52																		
Fawkham	07.57					08.02													
Meopham	08.01					08.12										08.50			
Sole Street	08.04															08.55			
Cuxton Road	08.09																		
Rochester Bge Jcn	08/12		08/17					08/28					08/39			08/58			
Chatham Goods																09.02		08.55	
Rochester	08.13		08.18					08.29					08.41						
Rochester	08.14		08.20					08.30					08.42				08/57		
CHATHAM	08.16		08.22					08.32					08.44						
CHATHAM	08.20		08.28					08.34					08.45				09/00		
GILLINGHAM	08.23		08.32					08.37					08.48						
GILLINGHAM			08.34														09/08		
Rainham			08.40																
Newington			08.46																
Western Jcn																			
Eastern Jcn																			
SITTINGBOURNE			08.52														09.30		
SITTINGBOURNE			08.55																
Murston Sdgs																			
Teynham			09.02																
FAVERSHAM			09.10																
FAVERSHAM			09.13		09.18														
Graveney Sdgs																			
Whitstable			09.23																
Chestfield			09.30																
HERNE BAY			09.35																
HERNE BAY			09.37																
Birchington			09.49																
Westgate			09.54																
MARGATE			09.59																
MARGATE			10.02																10.10
Broadstairs			10.09																10.19
Dumpton Park			10.14																10.23
RAMSGATE			10.18																10.26
Destination		Orp		S'oaks	Dover	Orp			Orp		S'oaks	Orp		S'oaks	Orp				Ashford

Train		06.40	
From		Fav	
Class	Pass	Goods	
Engine	DI 4-4-0	N 2-6-0	
FAVERSHAM	09.18		
Selling	09.25		
CANTERBURY E.	09.36		
CANTERBURY E.	09.38		
Bekesbourne	09.44		
Adisham	09.50	10.15	
Aylesham	09.54		
Snowdown	09.58		
Shepherdswell	10.03	10.25	
Kearsney	10.10		
DOVER PRIORY	10.15		
Destination			

Train			
From			
Class			
Engine			
SHEERNESS			
Queenborough			
Swale			
Redham Dock			
Kemsley			
Middle Jcn			
Eastern Jcn			
SITTINGBOURNE			
Destination			

WORKING TIMETABLE : RAMSGATE to VICTORIA (1955)

	Pass — L 4-4-0	07.40 Chatham Pass H 0-4-4T	08.23 S'oaks Pass EMU	Pass EMU	ECS EMU	Pass EMU	XP WC	Pass EMU	07.07 R'gate Pass L 4-4-0	09.00 Orp Pass EMU	08.20 M'stone Pass EMU	Pass EMU	Pass EMU	Pass EMU	XP WC	Pass EMU	09.16 Orp Pass L 4-4-0	07.02 C'bury Pass EMU	07.42 Dover Pass U1 2-6-0	09.02 S'oaks Pass EMU
RAMSGATE	07.07						07.20								07.35		07.42			
Dumpton Park	07.11						07.24								07.39		07.46			
Broadstairs	07.15						07.28								07.43		07.50			
MARGATE	07.21						07.34								07.49		07.56			
MARGATE	07.23						07.37								07.51					
Westgate	07.28														07.56					
Birchington	07.33														08.01					
HERNE BAY	07.44						07.52								08.12					
HERNE BAY	07.45						07.54								08.13					
Chestfield	07.51														08.18					
Whitstable	07.56						08.02								08.23					
Graveney																				
British Fruit																				
FAVERSHAM	08.06																		08.39	
FAVERSHAM	(08.15)						08/12		08.15						08/33				(08.48)	
Teynham																				
SITTINGBOURNE									08.26											
SITTINGBOURNE		08.13					08/20		08.27						08/40					
Eastern Jcn		08/14																		
Western Jcn																				
Newington																				
Rainham																				
GILLINGHAM									08.41											
GILLINGHAM			08.15	08.17	08.21	08/31		08.37								08.43				
CHATHAM			08.18		08.24			08.40								08.46				
CHATHAM			08.20	08/22	08.27	08/34		08.43								08.47	08/52			
Rochester			08.21		08.28			08.44								08.48				
Rochester			08.22	08/25	08.29	08/35		08.45								08.49	08/53			
Chatham Goods																				
Rochester Bge Jcn			08/24	08/26	08/30	08/36		08/46								08/51	08/54			
Cuxton Road																				
Sole Street			08.34		08.37	08/47					08.49					09/00	09/05			
Meopham			08.36								08.52									
Longfield																				
Fawkham			08.41								08.56									
Farningham Road			08.45								09.01									
SWANLEY		08.45	08.53			08/57				09.01	09.06	09.04			09/15	09.12				09.24
St Mary Cray		08.50								09.09										09.29
St Mary Cray Jcn		08/52	08/58			09/02				09/06	09/11					09/17	09/20			09/31
		Main	Main							Local	Main					Main	Main	Local		Main
Bickley Jcn		08/53	08/59							09/05	09/07					09/12	09/18	09/21		09/32
Bickley		08.54								09.09						09.14	09.23			09.34
BROMLEY SOUTH		08.56	09.03						09.10	09.12	09.16					09.21	09.26			09.36
BROMLEY SOUTH		08.57	09.04						09.11	09.13	09.17					09.22	09.31			09.37
Shortlands		09.00							09.14	09.15	09.20						09.34			09.40
Beckenham Jcn			09/08						09.17							09/26	09.37			
Kent House									09.19								09.39			
Penge East									09.21								09.41			
Sydenham Hill									09.24								09.44			
W. Dulwich									09.26								09.46			
Herne Hill			09/17						09.28							09.33	09.48	09.40		
Brixton									09.30							09.34	09.50	09.42		
VICTORIA									09.37							09.41	09.56	09.48		
Destination		S'ness	Bfs	H. Via		C. St	C. St	CX		H. Via	H. Via					C. St				H. Via

WORKING TIMETABLE : DOVER - FAVERSHAM (1955)

	Pass U1 2-6-0
Train	
From	
Class	Pass
Engine	U1 2-6-0
DOVER PRIORY	07.42
Dover Gas	
Kearsney	07.48
Shepherdswell	07.56
Snowdown	08.01
Aylesham	08.04
Adisham	08.07
Bekesbourne	08.13
CANTERBURY E.	08.18
CANTERBURY E.	08.20
Selling	08.33
FAVERSHAM	08.39
Destination	Ctm

WORKING TIMETABLE : SITTINGBOURNE - SHEERNESS (1955)

Train	07.40
From	Ctm
Class	Pass
Engine	H 0-4-4T
SITTINGBOURNE	08.13
Eastern Jcn	08/14
Middle Jcn	08/15
Kemsley	08.18
Redham Dock	
Swale	
Queenborough	08.25
SHEERNESS	08.34
Destination	

	07.57	08.18	08.10			08.30	06.50	08.35		08.48		08.53	08.57		09.04	08.42	09.38	08.35	05.23
From	C. St	H. Via	H. Via			H. Via	F. Rd	Vic		H. Via		Bfs	H. Via		Bfs	CX	S'ness	Vic	H. Hill
Class	Pass	Pass	Pass	Pass	Pass	XP	Pass	Goods	Pass	Pass	Pass	Boat	Pass	Pass	Pass	Pass	Pass	Pass	Goods
Engine	EMU	EMU	EMU	EMU	EMU	BR5 4-6-0	EMU	C 0-6-0	L 4-4-0	EMU	EMU	MN	EMU	EMU	EMU	EMU	H 0-4-4T	L 4-4-0	N 2-6-0
VICTORIA		08.18			08.24	08.35				08.44			09.00		09.04				
Brixton		08.23			08.29					08.49			09.07		09.09				
Herne Hill		08.25	08.28		08.32	08/44				08.52			09.09		09.12				
W. Dulwich					08.34					08.54					09.14				
Sydenham Hill					08.36					08.56					09.16				
Penge East					08.39					08.59					09.19				
Kent House					08.41					09.01					09.21				
Beckenham Jcn		08/31	08/35		08.43	08/52				09.03		09/17			09.23				
		Main	Main	Local	Local	Main	Main			Main	Main	Main	Local	Local	Main	Local			
Shortlands		08/33	08/37	08.39	08.46	08.54	08.59			09.06	09/19	09.19	09.24		09.26	09.31			
BROMLEY SOUTH		08.34	08.41		08.48	08.55	09.01			09.08		09.12	09.21	09.33	09.26	09.28			
BROMLEY SOUTH		08.35	08.42		08.49	08.57	09.02			09.09		09.13	09.22	(09.37)	09.27	09.29			
Bickley			08.42	08.45	08.53		09.05			09.12		09.18	09.25		09.30	09.32			
Bickley Jcn		08/38		08/47	08/55	09/02	09/07			09/13		09/20	09/26		09/27	09/34			
St Mary Cray Jcn		08/39		08/48		09/07							09/27						
St Mary Cray				08.50			09.10						09.30						
SWANLEY		08.47		08.55		09.08	09.15						09.35						
Farningham Road		08.52																	
Fawkham		08.57																	
Meopham		09.01																	
Sole Street		09.04				09/18		09.25											
Cuxton Road		09.09				09/23													
Rochester Bge Jcn	09/07	09/12				09/27		09/45								09/38			
Chatham Goods								09.50											
Rochester	09.09	09.13														09.40			
Rochester	09.20	09.14														09.41			
CHATHAM	09.11	09.16				09.29										09.43			
CHATHAM	09.13	09.18				09.32			09.38							09.44			
GILLINGHAM	09.16	09.21							09.42							09.47			
GILLINGHAM						09/35			09.43										
Rainham																			
Newington																			
Western Jcn																			
Eastern Jcn																	09/57		
SITTINGBOURNE									09.55								09.58		
SITTINGBOURNE						09/45			(10.00)									10.00	10.07
Murston Sdgs																			
Teynham																			
FAVERSHAM																		10.11	10.27
FAVERSHAM						09/53												10.14	
Graveney Sdgs																			
Whitstable						10.02													
Chestfield																			
HERNE BAY						10.11													
HERNE BAY						10.14													
Birchington						10.26													
Westgate						10.31													
MARGATE						10.37													
MARGATE						10.40													
Broadstairs						10.48													
Dumpton Park						10.52													
RAMSGATE						10.56													
Destination					Orp		S'oaks			Orp	Orp	Dover	S'oaks		Orp			Dover	

	08.35
From	Vic
Class	Pass
Engine	L 4-4-0
FAVERSHAM	10.14
Selling	10.21
CANTERBURY E.	10.32
CANTERBURY E.	10.34
Bekesbourne	10.40
Adisham	10.46
Aylesham	10.50
Snowdown	10.54
Shepherdswell	10.59
Kearsney	11.06
DOVER PRIORY	11.11
Destination	

Train	
From	
Class	Pass
Engine	H 0-4-4T
SHEERNESS	09.38
Queenborough	09.45
Swale	09.49
Redham Dock	
Kemsley	09.53
Middle Jcn	09/56
Eastern Jcn	09/57
SITTINGBOURNE	09.58
Destination	

WORKING TIMETABLE : RAMSGATE to VICTORIA (1955)

Train	08.57		07.08		07.42			09.42	09.22	08.17		10.02		09.42			10.20		10.02
From	M'stone		Dover		Dover			Orp	S'oaks	Dover		Orp	Loco	S'oaks			Orp		S'oaks
Class	Pass	XP	Pass	Light	Pass	Pass	Pass	Pass	Pass	Pass	XP	Pass	Light	Pass	ECS	Pass	Pass	ECS	Pass
Engine	EMU	V 4-4-0	BR4 2-6-0	C 0-6-0	U1 2-6-0	EMU	2-6-2T	EMU	EMU	N 2-6-0	WC	EMU	WC	EMU	EMU	EMU	EMU	C 0-6-0	EMU
RAMSGATE			08.05							08.25			08.30						
Dumpton Park			08.09							08.29									
Broadstairs			08.13							08.33									
MARGATE			08.19							08.39			08.46						
MARGATE										08.41									
Westgate										08.46									
Birchington																			
HERNE BAY										08.59									
HERNE BAY		08.20								09.00									
Chestfield		08.26																	
Whitstable		08.31								09.08									
Graveney																			
British Fruit																			
FAVERSHAM		08.41								09.10									
FAVERSHAM		08.42			08.48					09.18									
Teynham					08.57														
SITTINGBOURNE		08.53			09.03														
SITTINGBOURNE		08.54		08.57	09.05		09.08			09.25									
Eastern Jcn							09/09												
Western Jcn																			
Newington					09.12														
Rainham					09.18														
GILLINGHAM				09.14	09.23														
GILLINGHAM		09.05	09.10		09.25					09.34				09.40			09.45		
CHATHAM		09.08	09.13		09.29									09.43					
CHATHAM		09.10	09.15							09.37				09.40	09.44		09.49		
Rochester			09.17												09.45				
Rochester		09.12	09.18							09.39				09.44	09.46		09.52		
Chatham Goods																			
Rochester Bge Jcn		09/13	09/19							09/40				09/45	09/47		09/53		
Cuxton Road																			
Sole Street		09.25								09/51				10/00					
Meopham																			
Longfield																			
Fawkham																			
Farningham Road																			
SWANLEY	09/31	09/35						09.41				10/01		10.04	10/13				10.24
St Mary Cray								09.46						10.09					10.29
St Mary Cray Jcn	09.36	09/40						09/48			10/16	10/11			10/19				10/31
	Local							Local	Main		Main	Local		Main	Main		Local		Main
Bickley Jcn	09/37							09/47	09/49			10/07		10/12	10/20		10/25		10/32
Bickley								09.49	09.51			10.09		10.14			10.29		10.34
BROMLEY SOUTH	09.40							09.51	09.54			10.11		10.16			10.31		10.36
BROMLEY SOUTH	09.41							09.52	09.57		10/10	10.12		10.17	10/22		10.32		10.37
Shortlands	09.43							09.54	10.00			10.14		10.20			10.34		10.40
Beckenham Jcn	09.45							09.57			10/12	10.17		10/27			10.37		
Kent House								09.59				10.19					10.39		
Penge East								10.01				10.21					10.41		
Sydenham Hill								10.05				10.25					10.45		
W. Dulwich								10.06				10.26					10.46		
Herne Hill	09.52				09.58			10.09	10.11		10/20	10.29		10/38			10.49		
Brixton					10.00			10.11			10/21	10.31		10/40			10.51		
VICTORIA					10.06			10.16			10.27	10.36					10.56		
Destination	H. Via	C. St	CX	Loco			S'ness		H. Via					H. Via	S. Lane	C. St		Strood	H. Via

WORKING TIMETABLE : DOVER - FAVERSHAM (1955)

Train	
From	
Class	Pass
Engine	N 2-6-0
DOVER PRIORY	08.17
Dover Gas	
Kearsney	08.23
Shepherdswell	08.30
Snowdown	08.35
Aylesham	08.38
Adisham	08.41
Bekesbourne	08.47
CANTERBURY E.	08.52
CANTERBURY E.	08.54
Selling	
FAVERSHAM	09.10
Destination	

WORKING TIMETABLE : SITTINGBOURNE - SHEERNESS (1955)

Train	
From	
Class	Pass
Engine	2-6-2T
SITTINGBOURNE	09.08
Eastern Jcn	09/09
Middle Jcn	09/10
Kemsley	09.13
Redham Dock	
Swale	09.19
Queenborough	09.24
SHEERNESS	09.30
Destination	

WORKING TIMETABLE : VICTORIA to RAMSGATE (1955)

Train	08.40	08.52		09.03	09.11	10.10				08.52			09.30					05.23	
From	H. Jcn	C. St		Bfs	Bfs	S'ness				C. St			H. Via					H. Hill	
Class	Goods	Pass	Pass	Pass	Pass	Pass	Pass	Light	2 Light	Pass	Pass	XP	Pass	Pass	Pass	ECS	Pass	Goods	Pass
Engine	C 0-6-0	EMU	EMU	EMU	EMU	2-6-2T	EMU	C 0-6-0	2-6-4T	EMU	E1 4-4-0	BR5 4-6-0	EMU	EMU	EMU	EMU	EMU	N 2-6-0	L 4-4-0
VICTORIA		09.18					09.24					09.35	09.40		09.44	09.47	09.54		
Brixton		09/23					09.29						09.46		09.49	09.53	10.00		
Herne Hill		09/25					09.32					09.44	09.48		09.52	09.54	10.02		
W. Dulwich							09.34								09.54				
Sydenham Hill							09.36								09.56				
Penge East							09.39								09.59				
Kent House							09.41								10.01				
Beckenham Jcn		09/31					09.43					09/52	09.56		10.03				
		Main		Local	Main		Main					Main	Main	Local	Main				
Shortlands		09/32			09.39		09.46					09/55	09.59	09.59	10.06				
BROMLEY SOUTH		09.34		(09.33)	09.41		09.49					09.56	10.00	10.01	10.08				
BROMLEY SOUTH		09.35		09.37	09.42		09.49					09.57	10.01	10.02	10.09				
Bickley				09.40	09.45		09.52						10.04	10.05	10.12				
Bickley Jcn		09/38			09/46		09/54					10/02	10/05	10/06	10/13				
St Mary Cray Jcn		09/39			09/47								10/07						
St Mary Cray				09.50										10.10					
SWANLEY		09.47		09.55								10/08		10.15					
Farningham Road		09.52																	
Fawkham		09.57																	
Meopham		10.01																	
Sole Street		10.04										10/18							
Cuxton Road											10.09	10/23							
Rochester Bge Jcn		10/08									10/12	10/27							
Chatham Goods	09.55																		
Rochester		10.09									10.13								
Rochester	09/57	10.10									10.14								
CHATHAM		10.12									10.16								
CHATHAM	10.00	10.18							10.27			10.31							10.46
GILLINGHAM		10.21							10.30			10.35							10.50
GILLINGHAM	10.07											10.36							10.51
Rainham																			10.55
Newington	10.25																		
Western Jcn	10.30																		
Eastern Jcn						10/30													
SITTINGBOURNE						10.31						10.48							11.06
SITTINGBOURNE												10.50							11.08
Murston Sdgs																			
Teynham																			
FAVERSHAM												11.01							11.19
FAVERSHAM												11.03						11.15	
Graveney Sdgs																			
Whitstable												11.13							
Chestfield												11.18							
HERNE BAY												11.24							
HERNE BAY												11.26							
Birchington												11.38							
Westgate												11.43							
MARGATE												11.48							
MARGATE								10.50	11.27		11.44	11.50							
Broadstairs											11.52	11.58							
Dumpton Park											11.56	12.02							
RAMSGATE								11.00	11.43		11.59	12.06							
Destination	Q'boro			S'oaks	Orp			Loco	Loco			Hastings	Orp	S'oaks	Orp	S. Hill		Dover	

WORKING TIMETABLE : FAVERSHAM to DOVER (1955)

Train	06.40	05.23
From	Fav	H. Hill
Class	Goods	Goods
Engine	N 2-6-0	N 2-6-0
FAVERSHAM		11.15
Selling		
CANTERBURY E.		11.48
CANTERBURY E.		12.10
Bekesbourne		
Adisham		
Aylesham		
Snowdown		12.35
Shepherdswell	11.35	
Kearsney		
DOVER PRIORY	11/55	
Destination	Town	

WORKING TIMETABLE : SHEERNESS to SITTINGBOURNE (1955)

Train		
From		
Class	Pass	Pass
Engine	2-6-2T	H 0-4-4T
SHEERNESS	10.10	11.18
Queenborough	10.16	11.25
Swale		
Redham Dock		
Kemsley	10.25	11.33
Middle Jcn	10/28	11.36
Eastern Jcn	10/29	
SITTINGBOURNE	10.31	
Destination		Gill

WORKING TIMETABLE : RAMSGATE to VICTORIA (1955)

Train		07.51		10.42	10.22		04.50		10.48	09.20	11,00		10.42				07.36	11.22	11.02	
From		A'ford		Orp	S'aoks		L. Bge		Orp	Dover	Orp		S'oaks				M'stone	Orp	S'oaks	
Class	Pass	Pass	Goods	Pass	Pass	Pass	Pass	Pass	ECS	XP	Pass	ECS	Pass	Pass	Pass	XP	Pass	Pass	Pass	Pass
Engine	EMU	2-6-2T	C 0-6-0	EMU	EMU	EMU	E1 4-4-0	V 4-4-0	EMU	WC	EMU	E1 4-4-0	EMU	EMU	H 0-4-4T	BR5 4-6-0	2-6-2T	EMU	EMU	EMU
RAMSGATE							08.44	08.52								09.25	09.37			
Dumpton Park							08.48	08.56								09.29	09.41			
Broadstairs							08.52	09.00								09.33	09.45			
MARGATE							08.58	09.07								09.39	09.51			
MARGATE							09.01									09.42				
Westgate							09.06									09.47				
Birchington							09.11									09.52				
HERNE BAY							09.22									10.03				
HERNE BAY							09.23									10.05				
Chestfield							09.29													
Whitstable							09.34									10.14				
Graveney																				
British Fruit																				
FAVERSHAM		09.41					09.44			10/09						10.24				
FAVERSHAM							09.47									10.26				
Teynham							09.56													
SITTINGBOURNE							10.02									10.37				
SITTINGBOURNE							10.03			10/17					10.19	10.39				
Eastern Jcn															10/20					
Western Jcn																				
Newington																				
Rainham																				
GILLINGHAM							10.17													
GILLINGHAM	09.54	10.00	10.08				10.18			10/27			10.40			10/50				10.54
CHATHAM	09.57		10.11				10.22			10.30			10.43							10.57
CHATHAM	09.59		10/05	10.15						10.32		10.35	10.48			10/53				10.59
Rochester	10.00			10.16									10.48							11.00
Rochester	10.01		10/08	10.17						10/34		10/37	10.49			10/55				11.01
Chatham Goods			10.10																	
Rochester Bge Jcn	10/03		10/18							10/35		10/38	10/50			10/56				11/03
Cuxton Road																				
Sole Street	10.13									10/47						11/08				11.13
Meopham	10.15																			11.15
Longfield																				
Fawkham	10.20																			11.20
Farningham Road	10.24																			11.24
SWANLEY	10.32				10.41					10/59			11.04			11/18			11.24	11.32
St Mary Cray					10.46								11.09						11.29	
St Mary Cray Jcn	10/38				10.48					11/04			11/11			11/24			11/31	11/38
	Main			Local		Main		Local	Main	Local		Main				Main		Local	Main	Main
Bickley Jcn	10/39			10/47	10/49				10/52	11/05	11/05		11/12			11/25		11/27	11/32	11/39
Bickley				10.49	10.51				10.54		11.09		11.14					11.29	11.34	
BROMLEY SOUTH	10.42			10.51	10.53					11.08	11.11		11.16			11.28		11.31	11.36	11.42
BROMLEY SOUTH	10.43			10.52	10.57					11.09	11.12		11.17	11.20		11.30		11.32	11.37	11.43
Shortlands				10.54	11.00						11.14							11.34	11.40	
Beckenham Jcn	10/47			10.57						11/13			11.17			11/34		11.37		11/47
Kent House				10.59									11.19					11.39		
Penge East				11.01									11.21					11.41		
Sydenham Hill				11.04									11.24					11.44		
W. Dulwich				11.06									11.26					11.46		
Herne Hill	10/53			11.09						11/21			11.28			11/42		11.48		11/53
Brixton	10/54			11.11						11/22			11.30			11/43		11.51		11/54
VICTORIA	10.59			11.16						11.28			11.36			11.44		11.56		11.59
Destination					CX	H. Via	Strood		C. St		H. Via				S'ness				H. Via	

WORKING TIMETABLE : DOVER - FAVERSHAM (1955)

Train	07.51				
From	A'ford				
Class	Pass			XP	
Engine	2-6-4T			WC	
DOVER PRIORY	08.46			09.20	
Dover Gas					
Kearsney	08.52			09.27	
Shepherdswell	08.59			09.36	
Snowdown	09.04				
Aylesham	09.07			09.42	
Adisham	09.10				
Bekesbourne	09.16				
CANTERBURY E.	09.21			09.52	
CANTERBURY E.	09.22			09.54	
Selling	09.35				
FAVERSHAM	09.41			10/09	
Destination				Vic	

WORKING TIMETABLE : SITTINGBOURNE - SHEERNESS (1955)

Train					08.40	
From					H. Jcn	
Class				Pass	Goods	
Engine				H 0-4-4T	C 0-6-0	
SITTINGBOURNE				10.19		
Eastern Jcn				10/20		
Middle Jcn				10/21	10/32	
Kemsley				10.24	10/36	
Redham Dock						
Swale						
Queenborough				10.33	10/49	
SHEERNESS				10.39		
Destination						

WORKING TIMETABLE : VICTORIA to RAMSGATE (1955)

Train	09.42		09.51	06.50		09.05		10.11	10.28				11.40		10.31		10.50	10.42	10.51	
From	CX		H. Via	F. Rd		CX		H. Via	H. Grn				Fav		H. Via		H. Grn	CX	H. Via	
Class	Pass	Boat	Pass	Goods	Pass	Pass	Pass	Pass	Goods	Pass	Goods	Goods	XP	XP	Pass	Pass	Goods	Pass	Pass	Pass
Engine	EMU	MN	EMU	C 0-6-0	EMU	EMU	EMU	EMU	N1 2-6-0	EMU	N 2-6-0	N 2-6-0	V 4-4-0	BR5 4-6-0	EMU	EMU	N 2-6-0	EMU	EMU	EMU
VICTORIA		10.00			10.04		10.18			10.24				10.35		10.44				11.04
Brixton		10/07			10.09		10.23			10.29						10.49				11.09
Herne Hill		10/09			10.12		10.25			10.32				10.46		10.52				11.12
W. Dulwich					10.14					10.34						10.54				11.14
Sydenham Hill					10.16					10.36						10.56				11.16
Penge East					10.19					10.39						10.59				11.19
Kent House					10.21					10.41						11.01				11.21
Beckenham Jcn		10/17			10.23		10/31			10.43				10/55		11.03				11.23
		Main	Local		Main		Main	Local		Main				Main	Local	Main		Local		Main
Shortlands		10/19	10.19		10.26		10.39			10.46				10/57	10.59	11.06		11.19		11.26
BROMLEY SOUTH			10.21		10.28		10.34	10.41		10.48				10.58	11.01	11.08		11.21		11.28
BROMLEY SOUTH		10/20	10.22		10.29	10.35		10.42		1049				11.01	11.04	11.09		11.22		11.29
Bickley			10.25		10.32			10.45		10.52					11.07	11.12		11.25		11.32
Bickley Jcn		10/22	10/26		10/33	10/38		10/46		10/53				11/06	11/09	11/13		11/26		11/33
St Mary Cray Jcn			10/27			10/39		10/47	10/51						11/10	11/14		11/27		
St Mary Cray			10.30					10.50	10/55						11.12	11/18		11.30		
SWANLEY			10.35			10.47		10.55	11/03					11/12	11.17		11/26	11.35		
Farningham Road						10.51											11/32			
Fawkham						10.56														
Meopham						11.01														
Sole Street						11.04								11/22			11/51			
Cuxton Road						11/09								11/27						
Rochester Bge Jcn	10/39					11/08								11/31				11/39	11/12	
Chatham Goods				10.55																
Rochester	10.40					11.09												11.40	11.13	
Rochester	10.41			10/57		11.10								11/32				11.41	11.14	
CHATHAM	10.44					11.12								11.33				11.44	11.16	
CHATHAM	10.50			11/00		11.14								11.35				11.46	11.18	
GILLINGHAM	10.53			11.07		11.17												11.49	11.21	
GILLINGHAM														11/38						
Rainham																				
Newington																				
Western Jcn																				
Eastern Jcn																				
SITTINGBOURNE														11.49						
SITTINGBOURNE														11.51						
Murston Sdgs																				
Teynham																				
FAVERSHAM														12.02						
FAVERSHAM													11.40	12.05						
Graveney Sdgs											11.47	11.49								
Whitstable												11.57		12.15						
Chestfield														12.21						
HERNE BAY														12.27						
HERNE BAY														12.29						
Birchington														12.41						
Westgate														12.46						
MARGATE														12.51						
MARGATE													12.36	12.54						
Broadstairs													12.43	13.02						
Dumpton Park													12.47	13.07						
RAMSGATE													12.50	13.10						
Destination		Dover	S'oaks		Orp		S'oaks	A'ford		Orp			C. Cross		S'oaks	Orp		S'oaks		Orp

WORKING TIMETABLE : FAVERSHAM to DOVER (1955)

Station	Train	From	Class	Engine
FAVERSHAM				
Selling				
CANTERBURY E.				
CANTERBURY E.				
Bekesbourne				
Adisham				
Aylesham				
Snowdown				
Shepherdswell				
Kearsney				
DOVER PRIORY				
Destination				

WORKING TIMETABLE : SHEERNESS to SITTINGBOURNE (1955)

Station	Train	From	Class	Engine
SHEERNESS				
Queenborough				
Swale				
Redham Dock				
Kemsley				
Middle Jcn				
Eastern Jcn				
SITTINGBOURNE				
Destination				

WORKING TIMETABLE : RAMSGATE to VICTORIA (1955)

Train		11.42	06.56	11.22		09.42			12.02	11.42	11.19	11.18			09.58	12.22	12.02			
From		Orp	H. Via	S'oaks		A'ford			Orp	S'oaks	Dover	S'ness			A'ford	Orp	S'oaks			
Class	Pass	Pass	Pass	Pass	Pass	Pass	Goods	Pass	Pass	Pass	Pass	Pass	Pass	Goods	Pass	Pass	Pass	Pass	ECS	Pass
Engine	EMU	EMU	E1 4-4-0	EMU	2-6-2T	2-6-4T	N 2-6-0	EMU	EMU	EMU	D1 4-4-0	H 0-4-4T	C 0-6-0	N 2-6-0	EMU	EMU	EMU	EMU	2-6-2T	EMU
RAMSGATE			10.37			10.50														
Dumpton Park			10.41			10.54														
Broadstairs			10.45			10.58														
MARGATE			10.51			11.04														
MARGATE																				
Westgate																				
Birchington																				
HERNE BAY																				
HERNE BAY																				
Chestfield																				
Whitstable																				
Graveney																				
British Fruit																				
FAVERSHAM											12.16									
FAVERSHAM																				
Teynham																				
SITTINGBOURNE																				
SITTINGBOURNE					11.00								11.53							
Eastern Jcn					11/01								11/54							
Western Jcn												11/37								
Newington																				
Rainham																				
GILLINGHAM												11.49								
GILLINGHAM	11.07							11.42							11.54	12.07		12.15		12.40
CHATHAM	11.10							11.45							11.57	12.10		12.20		12.43
CHATHAM	11.12							11.47							11.58	12.12				12.45
Rochester	11.13							11.48							12.00	12.13				12.47
Rochester	11.14							11.49							12.01	12.14				12.49
Chatham Goods							11.24													
Rochester Bge Jcn	11/15						11/28	11/50							12/03	12/15				12/50
Cuxton Road																				
Sole Street															12.13					
Meopham															12.15					
Longfield																				
Fawkham															12.20					
Farningham Road															12.24					
SWANLEY				11.44										12/15	12.32		12.24			
St Mary Cray				11.49													12.29			
St Mary Cray Jcn				11/51										12/22	12/38		12/31			
	Local			Main				Local	Main						Main	Local	Main			
Bickley Jcn	11.47			11/52				12/07	12/12						12/39	12/27	12/32			
Bickley	11.49			11.54				12.09	12.14							12.29	12.34			
BROMLEY SOUTH	11.51			11.56				12.11	12.16						12.42	12.31	12.36			
BROMLEY SOUTH	11.52			11.57				12.12	12.17						12.43	12.32	12.37			
Shortlands	11.54			12.00				12.14	12.20							12.34	12.40			
Beckenham Jcn	11.57							12.17							12/47	12.37				
Kent House	11.59							12.19								12.39				
Penge East	12.01							12.21								12.41				
Sydenham Hill	12.04							12.24								12.44				
W. Dulwich	12.06							12.26								12.46				
Herne Hill	12.09							12.28							12/53	12.48				
Brixton	12.11							12.31							12/54	12.51				
VICTORIA	12.16							12.36							12.59	12.56				
Destination	CX			H. Via	S'ness		H. Jcn	C. St	H. Via				S'ness	H. Grn			H. Via	CX		C. St

WORKING TIMETABLE : DOVER - FAVERSHAM (1955)

Train	10.00	
From	Town	
Class	Goods	Pass
Engine	N 2-6-0	D1 4-4-0
DOVER PRIORY	10/10	11.19
Dover Gas		
Kearsney		11.25
Shepherdswell	10/30	11.32
Snowdown	10.35	11.37
Aylesham		11.40
Adisham		11.43
Bekesbourne		11.49
CANTERBURY E.		11.54
CANTERBURY E.		11.57
Selling		12.10
FAVERSHAM		12.16
Destination		

WORKING TIMETABLE : SITTINGBOURNE - SHEERNESS (1955)

Train			
From			
Class	Pass	Pass	Light
Engine	2-6-2T	C 0-6-0	C 0-6-0
SITTINGBOURNE	11.00	11.53	
Eastern Jcn	11/01	11/54	
Middle Jcn	11/02	11/55	
Kemsley	11.05	11.58	
Redham Dock			
Swale	11.14	12.04	
Queenborough	11.19	12.07	12.23
SHEERNESS	11.29	12.13	12.28
Destination			

WORKING TIMETABLE : VICTORIA to RAMSGATE (1955)

Train			11.33		10.55		11.11	10.54	12.18						12.15	10.50	11.31	
From			Q'boro		C. St		H. Via	H. Hill	S'ness						H. Jcn	H. Grn	H. Via	
Class	Goods		Goods	Goods	Pass	Pass	Pass	Goods	Pass	Pass	Pass	Pass	Pass	Pull	Goods	Goods	Pass	Pass
Engine	N 2-6-0	2-6-2T	C 0-6-0	N 2-6-0	EMU	EMU	EMU	N 2-6-0	EMU	2-6-2T	2-6-2T	L 4-4-0	C 0-6-0	BR5 4-6-0	C 0-6-0	N 2-6-0	EMU	EMU
VICTORIA						11.18	11.24								11.35				11.44
Brixton						11/23	11.29												11.49
Herne Hill	10.54					11/25									11/44				11.52
W. Dulwich							11.34												11.54
Sydenham Hill							11.36												11.56
Penge East							11.39												11.59
Kent House							11.41												12.01
Beckenham Jcn	11/17					11/31	11.43								11/51				12.03
	Local					Main	Main								Main		Main	Local	Main
Shortlands					11.39	11.33	11.46								11.55		11.59		12.06
BROMLEY SOUTH					11.41	11.34	11.48								11.56		12.01		12.08
BROMLEY SOUTH	11/27				11.42	11.35	11.49								11.58		12.02		12.09
Bickley	11.35				11.45		11.52	11.48									12.05		12.12
Bickley Jcn					11/46	11/38	11/53	11/49							12/03		12/06		12/13
St Mary Cray Jcn					11/47	11/39	11/51										12/07		
St Mary Cray					11.50		11.55										12.10		
SWANLEY					11.55	11.47	12/03								12/09		12.15		
Farningham Road						11.52													
Fawkham						11.57													
Meopham						12.01													
Sole Street						12.04									12/19		12.25		
Cuxton Road						12.09									12/24		12.35		
Rochester Bge Jcn					12/08	12/12									12/28	12/30	12/40		
Chatham Goods																12.35	12.45		
Rochester					12.09	12.13													
Rochester					12.10	12.14									12/29				
CHATHAM					12.12	12.16									12.30				
CHATHAM					12.14	12.17									12.33				
GILLINGHAM					12.17	12.20									12.37				
GILLINGHAM															12.38				
Rainham																			
Newington																			
Western Jcn																			
Eastern Jcn			12/05						12/37										
SITTINGBOURNE			12.09						12.38						12.50				
SITTINGBOURNE			(13.00)												12.52				
Murston Sdgs																			
Teynham															12.58				
FAVERSHAM															13.07				
FAVERSHAM		12.06		12.13											13.10				
Graveney Sdgs																			
Whitstable															13.20				
Chestfield																			
HERNE BAY				12.37											13.29				
HERNE BAY															13.31				
Birchington															13.43				
Westgate															13.48				
MARGATE															13.53				
MARGATE										13.20	13.40	13.50			13.58				
Broadstairs										13.28	13.49	13.57			14.06				
Dumpton Park										13.32	13.53	14.01			14.10				
RAMSGATE										13.35	13.56	14.04			14.14				
Destination			Dover				S'oaks	A'ford	Orp	C'bury	M'stone	M'stone						S'oaks	Orp

WORKING TIMETABLE : FAVERSHAM to DOVER (1955)

Train			05.23	05.23
From			H. Hill	H. Hill
Class	Pass	ECS	Goods	Goods
Engine	2-6-2T	2-6-2T	N 2-6-0	N 2-6-0
FAVERSHAM	12.06			
Selling	12.13			
CANTERBURY E.	12.25			
CANTERBURY E.	12.27			
Bekesbourne	12.33			
Adisham	12.39			
Aylesham	12.43			
Snowdown	12.47		13.17	
Shepherdswell	12.53			
Kearsney	13.02		13.30	13.45
DOVER PRIORY	13.07			13/55
Destination				Town

WORKING TIMETABLE : SHEERNESS to SITTINGBOURNE (1955)

Train		11.33	11.33			
From		Q'boro	Q'boro			
Class	Goods	Goods	Goods			Pass
Engine	C 0-6-0	C 0-6-0	C 0-6-0			2-6-2T
SHEERNESS						12.18
Queenborough	11.33					12.24
Swale						12.29
Redham Dock	11.40	11.52				
Kemsley		11.56	11.59			12.33
Middle Jcn			12/04			12/36
Eastern Jcn			12/05			12/37
SITTINGBOURNE			12.09			12.38
Destination						

WORKING TIMETABLE : RAMSGATE to VICTORIA (1955)

Train	12.42	12.22	11.00	13.00	12.42	13.22	13.02				13.42	13.22	06.05	10.00		10.45		12.56	10.12	
From	Orp	S'oaks	S'well	Orp	S'oaks	Orp	S'oaks				Orp	S'oaks	Read'g	Dover		A'ford		Chatham	Ton'bge	
Class	Pass	Pass	Goods	Pass	Pass	Pass	Pass	Pass	XP	Pass	Pass	Pass	Pass	Goods	Mxd	Pass	Goods	Pass	Pass	Goods
Engine	EMU	EMU	N 2-6-0	EMU	EMU	EMU	EMU	EMU	BR5 4-6-0	EMU	EMU	EMU	L 4-4-0	N 2-6-0	2-6-2T	V 4-4-0	C 0-6-0	2-6-2T	C 0-6-0	N 2-6-0
RAMSGATE									11.15				11.25			11.44	11.59	12.34		
Dumpton Park									11.19				11.29			11.48		12.38		
Broadstairs									11.23				11.33			11.52	12.10	12.42		
MARGATE									11.29				11.39			11.58		12.48		
MARGATE									11.32											
Westgate									11.37											
Birchington									11.42											
HERNE BAY									11.54											
HERNE BAY									11.56											
Chestfield									12.02											
Whitstable									12.08											
Graveney																				13.20
British Fruit																				13.27
FAVERSHAM			11.52						12.18					12.06						
FAVERSHAM			12.02						12.24					12.35						
Teynham									12.33											
SITTINGBOURNE									12.39									(13.20)		
SITTINGBOURNE			12/18						12.42					12/53	12.56			13.26		
Eastern Jcn															12/57			13/27		
Western Jcn																				
Newington									12.50											
Rainham									12.56											
GILLINGHAM			12.42						13.01											
GILLINGHAM			12.44					12.54	13.02	13.10				13/17						
CHATHAM								12.57	13.06	13.13										
CHATHAM			12/48					12.58	13.11	13.15				13/22						
Rochester								13.00	13.13	13.16										
Rochester			12/52					13.01	13.14	13.17				13/27						
Chatham Goods																				
Rochester Bge Jcn			12/54					13/03	13/16	13/18				13/29						
Cuxton Road																				
Sole Street							12.13		13/29											
Meopham							13.15													
Longfield																				
Fawkham							13.20													
Farningham Road							13.24													
SWANLEY		12.44		13.04		13.24	13.32		13/40			13.44								
St Mary Cray		12.49		13.09		13.29						13.49								
St Mary Cray Jcn		12/51		13/11		13/31	13/38		13/45			13/51								
	Local	Main		Local	Main	Local	Main	Local	Main		Local	Main								
Bickley Jcn	12/47	12/52		13/05	13/12	13/27	13/32	13/39	13/46		13/47	13/52								
Bickley	12.49	12.54		13.09	13.14	13.29	13.34				13.49	13.54								
BROMLEY SOUTH	12.51	12.56		13.11	13.16	13.31	13.36	13.42	13.49		15.52	13.56								
BROMLEY SOUTH	12.52	12.57		13.12	13.17	13.32	13.37	14.43	13.51		13.53	13.57								
Shortlands	12.54	13.00		13.14	13.20	13.34	13.40				13.55	14.00								
Beckenham Jcn	12.57			13.17		13.37		13/47	13/55		13.58									
Kent House	12.59			13.19		13.39					14.00									
Penge East	13.01			13.21		13.41					14.02									
Sydenham Hill	13.04			13.24		13.44					14.05									
W. Dulwich	13.06			13.26		13.46					14.07									
Herne Hill	13.08			13.29		13.48		13/53	14/03		14.10									
Brixton	13.11			13.31		13.51		13/54	14/04		14.12									
VICTORIA	13.16			13.36		13.56		13/59	14.17		14.10									
Destination		H. Via	Hoo Jn	H. Via		H. Via			CX		H. Via			Hoo Jn	S'ness			S'ness		

WORKING TIMETABLE : DOVER - FAVERSHAM (1955)

Train		10.00
From		Town
Class	Goods	Goods
Engine	N 2-6-0	N 2-6-0
DOVER PRIORY		
Dover Gas		
Kearsney		
Shepherdswell	11.00	
Snowdown		11.14
Aylesham		
Adisham		
Bekesbourne		
CANTERBURY E.		
CANTERBURY E.	11/24	11/39
Selling	11/42	11/57
FAVERSHAM	11.52	12.06
Destination	H. Jcn	H, Jcn

WORKING TIMETABLE : SITTINGBOURNE - SHEERNESS (1955)

Train			12.56
From			Ctm
Class	Mxd	Light	Pass
Engine	2-6-2T	C 0-6-0	2-6-2T
SITTINGBOURNE	12.56		13.26
Eastern Jcn	12/57		13/27
Middle Jcn	12/58		13/28
Kemsley	13.01		13.31
Redham Dock			
Swale	13.07		
Queenborough	13.11	13.28	13.42
SHEERNESS	13.17	13.33	13.48
Destination			

WORKING TIMETABLE : VICTORIA to RAMSGATE (1955)

Station	11.42 CX Pass EMU	11.51 H.Via Pass EMU	Pass EMU	L 4-4-0	11.33 Q'boro Goods N 2-6-0	2-6-2T	11.56 C.St Pass EMU	12.11 H.Via Pass EMU	Pass EMU	Pass EMU	12.13 Fav Goods N 2-6-0	13.20 S'ness Pass C 0-6-0	Boat WC	XP V 4-4-0	12.13 Fav Goods N 2-6-0	XP BR5 4-6-0	D1 4-4-0	Pass 2-6-4T	XP WC
VICTORIA			12.04				12.18		12.24				12.30			12.35			
Brixton			12.09				12.23		12.29				12/37						
Herne Hill			12.12				12.25		12.32							12/44			
W. Dulwich			12.14						12.34				(via						
Sydenham Hill			12.16						12.36				Cat-						
Penge East			12.19						12.39				ford)						
Kent House			12.21						12.41										
Beckenham Jcn			12.23				12/31		12.43							12/52			
(lines)		Local	Main				Local	Local	Main				Local			Main			
Shortlands		12.19	12.26				12/33	12.39	12.46				12/51			12/54			
BROMLEY SOUTH		12.21	12.28				12.34	12.41	12.48							12.55			
BROMLEY SOUTH		12.22	12.29				12.35	12.42	12.49				12/52			12.57			
Bickley		12.25	12.32					12.45	12.52										
Bickley Jcn		12/26	12/33				12/38	12/46	12/53				12/56			13/02			
St Mary Cray Jcn		12.27					12/39	12/47											
St Mary Cray		12.30						12.50											
SWANLEY		12.35					12.47	12.55								13/08			
Farningham Road							12.52												
Fawkham							12.57												
Meopham							13.01												
Sole Street							13.04									13/18			
Cuxton Road							13/09									13/23			
Rochester Bge Jcn	12/39						13/12	13/08								13/27			
Chatham Goods																			
Rochester	12.40						13.13	13.09											
Rochester	12.41						13.14	13.10								13/28			
CHATHAM	12.43						13.16	13.12											
CHATHAM	12.46					12.56	13.18	13.13								13.33			
GILLINGHAM	12.49					13.00	13.21	13.16								13.36			
GILLINGHAM						13.01										13.38			
Rainham						13.06													
Newington						13.13													
Western Jcn																			
Eastern Jcn												13/40							
SITTINGBOURNE						13.20						13.41				13.50			
SITTINGBOURNE					13.00	(13.26)										13.53			
Murston Sdgs																			
Teynham																13.59			
FAVERSHAM					13.16											14.08			
FAVERSHAM				13.13	13.45											14.12	14.20		
Graveney Sdgs																			
Whitstable																14.22			
Chestfield																14.28			
HERNE BAY																14.34			
HERNE BAY										13.45						14.37			
Birchington										14/05						14.49			
Westgate										14.10					14.49	14.55			
MARGATE															14/51	15.01			
MARGATE														14.45		15.05		15.15	15.25
Broadstairs														14.51		15.13		15.21	15.31
Dumpton Park														14.55		15.18		15.25	15.35
RAMSGATE														14.59		15.22		15.29	15.39
Destination		S'oaks	Orp	Dover	Dover	S'ness		S' oaks	Orp			Dover	C. Street				Dover	Hastings	C. Cross

WORKING TIMETABLE : FAVERSHAM to DOVER (1955)

Station	Pass L 4-4-0	08.40 H.Jcn Goods N 2-6-0	O1 0-6-0	Pass D1 4-4-0	08.40 H.Jcn Goods N 2-6-0
FAVERSHAM	13.13	13.45		14.20	
Selling	13.20			14.27	
CANTERBURY E.	13.31			14.38	
CANTERBURY E.	13.33		14/15	14.42	
Bekesbourne	13.39			14.48	
Adisham	13.45			14.54	
Aylesham	13.49			14.58	
Snowdown	13.53		14.40	15.02	15.18
Shepherdswell	13.58		14.42	15.07	15.28
Kearsney	14.05			15.14	
DOVER PRIORY	14.10		15/02	15.19	
Destination			Town		

WORKING TIMETABLE : SHEERNESS to SITTINGBOURNE (1955)

Station	Pass C 0-6-0	Light	Pass 2-6-4T
SHEERNESS	13.20	13.55	14.08
Queenborough	13.26	14.00	14.14
Swale	13.31		
Redham Dock			
Kemsley	13.36		14.21
Middle Jcn	13/39		14/24
Eastern Jcn	13/40		
SITTINGBOURNE	13.41		
Destination			Gill

WORKING TIMETABLE : RAMSGATE to VICTORIA (1955)

Train	13.20		14.02	13.42	14.22	14.02		14.35	13.10	14.42	12.37		14.22		13.20			15.02	14.08	14.22
From	Whit		Orp	Orp	Orp	S'oaks		Orp	Dover	Orp	Dover		S'oaks		Whit			Orp	S'ness	Gill
Class	Goods	Pass	Pass	Pass	Pass	Pass	Pass	Pass	Boat	Pass	Pass	Pass	Pass	Pass	Goods	Pcls	Pass	Pass	Pass	Pcls
Engine	N 2-6-0	EMU	EMU	EMU	EMU	EMU	EMU	EMU	MN 4-6-2	EMU	E1 4-4-0	EMU	EMU	C 0-6-0	N 2-6-0	C 0-6-0	EMU	EMU	2-6-2T	C 0-6-0
RAMSGATE																				
Dumpton Park																				
Broadstairs																				
MARGATE																				
MARGATE																				
Westgate																				
Birchington																				
HERNE BAY																				
HERNE BAY																				
Chestfield																				
Whitstable																				
Graveney	13.29																			
British Fruit	13.35														13.45					
FAVERSHAM											13.30				13.50					
FAVERSHAM											13.32									
Teynham											13.41									
SITTINGBOURNE											13.47									
SITTINGBOURNE											13.48			13.55						
Eastern Jcn														13/56						
Western Jcn																			14/25	
Newington											13.55									
Rainham											14.01									
GILLINGHAM											14.06								14.36	
GILLINGHAM		13.40				13.54					14.10						14.22	14.32		
CHATHAM		13.43				13.57					14.13						14.26	14.35		
CHATHAM		13.47				13.58					14.15					(14.43)		14.37		14.43
Rochester		13.48				14.00					14.16							14.38		14.45
Rochester		13.49				14.01					14.17							14.39		(14.56)
Chatham Goods																				
Rochester Bge Jcn		13/50				14/03					14/18							14/40		
Cuxton Road																				
Sole Street						14.13														
Meopham						14.15														
Longfield																				
Fawkham						14.20														
Farningham Road						14.24														
SWANLEY			14.04		14.24	14.32							14.44							
St Mary Cray			14.09		14.29								14.49							
St Mary Cray Jcn			14/11		14/31	14/38							14/51							
			Local	Main	Local	Main	Main	Main		Local	Local		Main					Local		
Bickley Jcn			14/07	14/12	14/27	14/32	14/39	14/41		14/43	14/47		14/52					15/07		
Bickley			14.09	14.14	14.29	14.34	14.40	14.42			14.49		14.54					15.09		
BROMLEY SOUTH			14.11	14.16	14.31	14.36	14.42	14.44			14.51		14.56					15.11		
BROMLEY SOUTH			14.12	14.17	14.32	14.37	14.43	14.46		14/46	14.52		14.57					15.12		
Shortlands			14.14	14.20	14.34	14.40		14.49		14/48	14.54		15.00					15.14		
Beckenham Jcn			14.17		14.37		14/47				14.57									
Kent House			14.19		14.39						14.59							15.19		
Penge East			14.21		14.41						15.01							15.21		
Sydenham Hill			14.24		14.44						15.04							15.24		
W. Dulwich			14.26		14.46						15.06							15.26		
Herne Hill			14.29		14.49	14/53		14/58			15.08							15.29		
Brixton			14.31		14.51	14/54		14/59			15.11							15.31		
VICTORIA			14.36		14.56	14.59		15.05			15.16							15.36		
Destination		CX		H. Via		H. Via		H. Via					CX	H. Via	S'ness			CX		

WORKING TIMETABLE : DOVER - FAVERSHAM (1955)

Train		
From		
Class		Loco
		Light
Engine	Pass	
	E1 4-4-0	N 2-6-0
DOVER PRIORY	12.37	12/45
Dover Gas		
Kearsney	12.43	
Shepherdswell	12.50	13.05
Snowdown	12.55	
Aylesham	12.58	
Adisham	13.01	
Bekesbourne	13.07	
CANTERBURY E.	13.12	
CANTERBURY E.	13.14	
Selling		
FAVERSHAM	13.30	
Destination	Ctm	

WORKING TIMETABLE : SITTINGBOURNE - SHEERNESS (1955)

Train	
From	
Class	
	Pass
Engine	C 0-6-0
SITTINGBOURNE	13.55
Eastern Jcn	13/56
Middle Jcn	13/57
Kemsley	14.00
Redham Dock	
Swale	14.06
Queenborough	14.10
SHEERNESS	14.20
Destination	

WORKING TIMETABLE : VICTORIA to RAMSGATE (1955)

Train	11.00	12.31		12.42	10.50	12.47				12.51	12.55	13.11		11.00	11.00	13.31		13.50	13.51	13.42
From	H. Via	H. Via		CX	CX	H. Grn	H. Grn		H. Via	C. St	H. Via		H. Via	H. Via	H. Via		H. Grn	H. Via	CX
Class	Pcls	Pass	Pass	Pass	Pass	Goods	Goods	Boat	Pass	Pass	Pass	Pass	Pcls	Pcls	Pass	Pass	Goods	Pass	Pass
Engine	E1 4-4-0	EMU	EMU	EMU	C 0-6-0	N 2-6-0		BR7	EMU	EMU	EMU	EMU	E1 4-4-0	E1 4-4-0	EMU	EMU	N 2-6-0	EMU	EMU
VICTORIA		12.44						13.00	13.04		13.18	13.24				13.44			
Brixton		12.49						13.07	13.09		13.23	13.29				13.49			
Herne Hill		12.52						13.08	13.12		13.25	13.32				13.52			
W. Dulwich		12.54							13.14			13.34				13.54			
Sydenham Hill		12.56							13.16			13.36				13.59			
Penge East		12.59							13.19			13.39				14.01			
Kent House		13.01							13.21			13.41				14.03			
Beckenham Jcn		13.03						13/16	13.23		13/31	13.43				14.06			
		Local	Main					Main	Local	Main	Local	Local			Main	Local		Main	Local
Shortlands		12.59	13.06					13/18	13.19	13.26	13/32	13/39			13.46	13.59		14.08	14.19
BROMLEY SOUTH		13.01	13.08						13.21	13.28	13.34	13.41			13.48	14.01		14.09	14.21
BROMLEY SOUTH		13.02	13.09					13/19	13.22	13.29	13.35	13.42			13.49	14.02		14.12	14.22
Bickley			13.06						13.12	13.25	13.32			14/13	13.45	13.57		14.05	14.25
Bickley Jcn		13/07	13/13						13/22	13/26	13/33	13/38			13/46	13/58		14/06	14/26
St Mary Cray Jcn	13/06	13/08				13/11			13/27			13/39			13/47		14/07	14/18	14/27
St Mary Cray	13.11	13/14							13.30		13.50				14.10			14/22	14.30
SWANLEY	13/12	13.16				13/22			13.35		13.47	13.55			14.15			14.35	14/30
Farningham Road											13.52								
Fawkham											13.57								
Meopham											14.01								
Sole Street	13/24										14.04								
Cuxton Road	13/29										14.09								
Rochester Bge Jcn	13/33			13/39							14.08	14/12							14/39
Chatham Goods					13.59														
Rochester	13.34			13.40							14.09	14.13							14.40
Rochester	13.38			13.41	14/01						14.10	14.14							14.41
CHATHAM				13.43							14.12	14.16							14.43
CHATHAM	13.40			13.45	14.03						14.13	14.18							14.46
GILLINGHAM				13.48							14.16	14.21							14.49
GILLINGHAM	13.43			14/11															
Rainham	13.49																		
Newington																			
Western Jcn																			
Eastern Jcn																			
SITTINGBOURNE	14.01			14.32															
SITTINGBOURNE	14.08																		
Murston Sdgs																			
Teynham																			
FAVERSHAM	14.20																		
FAVERSHAM	14.33																		
Graveney Sdgs																			
Whitstable	14.43												14.53						
Chestfield																			
HERNE BAY													15.00						
HERNE BAY													15.06						
Birchington													15.18	15.26					
Westgate														15.30					
MARGATE														15.38					
MARGATE													15.44						
Broadstairs													15.51						
Dumpton Park																			
RAMSGATE													16.06						
Destination		S'oaks	Orp				Ton'bge	Dover	S'oaks	Orp	S'oaks	Orp			S'oaks	Orp	A'ford	S'oaks	

WORKING TIMETABLE : FAVERSHAM to DOVER (1955)

Train	08.40
From	H. Jcn
Class	Goods
Engine	N & O1
FAVERSHAM	
Selling	
CANTERBURY E.	
CANTERBURY E.	
Bekesbourne	
Adisham	
Aylesham	
Snowdown	
Shepherdswell	15.48
Kearsney	15/58
DOVER PRIORY	16/08
Destination	Town

WORKING TIMETABLE : SHEERNESS to SITTINGBOURNE (1955)

Train	
From	
Class	
Engine	
SHEERNESS	
Queenborough	
Swale	
Redham Dock	
Kemsley	
Middle Jcn	
Eastern Jcn	
SITTINGBOURNE	
Destination	

WORKING TIMETABLE : RAMSGATE to VICTORIA (1955)

Train		14.42	13.05		15.18	14.22	15.04			11.59			13.55	15.42		15.22			11.15	16.02
From		S'oaks	Dover		Orp	Gill	S'oaks			Rams			S'down	Orp		S'oaks		Loco	C. Cross	Orp
Class	Pass	Pass	Pass	XP	Pass	Pcls	Pass	Pass	Pass	Goods	ECS	Pass	Goods	Pass	Pass	Pass	XP	Light	XP	Pass
Engine	EMU	EMU	L 4-4-0	BR5	EMU	C 0-6-0	EMU	EMU	C 0-6-0	C 0-6-0	D1 4-4-0	EMU	N 2-6-0	EMU	EMU	EMU	BR5	4MTT & V	WC	EMU
RAMSGATE				13.10													13.55	14.00	14.17	
Dumpton Park				13.14													13.59		14.21	
Broadstairs				13.18						13.42							14.03		14.25	
MARGATE				13.25						13.50							14.09	14.17	14.41	
MARGATE				13.29													14.12			
Westgate				13.34													14.17			
Birchington				13.39													14.22			
HERNE BAY				13.50													14.33			
HERNE BAY				13.52													14.35			
Chestfield				13.58													14.41			
Whitstable				14.03													14.47			
Graveney																				
British Fruit																				
FAVERSHAM			14.02	14.13									14.50				14.57			
FAVERSHAM			14.19										(15.20)				15.01			
Teynham																				
SITTINGBOURNE			14.30																	
SITTINGBOURNE			14.32						14.43								15/11			
Eastern Jcn									14/44											
Western Jcn																				
Newington																				
Rainham																				
GILLINGHAM			14.45																	
GILLINGHAM		14.41	14.46				14.54			14.57	15.10						15/22			
CHATHAM		14.44	14.50				14.57			15.01	15.13									
CHATHAM		14.47	14.53				14.58				15.15						15/25			
Rochester		14.48					15.00				15.16									
Rochester		14.49	14/55			14.56	15.01				15.17						15/27			
Chatham Goods																				
Rochester Bge Jcn		14/50	14/56			14/57	15/03				15/18						15/28			
Cuxton Road																				
Sole Street			15/09				15.13										15/39			
Meopham							15.15													
Longfield																				
Fawkham							15.20													
Farningham Road							15.24													
SWANLEY		15.04		15/19	15.24		15.32								15.44		15/50			
St Mary Cray		15.09			15.29										15.49					
St Mary Cray Jcn		15/11			15/31		15/38									15/51	15/55			
		Main	Main	Local	Main		Main							Local		Main				Local
Bickley Jcn		15/12	15/25	15/23	15/33		15/39							15/47		15/52	15/56			16/07
Bickley		15.14	15/26	15.29	15.34									15.49	15.51	15.54				16.09
BROMLEY SOUTH		15.16	15.28	15.31	15.37		15.42							15.51	15.53	15.56	15.59			16.11
BROMLEY SOUTH		15.17	15.29	15.32	15.37		15.43							15.52	15.54	15.57	16.00			16.12
Shortlands		15.20	15/31	15.35			15.45							15.54	15/56	16.00				16.14
Beckenham Jcn			15/33	15.38			15/47							15.57			16/04			16.17
Kent House				15.40										15.59						16.19
Penge East				15.42										16.01						16.21
Sydenham Hill				15.45										16.04						16.24
W. Dulwich				15.47										16.06						16.26
Herne Hill			15/41	15.49			15.53							16.09			16/12			16.29
Brixton				15.51			15/55							16.11			16/13			16.31
VICTORIA			15.48	15.57			16.00							16.16			16.20			16.36
Destination		C. St	H. Via			Strood	H. Via		S'ness		CX			H. Via	H. Via					

WORKING TIMETABLE : DOVER - FAVERSHAM (1955)

Train					14.02	14.02	
From					Town	Town	
Class		Pass			Goods	Goods	Goods	Pass
Engine		L 4-4-0			N 2-6-0	N 2-6-0	N 2-6-0	2-6-4T
Kearsney		13.11						14.46
Shepherdswell		13.19				14.27	14.45	14.54
Snowdown		13.24			13.55			14.59
Aylesham		13.27						15.02
Adisham		13.30					14.55	15.05
Bekesbourne		13.36						15.11
CANTERBURY E.		13.41						15.16
CANTERBURY E.		13.43			14/20			
Selling		13.56						
FAVERSHAM		14.02			14.50			
Destination					F'ham			

WORKING TIMETABLE : SITTINGBOURNE - SHEERNESS (1955)

Train	
From	
Class	Pass
Engine	C 0-6-0
SITTINGBOURNE	14.43
Eastern Jcn	14/44
Middle Jcn	14/45
Kemsley	14.48
Redham Dock	
Swale	14.54
Queenborough	14.59
SHEERNESS	15.05
Destination	

WORKING TIMETABLE : VICTORIA to RAMSGATE (1955)

	1	2	3	4	5	6	7	8	9	10	11	12	13	14	15	16	17	18
Train		10.50				13.55		14.11	15.20		14.31		12.25	14.35	14.51	14.42		16.15
From		H. Grn				C. St		H. Via	S'ness		H. Via		B'frs	Vic	H. Via	CX		S'ness
Class	Pcls	Light	Goods	Pass	XP	Pass	Pass	Pass	Pass	Pass	Pass	XP	Goods	Pass	Pass	Pass	Pass	Pass
Engine	C 0-6-0	N 2-6-0	C 0-6-0	2-6-4T	WC	EMU	EMU	EMU	C 0-6-0	EMU	WC	EMU	C 0-6-0	EMU	EMU	EMU	EMU	2-6-2T
VICTORIA						14.04		14.18		14.24	14.35			14.44			15.04	
Brixton						14.09		14/23		14.29				14.49			15.09	
Herne Hill						14.12		14/25		14.32	14/44			14.52			15.12	
W. Dulwich						14.14				14.34				14.54			15.14	
Sydenham Hill						14.16				14.36				14.56			15.16	
Penge East						14.19				14.39				14.59			15.19	
Kent House						14.21				14.41				15.01			15.21	
Beckenham Jcn						14.23		14/31		14.43	14/52			15.03			15.23	
(route)						Main	Local	Local		Main	Main	Local		Main	Local		Main	
Shortlands						14.26	14/33	14.39		14.46	14/54	14.59		15.06	15.19		15.26	
BROMLEY SOUTH						14.28	14.34	14.41		14.48	14.55	15.01		15.08	15.21		15.28	
BROMLEY SOUTH						14.29	14.35	14.42		14.49	14.57	15.02		15.09	15.22		15.29	
Bickley						14.32		14.45		14.52		15.05		15.12	15.25		15.32	
Bickley Jcn						14/33	14/38	14/46		14/53	15/02	15/06		15/13	15/26		15/33	
St Mary Cray Jcn						14/39		14/47			15/03	15/07	15/11					
St Mary Cray								14.50				15.10	15/15					
SWANLEY							14.47	14.55			15/08	15.15	15/23		15.35			
Farningham Road							14.52						15/29					
Fawkham							14.57											
Meopham							15.01											
Sole Street							15/04				15/18		15.48					
Cuxton Road							15/09				15/23							
Rochester Bge Jcn						15/08	15/12				15/27			15/39				
Chatham Goods																		
Rochester						15.09	15.13							15.40				
Rochester	14.54					15.10	15.14				15/28			15.41				
CHATHAM	14.56					15.12	15.16				15.29			15.43				
CHATHAM	15.20					15.13	15.18				15.32			15.46				
GILLINGHAM	15.24					15.16	15.21				15.36			15.49				
GILLINGHAM											15.38							
Rainham																		
Newington																		
Western Jcn																		
Eastern Jcn									15/41									16/35
SITTINGBOURNE									15.41		15.50							16.36
SITTINGBOURNE			14.48								15.52							
FAVERSHAM			15.04								16.03							
FAVERSHAM		14.35									16.06			16.11				
Graveney Sdgs																		
Whitstable														16.21				
Chestfield														16.27				
HERNE BAY														16.33				
HERNE BAY														16.35				
Birchington														16.47				
Westgate														16.52				
MARGATE														16.58				
MARGATE			16.22	16.55										17.01				
Broadstairs			16.30	17.03										17.09				
Dumpton Park			16.34	17.07										17.14				
RAMSGATE			16.38	17.11										17.18				
Destination		C'bury		Ashford	C. Cross	Orp		S'oaks		Orp	Dover	S'oaks		Orp	S'oaks		Orp	

WORKING TIMETABLE : FAVERSHAM to DOVER (1955)

	Light	Pass		XP
Train				14.35
From				Vic
Class	Light	Pass		XP
Engine	N 2-6-0	2-6-4T		WC
FAVERSHAM	14.35			16.06
Selling				16.13
CANTERBURY E.	14.55			16.24
CANTERBURY E.		15.43		16.26
Bekesbourne		15.49		16.33
Adisham		15.55		16.39
Aylesham		15.59		16.43
Snowdown		16.03		16.47
Shepherdswell		16.08		16.52
Kearsney		16.15		16.59
DOVER PRIORY		16.20		17.06
Destination				

WORKING TIMETABLE : SHEERNESS to SITTINGBOURNE (1955)

	Pass	Pass
Train		
From		
Class	Pass	Pass
Engine	C 0-6-0	2-6-2T
SHEERNESS	15.20	16.15
Queenborough	15.26	16.21
Swale	15.31	16.27
Redham Dock		
Kemsley	15.36	16.31
Middle Jcn	15/39	16/34
Eastern Jcn	15/40	16/35
SITTINGBOURNE	15.41	16.36
Destination		

WORKING TIMETABLE : RAMSGATE to VICTORIA (1955)

Train →	12.28	15.42			16.23	16.02		16.39	13.55		15.28	16.22		17.05	17.20		17.05	
From	M'stone	S'oaks			Orp	S'oaks		Orp	S'down		Dover	S'oaks		Orp	S. Hill		Orp	
Class	Pass	Pass	Pass	Pass	Pass	Pass	Pass	Pass	Goods	Pass	Pass	Pass	Goods	Pass	ECS	Pass	Pass	Pass
Engine	2-6-2T	EMU	EMU	2-6-2T	EMU	EMU	EMU	EMU	N 2-6-0	EMU	2-6-2T	EMU	C 0-6-0	EMU	EMU	EMU	EMU	EMU
RAMSGATE	14.25																	
Dumpton Park	14.29																	
Broadstairs	14.33																	
MARGATE	14.39																	
MARGATE																		
Westgate																		
Birchington																		
HERNE BAY																		
HERNE BAY																		
Chestfield																		
Whitstable																		
Graveney																		
British Fruit																		
FAVERSHAM											16.23							
FAVERSHAM				15.11														
Teynham				15.20														
SITTINGBOURNE				15.26														
SITTINGBOURNE				15.28					15/36	16.00								
Eastern Jcn										16/01								
Western Jcn																		
Newington				15.35														
Rainham				15.41														
GILLINGHAM				15.46														
GILLINGHAM		15.42		15.47		15.54			15/58		16.10						16.40	
CHATHAM		15.45		15.51		15.57					16.13						16.43	
CHATHAM		15.47				15.58			16/00		16.15						16.45	
Rochester		15.48				16.00					16.16						16.47	
Rochester		15.49				16.01					16.17						16.49	
Chatham Goods									16.05									
Rochester Bge Jcn		15/50				16/03					16/18						16/50	
Cuxton Road																		
Sole Street						16.13							17.03					
Meopham						16.15							17.08					
Longfield																		
Fawkham						16.20												
Farningham Road						16.24												
SWANLEY		16.04			16.24	16.33												
St Mary Cray		16.09			16.29													
St Mary Cray Jcn		16/11			16/31	16/38												
(route)		Main			Local	Local	Main	Main		Local	Main			Local			Main	Local
Bickley Jcn		16/13			16/28	16/32	16/39	16/44			16/53			17/06			17/10	
Bickley		16.14		16.22	16.29	16.34		16.42		16.45	16.54			17.07			17.11	17.14
BROMLEY SOUTH		16.16		16.24	16.31	16.36	16.42	16.44		16.47	16.56			17.09			17.13	17.16
BROMLEY SOUTH		16.17		16.25	16.32	16.37	16.40	16.43		16.45	16.57	16.48		17.10			17.14	17.17
Shortlands		16.20		16.28	16.35	16.40		16.48		16.52	17.00			17.12			17/16	17.20
Beckenham Jcn				16.31	16.38		16/47	16.51		16.56				17.16				
Kent House				16,33	16.40			16.53		16.58				17.18				
Penge East				16.35	16.42			16.55		17.00				17.20				
Sydenham Hill				16.38	16.45			16.58		17.04				17.23				
W. Dulwich				16.41	16.47			17.00		17.06				17.25				
Herne Hill				16.43	16.49		16/54	17.08						17.28	17.30			
Brixton				16.45	16.51		16/55	17.10						17.30	17/32			
VICTORIA				16.51	16.57		17.00	17.16						17.35	17.38			
Destination		H. Via	C. St			H. Via		H. Via	S'ness	CX		H. Via		C. St	H. Via		H. Via	H. Via

WORKING TIMETABLE : DOVER - FAVERSHAM (1955)

Train		14.02
From		Town
Class	Pass	Goods
Engine	2-6-2T	N 2-6-0
Kearsney	15.34	
Shepherdswell	15.41	
Snowdown	15.45	
Aylesham	15.48	
Adisham	15.51	16.10
Bekesbourne	15.57	16.20
CANTERBURY E.	16.02	
CANTERBURY E.	16.04	
Selling	16.17	
FAVERSHAM	16.23	
Destination		

WORKING TIMETABLE : SITTINGBOURNE - SHEERNESS (1955)

Train	
From	
Class	Pass
Engine	2-6-2T
SITTINGBOURNE	16.00
Eastern Jcn	16/01
Middle Jcn	16/02
Kemsley	16.05
Redham Dock	
Swale	16.11
Queenborough	16.16
SHEERNESS	16.26
Destination	

WORKING TIMETABLE : VICTORIA to RAMSGATE (1955)

Train	14.55		15.11			XP		15.31	15.47	15.51	16.04		ECS	15.42	16.55	16.14		16.11	
From	C. St		H. Via					H. Via		H. Via	H. Via			CX	Strood	C. St		H. Via	
Class	Pass	Pass	Pass	Pass	Pass	XP	Pass	Pass	Pass	Pass	Pass	Pass	ECS	Pass	Pass	Pass	Pass	Pass	Pass
Engine	EMU	U1 2-6-0	EMU	EMU	EMU	BR5 4-6-0	2-6-2T	EMU	EMU	EMU	EMU	EMU	2-6-2T	2-6-2T	EMU	D1 4-4-0	EMU	EMU	EMU
VICTORIA			15.18		15.24	15.35			15.44		16.04			16.06		16.18		16.22	
Brixton			15/23		15.29				15.49		16.09			16/15		16/23		16.27	
Herne Hill			15.25		15.32	15/44			15.52	15.59	16.11	16.15				16/25		16.30	
W. Dulwich					15.34				15.54	16.01	16.13	16.17						16.32	
Sydenham Hill					15.36				15.56	16.03	16.15	16.19						16.34	
Penge East					15.39				15.59	16.06	16.18							16.37	
Kent House					15.41				16.01	16.08	16.20							16.39	
Beckenham Jcn			15/31		15.43	15/52			16.03	16.10	16.23	16.26				16/31		16.41	
			Local	Local	Main	Main		Local	Main	Main	Local	Main	Local			Main		Local	Local
Shortlands			15/32	15.39	15.46	15/54		15.59	16.06	16/13	16/19	16.25	16.29			16/32		16.39	16.44
BROMLEY SOUTH			15.34	15.41	15.48	15.55		16.01	16.08	16.15	16.21	16.27	16.30			16.34		16.41	16.47
BROMLEY SOUTH			15.35	15.42	15.49	15.57		16.02	16.09	16.16	16.22	16.28	16.31			16.35		16.42	16.50
Bickley				15.45	15.52			16.05	16.12	16.19	16.25	16.31	16.34					16.45	16.53
Bickley Jcn			15/38	15/46	15/53	16/02		16/06	16/13	16/21	16/26		16/36			16/38		16/46	16/54
St Mary Cray Jcn			15/39	15/47				16/07			16/27					16/39		16/47	
St Mary Cray				15.50				16.10			16.30								16.50
SWANLEY			15.51	15.55		16.08		16.15			16.35					16.48		16.55	
Farningham Road			15.56													16.53			
Fawkham			16.01													16.58			
Meopham			16.05													17.02			
Sole Street			16.08			16/18										17.05			
Cuxton Road			16/13			16/23										17/10			
Rochester Bge Jcn	16/08		16/16			16/27								16/40	16/57	17/09		17/13	
Chatham Goods																			
Rochester	16.09		16.17											16.41	16.58	19.10		17.14	
Rochester	16.10		16.18			16/28								16.42	17.00	17.11		17.15	
CHATHAM	16.12		16.20			16.29								16.43	17.03	17.13		17.17	
CHATHAM	16.13		16.22			16.32							16.37	16.45	17.06	17.14		17.19	
GILLINGHAM	16.16		16.25										16.41	16.48	17.10	17.17		17.22	
GILLINGHAM						16/34							16.43		17.11				
Rainham													16.48		17.16				
Newington													16.54						
Western Jcn																			
Eastern Jcn																			
SITTINGBOURNE						16.46							17.02		17.26				
SITTINGBOURNE						16.48									(17.31)				
Murston Sdgs																			
Teynham																			
FAVERSHAM						16.59													
FAVERSHAM						17.01	17.12												
Graveney Sdgs																			
Whitstable						17.11													
Chestfield						17.17													
HERNE BAY						17.23													
HERNE BAY						17.25													
Birchington						17.37													
Westgate						17.43													
MARGATE						17.48													
MARGATE		17.35				17.51													
Broadstairs		17.42				17.59													
Dumpton Park		17.46				18.04													
RAMSGATE		17.50				18.08													
Destination		Dover		S' Oaks	Orp	Dover		S'oaks	Orp	Orp	S'oaks			Orp	C. St			S'oaks	Orp

WORKING TIMETABLE : FAVERSHAM to DOVER (1955)

Train							
From							
Class			Pass			ECS	
Engine			2-6-2T				
FAVERSHAM			17.12				
Selling			17.19				
CANTERBURY E.			17.30				
CANTERBURY E.			17.34				
Bekesbourne			17.40				
Adisham			17.46				
Aylesham			17.50				
Snowdown			17.54				
Shepherdswell			17.59				
Kearsney			18.11			18.55	
DOVER PRIORY			18.17			18.59	
Destination							

WORKING TIMETABLE : SHEERNESS to SITTINGBOURNE (1955)

Train
From
Class
Engine
SHEERNESS
Queenborough
Swale
Redham Dock
Kemsley
Middle Jcn
Eastern Jcn
SITTINGBOURNE
Destination

WORKING TIMETABLE : RAMSGATE to VICTORIA (1955)

	17.13	16.48		17.04	16.49					17.45	17.26		17.16	15.00	18.00	16.58	18.00	16.20		13.15
Train	17.13	16.48		17.04	16.49					17.45	17.26		17.16	15.00	18.00	16.58	18.00	16.20		13.15
From	Orp	S'oaks		S'oaks	M'stone					Orp	S'oaks		M'stone	C'bury	Orp	Dover	Orp	C'bury		C. Cross
Class	Pass	Pass	Pass	Pass	Pass	Pass	XP	Pass	Pass	Pass	Pass	Goods	Pass	Pass	Pass	Boat	Pass	Goods	Pass	XP
Engine	EMU	EMU	EMU	EMU	EMU	EMU	BR5 4-6-0	EMU	EMU	EMU	EMU	C 0-6-0	2-6-4T	EMU	EMU	BR7	EMU	N 2-6-0	2-6-2T	WC
RAMSGATE							15.22							15.33						16.02
Dumpton Park							15.26							15.37						16.06
Broadstairs							15.31							15.40						16.10
MARGATE							15.37							15.47						16.16
MARGATE							15.40				15.45									
Westgate							15.45				15/50									
Birchington							15.50				15.55									
HERNE BAY							16.02													
HERNE BAY							16.04													
Chestfield							16.10													
Whitstable							16.16													
Graveney																				
British Fruit																				
FAVERSHAM							16.26												16.54	
FAVERSHAM							16.31												(17.30)	
Teynham							16.40													
SITTINGBOURNE							16.46													
SITTINGBOURNE							16.48												16.56	
Eastern Jcn																			16/57	
Western Jcn																				
Newington																				
Rainham																				
GILLINGHAM							17.01													
GILLINGHAM						16.54	17.02		17.10											
CHATHAM						16.57	17.06		17.13											
CHATHAM						16.59	17.10		17.15											
Rochester						17.00			17.17											
Rochester						17.01	17/12		17.18											
Chatham Goods																				
Rochester Bge Jcn							17/03	17/13	17/19											
Cuxton Road																				
Sole Street							17.13	17/27												
Meopham							17.15													
Longfield																				
Fawkham							17.20													
Farningham Road							17.24													
SWANLEY		17.08		17.24	17.29	17.33	17/39				17.45		17.57							
St Mary Cray		17.13		17.29							17.50									
St Mary Cray Jcn			17/15	17/31	17/36	17/39	17/44				17/52		18/02							
	Local	Main	Local	Main	Local	Main	Main	Local		Local	Main			Local	Local	Main				
Bickley Jcn	17/18	17/16		17/32	17/37	17/40	17/45			17/50	17/53			18/03	18/05	18/10				
Bickley	17.19	17.18	17.34	17.34				17.49		17.54	17.55				18.07					
BROMLEY SOUTH	17.21	17.19	17.36	17.36	17.39	17.43	17.48	17.51		17.57	17.56		18.06		18.10	(18.10)				
BROMLEY SOUTH	17.22	17.24	17/37	17.37	17.40	17.44	17.50	17.52		17.58	17.57		18.08	(18.14)	18.13		18.14			
Shortlands	17.25	17.27	17/39	17.40	17/43	17/46		17.54		18.00	18.00						18.16			
Beckenham Jcn	17.28		17.41		17/46	17.50	17/54	17.57		18.04			18/12			18/16	18.19			
Kent House	17.32							17.59		18.06							18.21			
Penge East	17.34							18.01		18.08							18.23			
Sydenham Hill	17.37							18.04									18.26			
W. Dulwich	17.40							18.06		18.12							18.28			
Herne Hill	17.43		17.48		17/53	17.57	18/03	18.09		18.15				18/18		18/23	18.30			
Brixton	17.45				17/54	17.58	18/04	18.11						18/19		18/24	18.32			
VICTORIA	17.51				17.59	18.03	18.12	18.16						18.24		18.30	18.38			
Destination		H. Via	H. Via	H. Via					CX	H. Via	H. Via								S'ness	

WORKING TIMETABLE : DOVER - FAVERSHAM (1955)

		14.02			16.20
Train		14.02			16.20
From		Town			C'bury
Class	Goods	Goods			Goods
Engine	N 2-6-0	N 2-6-0			N 2-6-0
DOVER PRIORY					
Dover Gas					
Kearsney					
Shepherdswell					
Snowdown					
Aylesham					
Adisham					
Bekesbourne		16.34			
CANTERBURY E.		16.44			
CANTERBURY E.	16.20	(18.25)			
Selling	16.38				
FAVERSHAM					16.54
Destination					

WORKING TIMETABLE : SITTINGBOURNE - SHEERNESS (1955)

	Pass
Train	
From	
Class	Pass
Engine	2-6-2T
SITTINGBOURNE	16.56
Eastern Jcn	16/57
Middle Jcn	16/58
Kemsley	17.01
Redham Dock	
Swale	17.07
Queenborough	17.11
SHEERNESS	17.21
Destination	

WORKING TIMETABLE : VICTORIA to RAMSGATE (1955)

Train	16.32	17.10	16.55	16.26		16.45	16.32	16.20	16.40	16.31			16.45	17.40	16.51	16.42		17.15	17.04
From	C. Street	S'ness	Strood	H. Via		C. Street	C. Street	C. St	H. Via	H. Via			H. Via	S'ness	H. Via	CX		C. Street	H. Via
Class	Pass	Pass	Pass	Pass	Pass	XP	Pass	Pass	Pass	Pass	XP	Pass	Pass	Pass	Pass	Pass	Pass	XP	Pass
Engine	L1 4-4-0	2-6-2T	D1 4-4-0	EMU	EMU	WC	L1 4-4-0	EMU	EMU	EMU	V 4-4-0	EMU	EMU	2-6-2T	EMU	EMU	EMU	WC	EMU
VICTORIA						16.34							16.44		16.52				17.04
Brixton						16.39							16.49		16/57				17.09
Herne Hill				16.40	16.42				16/50				16.52					17.12	17.15
W. Dulwich				16.43									16.54		16.59				17.18
Sydenham Hill				16.45									16.56		17.01				17.20
Penge East				16.40									16.59		17.04			17.19	17.24
Kent House				16.50									17.01		17.06			17.21	17.26
Beckenham Jcn				16.52					16/57				17.03		17.09			17.23	17.28
				Main				Main	Local				Main		Local	Main	Local	Main	Main
Shortlands				16.55				16/59	16.59				17.06		17/08	17.11	17/19	17.27	17.31
BROMLEY SOUTH				16.56				17.00	17.01				17.09		17.13	17.21		17.28	17.33
BROMLEY SOUTH				16.57				17.01	17.02				17.11		17.12	17.14	17.22	17.29	17.34
Bickley				17.00					17.05				17.14		17.17		17.25	17.32	17.34
Bickley Jcn				17/02					17/06				17/15		17/14		17/26		17/34
St Mary Cray Jcn	16/55					17/03		17/06	17/08						17/15		17/27	17/34	
St Mary Cray									17/11								17/30		
SWANLEY	17/00					17/08		17.12	17.16						17.21		17.35	17/39	
Farningham Road									17.17										
Fawkham									17.22										
Meopham									17.26										
Sole Street	17/10					17/18			17.29									17/49	
Cuxton Road	17/15					17/23			17/34									17/54	
Rochester Bge Jcn	17/19					17/26	17/33		17/37								17/43	17/54	
Chatham Goods																			
Rochester	17.20						17.34		17.38								17.44		
Rochester	17.21					17/27	17.35		17.39								17.45	17/56	
CHATHAM	17.23						17.37		17.41								17.47		
CHATHAM	(17.30)					17/28	17.38		17.43								17.49	17/59	
GILLINGHAM							17.34	17.41	17.46								17.52		
GILLINGHAM						17/30	17.35												18/02
Rainham							17.40												
Newington							17.47												
Western Jcn																			
Eastern Jcn		17/28													17/57				
SITTINGBOURNE		17.29					17.53								18.00				
SITTINGBOURNE			17.31			17/40	17.56												18/11
Murston Sdgs																			
Teynham							18.02												
FAVERSHAM			17.42			17.49	18.11												
FAVERSHAM			17.52			17.53	(18.24)												18/19
Graveney Sdgs																			
Whitstable						18.03													18.28
Chestfield						18.09													
HERNE BAY						18.13													18.36
HERNE BAY						18.14													18.38
Birchington						18.26													
Westgate						18.31													
MARGATE						18.36													18.53
MARGATE						18.39					18.50								18.56
Broadstairs						18.47					18.58								19.04
Dumpton Park						18.51					19.01								19.08
RAMSGATE						18.55					19.06								19.12
Destination			Dover	Orp				S'oaks	C. Cross	Orp	M'stone				S' oaks		Orp		

WORKING TIMETABLE : FAVERSHAM to DOVER (1955)

Train	16.55
From	Strood
Class	Pass
Engine	D1 4-4-0
FAVERSHAM	17.52
Selling	17.59
CANTERBURY E.	18.10
CANTERBURY E.	18.16
Bekesbourne	18.23
Adisham	18.29
Aylesham	18.33
Snowdown	18.37
Shepherdswell	18.43
Kearsney	18.54
DOVER PRIORY	19.02
Destination	

WORKING TIMETABLE : SHEERNESS to SITTINGBOURNE (1955)

Train			
From			
Class	Pass	Goods	Pass
Engine	2-6-2T	C 0-6-0	2-6-2T
SHEERNESS	17.10	17.24	17.40
Queenborough	17.16	17.34	18.12
Swale	17.20		18.17
Redham Dock			
Kemsley	17.24		18.21
Middle Jcn	17/27		18/24
Eastern Jcn	17/28		18/25
SITTINGBOURNE	17.29		18.26
Destination			

WORKING TIMETABLE : RAMSGATE to VICTORIA (1955)

Train From Class Engine	Pass 2-6-2T	15.45 M'gate Goods C 0-6-0	17.05 Sole St Goods C 0-6-0	17.44 S'oaks Pass EMU	17.05 Sole St Goods C 0-6-0	Pass EMU	17.15 Dover Boat WC	18.20 Orp Pass EMU	Pass EMU	18.02 S'oaks Pass EMU	Pass EMU	16.18 Dover Pass L 4-4-0	Pass BR5 4-6-0	16.20 C'bury Goods N 2-6-0	Pass 2-6-2T	Pass EMU	07.35 Birk'hd XP V 4-4-0	Pull WC	18.42 Orp Pass EMU	Pcls N 2-6-0
RAMSGATE													16.15				16.32	17.05		17.10
Dumpton Park													16.19				16.36	17.09		
Broadstairs													16.23				16.40	17.13		17.24
MARGATE													16.30				16.46	17.19		17.30
MARGATE													16.34					17.21		(18.00)
Westgate													16.39							
Birchington		16.20											16.44							
HERNE BAY		16.40											16.55					17.36		
HERNE BAY		(18.10)											16.57					17.38		
Chestfield													17.03							
Whitstable													17.09					17.47		
Graveney																				
British Fruit																				
FAVERSHAM												17.16	17.19							
FAVERSHAM													17.25		17.30			17/57		
Teynham															17.42					
SITTINGBOURNE													17.36							
SITTINGBOURNE	17.29												17.38			17.57		18/05		
Eastern Jcn	17/30															17/58				
Western Jcn																				
Newington														17.46						
Rainham														17.52						
GILLINGHAM														17.57						
GILLINGHAM								17.50	17.54					17.59		18.08		18/14		
CHATHAM								17.53	17.57					18.03		18.11				
CHATHAM								17.55	17.59					(18.20)		18.12		18/17		
Rochester								17.56	18.00							18.14				
Rochester								17.57	18.01							18/19				
Chatham Goods																				
Rochester Bge Jcn								17/58	18.03							18/16		18/20		
Cuxton Road																				
Sole Street										18.13						18/30				
Meopham			17.35							18.15										
Longfield Sdg			17.43		18.00															
Fawkham					18.05					18.20										
Farningham Road					18.14					18.24										
SWANLEY				18.04					18.24	18.33						18/40				
St Mary Cray				18.09					18.29											
St Mary Cray Jcn				18/11					18/31	18/38						18/45				
				Main		Local	Local	Main	Main		Main					Main			Local	
Bickley Jcn				18.14			18/30	18.25	18.32	18/39						18/46			18/47	
Bickley				18.16		18.20		18.30	18.34										18.49	
BROMLEY SOUTH				18.17		18.22		18.33	18.36	18.41									18.51	
BROMLEY SOUTH				18.20		18.23	18/33	18.34	18.37	18.43						18/48			18.52	
Shortlands						18/25		18.36	18.40										18.54	
Beckenham Jcn						18/27	18/36	18.39		18/47						18/51			18.57	
Kent House								18.41											18.59	
Penge East								18.43											19.01	
Sydenham Hill								18.46											19.04	
W. Dulwich								18.48											19.06	
Herne Hill						18.34	18/43	18.50		18/54						18/58			19.08	
Brixton							18/44	18.52		18/55						18/59			19.11	
VICTORIA							18.50	18.58		19.00						19.05			19.16	
Destination	S'ness			H. Via		H. Via		C. St	H. Via						S'ness	CX				

WORKING TIMETABLE : DOVER - FAVERSHAM (1955)

Train From Class Engine	Pass L 4-4-0
DOVER PRIORY	16.18
Dover Gas	
Kearsney	16.24
Shepherdswell	16.31
Snowdown	16.35
Aylesham	16.38
Adisham	16.41
Bekesbourne	16.49
CANTERBURY E.	16.54
CANTERBURY E.	16.57
Selling	17.10
FAVERSHAM	17.16
Destination	

WORKING TIMETABLE : SITTINGBOURNE - SHEERNESS (1955)

Train From Class Engine	Pass 2-6-2T	Pass 2-6-2T
SITTINGBOURNE	17.29	17.57
Eastern Jcn	17/30	17/58
Middle Jcn	17/31	17/59
Kemsley	17.34	18.02
Redham Dock		
Swale	17.40	
Queenborough	17.44	18.09
SHEERNESS	17.52	18.18
Destination		

WORKING TIMETABLE : VICTORIA to RAMSGATE (1955)

Train	17.07	16.32		18.06	17.21		17.11	17.17	17.21		17.12	17.27	17.45			17.42	17.31	17.42		17.21
From	C. St	C. Street	Light	S'ness	C. Street		H. Via	H. Via	C. Street		CX	H. Via	C. Street			CX	H. Via	H. Via		C. Street
Class	Pass	Pass		Pass	Pass	Pass	Pass	Pass	Pass	Pass	Pass	Pass	XP	Pass	Pass	Pass	Pass	Pass	Pass	Pass
Engine	EMU	L1 4-4-0	2-6-2T	2-6-2T	U1 2-6-0	EMU	EMU	EMU	2-6-2T	EMU	EMU	EMU	WC	C 0-6-0	EMU	EMU	EMU	EMU	EMU	U1 2-6-0
VICTORIA						17.20				17.24					17.35				17.44	
Brixton						17.26				17.29					17.41				17.49	
Herne Hill						17.28	17.30			17.33		17.41			17.43		17.45	17.52	17.54	
W. Dulwich						17.32				17.35		17.43			17.45		17.47	17.54	17.56	
Sydenham Hill										17.38					17.43		17.47		17.56	
Penge East							17.37			17.41					17.46		17.50		17.59	
Kent House							17.39			17.43					17.48		17.52		18.01	
Beckenham Jcn						17/34	17.41			17.45					17.50		17.54		18.03	
(class)						Local	Local	Main		Local		Main			Main		Local	Local	Main	
Shortlands						17/35	17.39	17.44		17.48		17.53			17.57		17.59	18.04	18.06	
BROMLEY SOUTH						17.38	17.41	17.45		17.50		17.54			18.01		18.01	18.07	18.08	
BROMLEY SOUTH						17.39	17.41	17.45			17.51	17.55			18.03	18.02		18.08	18.09	
Bickley							17.45	17.49			17.54	18.02				18.05		18.08	18.12	
Bickley Jcn							17/42	17/46			17/51		18/04			18/06		18/11	18/13	
St Mary Cray Jcn					17/41	17/43	17/47						18/05			18/08	18/12			
St Mary Cray						17.46	17.50										18.10		18.15	
SWANLEY					17/46	17.53	17.55						18/10				18.15	18.20		
Farningham Road																		18.25		
Fawkham						18.01												18.30		
Meopham																		18.34		
Sole Street					17/57	18/07							18/20					18.37		
Cuxton Road					18.02	18/11							18/25					18/42		
Rochester Bge Jcn	18/02				18/06	18/14					18/21		18/29			18/38		18/45		
Chatham Goods																				
Rochester	18.03				18.08	18.15					18.22					18.39		18.46		
Rochester	18.04				18.09	18.15					18.23		18/30			18.40		18.47		
CHATHAM	18.06				18.11	18.17					18.25		18.31			18.42		18.49		
CHATHAM	18.07				18.14	18.18			18.21		18.26		18.33	18.38		18.43		18.51		
GILLINGHAM	18.10				18.18	18.21			18.24		18.29			18.42		18.46		18.54		
GILLINGHAM					18.19				18.26				18/37	18.43						
Rainham					18.24															
Newington									18.35											
Western Jcn									18/41											
Eastern Jcn				18/25																
SITTINGBOURNE				18.26	18.34									18.55						
SITTINGBOURNE		18.15			18.35								18/47							
Murston Sdgs																				
Teynham			18.23		18.41															
FAVERSHAM					18.50								18.55							
FAVERSHAM		18.24			(19.00)								18.57							19.00
Graveney Sdgs																				
Whitstable		18.34											19.07							
Chestfield		18.39											19.12							
HERNE BAY		18.45											19.18							
HERNE BAY		18.46											19.20							
Birchington		18.58											19.32							
Westgate		19.03											19.37							
MARGATE		19.08											19.42							
MARGATE		19.11											19.45							
Broadstairs		19.19											19.53							
Dumpton Park		19.23											19.57							
RAMSGATE		19.27											20.02							
Destination							S'oaks	Orp	S'ness			Orp			Orp		S'oaks		Orp	Dover

WORKING TIMETABLE : FAVERSHAM to DOVER (1955)

Train	17.21
From	C. St
Class	Pass
Engine	U1 2-6-0
FAVERSHAM	19.00
Selling	19.07
CANTERBURY E.	19.18
CANTERBURY E.	19.23
Bekesbourne	19.29
Adisham	19.35
Aylesham	19.39
Snowdown	19.43
Shepherdswell	19.49
Kearsney	20.00
DOVER PRIORY	20.06
Destination	

WORKING TIMETABLE : SHEERNESS to SITTINGBOURNE (1955)

Train	
From	
Class	Pass
Engine	2-6-2T
SHEERNESS	18.06
Queenborough	18.12
Swale	18.17
Redham Dock	
Kemsley	18.21
Middle Jcn	18/24
Eastern Jcn	18/25
SITTINGBOURNE	18.26
Destination	

WORKING TIMETABLE : RAMSGATE to VICTORIA (1955)

Train	18.22	16.15	17.09		16.20	19.07	18.42		17.40	19.20	18.10	19.20	19.02		17.22		15.36	17.10	
From	S'oaks	R'gate	Dover		C'bury	Orp	S'oaks		Dover	Orp	Dover	Orp	S'oaks		R'gate		M'stone	R'gate	
Class	Pass	Pass	Pass	Pass	Goods	Pass	Pass	Pass	Pass	Pass	Boat	Pass	Pass	Pass	Pass	Pass	Pass	Pcls	Goods
Engine	EMU	BR5 4-6-0	2-6-4T	EMU	N 2-6-0	EMU	EMU	BR5 4-6-0	D1 4-4-0	EMU	MN	EMU	EMU	EMU	BR5 4-6-0	EMU	2-6-4T	N 2-6-0	BR5 4-6-0
RAMSGATE								17.22									17.35		18.00
Dumpton Park								17.26									17.39		
Broadstairs								17.30											18.10
MARGATE								17.36									17.49		
MARGATE								17.39										18.00	
Westgate								17.44										18.04	
Birchington								17.49											
HERNE BAY								18.00											
HERNE BAY								18.02											
Chestfield								18.08											
Whitstable								18.12											
Graveney																			
British Fruit																			
FAVERSHAM			18.01					18.23	18.30										
FAVERSHAM			18.03												18.36				
Teynham			18.12		18.21														
SITTINGBOURNE			18.18		18.27														
SITTINGBOURNE			18.19		(18.56)										18.49				
Eastern Jcn																			
Western Jcn																			
Newington			18.26																
Rainham			18.32																
GILLINGHAM			18.37												19.01				
GILLINGHAM			18.38	18.42										18.54	19.03	19.09			
CHATHAM		(18.03)	18.42	18.45										18.57	19.07	19.12			
CHATHAM		18.20		18.47										18.59	19.10	19.14			
Rochester				18.48										19.00		19.15			
Rochester		18/22		18.49										19.01	19.12	19.17			
Chatham Goods																			
Rochester Bge Jcn		18/23		18/50										19/03	19/13	19/18			
Cuxton Road																			
Sole Street		18/36												19.13	19/25				
Meopham														19.15					
Longfield																			
Fawkham														19.19					
Farningham Road														19.24					
SWANLEY		18.51											19.24	19.33	19/36				
St Mary Cray													19.29						
St Mary Cray Jcn		18/57											19/31	19/38	19/41				
	Main	Main				Local	Main		Local	Main			Main	Main	Local				
Bickley Jcn	18/52	18/58				19/12	19/12		19/25	19/29			19/32	19/39	19/42				
Bickley	18.54					19.14	19.14		19.30				19.34						
BROMLEY SOUTH	18.56	19.01				19.16	19.16		19.32		(19.32)		19.36	19.42	19.45				
BROMLEY SOUTH	18.57	19.03				19.17	19.17		(19.33)	19.32	19.33		19.37	19.43	19.47				
Shortlands	19.00					19.19	19.20			19.33	19.35		19.40						
Beckenham Jcn		19.07				19.22				19.35	19.38			19/47	19/52				
Kent House											19.40								
Penge East						19.25					19.42								
Sydenham Hill											19.45								
W. Dulwich											19.47								
Herne Hill		19/15				19.31				19/43	19.50			19/53	20/00				
Brixton		19/16				19.33				19/44	19.52			19/54	20/01				
VICTORIA		19.22				19.38				19.50	19.57			19.59	20.07				
Destination	H. Via			C. St			H. Via						H. Via				CX		

WORKING TIMETABLE : DOVER - FAVERSHAM (1955)

Train		
From		
Class	Pass	XP
Engine	2-6-4T	D1 4-4-0
DOVER PRIORY	17.09	17.40
Dover Gas		
Kearsney	17.15	17.46
Shepherdswell	17.21	17.53
Snowdown	17.25	17.57
Aylesham	17.28	
Adisham	17.31	
Bekesbourne	17.36	
CANTERBURY E.	17.41	18.09
CANTERBURY E.	17.42	18.11
Selling	17.55	18.24
FAVERSHAM	18.01	18.30
Destination	Ctm	Vic

WORKING TIMETABLE : SITTINGBOURNE - SHEERNESS (1955)

Train	
From	
Class	
Engine	
SITTINGBOURNE	
Eastern Jcn	
Middle Jcn	
Kemsley	
Redham Dock	
Swale	
Queenborough	
SHEERNESS	
Destination	

WORKING TIMETABLE : VICTORIA to RAMSGATE (1955)

Train	17.47	17.50	17.51	17.57	18.16	18.04	17.50	19.05	18.23	18.06	18.11	17.57	18.24	18.27	19.28	18.31	18.42
From	H. Via	CX	H. Via	H. Via	C. Street	H. Via	CX	S'ness	C. Street	CX	H. Via	CX	H. Via	H. Via	S'ness	H. Via	CX
Class	Pass	Pass	Pass	Pass	XP	Pass	Pass	Pass	Pass	Pass	Pass	Pass	Pass	Pass	Pass	Pass	Pass
Engine	EMU	EMU	EMU	EMU	V 4-4-0	EMU	EMU	2-6-2T	V 4-4-0	EMU	EMU	EMU	EMU	EMU	2-6-2T	EMU	EMU
VICTORIA	17.53					18.04					18.18			18.24			
Brixton	17/58					18.09					18/23			18.29			
Herne Hill (Via Cat-ford)		17.58	18.08	18.12		18.16					18/24		18.28	18.32		18.38	
W. Dulwich		18.01	18.11	18.14		18.18								18.34		18.41	
Sydenham Hill		18.03	18.13	18.17		18.21								18.36		18.43	
Penge East		18.06	18.16	18.20		18.24								18.39		18.46	
Kent House		18.08	18.18	18.22										18.41		18.48	
Beckenham Jcn		18.10	18.20	18.24		18.28					18/32			18.43		18.50	
	Local	Main	Local	Main	Main	Main			Local		Main		Local	Main		Local	Main
Shortlands	18/09	18.13	18.19	18.23	18.27	18.31			18/33		18/39		18/44	18.46		18.53	18.59
BROMLEY SOUTH	18.11	18.14	18.21	18.24	18.28	18.33			18.35		18.41		18.47	18.49		18.54	19.01
BROMLEY SOUTH	18.12	18.15	18.22	18.25	18.29	18.35			18.36		18.42		18.48	18.52		18.55	19.02
Bickley		18.24	18.25	18.28		18.33				18.39		18.45		18/53		18.58	19.05
Bickley Jcn	18/15	18/26	18/26	18/30		18/35	18/40		18/38	18/46				18/51		19/06	
St Mary Cray Jcn	18/16		18/27			18/35			18/39	18/43	18/47		18/52			19/07	
St Mary Cray	18.18		18.30								18.50					19.10	
SWANLEY	18.23		18.35		18/40				18/48		18.55			18.59		19.15	
Farningham Road														19.04			
Fawkham														19.09			
Meopham														19.13			
Sole Street					18/50				18/58				19.16				
Cuxton Road					18/55				19/03				19/21				
Rochester Bge Jcn		18/51			18/59				19/07	19/09	19/16		19/24				19/39
Chatham Goods																	
Rochester		18.52							19.08	19.11	19.17		19.25				19.40
Rochester		18.53			19/00				19.09	19.13	19.18		19.26				19.41
CHATHAM		18.55						(18.55	19.11	19.15	19.20		19.28				19.43
CHATHAM		(19.04)			19/01			19.04	19.14	19.18	19.22		19.30				19.44
GILLINGHAM								19.07	19.18	19.21	19.25		19.33				19.47
GILLINGHAM					19/04				19.19								
Rainham									19.24								
Newington									19.30								
Western Jcn																	
Eastern Jcn								19/24					19/47				
SITTINGBOURNE								19.25	19.37				19.48				
SITTINGBOURNE					19/13			(19.30)	19.38				19.52				
Murston Sdgs																	
Teynham									19.44								
FAVERSHAM									19.53						20.03		
FAVERSHAM					19.21				19.57								
Graveney Sdgs																	
Whitstable					19.30												
Chestfield					19.35												
HERNE BAY					19.41												
HERNE BAY					19.42												
Birchington					19.54												
Westgate					19.59												
MARGATE					20.04												
MARGATE					20.06												
Broadstairs					20.14												
Dumpton Park					20.18												
RAMSGATE					20.22												
Destination	M'stone	Orp		S'oaks	Orp		Orp	Orp	Chatham	M'stone	Dover		S'oaks		Orp		S'oaks

WORKING TIMETABLE : FAVERSHAM to DOVER (1955)

Train	18.23
From	C.St
Class	Pass
Engine	V 4-4-0
FAVERSHAM	19.57
Selling	20.04
CANTERBURY E.	20.15
CANTERBURY E.	20.16
Bekesbourne	20.22
Adisham	20.28
Aylesham	20.32
Snowdown	20.36
Shepherdswell	20.41
Kearsney	20.48
DOVER PRIORY	20.53
Destination	

WORKING TIMETABLE : SHEERNESS to SITTINGBOURNE (1955)

Train		
From		
Class	Pass	Pass
Engine	2-6-2T	2-6-2T
SHEERNESS	19.05	19.28
Queenborough	19.13	19.36
Swale		
Redham Dock		
Kemsley	19.20	19.43
Middle Jcn	19/23	19/46
Eastern Jcn	19/24	19/47
SITTINGBOURNE	19.25	19.48
Destination	Ctm	Fav

WORKING TIMETABLE : RAMSGATE to VICTORIA (1955)

Train	15.45	15.45	17.10	17.10	16.20	16.20	19.42	19.22			14.02	20.02		19.05		20.04	19.42	19.57
From	M'gate	M'gate	R'gate	R'gate	C'bury	C'bury	Orp	S'oaks			Dover	Orp		S'ness		Orp	S'oaks	Bickley
Class	Goods	Goods	Pcls	Pcls	Goods	Goods	Pass	Pass	Goods	Pass	Goods	Pass	Goods	Pass	Pcls	ECS	Pass	Pcls
Engine	C 0-6-0	C 0-6-0	N 2-6-0	N 2-6-0	N 2-6-0	N 2-6-0	EMU	EMU	2-6-2T	EMU	N 2-6-0	EMU	N 2-6-0	C & LM2	EMU	EMU	EMU	EMU
RAMSGATE																		
Dumpton Park																		
Broadstairs																		
MARGATE																		
MARGATE																		
Westgate			18.12															
Birchington			18.16	18.22														
HERNE BAY				18.34														
HERNE BAY	18.10			(19.23)														
Chestfield	18.18	18.28																
Whitstable																		
Graveney																		
British Fruit																		
FAVERSHAM		18.45									19.18							
FAVERSHAM																		
Teynham								19.17										
SITTINGBOURNE								19.23						(19.25)				
SITTINGBOURNE					18.56			(19.58)						19.30				
Eastern Jcn																		
Western Jcn																		
Newington					19.07	19.28								19.37				
Rainham						19.34								19.43				
GILLINGHAM														19.48				
GILLINGHAM								19.40						19.49				
CHATHAM								19.43						19.53				
CHATHAM								19.47										
Rochester								19.48										
Rochester								19.49										
Chatham Goods													19.35					
Rochester Bge Jcn								19/50					19/40					
Cuxton Road																		
Sole Street													20/02					
Meopham																		
Longfield																		
Fawkham													20.10					
Farningham Road																		
SWANLEY							19.44							19.57				
St Mary Cray							19.49							20.05				
St Mary Cray Jcn							19/51							20/08				
							Local	Main				Local		Main		Local	Main	Local
Bickley Jcn							19/47	19/52				20/07		20/09		20/10	20/12	
Bickley							19.49	19.54				20.09				20.12	20.14	
BROMLEY SOUTH							19.51	19.56				20.11		20.14			20.16	(20.14)
BROMLEY SOUTH							19.52	19.57				20.12		(20.20)			20.17	20.20
Shortlands							19.54	20.00				20.14					20.20	
Beckenham Jcn							19.57					20.17						20.24
Kent House							19.59					20.19						
Penge East							20.01					20.21						
Sydenham Hill							20.04					20.24						
W. Dulwich							20.06					20.26						
Herne Hill							20.08					20.28						
Brixton							20.11					20.31						
VICTORIA							20.16					20.37						
Destination								H. Via	C. St								H. Via	

WORKING TIMETABLE : DOVER - FAVERSHAM (1955)

Train	14.02	14.02
From	Town	Town
Class	Goods	Goods
Engine	N 2-6-0	N 2-6-0
DOVER PRIORY		
Dover Gas		
Kearsney		
Shepherdswell		
Snowdown		
Aylesham		
Adisham		
Bekesbourne		
CANTERBURY E.		
CANTERBURY E.	18.25	
Selling	18.48	19.08
FAVERSHAM		19.18
Destination		

WORKING TIMETABLE : SITTINGBOURNE - SHEERNESS (1955)

Train	18.21
From	CTM
Class	Pass
Engine	2-6-2T
SITTINGBOURNE	
Eastern Jcn	
Middle Jcn	18/42
Kemsley	18.45
Redham Dock	
Swale	
Queenborough	18.56
SHEERNESS	19.02
Destination	

WORKING TIMETABLE : VICTORIA to RAMSGATE (1955)

Train			18.50		18.47	18.51		18.50					20.17	19.11			19.31		19.10	19.51	
From			Vic		H. Via	H. Via		CX					S'ness	H. Via			H. Via		CX	H. Via	
Class	Pass	Pass	Pass	Pass	Pass	Pass	Pass	Pass	Pass	Pass	Pass	Pass	Pass	Pass	XP	Pass	Pass	Pass	Pass	Pass	Pass
Engine	EMU	EMU	EMU	L 4-4-0	EMU	EMU	EMU	EMU	EMU	2-6-2T	WC	2-6-2T	EMU	EMU	WC	2-6-4T	EMU	EMU	EMU	EMU	2-6-2T
VICTORIA	18.50	18.44					19.04		19.18				19.24		19.35			19.44			
Brixton	18/55	18.49					19.09		19.23				19.29					19.49			
Herne Hill		18.52			18.58		19.12						19.32	19/25			19/44	19.52			
W. Dulwich	via	18.55	via		19.01		19.14						19.34					19.54			
Sydenham Hill	Cat-	18.57	Cat-		19.03		19.16						19.36					19.56			
Penge East	ford	19.00	ford		19.06		19.19						19.39					19.59			
Kent House	loop	19.02	loop		19.08		19.21						19.41					20.01			
Beckenham Jcn		19.04			19.10		19.23	19/31					19.43				19/52	20.03			
	Main	Local		Main	Local	Main		Local					Local	Main	Main		Local	Main		Local	
Shortlands	19.07	19/06		19.13	19.19	19.26		19/32					19.39	19.46	19/53		19.59	20.07		20.19	
BROMLEY SOUTH	19.09	19.09		19.14	19.21	19.28		19.34					19.41	19.48			20.01	20.08		20.21	
BROMLEY SOUTH	19.10	19.10		19.15	19.22	19.29		19.35					19.42	19.49	19/54		20.02	20.09		20.22	
Bickley	19.13			19.18	19.25	19.32							19.45	19.52			20.05	20.12		20.25	
Bickley Jcn	19/15	19/12		19/20	19/26	19/33		19/38					19/46	19/53	19/57		20/06	20/13		20/26	
St Mary Cray Jcn		19/13				19/27		19/39					19/47				20/07			20/27	
St Mary Cray						19.30							19.50				20.10			20.30	
SWANLEY				19.22		19.35			19.47				19.55		20.03		20.15			20.35	
Farningham Road				19.26					19.52												
Fawkham				19.31					19.57												
Meopham				19.36					20.01												
Sole Street				19.38					20.04						20/13						
Cuxton Road				19/41					20.09						20/18						
Rochester Bge Jcn				19/47					20/12	20/06					20/22	20/27					
Chatham Goods																					
Rochester				19.48					20.13	20.07						20.29					
Rochester				19.49					20.14	20.08					20/23	20.30					
CHATHAM				19.50					20.16	20.10					20.24	20.32					
CHATHAM				19.52					20.18	20.13					20.26	20.34					20.38
GILLINGHAM				19.55					20.21	20.16						20.37					20.42
GILLINGHAM															20/30						20.43
Rainham																					20.48
Newington																					20.54
Western Jcn																					
Eastern Jcn												20/34									
SITTINGBOURNE												20.35			20.40						21.01
SITTINGBOURNE															20.42						21.03
Murston Sdgs																					
Teynham																					21.08
FAVERSHAM															20.53						21.17
FAVERSHAM				20.05											20.56	21.01					
Graveney Sdgs																					
Whitstable				20.15											21.06						
Chestfield				20.20											21.12						
HERNE BAY				20.26											21.18						
HERNE BAY				20.27											21.20						
Birchington				20.39											21.32						
Westgate				20.44											21.37						
MARGATE				20.49											21.42						
MARGATE				20.56						21.20	21.28				21.45						
Broadstairs				21.02						21.26	21.34				21.53						
Dumpton Park				21.06						21.31	21.38				21.57						
RAMSGATE				21.10						21.35	21.42				22.01						
Destination			Orp		Orp	S'oaks		Orp		C'bury	C. Street		S'oaks	Orp		Dover	S'oaks		Orp	S'oaks	

WORKING TIMETABLE : FAVERSHAM to DOVER (1955)

Train	
From	
Class	Pass
Engine	2-6-4T
FAVERSHAM	21.01
Selling	21.08
CANTERBURY E.	21.19
CANTERBURY E.	21.23
Bekesbourne	21.29
Adisham	21.35
Aylesham	21.39
Snowdown	21.43
Shepherdswell	21.48
Kearsney	21.55
DOVER PRIORY	22.00
Destination	

WORKING TIMETABLE : SHEERNESS to SITTINGBOURNE (1955)

Train	
From	
Class	Pass
Engine	2-6-2T
SHEERNESS	20.17
Queenborough	20.23
Swale	
Redham Dock	
Kemsley	20.30
Middle Jcn	20/33
Eastern Jcn	20/34
SITTINGBOURNE	20.35
Destination	

WORKING TIMETABLE : RAMSGATE to VICTORIA (1955)

Train	17.32	16.12	20.18	19.57		20.02		20.42	21.22				16.15	18.00	17.10	17.10	19.17	16.20
From	A'ford	Ton'bge	Orp	Bickley		S'oaks		Orp	S'oaks				C. Cross		R'gate	R'gate	Teyn	C'bury
Class	Pass	Pass	Pass	Pcls	Pass	Pass	Pass	Pass	Pass	Goods	Pass	Pass	XP	Goods	Pcls	Pcls	Goods	Goods
Engine	2-6-4T	L 4-4-0	EMU	EMU	2-6-2T	EMU	EMU	EMU	EMU	N 2-6-0	D1	EMU	WC	BR5 4-6-0	N 2-6-0	N 2-6-0	C 0-6-0	N 2-6-0
RAMSGATE		18.30											18.39					
Dumpton Park		18.34											18.43					
Broadstairs		18.38											18.47	18.54				
MARGATE		18.44											18.53	19.02				
MARGATE		18.47												(20.08)				
Westgate		18.52																
Birchington		18.57																
HERNE BAY		19.09																
HERNE BAY		19.11													19.23			
Chestfield																		
Whitstable		19.20													19.31	19.44		
Graveney																		
British Fruit																		
FAVERSHAM	19.27	19.30														19.54		
FAVERSHAM											19.39							
Teynham																		
SITTINGBOURNE											19.50							
SITTINGBOURNE					19.45						19.51						19.58	
Eastern Jcn					19/46													
Western Jcn																		
Newington																	20.08	
Rainham											20.01							20.10
GILLINGHAM											20.06							
GILLINGHAM						19.54						20.08						20/18
CHATHAM						19.57						20.11						
CHATHAM						19.59						20.13						20/22
Rochester						20.00						20.15						
Rochester						20.01						20.17						20/26
Chatham Goods																		
Rochester Bge Jcn						20/03						20/18						20/28
Cuxton Road																		
Sole Street						20.13												
Meopham						20.15												
Longfield																		
Fawkham						20.20			20.22									
Farningham Road						20.24			20/29									
SWANLEY						20.33			20/47									
St Mary Cray																		
St Mary Cray Jcn						20/38			20/57									
			Main			**Main**	**Main**	**Local**	**Main**									
Bickley Jcn			20/23			20/32	20/39	20/47	20/52	21/01								
Bickley			20.29			20.34	20.49	2054										
BROMLEY SOUTH			20.32			20.36	20.42	20.51	20.56									
BROMLEY SOUTH			20.33			20.37	20.43	20.52	20.57	21/05								
Shortlands			20.35			20.40		20.54	21.00									
Beckenham Jcn			20.38	20.40			20/47	20.57		21.10								
Kent House			20.40	20.49				20.59										
Penge East			20.42	20.54				21.01										
Sydenham Hill			20.45					21.04										
W. Dulwich			20.47					21.06										
Herne Hill			20.50	20.59			20/53	21.08										
Brixton			20.51				20/54	21.11										
VICTORIA			20.57				20.59	21.16										
Destination				H. Via	S'ness	H. Via		H.Via		Waddon			CX					B'friars

WORKING TIMETABLE : DOVER - FAVERSHAM (1955)

Train	17.32
From	A'ford
Class	Pass
Engine	2-6-4T
DOVER PRIORY	18.30
Dover Gas	
Kearsney	18.36
Shepherdswell	18.44
Snowdown	18.49
Aylesham	18.52
Adisham	18.55
Bekesbourne	19.01
CANTERBURY E.	19.06
CANTERBURY E.	19.08
Selling	19.21
FAVERSHAM	19.27
Destination	

WORKING TIMETABLE : SITTINGBOURNE - SHEERNESS (1955)

Train	
From	
Class	Pass
Engine	2-6-2T
SITTINGBOURNE	19.45
Eastern Jcn	19/46
Middle Jcn	19/47
Kemsley	19.50
Redham Dock	
Swale	
Queenborough	20.01
SHEERNESS	20.07
Destination	

Train	19.42			21.22	19.55		20.11				20.31		21.05		20.51	20.42		20.45	21.22	22.11	
From	CX			S'ness	C.St		H.Via				H.Via		Hoo Jn		H.Via	CX		B'ham	S'ness	S'ness	
Class	Pass	Pass	Pass	Pass	Pass	Pass	Pass	Pass	Pass	XP	Pass	Pass	Goods	Boat	Pass	Pass	Pass	Goods	Pass	Pass	Light
Engine	EMU	2-6-4T	EMU	2-6-2T	EMU	EMU	EMU	EMU	EMU	V 4-4-0	EMU	EMU	C 0-6-0	WC&LI	EMU	EMU	EMU	C 0-6-0	2-6-2T	2-6-2T	L 4-4-0
VICTORIA			20.04				20.18		20.24	20.35		20.44		21.00			21.04				
Brixton			20.09				20/23		20.29			20.49		21.07			21.09				
Herne Hill			20.12				20.25		20.32		20/44	20.52		21.08			21.12				
W. Dulwich			20.14						20.34			20.54					21.14				
Sydenham Hill			20.16						20.36			20.56					21.16				
Penge East			20.19						20.39			20.59					21.19				
Kent House			20.21						20.41			21.01					21.21				
Beckenham Jcn			20.23				20/31		20.43		20/52	21.03		21.16			21.23				
			Main				Local		Local	Main	Main	Local		Main	Local	Main	Local				
Shortlands			20.26				20/32		20.39	20.46	20/53	20.59		21.06	21/18	21.19	21.26	21/27			
BROMLEY SOUTH			20.28				20.34		20.41	20.48	20.55	21.01		21.08		21.21	21.28	21/31			
BROMLEY SOUTH			20.29				20.35		20.42	20.49	20.56	21.02		21.09	21.20	21.22	21.29				
Bickley			20.32						20.45	20.52		21.05		21.12	21.22	21.25	21.32				
Bickley Jcn			20/33				20/38		20/46	20/53	21/01	21/06		21/13	21/23	21/26	21/33				
St Mary Cray Jcn							20/39		20/47		21/07				21/27						
St Mary Cray										20.50		21.10			21.30						
SWANLEY							20.47			20.55	21.07	21.15			21.35						
Farningham Road							20.52														
Fawkham							20.57														
Meopham							21.01														
Sole Street							21.04			21/17											
Cuxton Road							21.09			21/22											
Rochester Bge Jcn	20/39				21/08		21/12			21/26			21/32			21/39					
Chatham Goods													21.37								
Rochester	20.40				21.09		21.13									21.40					
Rochester	20.41				21.10		21.14			21/27						21.41					
CHATHAM	20.43				21.12		21.16			21.28						21.43					
CHATHAM	20.45				21.14		21.18			21.32						21.45					
GILLINGHAM	20.48				21.17		21.21			21.36						21.48					
GILLINGHAM										21.38											
Rainham																					
Newington																					
Western Jcn																					
Eastern Jcn				21/41																22/31	
SITTINGBOURNE				21.42						21.50										22.32	
SITTINGBOURNE				(22.05)						21.52									22.05		
Murston Sdgs																					
Teynham																			22.11		
FAVERSHAM										22.03									22.20		
FAVERSHAM										22.07											
Graveney Sdgs																					
Whitstable										22.17											
Chestfield										22.23											
HERNE BAY										22.29											
HERNE BAY										22.31											
Birchington										22.43											
Westgate										22.48											
MARGATE										22.53											
MARGATE		21.58								22.56											23.15
Broadstairs		22.04								23.04											
Dumpton Park		22.08								23.08											
RAMSGATE		22.12								23.12											23.30
Destination	Ashford		Orp				S'oaks		Orp		S'oaks	Orp		Paris	S'oaks		Orp				Loco

WORKING TIMETABLE : FAVERSHAM to DOVER (1955)

Train	
From	
Class	
Engine	
FAVERSHAM	
Selling	
CANTERBURY E.	
CANTERBURY E.	
Bekesbourne	
Adisham	
Aylesham	
Snowdown	
Shepherdswell	
Kearsney	
DOVER PRIORY	
Destination	

WORKING TIMETABLE : SHEERNESS to SITTINGBOURNE (1955)

Class	Pass	Goods	Pass
Engine	2-6-2T	C 0-6-0	2-6-2T
SHEERNESS	21.22		22.11
Queenborough	21.28	21.42	22.18
Swale	21.33		22.23
Redham Dock			
Kemsley	21.37	21/55	22.28
Middle Jcn	21/40	21/59	22/30
Eastern Jcn	21/41		22/31
SITTINGBOURNE	21.42		22.32
Destination	Fav	BLA	

WORKING TIMETABLE : RAMSGATE to VICTORIA (1955)

Train	21.02	20.42	21.10				19.48		21.22	21.02			19.17	21.42		21.59	21.22		22.00	21.59
From	Orp	S'oaks	Orp				Dover		Orp	S'oaks			Teyn	Orp		Gill	S'oaks		Orp	Gill
Class	Pass	Pass	ECS	Pass	Pass	Pass	Pass	Goods	Pass	Pass	Pass	Pcls	Goods	Pass	Pass	Pcls	Pass	XP	Pass	Pcls
Engine	EMU	EMU	EMU	EMU	2-6-2T	EMU	U1 2-6-0	C 0-6-0	EMU	EMU	EMU	EMU	C 0-6-0	EMU	EMU	EMU	EMU	BR5 4-6-0	EMU	EMU
RAMSGATE																		19.45		
Dumpton Park																		19.49		
Broadstairs																		19.53		
MARGATE																		19.59		
MARGATE																		20.02		
Westgate																		20.07		
Birchington																		20.12		
HERNE BAY																		20.23		
HERNE BAY																		20.25		
Chestfield																		20.31		
Whitstable																		20.37		
Graveney																				
British Fruit																				
FAVERSHAM							20.45											20.47		
FAVERSHAM																		20.50		
Teynham																				
SITTINGBOURNE																		21.01		
SITTINGBOURNE					20.51													21.03		
Eastern Jcn					20/52															
Western Jcn																				
Newington													20.58							
Rainham													21.04							
GILLINGHAM																		21.16		
GILLINGHAM				20.27		20.42					20.54	20.59				21.10		21.18		
CHATHAM				20.30		20.45					20.57	21.04				21.13	(21.04)	21.22		
CHATHAM				20.32		20.47					20.59	(21.19)				21.15	21.19	21.29		
Rochester				20.34		20.48					21.00					21.16	21.22			(21.22)
Rochester				20.35		20.49					21.01					21.17	(21.44)	21.31		21.44
Chatham Goods								20.55												
Rochester Bge Jcn				20/37		20/50		20/58			21/03					21/18		21/32		21/46
Cuxton Road																				
Sole Street				20.47							21.13							21.45		
Meopham				20.49							21.15									
Longfield																				
Fawkham				20.53							21.20									
Farningham Road				20.58							21.24									
SWANLEY				21.11						21.24	21.33					21.44	21/55			
St Mary Cray										21.29						21.49				
St Mary Cray Jcn				21/16						21/31	21/38					21/51			22/01	
	Local	Main	Local	Main					Local	Main	Main			Local		Main	Main		Local	
Bickley Jcn	21/07	21/12	21/14	21/17					21/27	21/32	21/39			21/47		21/52	22/02		22/05	
Bickley	21.09	21.14	21.16						21.29	21.34				21.49		21.54			22.09	
BROMLEY SOUTH	21.11	21.16		21.21					21.31	21.36	21.42			21.51		21.56	22.05		22.12	
BROMLEY SOUTH	21.12	21.17		21.22					21.32	21.37	21.43			21.52		21.57	22.07		22.13	
Shortlands	21.14	21.20							21.34	21.40				21.54		22.00			22.15	
Beckenham Jcn	21.17			21/25					21.37		21/47			21.57			22/11		22.18	
Kent House	21.19								21.39					21.59					22.20	
Penge East	21.21								21.41					22.01					22.22	
Sydenham Hill	21.24								21.44					22.04					22.25	
W. Dulwich	21.26								21.46					22.06					22.27	
Herne Hill	21.29			21/32					21.49		21/53			22.09			22/19		22.30	
Brixton	21.31			21/33					21.51		21/54			22.11			22/20		22.32	
VICTORIA	21.37			21.39					21.56		21.59			22.16			22/26		22.37	
Destination		H. Via				CX	H. Jcn			H. Via						CX	H. Via			C. St

WORKING TIMETABLE : DOVER - FAVERSHAM (1955)

Train		20.00	20.00
From		Town	Town
Class	Pass	Goods	Goods
Engine	U1 2-6-0	N 2-6-0	N 2-6-0
DOVER PRIORY	19.48	20/10	
Dover Gas			
Kearsney	19.54		
Shepherdswell	20.02	20.30	21.00
Snowdown	20.07		
Aylesham	20.10		
Adisham	20.13		
Bekesbourne	20.19		
CANTERBURY E.	20.24		21.25
CANTERBURY E.	20.26		(22.16)
Selling	20.39		
FAVERSHAM	20.45		
Destination			

WORKING TIMETABLE : SITTINGBOURNE - SHEERNESS (1955)

Train	
From	
Class	Pass
Engine	2-6-2T
SITTINGBOURNE	20.51
Eastern Jcn	20/52
Middle Jcn	20/53
Kemsley	20.56
Redham Dock	
Swale	
Queenborough	21.04
SHEERNESS	21.10
Destination	

WORKING TIMETABLE : VICTORIA to RAMSGATE (1955)

	20.55	21.11					21.31		21.51	21.42		22.36	21.54	21.55			23.13		23.07	22.00
From	C. St	H. Via					H. Via		H. Via	CX		Hoo Jn	N'fleet	C. St			S'ness		G'end	H. Grn
Class	Pass	Pass	Pass	Pass	XP	Pass	Pass	Pass	Pass	Pass	Pass	Goods	Goods	Pass	Pass	Pass	Pass	Pass	P&P	Goods
Engine	EMU	EMU	EMU	EMU	WC	2-6-4T	EMU	EMU	EMU	EMU	EMU	C 0-6-0	N 2-6-0	EMU	EMU	EMU	C & LM2	D1 4-4-0	H 0-4-4T	N 2-6-0
VICTORIA		21.18		21.24	21.35		21.44				22.04			22.18	22.24					
Brixton		21/23		21.29			21.49				22.09			22/23	22.29					
Herne Hill		21/25		21/32	21/44		21.52				22.12			22/25	22.32					
W. Dulwich				21.34			21.54				22.14				22.34					
Sydenham Hill				21.36			21.56				22.16				22.36					
Penge East				21.39			21.59				22.19				22.39					
Kent House				21.41			22.01				22.21				22.41					
Beckenham Jcn		21/31		21.43	21/52		22.03				22.23			22/31	22.43					
		Local	Local	Main	Local		Local	Main	Local		Main			Main	Local					
Shortlands		21/32	21/39	21.46	21/53		21.59	22.06	22.19		22.26			22/32	22/46					
BROMLEY SOUTH		21.34	21.41	21.48			22.01	22.08	22.21		22.28			22.34	22.48					
BROMLEY SOUTH		21.35	21.42	21.49	21/55		22.02	22.09	22.22		22.29			22.35	22.49					
Bickley			21.45	21.52			22.05	22.12	22.25		22.32				22.52					
Bickley Jcn		21/38	21/46	21/53	21/58		22/06	22/13	22/26		22/33			22/38	22/53					
St Mary Cray Jcn		21/39	21/47				22/07		22/27											22/40
St Mary Cray				21.50			22.10		22.30											22.44
SWANLEY		21.47	21.55		22.04		22.15		22.35											22.52
Farningham Road		21.52													22.52					22/58
Fawkham		21.57													22.57					23/17
Meopham		22.01													23.01					
Sole Street		22.04			22/14										23.04					23/25
Cuxton Road		22.09			22/19										23.09					
Rochester Bge Jcn	22/08	22/12			22/23					22/39		22/51	23/02	23/08	23/12				23/24	23/33
Chatham Goods													23.05							23.37
Rochester	22.09	22.13								22.40				23.09	23.13				23.26	
Rochester	22.10	22.14			22/24					22.41		22/53		23.10	23.14				23.28	
CHATHAM	22.12	22.16			22.25					22.43				23.12	23.16				23.30	
CHATHAM	22.14	22.18			22.28					22.46		22/56		23.14	23.18			23.22	23.32	
GILLINGHAM	22.17	22.21								22.49				23.17	23.21			23.26	23.36	
GILLINGHAM					22/31							23/04			23.27					
Rainham												23.10			23.32					
Newington																				
Western Jcn																				
Eastern Jcn																	23/30			
SITTINGBOURNE					22.42												23.31		23.42	
SITTINGBOURNE					22.43														23.44	
Murston Sdgs																				
Teynham																				
FAVERSHAM					22.54														23.55	
FAVERSHAM					22.56	22.57														
Graveney Sdgs																				
Whitstable					23.06															
Chestfield					23.11															
HERNE BAY					23.17															
HERNE BAY					23.18															
Birchington					23.31															
Westgate					23.36															
MARGATE					23.41															
MARGATE					23.44															
Broadstairs					23.52															
Dumpton Park					23.56															
RAMSGATE					00.00															
Destination			S'oaks	Orp		Dover	S'oaks	Orp	S'oaks		Orp					Orp				

WORKING TIMETABLE : FAVERSHAM to DOVER (1955)

Train	
From	
Class	Pass
Engine	2-6-4T
FAVERSHAM	22.57
Selling	23.04
CANTERBURY E.	23.15
CANTERBURY E.	23.18
Bekesbourne	23.24
Adisham	23.30
Aylesham	23.34
Snowdown	23.38
Shepherdswell	23.43
Kearsney	23.50
DOVER PRIORY	23.55
Destination	

WORKING TIMETABLE : SHEERNESS to SITTINGBOURNE (1955)

Train	
From	
Class	Pass
Engine	C & 2MT
SHEERNESS	23.13
Queenborough	23.19
Swale	
Redham Dock	
Kemsley	23.26
Middle Jcn	23/29
Eastern Jcn	23/30
SITTINGBOURNE	23.31
Destination	

WORKING TIMETABLE : RAMSGATE to VICTORIA (1955)

	Train	Train	Train	Train	Train	Train	Train	Train	Train	Train	Train	Train	Train	Train	Train	Train	Train	Train	Train
Train	21.42	20.00	17.58	18.00		19.17		17.10	22.20	22.02		17.10		17.10	22.42	22.25	17.10	22.55	
From	S'oaks	G'end	M'stone	R'gate		Teyn		R'gate	Orp	S'oaks		R'gate		R'gate	Orp	S'oaks	R'gate	Orp	
Class	Pass	Goods	Pass	Goods	Pass	Goods	Pass	Pcls	Pass	Pass	Pass	Pcls	Pass	Pcls	Pass	Pass	Pcls	Pass	Pass
Engine	EMU	C 0-6-0	2-6-4T	BR5 4-6-0	2-6-2T	C 0-6-0	EMU	N 2-6-0	EMU	EMU	EMU	N 2-6-0	EMU	N 2-6-0	EMU	EMU	N 2-6-0	EMU	C 0-6-0
RAMSGATE			19.53																
Dumpton Park			19.57																
Broadstairs			20.01																
MARGATE			20.07																
MARGATE				20.08															
Westgate				20/17															
Birchington				20.24															
HERNE BAY																			
Chestfield																			
Whitstable																			
Graveney																			
British Fruit																			
FAVERSHAM																			
FAVERSHAM								21.15											21.40
Teynham								21.23				21.25							21.49
SITTINGBOURNE												21.34							21.55
SITTINGBOURNE					21.10							21.46							22.00
Eastern Jcn					21/11														22/01
Western Jcn																			
Newington																			
Rainham						21.34						21.56		22.01					
GILLINGHAM						21.40													
GILLINGHAM							21.40			21.54	21.58								
CHATHAM							21.43			21.57	22.01								
CHATHAM							21.46			21.59	22.03	22/10							
Rochester							21.48			22.00	22.05								
Rochester							21.49			22.01	22.08	22/12							
Chatham Goods																			
Rochester Bge Jcn							21/50			22/03	22/09	22/13							
Cuxton Road																			
Sole Street										22.13		22/27							
Meopham										22.15									
Longfield																			
Fawkham										22.20									
Farningham Road		21.58								22.24									
SWANLEY	22.04	22/09							22.24	22.33		22/40			22.44				
St Mary Cray	22.09	22/16							22.29						22.49				
St Mary Cray Jcn	22/11	22/19							22/31	22/38		22/45			22/51				
	Main								Local	Main	Main				Main	Local	Main		Local
Bickley Jcn	22/12								22/27	22/32	22/39	22/46			22/47	22/52			23/00
Bickley	22.14								22.29	22.34					22.49	22.54			23.02
BROMLEY SOUTH	22.16								22.31	22.36	22.42				22.51	22.56			23.04
BROMLEY SOUTH	22.17								22.32	22.37	22.43	22/49			22.52	22.57			23.05
Shortlands	22.20								22.34	22.40					22.54	23.00			23.07
Beckenham Jcn									22.37		22/47	22/53			22.57				23.11
Kent House									22.39						22.59				23.13
Penge East									22.41						23.01				23.15
Sydenham Hill									22.44						23.04				23.19
W. Dulwich									22.46						23.06				23.21
Herne Hill									22.49		22/53	23.05			23.09		23.16		23.24
Brixton									22.51		22/54				23.11		23/19		23.26
VICTORIA									22.57		22.59				23.16		23.26		23.32
Destination	H. Via	BLA			S'ness		CX			H. Via		CX		H. Via					S'ness

WORKING TIMETABLE : DOVER - FAVERSHAM (1955)

Train	
From	
Class	
Engine	
DOVER PRIORY	
Dover Gas	
Kearsney	
Shepherdswell	
Snowdown	
Aylesham	
Adisham	
Bekesbourne	
CANTERBURY E.	
CANTERBURY E.	
Selling	
FAVERSHAM	
Destination	

WORKING TIMETABLE : SITTINGBOURNE - SHEERNESS (1955)

	Train	Train
Train		
From		
Class	Pass	Pass
Engine	2-6-2T	C 0-6-0
SITTINGBOURNE	21.10	22.00
Eastern Jcn	21/11	22/01
Middle Jcn	21/12	22/02
Kemsley	21.15	22.05
Redham Dock		
Swale	21.21	22.11
Queenborough	21.25	22.15
SHEERNESS	21.35	22.24
Destination		

WORKING TIMETABLE : VICTORIA to RAMSGATE (1955)

Train	22.31		22.51		22.42	22.46		23.10		23.26
From	H. Via		H. Via		CX	CX		BLA		H. Via
Class	Pass	Pass	Pass	Pass	Pass	Pass	Goods	Goods	Pass	Pass
Engine	EMU	EMU	EMU	EMU	EMU	EMU	2-6-4T	BR4 4-6-0	EMU	EMU
VICTORIA		22.44		23.04					23.30	
Brixton		22.49		23.09					23.35	
Herne Hill		22.52		23.12					23.38	
W. Dulwich		22.54		23.14					23.40	
Sydenham Hill		22.56		23.16					23.42	
Penge East		22.59		23.19					23.45	
Kent House		23.01		23.21					23.47	
Beckenham Jcn		23.03		23.23					23.49	
	Local	Main	Local	Main					Main	Local
Shortlands	22.59	23.06	23.19	23.26					23.52	23.54
BROMLEY SOUTH	23.01	23.08	23.21	23.28					23.54	23.57
BROMLEY SOUTH	23.02	23.09	23.22	23.29					23.58	23.58
Bickley	23.05	23.12	23.25	23.32					00.01	00.01
Bickley Jcn	23/06	23/13	23/26	23/33					00/02	00/02
St Mary Cray Jcn	23/07		23/27					23/48		00/03
St Mary Cray	23.10		23.30					23/51		00.06
SWANLEY	23.15		23.35					23/58		00.11
Farningham Road							23.40			
Fawkham										
Meopham										
Sole Street							00/00			
Cuxton Road										
Rochester Bge Jcn					23/41	00/04	00/20			
Chatham Goods							00.24			
Rochester					23.42	00.05				
Rochester					23.43	00.06				
CHATHAM					23.45	00.08				
CHATHAM					23.47	00.10				
GILLINGHAM					23.50	00.13				
GILLINGHAM										
Rainham										
Newington										
Western Jcn										
Eastern Jcn										
SITTINGBOURNE										
SITTINGBOURNE										
Murston Sdgs										
Teynham										
FAVERSHAM										
FAVERSHAM										
Graveney Sdgs										
Whitstable										
Chestfield										
HERNE BAY										
HERNE BAY										
Birchington										
Westgate										
MARGATE										
MARGATE										
Broadstairs										
Dumpton Park										
RAMSGATE										
Destination	S'oaks	Orp	S'oaks	Orp				Dover	Orp	S'oaks

WORKING TIMETABLE : FAVERSHAM to DOVER (1955)

Train	
From	
Class	
Engine	
FAVERSHAM	
Selling	
CANTERBURY E.	
CANTERBURY E.	
Bekesbourne	
Adisham	
Aylesham	
Snowdown	
Shepherdswell	
Kearsney	
DOVER PRIORY	
Destination	

WORKING TIMETABLE : SHEERNESS to SITTINGBOURNE (1955)

Train	
From	
Class	
Engine	
SHEERNESS	
Queenborough	
Swale	
Redham Dock	
Kemsley	
Middle Jcn	
Eastern Jcn	
SITTINGBOURNE	
Destination	

WORKING TIMETABLE : RAMSGATE to VICTORIA (1955)

Train	18.00	21.13	21.42		22.40		20.40	19.35	23.08			21.10	19.12	19.15		21.42	
From	R'gate	Dover	Q'boro		S'oaks		A'ford	Rams	S'oaks			Rams	Ton'bge	C. Cross		Q'boro	
Class	Goods	Pass	Goods	Pass	Pass	Pass	Goods	Pass	Pass	Pass	Goods	Pass	Pass	XP	Pass	Goods	Goods
Engine	BR5 4-6-0	2-6-4T	C 0-6-0	EMU	EMU	L1 4-4-0	N1 2-6-0	E1 4-4-0	EMU	EMU	C 0-6-0	L1 4-4-0	L 4-4-0	WC	2-6-2T	C 0-6-0	BR5 4-6-0
RAMSGATE						21.10							21.35	21.48			
Dumpton Park						21.14							21.39	21.52			
Broadstairs						21.19							21.43	21.56			
MARGATE						21.25							21.49	22.02			
MARGATE						21.28											
Westgate						21.33											
Birchington	21.08					21.38											
HERNE BAY	21.48					21.49											
HERNE BAY						21.51											
Chestfield						21.57											
Whitstable						22.02											
Graveney																	
British Fruit																	
FAVERSHAM	22.10					22.12											
FAVERSHAM						22.15										22.35	
Teynham						22.24											
SITTINGBOURNE						22.30											
SITTINGBOURNE						22.33									22.45	22/50	
Eastern Jcn															22/46		
Western Jcn			22/02														
Newington			22/08														
Rainham			22/14			22.43											
GILLINGHAM			22.22			22.48											
GILLINGHAM			22.40	22.45		22.49				22.54							23/16
CHATHAM				22.48		22.53				22.57	(22.53)						
CHATHAM			22/44	22.50		(23.02)				22.59	23.02						23/18
Rochester				22.51						23.00	23.04						
Rochester			22/46	22.52		23.06				23.01		23.05					
Chatham Goods			22.48													23.15	23.21
Rochester Bge Jcn				22/53		23/07				23/03		23/06				23/20	
Cuxton Road																	
Sole Street										23.13							
Meopham										23.15							
Longfield																	
Fawkham										23.20							
Farningham Road										23.24							
SWANLEY				23.00			23/05	23.18	23.27	23.33							
St Mary Cray				23.05					23.32								
St Mary Cray Jcn				23/07			23/15	23/24	23/35	23/38							
				Main				Main	Main	Local							
Bickley Jcn				23/08				23/25	23/36	23/39							
Bickley				23.10					23.37								
BROMLEY SOUTH				23.12				23.30	23.42	23.42							
BROMLEY SOUTH				23.13				23.32	23.43	23.43	23.45						
Shortlands				23.15				23.34	23.45	23.46							
Beckenham Jcn								23.36		23.49	00/53						
Kent House										23.51							
Penge East										23.53							
Sydenham Hill										23.56							
W. Dulwich										23.59							
Herne Hill								23/45		00.01	00.13						
Brixton										00.03							
VICTORIA										00.09							
Destination				S. Grn	Bfs	C. Cross	H. Grn	H. Via	H. Via			CX			S'ness	BLA	

WORKING TIMETABLE : DOVER - FAVERSHAM (1955)

Train		19.35
From		S'cliffe
Class	Pass	Goods
Engine	2-6-4T	N 2-6-0
DOVER PRIORY	21.13	21/50
Dover Gas		
Kearsney	21.19	
Shepherdswell	21.27	
Snowdown	21.32	22.25
Aylesham	21.35	
Adisham	21.38	
Bekesbourne	21.44	
CANTERBURY E.	21.49	
CANTERBURY E.	21.51	
Selling	22.04	
FAVERSHAM	22.10	
Destination		

WORKING TIMETABLE : SITTINGBOURNE - SHEERNESS (1955)

Train	
From	
Class	Pass
Engine	2-6-2T
SITTINGBOURNE	22.45
Eastern Jcn	22/46
Middle Jcn	22/47
Kemsley	22.50
Redham Dock	
Swale	
Queenborough	22.57
SHEERNESS	23.04
Destination	

The C class 0-6-0's first appeared in 1900 and set a record by remaining as the standard goods engine in Kent for almost sixty years; their only rival being the N 2-6-0 which took over most of the long distance work to and from London and the Kent coalfield. To see the class at their best and busiest all one had to do was to stand for an hour within earshot of Hoo Junction, Gravesend, where the full and honest bark of these engines was almost continuous. 31715 was one of eight based at Faversham whose duties involved long hours at work between Hoo Junction, the Medway towns, Sheerness, Faversham and Margate. Curiously they had no booked duties over the Dover road to the Kent Coalfields the reason being that N 2-6-0's were preferred because of their greater haulage capabilities over the severe gradients. 31715, pictured on Faversham shed in August 1957, was withdrawn in November 1961 after a working life of sixty-one years. (L.G. Marshall)

Although modified from time to time, the South Eastern O1 0-6-0 dated from 1878 and remained in service until 1961. The longevity of the class was in part due to their very wide route availability which allowed them to run on the busy Tilmanstone - Shepherdswell colliery branch from which the standard C class 0-6-0 was prohibited. Twenty-three of the original fifty-nine engines were in traffic by the start of the decade but by the autumn of 1951 this had been reduced to eight: four at Ashford and four at Dover to work the Kent & East Sussex (Headcorn to Robertsbridge) and the Tilmanstone branch respectively. 31430 stands on Dover loco in July 1958, coaled and ready for its turn on the Tilmanstone branch. (L.G. Marshall)

Train	20.00	22.47	18.50	21.36	21.15	22.35		23.02
From	Dover	Dover	Dover	Ashford	West M	Fav		C'bury
Class	Goods	Pass	Goods	Pass	Goods	Goods	Pass	Pass
Engine	N 2-6-0	U1 2-6-0	N 2-6-0	L 4-4-0	N 2-6-0	BR5 4-6-0	C 0-6-0	2-6-2T
RAMSGATE				22.25	22.41			23.38
Dumpton Park				22.45				23.42
Broadstairs				22.49				23.47
MARGATE				22.55				23.53
MARGATE			22/44					
Westgate								
Birchington								
HERNE BAY								
HERNE BAY			23/14					
Chestfield								
Whitstable								
Graveney								
British Fruit								
FAVERSHAM	22.50	23.38	23.40					
FAVERSHAM			(01.15)					
Teynham								
SITTINGBOURNE								
SITTINGBOURNE							23.52	
Eastern Jcn							23/53	
Western Jcn								
Newington								
Rainham								
GILLINGHAM								
GILLINGHAM								
CHATHAM								
CHATHAM								
Rochester								
Rochester								
Chatham Goods						23.35		
Rochester Bge Jcn						23/40		
Cuxton Road								
Sole Street						23/53		
Meopham								
Longfield								
Fawkham								
Farningham Road								
SWANLEY					00.19	00/10		
St Mary Cray					00.26	00/15		
St Mary Cray Jcn						00/22		
Bickley Jcn								
Bickley						00/26		
BROMLEY SOUTH								
BROMLEY SOUTH						00/29		
Shortlands								
Beckenham Jcn						00/35		
Kent House								
Penge East								
Sydenham Hill								
W. Dulwich								
Herne Hill						00.58		
Brixton								
VICTORIA								
Destination						S'ness		

Train	20.00	
From	Town	
Class	Goods	Pass
Engine	N 2-6-0	U1 2-6-0
DOVER PRIORY		22.47
Dover Gas		
Kearsney		22.53
Shepherdswell		23.00
Snowdown		23.05
Aylesham		23.08
Adisham		23.11
Bekesbourne		
CANTERBURY E.		23.19
CANTERBURY E.	22.16	23.22
Selling		
FAVERSHAM	22.50	23.38
Destination	H. Grn	

Train	
From	
Class	Pass
Engine	C 0-6-0
SITTINGBOURNE	23.52
Eastern Jcn	23/53
Middle Jcn	23/54
Kemsley	23.57
Redham Dock	
Swale	00.03
Queenborough	00.08
SHEERNESS	00.13
Destination	

VICTORIA
STATION WORKING : 1954/5

Train	Arrive	Engine	Shed	Dep	Destination
		C 0-6-0	S. Lane 71	00.01	Light to S. Lane loco
00.10 Stewarts Lane (Milk)	00.18	E2 0-6-0T	S. Lane 55		(Station pilot to 04.00)
01.05 Holborn Viaduct (Pcl)	01.38	E1 4-4-0	S. Lane 47		
01.13 East Croydon (Pcls)	01.42	LM4 2-6-4T	S. Lane 503		
		E1 4-4-0	S. Lane 47	01.50	Light to S. Lane Loco
01.55 Stewarts Lane (Milk)	02.02	BR5 4-6-0	S. Lane 15		
		BR5 4-6-0	S. Lane 15	02.15	Light to S. Lane Loco
		LM4 2-6-4T	S. Lane 503	02.20	Kensington Pcls
Light ex S. Lane loco	03.20	BR5 4-6-0	S. Lane 16		(For 03.30)
		BR5 4-6-0	S. Lane 16	03.30	Ramsgate
		E2 0-6-0T	S. Lane 55	04.00	Light to Victoria LBSCR
04.15 Stewarts Lane (ECS)	04.25	H 0-4-4T	S. Lane 53		(ECS for 05.10)
Light ex S. Lane loco	04.57	BR5 4-6-0	S. Lane 12		(For 05.10)
		BR5 4-6-0	S. Lane 12	05.10	Ramsgate
		H 0-4-4T	S. Lane 53	06.00	Stewarts Lane (Pcls)
Light ex Victoria (LBSCR)	06.05	E2 0-6-0T	S. Lane 55		(Pilot to 11.45)
07.40 Stewarts Lane (ECS)	07.50	BR5 4-6-0	S. Lane 10		(ECS for 08.35)
(On rear of 07.50 ECS)		BR5 4-6-0	S. Lane 14	07.55	Light to S. Lane CS
08.00 Victoria CS	08.05	E2 0-6-0T	S. Lane 55		(ECS for 09.00)
Light ex S. Lane loco	08.17	BR5 4-6-0	S. Lane 13		(For 08.35)
		BR5 4-6-0	S. Lane 13	08.35	Ramsgate
Light ex S. Lane loco	08.42	MN 4-6-2	S. Lane 2		(For 09.00)
		MN 4-6-2	S. Lane 2	09.00	Dover Marine
08.50 Stewarts Lane (ECS)	09.02	N 2-6-0	S. Lane 501		(ECS for 09.35)
07.20 Dover Marine	09.10	WC & L1	Dover 430/437		
09.05 Victoria CS	09.10	H 0-4-4T	S. Lane 54		(ECS for 10.00)
08.34 Cannon Street (ECS)	09.28	LM2 2-6-2T	S. Lane 50		
		BR5 4-6-0	S. Lane 14	09.35	Ramsgate
Light ex S. Lane loco	09.38	MN 4-6-2	S. Lane 3		(For 10.00)
(ECS of 07.20 Dover)		LM2 2-6-2T	S. Lane 50	09.42*	Victoria CS
		L1 4-4-0	Dover 437	09.45	Light to S. Lane loco
09.50 Victoria CS	09.55	LM2 2-6-2T	S. Lane 50		(ECS for 10.35 Ramsgate)
		MN 4-6-2	S. Lane 3	10.00	Dover Marine
08.25 Ramsgate	10.27	WC 4-6-2	Rams 473		
		BR5 4-6-0	S. Lane 10	10.35	Ramsgate
		WC 4-6-2	Rams 473	10.40*	Victoria CS
10.40 Stewarts Lane (ECS)	10.50	BR5 4-6-0	S. Lane 15		
09.20 Dover Priory	11.28	WC 4-6-2	Dover 431		
		BR5 4-6-0	S. Lane 11	11.35	Ramsgate (Pullman)
		WC 4-6-2	Dover 431	11.40*	Victoria CS
11.35 Victoria CS	11.40	LM2 2-6-2T	S. Lane 50		(ECS for 12.30)
11.30 Stewarts Lane (Coal)	11.45	WC 4-6-2	Rams 473		
09.25 Ramsgate	11.49	BR5 4-6-0	S. Lane 16		
		BR5 4-6-0	S. Lane 16	12.00*	Victoria CS
11.55 Victoria CS	12.00	E2 0-6-0T	S. Lane 55		(ECS for 12.35)
11.50 Stewarts Lane (ECS)	12.02	LM2 2-6-2T	S. Lane 51		(ECS for 13.00)
		WC 4-6-2	Dover 430	12.30	Dover Marine
		BR5 4-6-0	S. Lane 15	12.35	Ramsgate
Light ex S. Lane loco	12.45	BR7 4-6-2	S. Lane 4		(For 13.00)
		BR7 4-6-2	S. Lane 4	13.00	Folkestone Harbour
		WC 4-6-2	Rams 473	13.42	Stewarts Lane coal
13.45 Victoria CS	13.49	E2 0-6-0T	S. Lane 55		(ECS for 14.35)
11.15 Ramsgate	14.10	BR5 4-6-0	S. Lane 12		
		BR5 4-6-0	S. Lane 12	14.20*	Victoria CS
Light ex S. Lane loco	14.22	WC 4-6-2	Dover 431		(For 14.35)
		WC 4-6-2	Dover 431	14.35	Ramsgate
14.50 Victoria CS	14.55				
13.10 Dover Marine	15.05	MN 4-6-2	S. Lane 3		
Light ex S. Lane loco	15.22	BR5 4-6-0	S. Lane 16		(For 15.35)
		MN 4-6-2	S. Lane 3	15.32*	Victoria CS
		BR5 4-6-0	S. Lane 16	15.35	Ramsgate
13.10 Ramsgate	15.48	BR5 4-6-0	S. Lane 13		
Light ex S. Lane loco	15.50	E1 4-4-0	S. Lane 47		Shunt vans of 13.10 ex Ramsga
Light ex Victoria CS	15.55	LM2 2-6-2T	S. Lane 50		(For 16.06 ECS)
		BR5 4-6-0	S. Lane 12	16.00	Stewarts Lane (ECS)
15.48 Victoria CS	16.02	E2 0-6-0T	S. Lane 55		(ECS for 16.06 ECS)
		LM2 2-6-2T	S. Lane 50	16.06	Cannon Street (ECS)
		E1 4-4-0	S. Lane 47	16.15	Light to S. Lane CS
13.55 Ramsgate	16.20	V 4-4-0	Rams 481		
		BR5 4-6-0	S. Lane 13	16.40	Stewarts Lane (ECS)
15.22 Ramsgate	18.12	BR5 4-6-0	S. Lane 14		(Forms 19.35)
16.58 Dover Marine	18.30	BR7 4-6-2	S. Lane 4		
Light ex S. Lane loco	18.32	L1 4-4-0	Dover 437		(For 18.52 ECS)
17.15 Dover Marine	18.50	WC 4-6-2	Dover 430		
(Stock of 16.58 ex Dover)		L1 4-4-0	Dover 437	18.52	Stewarts Lane (ECS)
18.50 Stewarts Lane (Milk)	18.58	H 0-4-4T	S. Lane 53		(LBSCR Transfer pilot)
17.05 Ramsgate (Pullman)	19.05	WC 4-6-2	Rams 470		
		WC 4-6-2	Dover 430	19.10*	Victoria CS
Light ex Victoria CS	19.15	N 2-6-0	S. Lane 60		(For 19.26 ECS)
16.15 Ramsgate	19.22	BR5 4-6-0	S. Lane 10		
Light ex S. Lane loco	19.25	WC 4-6-2	Rams 473		(For 19.35)
(Stock of 17.05 ex Ramsgate)		N 2-6-0	S. Lane 60	19.26	Stewarts Lane (ECS)
		WC 4-6-2	Rams 473	19.35	Ramsgate
		BR5 4-6-0	S. Lane 10	19.38*	Victoria CS
18.10 Dover Marine	19.50	MN 4-6-2	S. Lane 2		
19.50 Victoria CS	19.55				
(LBSCR Transfer pilot)		H 0-4-4T	S. Lane 53	20.00	Light to S. Lane Loco
20.00 Victoria CS	20.05	E1 4-4-0	S. Lane 47		(Forms 21.00)
17.40 Dover Priory	20.07	BR5 4-6-0	S. Lane 11		(Forms 20.20 ECS)
		MN 4-6-2	S. Lane 2	20.08*	Victoria CS
Light ex S. Lane loco	20.12	V 4-4-0	Rams 481		(For 20.35)
		BR5 4-6-0	S. Lane 14	20.20	Stewarts Lane (ECS)
		V 4-4-0	Rams 481	20.35	Ramsgate
Light ex S. Lane loco	20.45	WC & L1	Dover 430/437		(For 21.00)
		WC & L1	Dover 430/437	21.00	Dover Marine
21.00 Stewarts Lane (ECS)	21.10	BR5 4-6-0	S. Lane 10		
Light ex S. Lane loco	21.22	WC 4-6-2	Rams 470		(For 21.35)
		WC 4-6-2	Rams 470	21.35	Ramsgate
19.45 Ramsgate	22.26	BR5 4-6-0	S. Lane 16		
Light ex Victoria (LBSCR)	22.30	N 2-6-0	S. Lane 508		
		N 2-6-0	S. Lane 508	22.50	Stewarts Lane (ECS)
17.10 Ramsgate (Pcls)	23.26	N 2-6-0	S. Lane 63		
Light ex S. Lane loco	23.27	H 0-4-4T	S. Lane 54		(Station Pilot to 09.00)
23.16 Holborn Viaduct (Pcls)	23.36	C 0-6-0	S. Lane 71		
		N 2-6-0	S. Lane 63	23.45	Light to S. Lane Loco

* Stock propelled by inward engine

Because the South Eastern suburban service had been electrified in stages between 1925 and 1938, Victoria was not the most interesting of London's stations from which to watch trains - unless, of course, one happened to be fascinated by electric multiple-units. Main line steam was confined to the Ramsgate expresses and Continental boat trains and although these amounted (in the quietest period of the year) to only seventeen departures, they did include some elements of variety.

The most surprising element of the steam working at Victoria was the absence of light Pacifics and given the post-war invasion of 130 engines, one might have expected them to have featured prominently in the operation of the line's expresses. In fact the greater part of the Ramsgate express duties were worked by Stewarts Lane 4-6-0's - King Arthur N15's until 1955 and thereafter new BR Standard 5MT's - and this included the 11.35 'Thanet Belle' Pullman.

It was only during the evening when engines from Ramsgate took over some of the services that the monopoly of the 4-6-0's was broken: the 19.35 and 21.35 expresses being Pacific-worked whilst the 20.35 was booked to a Schools 4-4-0.

The boat trains were deemed to be beyond what was reasonable for a class 5 engine to work and therefore Pacifics were used for all five daily departures although there were variations between services. The two morning departures were heavily loaded trains and were diagrammed to Merchant Navy pacifics; the only time when a class 8 engine could be seen at Victoria. The two midday services were lighter and did not therefore warrant anything larger than a class 7. One of the services was booked to a Dover light Pacific whilst the other - the Golden Arrow - was the province of one of the two Britannia Pacifics based at Stewarts Lane. The odd-man out was the Night Ferry and being too heavy even for a Merchant Navy was diagrammed to the incongruity of a light Pacific paired with an L1 4-4-0.

Any interest that might have been provided by the empty stock working was absent because many inward services were simply propelled into the carriage sidings by the train engine. A handful of services were based at Stewarts Lane and were worked in the conventional way, some producing the best variety of steam - N 2-6-0's, E2 0-6-0T's and 4-4-0's - that the station was capable of producing.

8 DA3 DEC I 9 2 5 H4 G
FG2 G9DC K DE: 9C7 8FG62 B (1-0/ . y

GWMS	2WRN 6SOSN	FPNM	5 NV 5 NtbSLfRTS		
23.50 Stewarts Lane (Pcls)	00.17	E1 4-4-0	S. Lane 47		
		E1 4-4-0	S. Lane 91	00.30	Light to B. Arms loco
00.35 Cannon St (Pcls)	00.43	E1 4-4-0	S. Lane 45		
		E1 4-4-0	S. Lane 47	01.05	Victoria (Pcls)
		E1 4-4-0	S. Lane 45	01.30	Light to Ewer St loco
Station Pilot		LM2 2-6-2T	S. Lane 50	02.45	Light to Southwark
Light ex Ewer St loco	02.45	E1 4-4-0	S. Lane 45		
		E1 4-4-0	S. Lane 45	03.00	Ramsgate via Chatham
03.05 Southwark (Pcls)	03.20	LM2 2-6-2T	S. Lane 50		
		LM2 2-6-2T	S. Lane 50	04.15	Light to Ludgate Hill
05.30 Rotherhithe Rd	06.00	E1 4-4-0	BLA 90		
		E1 4-4-0	BLA 90	06.56	Margate via Ashford
Light ex Ludgate Hill	10.37	LM2 2-6-2T	BLA 107		
		LM2 2-6-2T	BLA 107	11.00	Ramsgate via Chatham (Pcls)
11.30 Rotherhithe Road	11.55	LM2 2-6-2T	BLA 109		
		LM2 2-6-2T	BLA 109	12.16	Light to Blackfriars
Light ex Ewer St loco	19.39	LM2 2-6-2T	BLA 109		
19.15 Clapham Jcn (Pcls)	19.59	H 0-4-4T	S. Lane 54		(Engine works pilot to 21.30)
		LM2 2-6-2T	BLA 109	20.33	London Bridge (Perish)
		H 0-4-4T	S. Lane 54	21.30	Light to Ludgate Hill
Light ex Ludgate Hill	21.50	LM2 2-6-2T	S. Lane 50		(Becomes Station Pilot)
22.30 Rotherhithe Road	23.00	LM2 2-6-2T	BLA 108		
Light ex Blackfriars	23.07	C 0-6-0	S. Lane 71		
		C 0-6-0	S. Lane 71	23.16	Victoria (Pcls)
		LM2 2-6-2T	BLA 108	23.20	Light to Blackfriars
19.35 Ramsgate via Dover	23.58	E1 4-4-0	S. Lane 91		

STEWARTS LANE MPD : ENGINE MOVEMENTS (WINTER 1955)

Inward Working	On Shed	Engine	Diagram	Off Shed	To Work
23.16 Holborn V - Victoria Pcls	00.08	C 0-6-0	SL. 71		(For 01.48)
Victoria Pilot	00.10	E2 0-6-0T	SL. 55		(For 23.55)
		N 2-6-0	SL. 61	00.25	01.35 Gds Herne Hill - Faversham
19.29 Chichester - Victoria Pcls	00.28	LM4 2-6-4T	SL. 502		(For 04.15
23.45 Gds Bromley S - Herne Hill	00.42	C 0-6-0	HG 200		(For 02.00)
		C 0-6-0	SL. 70	01.48	02.32 Gds Herne Hill - Gillingham
01.05 Holborn V - Victoria Pcls	01.58	E1 4-4-0	SL. 47		(For 04.10)
		C 0-6-0	HG 200	02.00	02.35 Clapham Jcn - Mottingham Milk
23.38 Gds Horsham - Battersea	02.00	N 2-6-0	SL. 501		(For 03.50)
18.00 Gds Ramsgate - Herne Hill	02.15	BR5 4-6-0	SL.15		(For 03.10)
01.45 Gds Norwood - Battersea	02.45	N 2-6-0	SL. 60		(For 09.05)
00.25 Gds Hoo Jcn - Herne Hill	02.45	C 0-6-0	HG 187		(For 10.20)
23.50 Gillingham - Herne Hill Gds	02.50	C 0-6-0	SL. 70		(For 05.35)
		P 0-6-0	SL. 78	02.55	Stewarts Lane pilot
01.10 Gds Three Bridges - Battersea	03.00	N 2-6-0	SL. 509		(For 05.43)
		BR5 4-6-0	SL.16	03.10	03.30 Victoria - Ramsgate
		U1 2-6-0	SL. 508	03.10	03.45 Battersea - Three Bridges Gds
02.45 Kensington - S. Lane Milk	03.25	H 0-4-4T	SL. 53		(For 04.05)
		N 2-6-0	SL. 501	03.50	04.15 Battersea - Norwood Gds
Stewarts Lane Pilot	04.05	P 0-6-0	SL. 78		(For 05.55)
		H 0-4-4T	SL. 53	04.05	04.15 S. Lane -Victoria ECS
		E1 4-4-0	SL. 46	04.10	04.25 S. Lane - Ludgate Hill ECS
Victoria (LBSCR) Pilot	04.10	H 0-4-4T	SL. 506		(For 06.15)
		LM4 2-6-4T	SL. 502	04.15	04.30 S. Lane - Victoria Milk
03.00 Pcls Clapham Jcn - Kensington	04.15	LM4 2-6-4T	SL. 503		(For 05.43)
		N 2-6-0	SL. 62	04.30	05.23 Gds Herne Hill - Dover
		E2 0-6-0T	SL. 76	04.45	Herne Hill Pilot
		BR5 4-6-0	SL.12	04.50	05.10 Victoria - Ramsgate
		H 0-4-4T	SL. 52	04.55	S. Lane Pilot
		C 0-6-0	SL. 516	05.10	05.40 Battersea - Norwood Gds
01.15 Gds Worthing - Battersea	05.15	BR5 4-6-0	SL.13		(For 08.10)
		C 0-6-0	SL. 71	05.35	06.40 Kensington - Clapham Jcn Milk
South Lambeth Pilot	05.35	57xx 0-6-0	OOC 262		(For 07.00)
		LM4 2-6-4T	SL. 503	05.43	06.29 Victoria - T. Wells
		N 2-6-0	SL. 509	05.43	06.15 Victoria - New Cross Gate (Pcls)
		P 0-6-0	SL. 78	05.55	Stewarts Lane pilot
03.25 Sevenoaks - Herne Hill Gds	06.14	N 2-6-0	SL. 64		(For 10.15)
		H 0-4-4T	SL. 506	06.15	Victoria (LBSCR) Pilot
04.00 Gds Ferme Park - Battersea	06.20	W 2-6-4T	SL. 514		(For 07.00)
Stewarts Lane Pilot	06.35	P 0-6-0	SL. 78		(For 07.55)
		57xx 0-6-0	OOC 262	07.00	South Lambeth Pilot
06.20 Norwood - Battersea Gds	07.15	N 2-6-0	SL. 501		(For 10.50)
		BR5 4-6-0	SL.10	07.25	07.40 S. Lane - Victoria ECS
		BR5 4-6-0	SL.14	07.25	07.40 S. Lane - Victoria ECS (On rear)
		E2 0-6-0T	SL. 519	07.50	Battersea Yard pilot
		P 0-6-0	SL. 78	07.55	Stewarts Lane pilot
		BR5 4-6-0	SL.13	08.10	08.35 Victoria - Ramsgate
Battersea Yard pilot	08.25	E2 0-6-0T	SL. 520		(For 17.50)
		MN 4-6-2	SL. 2	08.35	09.00 Victoria - Dover (M)
		N 2-6-0	SL. 60	09.05	09.50 Victoria (E) - Eardley ECS
		MN 4-6-2	SL. 3	09.30	10.00 Victoria - Dover (M)
		LM4 2-6-4T	SL. 511	09.32	10.08 Victoria - Tunbridge Wells
07.10 Dover (M) - Victoria (Pilot)	10.00	L1 4-4-0	Dvr 437		(For 18.27)
07.10 Dover (M) - Victoria	10.00	WC 4-6-2	Dvr 430		(For 11.40)
		N 2-6-0	SL. 64	10.15	10.54 Gds Herne Hill - Ashford
09.48 Ludgate Hill - S. Lane ECS	10.15	E1 4-4-0	SL. 47		(For 15.40)
		C 0-6-0	HG 194	10.20	Wandsworth Road Pilot
		BR5 4-6-0	SL.11	10.25	10.40 S. Lane - Victoria ECS (On rear)
		BR5 4-6-0	SL.15	10.25	10.40 S. Lane - Victoria ECS
08.23 Uckfield - Victoria	10.26	BR4 2-6-4T	BTN 742		(For 17.35)
08.24 Forest Row - Victoria		LM4 2-6-4T	TB 674		(For 16.10)
		N 2-6-0	SL. 501	10.50	11.00 S. Lane - Clapham Jn ECS
08.25 Ramsgate - Victoria	10.50	WC 4-6-2	Ram 473		(For 19.15)
		W 2-6-4T	SL. 513	11.00	11.30 Battersea - Norwood Gds
10.35 Ludgate Hill - S. Lane ECS	11.00	H 0-4-4T	SL. 54		(For 12.35)
08.45 Wandsworth Rd - Battersea	11.10	C 0-6-0	SL. 74		(For 17.20)
09.33 T. Wells - Victoria	11.12	LM4 2-6-4T	SL. 501		(For 15.22)
11.00 Ludgate Hill - S. Lane ECS	11.30	C 0-6-0	SL. 71		(For 15.15)
		WC 4-6-2	Dvr 430	11.40	11.50 S. Lane - Victoria ECS (On rear)
09.22 Dover (P) - Victoria	11.50	WC 4-6-2	Dvr 431		(For 14.15)
		N 2-6-0	SL. 509	12.00	12.30 Battersea - Norwood Gds
09.57 Cannon St - Grove Park ECS	12.06	C 0-6-0	SL. 72		(For 14.15)

Inward Working	On Shed	Engine	Diagram	Off Shed	To Work
09.25 Ramsgate - Victoria	12.20	BR5 4-6-0	SL.16		(For 15.15)
		BR7 4-6-2	SL. 4	12.35	13.00 Victoria - Dover (M)
		H 0-4-4T	SL. 54	12.35	12.45 S. Lane - Kensington Milk
Bank 12.35 ex Victoria	12.45	E2 0-6-0T	SL. 55		(For 13.30)
Bank 13.00 ex Victoria	13.15	LM2 2-6-2T	SL.51		(For 16.00)
Herne Hill Pilot	13.16	E2 0-6-0T	SL. 75		(For 21.45)
		E2 0-6-0T	SL. 55	13.30	13.45 Victoria CS - Victoria ECS
12.50 Mottingham - Clapham Jcn Milk	13.55	C 0-6-0	HG 200		(For 16.30)
		C 0-6-0	SL. 72	14.15	14.55 Herne Hill - Brockley Lane Gds
		WC 4-6-2	Dvr 431	14.15	14.35 Victoria - Dover (P)
13.15 Gds Norwood - Battersea	14.15	W 2-6-4T	SL. 513		(For 17.15)
14.00 Clapham Jcn - S. Lane Milk	14.20	H 0-4-4T	SL. 54		(For 16.50)
		C 0-6-0	SL. 71	15.15	15.30 S. Lane - Ludgate Hill ECS
		BR5 4-6-0	SL.16	15.15	15.35 Victoria - Ramsgate
		LM4 2-6-4T	SL. 502	15.22	17.19 Eardley - Victoria ECS
14.43 Gds Norwood - Battersea	15.25	N 2-6-0	SL. 509		(For 19.50)
13.05 Dover (M) - Victoria	15.30	MN 4-6-2	SL. 3		(For 09.30)
Stewarts Lane Pilot	15.35	P 0-6-0	SL. 78		(For 02.55)
		E1 4-4-0	SL. 47	15.40	16.35 S. Lane - Ludgate Hill ECS
		LM2 2-6-2T	SL.51	16.00	16.15 S. Lane - Ludgate Hill ECS
13.47 T. Wells - Victoria	16.05	LM4 2-6-4T	SL. 511		(For 17.15)
		LM4 2-6-4T	TB 674	16.10	16.50 Victoria - Brighton
		C 0-6-0	HG 200	16.30	16.45 S. Lane - Ludgate Hill ECS
16.00 Victoria - S. Lane ECS	16.40	BR5 4-6-0	SL.12		(For 04.50)
		H 0-4-4T	SL. 54	16.50	17.00 S. Lane - Wood Lane Milk
16.40 Victoria - S. Lane ECS (On rear)	17.00	WC 4-6-2	Ram 481		(For 20.05)
16.40 Victoria - S. Lane ECS	17.00	BR5 4-6-0	SL.13		(For 22.20)
		LM4 2-6-4T	SL. 511	17.15	17.50 Victoria - Tunbridge Wells
		W 2-6-4T	SL. 513	17.15	17.45 Battersea - Lillie Bridge Gds
16.06 Victoria - Ludgate Hill ECS	17.15	LM2 2-6-2T	SL.50		(For 18.45)
		C 0-6-0	SL. 74	17.20	19.50 Wandsworth Rd - Herne Hill
Herne Hill Pilot	17.30	C 0-6-0	HG 194		(For 19.05)
		BR4 2-6-4T	BTN 742	17.35	18.10 Victoria - Uckfield
		E2 0-6-0T	SL. 520	17.50	Battersea Yard pilot
Battersea Yard pilot	18.05	E2 0-6-0T	SL. 519		(For 07.50)
		L1 4-4-0	Dvr 437	18.27	18.52 Victoria - S. Lane (ECS)
		LM2 2-6-2T	SL.50	18.45	19.00 S. Lane - Ludgate Hill (Pcls)
		C 0-6-0	HG 194	19.05	19.37 Battersea - Hither Green Gds
17.36 E. Grinstead - Victoria	19.10	BR4 2-6-4T	BTN 741		(For 20.50)
18.52 Victoria - S. Lane (ECS)	19.10	L1 4-4-0	Dvr 437		(For 20.35 and couple to Dvr 430)
		WC 4-6-2	Ram 473	19.15	19.35 Victoria - Ramsgate
16.58 Dover (M) - Victoria	19.15	BR7 4-6-2	SL. 4		(For 12.35)
17.15 Dover (M) - Victoria	19.20	WC 4-6-2	Dvr 430		(For 20.35 and couple to Dvr 437)
18.50 S. Lane - Victoria (Vans)	19.30	H 0-4-4T	SL. 53		(For 21.55)
19.26 Victoria - S. Lane ECS (On rear)	19.45	WC 4-6-2	Ram 470		(For 21.15)
19.26 Victoria - S. Lane ECS	19.45	N 2-6-0	SL. 60		(For 00.25)
		N 2-6-0	SL. 509	19.50	20.24 Battersea - Three Bridges Gds
		WC 4-6-2	Ram 481	20.05	20.35 Victoria - Ramsgate
18.10 Dover (M) - Victoria	20.20	MN 4-6-2	SL. 2		(For 08.35)
S. Lane Pilot	20.25	H 0-4-4T	SL. 52		(For 04.55)
		WC 4-6-2	Dvr 430	20.35	21.00 Victoria - Dover (M)
		L1 4-4-0	Dvr 437	20.35	21.00 Victoria - Dover (M) (Pilot)
20.20 Victoria - S. Lane ECS (On rear)	20.45	BR5 4-6-0	SL.11		(For 10.25)
20.20 Victoria - S. Lane ECS	20.45	BR5 4-6-0	SL.14		(For 07.25)
		BR4 2-6-4T	BTN 741	20.50	21.30 Victoria - H. Heath Pcls
20.15 Gds Camberwell - Herne Hill	21.10	C 0-6-0	SL. 72		(For 22.45)
		WC 4-6-2	Ram 470	21.15	21.35 Victoria - Ramsgate
		E2 0-6-0T	SL. 75	21.45	Herne Hill Pilot
Bank 21.35 ex Victoria	21.45	BR5 4-6-0	SL.10		(For 07.25)
		H 0-4-4T	SL. 53	21.55	S. Lane Pilot
		BR5 4-6-0	SL.13	22.20	22.50 Gds Battersea - T. Bridges
22.03 Ludgate Hill - S. Lane Pcls	22.30	H 0-4-4T	SL. 54		(For 23.20)
		C 0-6-0	SL. 72	22.45	23.48 Blackfriars - Herne Hill Gds
21.15 Tunbridge Wells - Victoria	23.10	LM4 2-6-4T	SL. 511		(For 09.32)
22.50 Victoria - S. Lane ECS	23.15	U1 2-6-0	SL. 508		(For 03.10)
22.50 Victoria - S. Lane ECS (On rear)	23.15	BR5 4-6-0	SL.16		(For 10.25)
		H 0-4-4T	SL. 54	23.20	Victoria Pilot
22.14 Gds Merton Abbey - Battersea	23.20	C 0-6-0	SL. 516		(For 05.10)
17.10 Ramsgate - Victoria (Pcls)	23.30	N 2-6-0	SL. 63		(For 04.30)
22.54 Gds Herne Hill - S. Lane	23.30	E2 0-6-0T	SL. 76		(For 04.45)
		E2 0-6-0T	SL. 55	23.55	00.10 S. Lane - Victoria Milk

It might be assumed that because Victoria's suburban services had been electrified shortly after the grouping, Stewarts Lane Motive Power Depot enjoyed rather a quiet life. In fact the opposite was the case since any relief given by the arrival of the third rail was nullified by the closure of the LBSCR's Battersea shed; the work and engines of the latter being transferred to Stewarts Lane.

Stewarts Lane was therefore a joint depot in the sense that it provided engines and men for both the Chatham and Brighton sections and although the passenger workings of the LBSCR were almost exclusively worked by electric multiple-unit, engines had to be provided for the hourly Tunbridge Wells services and a relatively heavy goods timetable.

The shed also provided engines for a third category of work: the Dover and Folkestone boat trains which whilst numbering only five during the winter grew to eleven (plus specials) during the summer.

The allocation consisted (January 1955) of 106 engines of 18 classes which made the shed one of the most varied in London if not the country. With an engine ringing off every twenty minutes, it was also one of the busiest and was responsible for preparing seventy-two engines on the quietest winter weekday: fifty-seven being Stewarts Lane engines and the balance, fifteen, being foreign engines that had turned-round in London.

The shed's largest fleet consisted of seventeen West Country light Pacifics for which, incredibly, there were no basic diagrams. Occasionally one would substitute for a King Arthur 4-6-0 on a Ramsgate turn - a light Pacific could often be found on the 15.35 ex Victoria - but otherwise their duties revolved solely around the summer boat train service which, as mentioned earlier, could rise to eleven or more trains a day. The shed also housed three of the larger Merchant Navy engines and whilst these were generally reserved for the heavy 09.00 and 10.00 boat trains from Victoria, they did make rare visits to Thanet at times of engine shortage. Such outings however were uncommon in the extreme.

The Southern tended to allocate resources according to peak rather than optimum demand and even though its seventeen light Pacifics were 'busy' doing very little during the winter, the ranks of class 7 engines were augmented by two Britannia Pacifics - the same power classification as a West Country - which were placed in the boat train links. Their regular booking was on the 13.00 Victoria - Dover 'Golden Arrow'; a working that did not call for the full weight of a Merchant Navy.

The hardest work done by Stewarts Lane engines on a regular basis was performed by the shed's sixteen King Arthur 4-6-0's. The class handled most of the Victoria - Ramsgate expresses (the exceptions being the evening trains which were worked by Ramsgate Schools or Light Pacifics on their way home), most engines working one round trip to the coast although the engine of the 03.30 and the 15.35 departures from Victoria were diagrammed to the same engine whilst the engine of the 08.35 Victoria - Ramsgate later crossed the boundary with the LBSCR and completed its day with a

LOCOMOTIVE ALLOCATIONS & TRANSFERS : STEWARTS LANE (73A)

Loco	Class	Aug-50	Sep-50	Oct-50	Nov-50	Dec-50	Jan-51	Feb-51	Mar-51	Apr-51	May-51	Jun-51	Jul-51
35025	8P : MN 4-6-2 (1941)												
35026	8P : MN 4-6-2 (1941)												
35027	8P : MN 4-6-2 (1941)												
35028	8P : MN 4-6-2 (1941)												
34033	7P : WC 4-6-2 (1945)												
34034	7P : WC 4-6-2 (1945)			To Ex Jcn	X	X	X	X	X	X	X	X	X
34035	7P : WC 4-6-2 (1945)			To Brighton	X	X	X	X	X	X	X	X	X
34066	7P : WC 4-6-2 (1945)												
34067	7P : WC 4-6-2 (1945)												
34068	7P : WC 4-6-2 (1945)												
34069	7P : WC 4-6-2 (1945)												
34070	7P : WC 4-6-2 (1945)												
34071	7P : WC 4-6-2 (1945)												
34074	7P : WC 4-6-2 (1945)	X	X	Ex Dover		To Dover	X	X	X	X	X	X	X
34075	7P : WC 4-6-2 (1945)	X	X	Ex Dover		To Dover	X	X	X	X	X	X	X
34076	7P : WC 4-6-2 (1945)												
34083	7P : WC 4-6-2 (1945)								To Ramsgate	X	X	X	X
34084	7P : WC 4-6-2 (1945)								To Ramsgate	X	X	X	X
34085	7P : WC 4-6-2 (1945)								To Ramsgate	X	X	X	X
34087	7P : WC 4-6-2 (1945)	X	X	X	X	X	X	X	Ex Ramsgate				
34088	7P : WC 4-6-2 (1945)	X	X	X	X	X	X	X	Ex Ramsgate				
34090	7P : WC 4-6-2 (1945)	X	X	X	X	X	X	X	Ex Ramsgate				
34091	7P : WC 4-6-2 (1945)												
34092	7P : WC 4-6-2 (1945)												
34101	7P : WC 4-6-2 (1945)												
34102	7P : WC 4-6-2 (1945)												
34103	7P : WC 4-6-2 (1945)												
34104	7P : WC 4-6-2 (1945)												
70004	7MT 4-6-2 (1951)	X	X	X	X	X	X	X	X	X	X	NEW	
70014	7MT 4-6-2 (1951)	X	X	X	X	X	X	X	X	X	X	NEW	
31912	6F : W 2-6-4T (1931)												
31914	6F : W 2-6-4T (1931)												
31915	6F : W 2-6-4T (1931)								To H. Green	X	X	X	X
30793	5P : N15 4-6-0 (1926)												
30794	5P : N15 4-6-0 (1926)	X	X	X	Ex B. Arms								
30795	5P : N15 4-6-0 (1926)	X	X	X	X	Ex Ramsgate							
30796	5P : N15 4-6-0 (1926)											To Dover	X
30763	5P : N15 4-6-0 (1925)												
30764	5P : N15 4-6-0 (1925)												
30765	5P : N15 4-6-0 (1925)	X	X	X	X	Ex N. Elms							
30766	5P : N15 4-6-0 (1925)												
30767	5P : N15 4-6-0 (1925)	X	X	X	X	X	X	X	X	X	X	Ex Dover	
30768	5P : N15 4-6-0 (1925)	X	X	X	X	X	X	X	X	X	X	Ex Dover	
30769	5P : N15 4-6-0 (1925)	X	X	X	X	X	X	X	X	X	X	Ex Dover	
30772	5P : N15 4-6-0 (1925)	X	X	X	Ex E'leigh	To Dover	X	X	X	X	X	X	X
30773	5P : N15 4-6-0 (1925)	X	X	X	Ex Sarum	To Dover	X	X	X	X	X	X	X
30774	5P : N15 4-6-0 (1925)					To Dover	X	X	X	X	X	X	X
30775	5P : N15 4-6-0 (1925)					To Dover	X	X	X	X	X	X	X
30776	5P : N15 4-6-0 (1925)					To Dover	X	X	X	X	X	X	X
30777	5P : N15 4-6-0 (1925)	X	X	X	X	X	X	X	X	X	X	Ex N. Elms	
30778	5P : N15 4-6-0 (1925)			To E'leigh	X	X	X	X	X	X	X	Ex N. Elms	
30779	5P : N15 4-6-0 (1925)	X	X	X	X	X	X	X	X	X	X	Ex N. Elms	
30786	5P : N15 4-6-0 (1925)									To E'leigh	X	X	X
30791	5P : N15 4-6-0 (1925)	X	X	X	Ex N. Elms								
30792	5P : N15 4-6-0 (1925)	X	X	X	Ex N. Elms								
33036	5F : Q1 0-6-0 (1942)	X	X	X	X	X	X	X	X	X	X	X	Ex Ton
33037	5F : Q1 0-6-0 (1942)	X	X	X	X	X	X	X	X	X	X	X	Ex Ton
33038	5F : Q1 0-6-0 (1942)	X	X	X	X	X	X	X	X	X	X	X	Ex Ton
31409	5F : N 2-6-0 (1917)												
31410	5F : N 2-6-0 (1917)												
31411	5F : N 2-6-0 (1917)												
31412	5F : N 2-6-0 (1917)												
31413	5F : N 2-6-0 (1917)												
31414	5F : N 2-6-0 (1917)												
31810	5F : N 2-6-0 (1917)												
31811	5F : N 2-6-0 (1917)												
31812	5F : N 2-6-0 (1917)												
31813	5F : N 2-6-0 (1917)												
31814	5F : N 2-6-0 (1917)												
31815	5F : N 2-6-0 (1917)												
31816	5F : N 2-6-0 (1917)												
31817	5F : N 2-6-0 (1917)												To Dover
31818	5F : N 2-6-0 (1917)												To Dover
31859	5F : N 2-6-0 (1917)				To Ramsgate	X	X	X	X	X	X	X	
31899	4P : U1 2-6-0 (1925)	X	X	X	X	X	X	X	X	X	X	X	Ex Redhill
31900	4P : U1 2-6-0 (1925)	X	X	X	X	X	X	X	X	X	X	X	Ex Redhill
31901	4P : U1 2-6-0 (1925)	X	X	X	X	X	X	X	X	X	X	Ex B. Arms	
31902	4P : U1 2-6-0 (1925)	X	X	X	X	X	X	X	X	X	X	Ex B. Arms	
31903	4P : U1 2-6-0 (1925)				To B. Arms	X	X	X	X	X	X	X	X
31903	4P : U1 2-6-0 (1925)	X	X	X	X	X	X	X	X	X	X	Ex B. Arms	
31904	4P : U1 2-6-0 (1925)				To B. Arms	X	X	X	X	X	X	Ex B. Arms	
31905	4P : U1 2-6-0 (1925)												
31906	4P : U1 2-6-0 (1925)												
31907	4P : U1 2-6-0 (1925)												
31908	4P : U1 2-6-0 (1925)												
31909	4P : U1 2-6-0 (1925)												
31910	4P : U1 2-6-0 (1925)												
31793	4P : U 2-6-0 (R/B 2-6-4T) 1928			To Reading	X	X	X	X	X	X	X	X	X
31803	4P : U 2-6-0 (R/B 2-6-4T) 1928				To Guild	X	X	X	X	X	X	X	X
31623	4P : U 2-6-0 (1928)				To N. Elms	X	X	X	X	X	X	X	X

Battersea - Three Bridges freight. Most of the duties involved an element of empty carriage working between Stewarts Lane and Victoria.

The long reign of the King Arthur's came to an end in mid-1955 when the first of ten new BR5 4-6-0's arrived to take over the Ramsgate workings. Although this spelt the end of booked N15 work from Victoria, the number of new 4-6-0's was only just sufficient for the basic winter service and half the allocation of King Arthurs had to be retained at Stewarts Lane in order to cover the heavy summer traffic.

Schools 4-4-0's belonged more to the South Eastern than the Chatham road and were not strongly represented at Stewarts Lane which normally had only one of the class - 30915 'Brighton' was the resident example for quite a period during the 1950's - used primarily for Victoria - Newhaven relief boat trains. When not so employed the 4-4-0 was often used on the 09.35 Victoria to Ramsgate and the 15.22 Ramsgate to Victoria instead of the booked N15 4-6-0. Both classes, of course, were 5P.

The influx of modern designs ought to have consigned the once-familiar inside cylinder 4-4-0's to history yet for two reasons the type survived and indeed continued in traffic until the final days of steam. The first reason was that the volume of holiday traffic was of such a density that it was only with the greatest reluctance that main line engines of any sort were taken out of traffic; the other reason being the restrictions on the stretch of line between Herne Hill and Holborn Viaduct - from where many of the Division's parcels trains started - which was barred to all main line engines other than D, D1 and E1 4-4-0's.

Stewarts Lane usually had half a dozen of these engines - typically three E1 and three D1 4-4-0's - which were used for the 05.50 Cannon Street to Dover via Dartford: a two-day duty which included a considerable amount of empty carriage work in and around Holborn Viaduct. A third E1 was outbased at Gillingham but worked the 03.00 Holborn Viaduct to Ramsgate via Dartford. The Stewarts Lane D1 4-4-0's had less regular work than the E1's and their only booked diagram was for the 07.00 Cannon Street - Dartford - Ramsgate on Saturday mornings instead of the normal N 2-6-0. The reason for this was because the return working was the 21.10 Ramsgate to Holborn Viaduct via Ashford and Maidstone East.

Not all the E1 mileage was run in the shadow of Holborn Viaduct and for most of the 1950's it was always possible to have a run behind one of the class on a main line express. The best chance lay with the 11.50 Victoria to Margate, a seven-coach working which ran all the year round and in spite of numerous post-grouping developments continued to be diagrammed to an E1 4-4-0. Allowed only 24 minutes to run from Bromley South to Chatham - a stretch of line that included an heroic ascent of Sole Street and a dashing downhill run to the Medway - there were some who regarded it as altogether better value for money than the preceding 11.35 Pullman.

The BR Standard engines referred to above were not the only strangers to be received by Stewarts Lane since late 1950 saw a batch of new LMS 4MT 2-6-4T's arrive to take part in the Victoria - Tunbridge Wells West service: one of the few sections of the LBSCR not to have been electrified. These large and efficient tanks were followed twelve months later by the smaller but equally efficient LMS 2-6-2T's which assisted with the Cannon Street empty stock workings and shunted the carriage sidings at Victoria and Holborn. The hours worked by these engines were long and both diagrams called for almost twenty-three hours continuous steaming.

Expectations that the 2-6-2T's would replace the H 0-4-4T's of 1904 proved to be false and after half a century of use, Stewarts Lane had nine of the class on its books with four being in traffic each day and giving no quarter

Loco	Class	Aug-50	Sep-50	Oct-50	Nov-50	Dec-50	Jan-51	Feb-51	Mar-51	Apr-51	May-51	Jun-51	Jul-51
								LOCOMOTIVE ALLOCATIONS & TRANSFERS : STEWARTS LANE (73A)					
42070	4MT 2-6-4T (1948)	X	X	X	NEW	To Ramsgate	X	X	X	X	X	X	X
42071	4MT 2-6-4T (1948)	X	X	X	NEW	To Ashford	X	X	X	X	X	X	X
42072	4MT 2-6-4T (1948)	X	X	X	NEW	To Ashford	X	X	X	X	X	X	X
42073	4MT 2-6-4T (1948)	X	X	X	NEW	To Ashford	X	X	X	X	X	X	X
42074	4MT 2-6-4T (1948)	X	X	X	NEW	To Ashford	X	X	X	X	X	X	X
42080	4MT 2-6-4T (1948)	X	X	X	X.	NEW							
42081	4MT 2-6-4T (1948)	X	X	X	X	NEW							
42082	4MT 2-6-4T (1948)	X	X	X	X	NEW							
42083	4MT 2-6-4T (1948)	X	X	X	X	NEW							
42084	4MT 2-6-4T (1948)	X	X	X	X	X	X	X	NEW				
31758	3P : L1 4-4-0 (1926)	X	X	X	X	X	X	X	X	X	X	X	Ex B. Arms
31759	3P : L1 4-4-0 (1926)	X	X	X	X	X	X	X	X	X	X	X	Ex B. Arms
31762	3P : L 4-4-0 (1914)					To Ton	X	X	X	X	X	X	X
31764	3P : L 4-4-0 (1914)					To Ton	X	X	X	X	X	X	X
31767	3P : L 4-4-0 (1914)					To St L.	X	X	X	X	X	X	X
31019	3P : E1 4-4-0 (1919)												
31067	3P : E1 4-4-0 (1919)												
31165	3P : E1 4-4-0 (1919)					To B. Arms	X	X	X	X	X	X	X
31504	3P : E1 4-4-0 (1919)												
31506	3P : E1 4-4-0 (1919)												
31145	3P : D1 4-4-0 (1921)											To Dover	X
31487	3P : D1 4-4-0 (1921)					To Fav	X	X	X	X	X	X	X
31743	3P : D1 4-4-0 (1921)												
31745	3P : D1 4-4-0 (1921)	X	X	X	X	Ex Ton			W/D	X	X	X	X
31749	3P : D1 4-4-0 (1921)												
32100	3F : E2 0-6-0T (1913)												
32101	3F : E2 0-6-0T (1913)												
32102	3F : E2 0-6-0T (1913)												
32103	3F : E2 0-6-0T (1913)												
32104	3F : E2 0-6-0T (1913)												
32105	3F : E2 0-6-0T (1913)												
32106	3F : E2 0-6-0T (1913)												
32107	3F : E2 0-6-0T (1913)												
32128	2F : E1 0-6-0T (1874)								To Soton	X	X	X	X
31234	2F : C 0-6-0 (1900)						To Gill	X	X	X	X	X	X
31573	2F : C 0-6-0 (1900)	X	X	X	X	X	Ex Gill						
31575	2F : C 0-6-0 (1900)												
31576	2F : C 0-6-0 (1900)												
31578	2F : C 0-6-0 (1900)												
31579	2F : C 0-6-0 (1900)	X	X	X	X	X	Ex Gill						
31580	2F : C 0-6-0 (1900)	X	X	X	X	X	X	X	X	X	X	X	Ex Ton
31581	2F : C 0-6-0 (1900)	X	X	X	X	X	X	X	X	X	X	X	Ex H. Greer
31582	2F : C 0-6-0 (1900)												
31583	2F : C 0-6-0 (1900)	X	X	X	X	X	X	X	X	X	X	X	Ex Gill
31584	2F : C 0-6-0 (1900)	X	X	X	X	X	X	X	X	X	X	X	Ex B. Arms
31681	2F : C 0-6-0 (1900)						To Gill	X	X	X	X	X	X
31683	2F : C 0-6-0 (1900)						To Gill	X	X	X	X	X	X
31714	2F : C 0-6-0 (1900)												To Fav
31716	2F : C 0-6-0 (1900)												To Ton
31717	2F : C 0-6-0 (1900)												To Ton
31718	2F : C 0-6-0 (1900)												
31719	2F : C 0-6-0 (1900)												
31721	2F : C 0-6-0 (1900)	X					X	X	X	X	X	X	Ex Ashford
31722	2F : C 0-6-0 (1900)						To B. Arms	X	X	X	X	X	X
31706	1P : R1 0-4-4T (1900)			To St L.	X	X	X	X	X	X	X	X	X
31660	1P : R 0-4-4T (1891)												
31005	1P : H 0-4-4T (1904)												
31177	1P : H 0-4-4T (1904)									To Ton	X	X	X
31184	1P : H 0-4-4T (1904)			To Ton	X	X	X	X	X	X	X	X	X
31261	1P : H 0-4-4T (1904)												
31263	1P : H 0-4-4T (1904)												
31265	1P : H 0-4-4T (1904)	X	X	X	Ex Ramsgate								
31266	1P : H 0-4-4T (1904)												
31269	1P : H 0-4-4T (1904)	X	X	X	Ex Ashford								
31295	1P : H 0-4-4T (1904)												To Fav
31307	1P : H 0-4-4T (1904)						To Gill	X	X	X	X	X	X
31311	1P : H 0-4-4T (1904)												
31319	1P : H 0-4-4T (1904)	X	X	Ex St. L									
31320	1P : H 0-4-4T (1904)	X	X	X	X	X	X	X	X	Ex Ton	X	X	X
31321	1P : H 0-4-4T (1904)												
31329	1P : H 0-4-4T (1904)												
30756	1F : '0756' 0-6-0T (1907)												
31555	0F : P 0-6-0T (1909)			To Dover	X	X	X	X	X	X	X	X	X
31558	0F : P 0-6-0T (1909)	X	X	Ex Dover									

to the more modern engines by working for around twenty-two hours per day. Two of the 0-4-4T's spent much of their time on the West London extension whilst the others worked as station pilots at Stewarts Lane Yard and Victoria Central. The reason for having twice as many engines as there were diagrams was partly because of the length of the workings - almost a full day in many cases - plus the additional empty stock workings that were called for during the summer months.

Amongst Stewarts Lane's allocation were three of the curious W 2-6-4T's - curious because the 2-6-4T arrangement was unusual in a goods engine - which worked to an LBSCR diagram involving trip workings between Battersea Yard and Norwood, Lillie Bridge, Ferme Park and Old Oak Common. The working was a long one and the engine that left Stewarts Lane at 11.00 on, for example, Monday to work the 11.30 Battersea - Norwood did not return to the shed until 06.20 on Wednesday. The W class did not generally find themselves in the public spotlight and the best chance of seeing one in Victoria station came during the summer when the 2-6-4T that normally rang off shed at 11.00 left four hours earlier to work the stock of the 06.10 Newhaven - Victoria boat express empty to Eardley before picking up its diagram with the 11.30 Battersea to Norwood goods.

For longer distance goods traffic, Stewarts Lane had nine N and four U1 2-6-0's; the former being used for preference since the U1's were unable to handle a full load on main line workings. In fact the only regular U1 turn at Stewarts Lane was for the 03.45 Battersea - Three Bridges goods and the 10.56 Brighton - Victoria via Eridge and Oxted. The same engine later worked the 15.52 Victoria to Brighton via

Loco	Class	Aug-51	Sep-51	Oct-51	Nov-51	Dec-51	Jan-52	Feb-52	Mar-52	Apr-52	May-52	Jun-52	Jul-52
35025	8P : MN 4-6-2 (1941)								To Ex Jcn	X	X	X	X
35026	8P : MN 4-6-2 (1941)												
35027	8P : MN 4-6-2 (1941)												
35028	8P : MN 4-6-2 (1941)												
34033	7P : WC 4-6-2 (1945)		To Plymouth	X	X	X	X	X	X	X	X	X	X
34066	7P : WC 4-6-2 (1945)												
34067	7P : WC 4-6-2 (1945)												
34068	7P : WC 4-6-2 (1945)												
34069	7P : WC 4-6-2 (1945)												
34070	7P : WC 4-6-2 (1945)												
34071	7P : WC 4-6-2 (1945)												
34076	7P : WC 4-6-2 (1945)								To Stratford	X	X	X	X
34087	7P : WC 4-6-2 (1945)												
34088	7P : WC 4-6-2 (1945)												
34090	7P : WC 4-6-2 (1945)												
34091	7P : WC 4-6-2 (1945)												
34092	7P : WC 4-6-2 (1945)												
34101	7P : WC 4-6-2 (1945)												
34102	7P : WC 4-6-2 (1945)												
34103	7P : WC 4-6-2 (1945)												
34104	7P : WC 4-6-2 (1945)												
70004	7MT 4-6-2 (1951)												
70014	7MT 4-6-2 (1951)												
31912	6F : W 2-6-4T (1931)												
31914	6F : W 2-6-4T (1931)												
30793	5P : N15 4-6-0 (1926)												
30794	5P : N15 4-6-0 (1926)												
30795	5P : N15 4-6-0 (1926)												
30763	5P : N15 4-6-0 (1925)												
30764	5P : N15 4-6-0 (1925)												
30765	5P : N15 4-6-0 (1925)												
30766	5P : N15 4-6-0 (1925)												
30767	5P : N15 4-6-0 (1925)												
30768	5P : N15 4-6-0 (1925)												
30769	5P : N15 4-6-0 (1925)												
30770	5P : N15 4-6-0 (1925)	X	X	X	X	X	X	X	X	X	X	Ex Dover	
30771	5P : N15 4-6-0 (1925)	X	X	X	X	X	X	X	X	X	X	Ex Dover	
30772	5P : N15 4-6-0 (1925)	X	X	X	X	X	X	X	X	X	X	Ex Dover	
30773	5P : N15 4-6-0 (1925)	X	X	X	X	X	X	X	X	X	X	Ex Dover	
30774	5P : N15 4-6-0 (1925)	X	X	X	X	X	X	X	X	X	X	Ex Dover	
30777	5P : N15 4-6-0 (1925)		To Dover	X	X	X	X	X	X	X	X	X	X
30778	5P : N15 4-6-0 (1925)		To Dover	X	X	X	X	X	X	X	X	X	X
30779	5P : N15 4-6-0 (1925)		To Dover	X	X	X	X	X	X	X	X	X	X
30791	5P : N15 4-6-0 (1925)												
30792	5P : N15 4-6-0 (1925)												
33036	5F : Q1 0-6-0 (1942)												
33037	5F : Q1 0-6-0 (1942)												
33038	5F : Q1 0-6-0 (1942)												
31409	5F : N 2-6-0 (1917)												
31410	5F : N 2-6-0 (1917)												
31411	5F : N 2-6-0 (1917)												
31412	5F : N 2-6-0 (1917)												
31413	5F : N 2-6-0 (1917)												
31414	5F : N 2-6-0 (1917)												
31810	5F : N 2-6-0 (1917)												
31811	5F : N 2-6-0 (1917)												
31812	5F : N 2-6-0 (1917)												
31813	5F : N 2-6-0 (1917)												
31814	5F : N 2-6-0 (1917)												
31815	5F : N 2-6-0 (1917)					To Gill	X	X	X	X	X	X	X
31816	5F : N 2-6-0 (1917)		To Gill	X	X	X	X	X	X	X	X	X	X
31892	4P : U1 2-6-0 (1925)	X	X	X	X	X	X	X	X	X	X	Ex B. Arms	
31893	4P : U1 2-6-0 (1925)	X	X	X	X	X	X	X	X	X	X	Ex B. Arms	
31899	4P : U1 2-6-0 (1925)		To H. Green	X	X	X	X	X	X	X	X	X	X
31899	4P : U1 2-6-0 (1925)	X	X	X	X	X	X	X	X	X	X	Ex H. Green	
31900	4P : U1 2-6-0 (1925)		To H. Green	X	X	X	X	X	X	X	X	X	X
31900	4P : U1 2-6-0 (1925)	X	X	X	X	X	X	X	X	X	X	Ex H. Green	
31901	4P : U1 2-6-0 (1925)												
31902	4P : U1 2-6-0 (1925)												
31903	4P : U1 2-6-0 (1925)												
31904	4P : U1 2-6-0 (1925)												
31905	4P : U1 2-6-0 (1925)												
31906	4P : U1 2-6-0 (1925)												
31907	4P : U1 2-6-0 (1925)											To N. Elms	X
31908	4P : U1 2-6-0 (1925)											To N. Elms	X
31909	4P : U1 2-6-0 (1925)											To N. Elms	X
31910	4P : U1 2-6-0 (1925)											To N. Elms	X

engaged with a miscellany of goods services between Norwood and Three Bridges but one of the engines had the interesting task of working the empty stock of the Bournemouth Belle between Stewarts Lane, where it was cleaned and maintained, and Clapham Junction prior to being handed over to a South Western engine and men.

The numerous of all goods engines at Stewarts Lane were the shed's twelve C 0-6-0's: a class that had been going strong since 1900 and showed few signs of loosening their grip on the Division's freight activities. Most of them covered the myriad LCDR services that radiated from Herne Hill whilst others were involved in the complex empty stock arrangements between Cannon Street and Stewarts Lane whereby trains were hauled from Cannon Street to Ludgate Hill by one engine and then, after reversal, from Ludgate Hill to Stewarts Lane by another.

Having been all but displaced by the N 2-6-0's on longer distance goods workings, the Stewarts Lane C's were not often seen the country side of Swanley although one of the class had a regular turn on the 02.32 Herne Hill to Gillingham, a stopping service that took over eight hours to cover the 32-mile distance. The engine returned with the rather faster (ie two hours and thirty-nine minutes) 23.40 to Herne Hill having spent the interim on local work in the Medway including an appearance with a rush-passenger working over the Allhallows branch.

If eight hours to reach the Medway seems excessive it was nothing as compared to the 05.40 goods from Battersea which took nearly seven hours to cover the ten miles to Norwood Junction. This was a Stewarts Lane LBSCR working for which a C 0-6-0 was used and in whose defence it must be pointed out that the train spent four hours shunting at New Wandsworth and another two at Wandsworth Common. On reaching Norwood Junction the 0-6-0 penetrated even more deeply into Brighton territory by working the 14.05 Norwood to Merton Abbey, a train which was routed via West Croydon, Waddon Marsh, Mitcham Junction and Wimbledon. There were not very many engines that could boast of visiting all three SR constituents in the same day.

While Stewarts Lane sent one of its 0-6-0's into darkest Brighton country, the shed used a pair of strangers for some of its local work. The 10.20 Wandsworth Road shunt and the 16.45 empty stock to Ludgate Hill (for the 18.18 Cannon Street - Ramsgate) were both worked by Hither Green C 0-6-0's although the crews for both turns came from Stewarts Lane. Territorial boundaries were jealously guarded by sheds and the use of Hither Green men on work traditionally associated with Stewarts Lane (or indeed any other shed) ran the risk of serious

Eridge and returned to London with the 20.00 Shoreham - Victoria parcels. On Saturdays another of the class worked to the coast with the 01.35 Herne Hill - Faversham goods, coming back to London with the 12.20 Ramsgate - Victoria express.

By contrast seven of the shed's nine N 2-6-0's were normally in traffic: four on the Chatham section and three on the Brighton. The Chatham engines were used on the express goods services from Herne Hill to Faversham (01.35), Dover (05.25) and Ashford via Maidstone East (10.54); the engines working the first pair of these services not returning to Stewarts Lane until the following day, each working therefore calling for two engines which alternated daily. Almost all their work was on goods services but one could be found on the 07.00 Cannon Street to Ramsgate via Dartford whilst engaged in the second day of the working which commenced with the 05.23 Herne Hill to Faversham.

The two LBSCR workings were mainly

Clean enough for the Royal Train. N15 30768 'Sir Balin' prepares to ring off shed to work a Victoria - Ramsgate express in 1954, a year before the class started to be replaced by BR Standard 5MT 4-6-0's. You had to go a long way in London (or indeed anywhere) to find engines as well cleaned as those of Stewarts Lane. (M. Bentley)

industrial relations problems.

Given the extent of electrification on the former LBSCR it was not surprising that ex-SECR motive power dominated the pre-grouping scene at Stewarts Lane so much so that, as seen above, a class C had to be used on one of the Brighton section goods services. To some extent the imbalance was addressed by the LBSCR E2 0-6-0T's which were used for both yard pilots at Herne Hill as well as the station pilot at Victoria (Eastern). Two other E2 were also used for the Battersea yard pilots. Strangely for a railway where engines were often diagrammed to spend twenty-four hours or more in steam, the E2 yard pilots worked relatively short shifts. The longest stretch of duty was the eighteen and a half hours by one of the Herne Hill engines whilst the day shift Battersea pilot spent barely ten hours in traffic. More typical was the Victoria station pilot whose turn of duty lasted for a fraction over twenty-four hours.

Although there were many instances of locomotive interchange between the constituent parts of the Southern, by and large engines tended to remain on their native metals and it was a point of note that all ten of the LBSCR E2 engines were allocated to the South Eastern: eight to Stewarts Lane and two to Dover. This was in spite of the fact the class was prohibited between Blackfriars and Holborn Viaduct plus the Kearsney loop at Dover.

Stewarts Lane had one engine that rarely if ever appeared in the popular railway press and was a legacy of the Great Western Railway's ownership of South Lambeth goods yard which was situated between Stewarts Lane and the south bank of the Thames. Six trains per day were booked to run from either Acton or Old Oak Common and, consisting of a 57xx 0-6-0 Pannier Tank and thirty-one loaded mineral wagons, they not only remained the responsibility of the Western but an Old Oak Common 57xx 0-6-0 was outbased at Stewarts Lane for a week at a time in order to shunt the yard. The

Loco	Class	Sep-51	Oct-51	Nov-51	Dec-51	Jan-52	Feb-52	Mar-52	Apr-52	May-52	Jun-52	Jul-52
	LOCOMOTIVE ALLOCATIONS & TRANSFERS : STEWARTS LANE (73A)											
42080	4MT 2-6-4T (1948)											
42081	4MT 2-6-4T (1948)											
42082	4MT 2-6-4T (1948)											
42083	4MT 2-6-4T (1948)							To Selby	X	X	X	X
42084	4MT 2-6-4T (1948)							To M'bro	X	X	X	X
42089	4MT 2-6-4T (1948)	X	X	X	X	X	X	Ex Brighton				
42090	4MT 2-6-4T (1948)	X	X	X	X	X	X	X	X	X	Ex Brighton	
42091	4MT 2-6-4T (1948)	X	X	X	X	X	X	Ex Brighton				
31758	3P : L1 4-4-0 (1926)					To Ashford	X	X	X	X	Ex Ashford	
31759	3P : L1 4-4-0 (1926)					To Ashford	X	X	X	X	Ex Ashford	
31019	3P : E1 4-4-0 (1919)											
31067	3P : E1 4-4-0 (1919)											
31504	3P : E1 4-4-0 (1919)											
31506	3P : E1 4-4-0 (1919)											
31743	3P : D1 4-4-0 (1921)											
31749	3P : D1 4-4-0 (1921)											
32100	3F : E2 0-6-0T (1913)											
32101	3F : E2 0-6-0T (1913)											
32102	3F : E2 0-6-0T (1913)											
32103	3F : E2 0-6-0T (1913)											
32104	3F : E2 0-6-0T (1913)											
32105	3F : E2 0-6-0T (1913)											
32106	3F : E2 0-6-0T (1913)											
32107	3F : E2 0-6-0T (1913)											
41290	2MT 2-6-2T (1946)	NEW										
41291	2MT 2-6-2T (1946)	X	X	X	X	X	X	X	X	X	Ex Eastbn	
41292	2MT 2-6-2T (1946)	X	X	X	NEW							
41293	2MT 2-6-2T (1946)	X	X	X	NEW						To E'leigh	X
41294	2MT 2-6-2T (1946)	X	X	X	NEW							
41295	2MT 2-6-2T (1946)	X	X	X	X	X	X	X	X	X	Ex B. Arms	
41296	2MT 2-6-2T (1946)	X	X	X	X	X	X	X	X	X	Ex T. Bges	
41297	2MT 2-6-2T (1946)	X	X	X	X	X	X	X	X	X	Ex T. Bges	
31573	2F : C 0-6-0 (1900)											
31575	2F : C 0-6-0 (1900)											
31576	2F : C 0-6-0 (1900)											
31578	2F : C 0-6-0 (1900)											
31579	2F : C 0-6-0 (1900)											
31580	2F : C 0-6-0 (1900)											
31581	2F : C 0-6-0 (1900)											
31582	2F : C 0-6-0 (1900)											
31583	2F : C 0-6-0 (1900)											
31584	2F : C 0-6-0 (1900)											
31718	2F : C 0-6-0 (1900)											
31719	2F : C 0-6-0 (1900)											
31721	2F : C 0-6-0 (1900)											
31660	1P : R 0-4-4T (1891)				To Gill	X	X	X	X	X	X	X
31005	1P : H 0-4-4T (1904)											
31158	1P : H 0-4-4T (1904)	X	X	X	Ex Ashford							
31261	1P : H 0-4-4T (1904)											
31263	1P : H 0-4-4T (1904)											
31265	1P : H 0-4-4T (1904)											
31266	1P : H 0-4-4T (1904)											
31269	1P : H 0-4-4T (1904)											
31311	1P : H 0-4-4T (1904)										To Redhill	X
31319	1P : H 0-4-4T (1904)											
31320	1P : H 0-4-4T (1904)											
31321	1P : H 0-4-4T (1904)											
31329	1P : H 0-4-4T (1904)				To Faversham	X	X	X	X	X	X	X
30756	1F : '0756' 0-6-0T (1907)				W/D	X	X	X	X	X	X	X
31557	0F : P 0-6-0T (1909)	X	X	X	Ex Dover							
31558	0F : P 0-6-0T (1909)											

engine ran light from Old Oak at 13.15 on Saturday afternoons and shunted the sidings until working back to the Western the following Saturday with the 18.10 empties from South Lambeth to Old Oak Common. Intermediate servicing was provided by Stewarts Lane loco between 06.00 and 07.00 each morning and at other times when needed. The continuous nature of the work made one wonder whether there was any scope for improvement by diesel shunting locomotives.

In addition to housing some of the largest engines of the Southern, Stewarts Lane was also the home of the smallest and from 1949 boasted at least one of the P class 0-6-0T's which shunted in Stewarts Lane carriage sidings between 03.00 and 15.35. Introduced in 1909 for lightweight push and pull duties, many of which ceased between 1914 and the grouping, it was almost astonishing that this class of seven diminutive engines survived for as long as it did and their longevity may have been due to the fact that there was almost nowhere on the Southern - the only prohibition was over the branch from Shepherdswell to Tilmanstone colliery - where the class was not allowed to work. The number of P 0-6-0T's allocated to Stewarts Lane fluctuated between one and three but the last example remained in traffic until February 1960, some nine months after electrification.

1950/1

The first years of the decade saw a considerable movement of engines - throughout the system, the Southern was no exception - as BR tried to settle down after the upheaval of the war years. With rationing and numerous constraints on industrial output it is no exaggeration to state that the war did not really come to a close until about 1952 and this was reflected in the dynamics of motive power allocation which fluctuated a great deal more than the train service which tended to remain unmoved by events.

During the latter months of 1950 the overall allocation fell from 112 to 106 locomotives most of which was accounted for by the departure of the shed's three U class 2-6-0's and the arrival of two batches of new LMS 4MT 2-6-4 tanks for the LBSCR services to Tunbridge Wells.

The arrival of these engines reawakened some misgivings in Kent, reviving some rather unsettling memories of events twenty-three years earlier when the Southern Railway had embarked upon a plan in which most SECR expresses would be worked by 2-6-4 tanks.

Loco	Class	Aug-52	Sep-52	Oct-52	Nov-52	Dec-52	Jan-53	Feb-53	Mar-53	Apr-53	May-53	Jun-53	Jul-53
35026	8P : MN 4-6-2 (1941)												
35027	8P : MN 4-6-2 (1941)												
35028	8P : MN 4-6-2 (1941)												
34066	7P : WC 4-6-2 (1945)												
34067	7P : WC 4-6-2 (1945)												
34068	7P : WC 4-6-2 (1945)												
34069	7P : WC 4-6-2 (1945)												
34070	7P : WC 4-6-2 (1945)												
34071	7P : WC 4-6-2 (1945)												
34087	7P : WC 4-6-2 (1945)												
34088	7P : WC 4-6-2 (1945)												
34090	7P : WC 4-6-2 (1945)												
34091	7P : WC 4-6-2 (1945)												
34092	7P : WC 4-6-2 (1945)												
34101	7P : WC 4-6-2 (1945)												
34102	7P : WC 4-6-2 (1945)												
34103	7P : WC 4-6-2 (1945)												
34104	7P : WC 4-6-2 (1945)												
70004	7MT 4-6-2 (1951)												
70014	7MT 4-6-2 (1951)												
70034	7MT 4-6-2 (1951)	X	X	X	X	X	X	X	X		Ex L'sight		To Stratford
31912	6F : W 2-6-4T (1931)												To H. Green
31914	6F : W 2-6-4T (1931)												
31915	6F : W 2-6-4T (1931)	X	X	X	X	X	X	X	X	X	X	X	Ex H. Green
61015	5P : B1 4-6-0 (1942)	X	X	X	X	X	X	X	X	X	Ex York		To York
61041	5P : B1 4-6-0 (1942)	X	X	X	X	X	X	X	X	X	Ex Norwich		To Darnall
61050	5P : B1 4-6-0 (1942)	X	X	X	X	X	X	X	X	X	Ex Norwich		To Norwich
61109	5P : B1 4-6-0 (1942)	X	X	X	X	X	X	X	X	X	Ex Stratford		To Stratford
61133	5P : B1 4-6-0 (1942)	X	X	X	X	X	X	X	X	X	Ex Eastf'd		To East'fd
61148	5P : B1 4-6-0 (1942)	X	X	X	X	X	X	X	X	X	Ex Th Jcn		To Th Jcn
61188	5P : B1 4-6-0 (1942)	X	X	X	X	X	X	X	X	X	Ex Colwick		To Colwick
61192	5P : B1 4-6-0 (1942)	X	X	X	X	X	X	X	X	X	Ex Colwick		To Colwick
61219	5P : B1 4-6-0 (1942)	X	X	X	X	X	X	X	X	X	Ex Carlisle		To Carlisle
61273	5P : B1 4-6-0 (1942)	X	X	X	X	X	X	X	X	X	Ex Darlington		Ex Darlington
61274	5P : B1 4-6-0 (1942)	X	X	X	X	X	X	X	X	X	Ex Darlington		Ex Darlington
61329	5P : B1 4-6-0 (1942)	X	X	X	X	X	X	X	X	X	Ex Stratford		To Stratford
61338	5P : B1 4-6-0 (1942)	X	X	X	X	X	X	X	X	X	Ex York		To York
61354	5P : B1 4-6-0 (1942)	X	X	X	X	X	X	X	X	X	Ex E'bro		To E'bro
30915	5P : V 4-4-0 (1930)	X	Ex Ramsgate										
30793	5P : N15 4-6-0 (1926)												
30794	5P : N15 4-6-0 (1926)												
30795	5P : N15 4-6-0 (1926)												
30763	5P : N15 4-6-0 (1925)												
30764	5P : N15 4-6-0 (1925)												
30765	5P : N15 4-6-0 (1925)												
30766	5P : N15 4-6-0 (1925)												
30767	5P : N15 4-6-0 (1925)												
30768	5P : N15 4-6-0 (1925)												
30769	5P : N15 4-6-0 (1925)								To Dover	X	X	X	X
30770	5P : N15 4-6-0 (1925)												
30771	5P : N15 4-6-0 (1925)												
30772	5P : N15 4-6-0 (1925)								To Ramsgate	X	X	X	X
30773	5P : N15 4-6-0 (1925)												
30774	5P : N15 4-6-0 (1925)												
30791	5P : N15 4-6-0 (1925)												
30792	5P : N15 4-6-0 (1925)												
33036	5F : Q1 0-6-0 (1942)		To Ton	X	X	X	X	X	X	X	X	X	X
33037	5F : Q1 0-6-0 (1942)		To H. Green	X	X	X	X	X	X	X	X	X	X
33038	5F : Q1 0-6-0 (1942)		To E'leigh	X	X	X	X	X	X	X	X	X	X
31409	5F : N 2-6-0 (1917)												
31410	5F : N 2-6-0 (1917)												
31411	5F : N 2-6-0 (1917)												
31412	5F : N 2-6-0 (1917)												
31413	5F : N 2-6-0 (1917)												
31414	5F : N 2-6-0 (1917)												
31810	5F : N 2-6-0 (1917)												
31811	5F : N 2-6-0 (1917)												
31812	5F : N 2-6-0 (1917)												
31813	5F : N 2-6-0 (1917)												
31814	5F : N 2-6-0 (1917)												
31891	4P : U1 2-6-0 (1925)	X	Ex B. Arms										To B. Arms
31892	4P : U1 2-6-0 (1925)												
31893	4P : U1 2-6-0 (1925)												
31899	4P : U1 2-6-0 (1925)												
31900	4P : U1 2-6-0 (1925)												
31901	4P : U1 2-6-0 (1925)												
31902	4P : U1 2-6-0 (1925)												
31903	4P : U1 2-6-0 (1925)												
31904	4P : U1 2-6-0 (1925)												
31905	4P : U1 2-6-0 (1925)												
31906	4P : U1 2-6-0 (1925)												

The column header above the table reads: LOCOMOTIVE ALLOCATIONS & TRANSFERS : STEWARTS LANE (73A)

Many railwaymen - not all of whom were in their dotage by any means - remembered too clearly the instability of the K-class tanks which had led initially to numerous derailments and eventually, in August 1927, to a full-scale disaster in which the derailment of one of the engines at 55 mph near Sevenoaks whilst working the 17.00 Charing Cross - Ramsgate business express resulted in the deaths of thirteen passengers and innumerable injuries. The class was peremptorily taken out of traffic and although the principal culprit was later determined to be the permanent way, the engines were rebuilt as 2-6-0 tender engines and never again took part in routine express work.

One product of the experiment had been to

SOUTH LAMBETH YARD (1955)					
Train	Arrive	Engine	Shed	Dep	Destination
23.30 Old Oak Common	00.05	57xx 0-6-0PT	OOC 264	02.30	Old Oak Common
02.45 Old Oak Common	03.20	57xx 0-6-0PT	OOC 265	04.00	EBV Old Oak Common
Pilot		57xx 0-6-0PT	OOC 263	05.30	S. Lane MPD
05.20 Acton	06.03	57xx 0-6-0PT	OOC 264	06.35	Old Oak Common
Light ex S. Lane MPD	07.10	57xx 0-6-0PT	OOC 263		Pilot
07.05 Old Oak Common	07.50	57xx 0-6-0PT	OOC 265	08.05	Light to Old Oak Common
08.30 Old Oak Common	09.05	57xx 0-6-0PT	OOC 264		
		57xx 0-6-0PT	OOC 263	10.00	Stewarts Lane Yard
Light ex Stewarts Lane Yard	10.30	57xx 0-6-0PT			Pilot
		57xx 0-6-0PT	OOC 264	13.25	Old Oak Common
13.15 EBV Old Oak Common *	13.55	57xx 0-6-0PT	OOC 265	15.55	Old Oak Common
18.00 EBV Old Oak Common	18.35	57xx 0-6-0PT	OOC 265	19.10	Old Oak Common
19.10 2 Light Old Oak Common	19.42	57xx 0-6-0PT	OOC 262/5	20.30	Park Royal
		57xx 0-6-0PT	OOC 262	21.50	Acton
21.10 Old Oak Common	21.45	57xx 0-6-0PT	OOC 265	22.00	Light to Old Oak Common

* Changeover engine on Saturdays

leave the Southern Railway with very strong feelings regarding the suitability of 2-6-4T locomotives for passenger work, misgivings that were rekindled when the LMS locomotives arrived on the scene in 1950.

Most of the objections came from the ex-SECR management who were anxious to ensure that the new engines did not find their way onto the kind of duties that the K class engines had been involved in. Trials galore were run on the South Eastern during the first few weeks and although the new locomotives were found to be free of the problems that had surrounded the earlier engines, the South Eastern nevertheless remained somewhat suspicious of the wheel arrangement and although no restrictions were placed on their movements, the SE allocation of LMS engines tended to be confined to stopping trains in East Kent.

The Brighton management did not share the misgivings of their neighbours and had been users of large tank engines for many years, albeit on a small scale because of the spread of electrification. Their principal steam service - Victoria to Tunbridge Wells - relied heavily on the ageing I3 4-4-2T's with occasional assistance from the two J class 4-6-2 tanks. Both classes were over forty years old and in a condition so parlous that four Q class 0-6-0's had to be found to keep the Victoria service operating. So serious was the position that it was to Tunbridge Wells that the first of the LMS 2-6-4T imports went.

By early 1951 4-4-2T's had become an unusual sight at Victoria and by September their replacement by LMS tanks at Tunbridge Wells was complete. The last I3 left the shed in September 1951 but not before witnessing the end of the LMS 2-6-4T monopoly which at Tunbridge Wells turned out to be very short-lived since the summer of 1951 saw many of the LMS engines being displaced by new BR Standard 2-6-4T's.

Although Tunbridge Wells engines worked the majority of the trains, the Stewarts Lane examples

played their part and were responsible for the 05.20, 06.29, 10.08, 14.08, 17.50 and 18.48 departures from Victoria.

Another 1950 landmark was the departure of the L class 4-4-0's from Stewarts Lane after nearly forty years service. With little main line work remaining and being more restricted (the L's were prohibited from running over the Sheerness branch or from Herne Hill to Holborn Viaduct) than the D or E classes of 4-4-0, the

L's were despatched to Ashford, Tonbridge, St Leonards and Ramsgate where they could be usefully employed on rural stopping services in East Kent whilst remaining available for main line duties during the summer peak.

1951/2

The year saw quite a number of engines exchanged for others as the backlog of maintenance was attacked but the total of engines at Stewarts Lane remained more or less constant at just over 100 engines. A number of N 2-6-0's were exchanged for a similar number of U1 moguls and three of the fascinatingly ugly Q1 0-6-0's arrived to see how they could manage in the W 2-6-4T workings.

The main event of the year was the arrival of two new Britannia Pacifics which was something of a surprise in view of the seventeen light Pacifics for which work was of a largely seasonal nature. After being tried on Waterloo - Bournemouth services - and after some lengthy

		LOCOMOTIVE ALLOCATIONS & TRANSFERS : STEWARTS LANE (73A)										
Loco	Class	Aug-52	Sep-52	Oct-52	Nov-52	Dec-52	Jan-53	Feb-53	Mar-53	Apr-53	May-53	Jun-53	Jul-53
42080	4MT 2-6-4T (1948)												
42081	4MT 2-6-4T (1948)												
42082	4MT 2-6-4T (1948)								To Brighton	X	X	X	X
42089	4MT 2-6-4T (1948)												
42090	4MT 2-6-4T (1948)												
42091	4MT 2-6-4T (1948)												
31758	3P : L1 4-4-0 (1926)										To Gill	X	X
31759	3P : L1 4-4-0 (1926)										To Gill	X	X
31785	3P : L1 4-4-0 (1926)	X	Ex B. Arms			To Ashford	X	X	X	X	X	X	X
31786	3P : L1 4-4-0 (1926)	X	Ex B. Arms			To E'leigh	X	X	X	X	X	X	X
31787	3P : L1 4-4-0 (1926)	X	Ex B. Arms			To E'leigh	X	X	X	X	X	X	X
31788	3P : L1 4-4-0 (1926)	X	Ex B. Arms			To E'leigh	X	X	X	X	X	X	X
31789	3P : L1 4-4-0 (1926)	X	Ex B. Arms			To E'leigh	X	X	X	X	X	X	X
31019	3P : E1 4-4-0 (1919)												
31067	3P : E1 4-4-0 (1919)												
31165	3P : E1 4-4-0 (1919)	X	X	X	X	X	X	X	Ex B. Arms		To B. Arms	X	X
31504	3P : E1 4-4-0 (1919)												
31506	3P : E1 4-4-0 (1919)												
31509	3P : D1 4-4-0 (1921)	X	X	X	X	X	X	X	X	X	Ex Gill		
31545	3P : D1 4-4-0 (1921)	X	X	X	X	X	X	X	X	X	Ex Gill		
31743	3P : D1 4-4-0 (1921)								To B. Arms	X	X	Ex B. Arms	X
31749	3P : D1 4-4-0 (1921)								To Redhill	X	X	X	X
32100	3F : E2 0-6-0T (1913)												
32101	3F : E2 0-6-0T (1913)												
32102	3F : E2 0-6-0T (1913)												
32103	3F : E2 0-6-0T (1913)												
32104	3F : E2 0-6-0T (1913)												
32105	3F : E2 0-6-0T (1913)												
32106	3F : E2 0-6-0T (1913)												
32107	3F : E2 0-6-0T (1913)												
31315	2P : E 4-4-0 (1905)	X	X	X	X	X	X	X	X	X	Ex Fav		
41290	2MT 2-6-2T (1946)												
41291	2MT 2-6-2T (1946)												
41292	2MT 2-6-2T (1946)												
41294	2MT 2-6-2T (1946)												
41295	2MT 2-6-2T (1946)												
41296	2MT 2-6-2T (1946)												
41297	2MT 2-6-2T (1946)								To T. Wells	X	X	X	X
31573	2F : C 0-6-0 (1900)												
31575	2F : C 0-6-0 (1900)												
31576	2F : C 0-6-0 (1900)												
31578	2F : C 0-6-0 (1900)												
31579	2F : C 0-6-0 (1900)												
31580	2F : C 0-6-0 (1900)												W/D
31581	2F : C 0-6-0 (1900)												
31582	2F : C 0-6-0 (1900)												
31583	2F : C 0-6-0 (1900)												
31584	2F : C 0-6-0 (1900)												
31718	2F : C 0-6-0 (1900)												
31719	2F : C 0-6-0 (1900)												
31721	2F : C 0-6-0 (1900)					To St L.	X	X	X	X	X	X	X
31005	1P : H 0-4-4T (1904)												
31158	1P : H 0-4-4T (1904)												
31261	1P : H 0-4-4T (1904)												
31263	1P : H 0-4-4T (1904)												
31265	1P : H 0-4-4T (1904)												
31266	1P : H 0-4-4T (1904)												
31269	1P : H 0-4-4T (1904)												
31319	1P : H 0-4-4T (1904)												
31320	1P : H 0-4-4T (1904)												
31321	1P : H 0-4-4T (1904)												To Brighton
31555	0F : P 0-6-0T (1909)	X	X	X	X	Ex Dover							
31557	0F : P 0-6-0T (1909)												
31558	0F : P 0-6-0T (1909)								To E'leigh	X	X	X	X

mechanical problems - the engines settled down to the Golden Arrow working from Victoria.

Another new class arrived at Stewarts Lane a month after the Britannias, LMS 2MT 41290 going into service in September 1951 and eventually being joined by three others of the class. Unlike the larger LMS engines, the 2-6-2T's were used on SECR diagrams and replaced a pair of H class 0-4-4T's, an R 0-4-4T and an LBSCR E1 0-6-0T.

The Stewarts Lane element of the 130-strong class was probably unique in that none of the engines had a booked turn on a passenger duty: a strange turn of affairs for a class designed to operate push and pull services on the London Midland & Scottish Railway. Two duties were covered at Stewarts Lane but since both had a duration of almost 24 hours four (sometimes six) engines were provided: a generous provision of spare capacity which in 1956 allowed 41296 to be sent away to far-off Barnstaple. Most of the work undertaken involved empty coaching stock in both directions between Stewarts Lane, Ludgate Hill and Cannon Street together with shunting duties at London Bridge and Southwark, generally keeping out of the public eye. To find them at Victoria meant picking one's times rather carefully although if one turned up at lunchtime both engines could be found side by side; one with the stock of the 12.30 Folkestone boat train and the other with the Golden Arrow. Their only other booked appearance was with the stock of the 10.35 Victoria to Ramsgate. (At the height of the summer with many additional trains running the 2-6-2T's became a little more apparent. The engine that brought in the 13.30 Folkestone/Calais stock had, in the space of ten minutes, to bank the service up to Grosvenor Bridge, run light to Victoria carriage sidings and reappear in the station with the empty stock for the 14.30 Dover/Ostend).

The final arrival of note during 1951 came in June with the transfer of two L1 4-4-0's from Bricklayers Arms. No specific diagrams were issued for the pair which remained useful for summer contingencies and remained at Stewarts Lane until January when they were reallocated to Ashford. Both engines later returned to Stewarts Lane for the 1952 summer season.

1952/3

Having amassed a number of BR and LM Standard designs, 1952 was a year of consolidation rather than change, the chief item of interest being an increase from twelve to seventeen in the shed's King Arthur 4-6-0's. This growth was partially matched by the loss of two Pacifics (Merchant Navy 35025 went to Exmouth Junction in March while West Country 34076 was sent on loan to Stratford, Great Eastern). The Newhaven boat trains also provided an excuse to allocate Schools 4-4-0

Loco	Class	Aug-53	Sep-53	Oct-53	Nov-53	Dec-53	Jan-54	Feb-54	Mar-54	Apr-54	May-54	Jun-54	Jul-54
35026	8P : MN 4-6-2 (1941)												
35027	8P : MN 4-6-2 (1941)												
35028	8P : MN 4-6-2 (1941)												
34017	7P : WC 4-6-2 (194!	X	X	X	X	X	X	X	Ex Ex Jcn				
34065	7P : WC 4-6-2 (194!	X	X	X	X	X	X	X	X	X	X	Ex N. Elms	
34066	7P : WC 4-6-2 (1945)												
34067	7P : WC 4-6-2 (1945)												
34068	7P : WC 4-6-2 (1945)												
34069	7P : WC 4-6-2 (1945)								To Ex Jcn	X	X	X	X
34070	7P : WC 4-6-2 (1945)												
34071	7P : WC 4-6-2 (1945)												
34087	7P : WC 4-6-2 (1945)												
34088	7P : WC 4-6-2 (1945)												
34090	7P : WC 4-6-2 (1945)												
34091	7P : WC 4-6-2 (1945)												
34092	7P : WC 4-6-2 (1945)												
34101	7P : WC 4-6-2 (1945)												
34102	7P : WC 4-6-2 (1945)												
34103	7P : WC 4-6-2 (1945)												
34104	7P : WC 4-6-2 (1945)												
70004	7MT 4-6-2 (1951)												
70014	7MT 4-6-2 (1951)												
31914	6F : W 2-6-4T (1931)												
31915	6F : W 2-6-4T (1931)												
30915	5P : V 4-4-0 (1930)												
30793	5P : N15 4-6-0 (1926)												
30794	5P : N15 4-6-0 (1926)												
30795	5P : N15 4-6-0 (1926)											To H. Green	X
30763	5P : N15 4-6-0 (1925)												
30764	5P : N15 4-6-0 (1925)												
30765	5P : N15 4-6-0 (1925)												
30766	5P : N15 4-6-0 (1925)												
30767	5P : N15 4-6-0 (1925)												
30768	5P : N15 4-6-0 (1925)												
30769	5P : N15 4-6-0 (192.	X	X	X	X	X	X	X	X	X	Ex Dover		
30770	5P : N15 4-6-0 (1925)												
30771	5P : N15 4-6-0 (1925)												
30773	5P : N15 4-6-0 (1925)												
30774	5P : N15 4-6-0 (1925)												
30791	5P : N15 4-6-0 (1925)												
30792	5P : N15 4-6-0 (1925)												
31409	5F : N 2-6-0 (1917)												
31410	5F : N 2-6-0 (1917)												
31411	5F : N 2-6-0 (1917)												
31412	5F : N 2-6-0 (1917)												
31413	5F : N 2-6-0 (1917)												
31414	5F : N 2-6-0 (1917)												
31810	5F : N 2-6-0 (1917)												
31811	5F : N 2-6-0 (1917)												
31812	5F : N 2-6-0 (1917)												
31813	5F : N 2-6-0 (1917)		To Sarum	X	X	X	X	X	X	X	X	X	X
31814	5F : N 2-6-0 (1917)		To Sarum	X	X	X	X	X	X	X	X	X	X
31815	5F : N 2-6-0 (1917)	X	Ex Gillingham								Ex Gillingham	X	X
31816	5F : N 2-6-0 (1917)	X	Ex Gillingham								Ex Gillingham	X	X
31892	4P : U1 2-6-0 (1925)		To H. Green	X	X	X	X	X	X	X	X	X	X
31893	4P : U1 2-6-0 (1925)		To H. Green	X	X	X	X	X	X	X	X	X	X
31899	4P : U1 2-6-0 (1925!		To Redhill	X	X	X	X	X	X	X	X	X	X
31900	4P : U1 2-6-0 (1925)		To Redhill	X	X	X	X	X	X	X	X	Ex Redhill	
31901	4P : U1 2-6-0 (1925)												
31902	4P : U1 2-6-0 (1925)												
31903	4P : U1 2-6-0 (1925)												
31904	4P : U1 2-6-0 (1925)												
31905	4P : U1 2-6-0 (1925)												
31906	4P : U1 2-6-0 (1925)												
31907	4P : U1 2-6-0 (1925!	X	X	X	X	X	X	X	X	X	X	Ex N. Elms	
31908	4P : U1 2-6-0 (1925!	X	X	X	X	X	X	X	X	X	X	Ex N. Elms	

30915 to Stewarts Lane; not a class generally associated with the shed. As a rule the 09.31 Victoria - Newhaven/Dieppe was worked by Newhaven men and one of the three 7P electric locomotives whilst any relief trains were handled by Brighton-based H2 Atlantics. Plans to release a second electric locomotive for the relief trains never came to fruition - the three engines carried out a busy programme of goods work - and as the number of Atlantics and their reliability decreased action was required. The arrangement by which the Atlantics worked the relief trains were not sound - a great deal of light engine running between Brighton and London was involved - and eventually the matter was resolved by the provision of 30915 which became a settled feature of the Newhaven workings for some years.

On the more everyday front, 30756, the exiled PDSWJR 0-6-0T, was taken out of traffic at the end of 1951 and replaced by an additional P 0-6-0T.

1953/4

1953 was both the best and worst of times. For passengers it was a trying year whilst for enthusiasts it produced an array of engines that lay beyond the scope of imaginings! In March freak meteorological conditions produced flooding on a scale previously unknown and while East Anglia took the brunt of the weather, several miles of the main line between Herne Bay and Birchington were completely washed away. This had two lasting effects: one being that the direct line from London to Thanet no longer existed and the other being to assure the future of the Station Master at Herne Bay who practically devised an emergency timetable, with the engine and mens diagrams, on the back of an envelope and put into practice.

There was no stranger a sight on the Southern than an LNER B1 4-6-0 at Stewarts Lane but for a short time during the Spring of 1953 no less than fourteen were borrowed from a variety of East Coast sheds to shore up a temporary withdrawal of SR light Pacifics. 61133 of Glasgow (Eastfield) stands on Stewarts Lane during the crisis. (M. Millar)

Reinstating the track was an engineering task of considerable magnitude and it was not until the last few days of May that Herne Bay and Birchington were once again connected. In the meantime the wartime connection between the LCDR and SER at Canterbury had been reinstated with trains running from Victoria to Birchington via Faversham, Canterbury West, Minster, Ramsgate and Margate. Connections to Whitstable and Herne Bay were operated by a push and pull service from Faversham.

None of this had much effect on the allocation at Stewarts Lane - although the emergency timetable posed tremendous problems with the drivers and guards workings - but just as conditions at Herne Bay were at their worst, the entire fleet of Southern Pacifics had to be grounded because of suspected axle problems.

It was a job tailor-made for the British Transport Commission who in theory ran the railway even though most decisions were taken at Regional or District level - just as they had been since 1923. The BTC were in the first place able to act as a forceful liaison between the South Eastern and the rest of British Railways and at the same time were anxious to get the message across that locomotives did not necessarily have to remain forever on their parent tracks. The result was that very speedy arrangements were made for fourteen LNER B1 4-6-0's to be lent to Stewarts Lane for their Ramsgate services; the visitors being despatched from

Loco	Class	Aug-53	Sep-53	Oct-53	Nov-53	Dec-53	Jan-54	Feb-54	Mar-54	Apr-54	May-54	Jun-54	Jul-54
	LOCOMOTIVE ALLOCATIONS & TRANSFERS : STEWARTS LANE (73A)												
42080	4MT 2-6-4T (1948)												
42081	4MT 2-6-4T (1948)												
42089	4MT 2-6-4T (1948)												
42090	4MT 2-6-4T (1948)												
42091	4MT 2-6-4T (1948)												
30537	4F : Q 0-6-0 (1938)	X	X	X	X	X	X	X	X	X	X	Ex Norwood	
30538	4F : Q 0-6-0 (1938)	X	X	X	X	X	X	X	X	X	X	Ex Norwood	
31019	3P : E1 4-4-0 (1919)												
31067	3P : E1 4-4-0 (1919)												
31504	3P : E1 4-4-0 (1919)												
31506	3P : E1 4-4-0 (1919)												
31509	3P : D1 4-4-0 (1921)						To Gillingham	X	X	X	X	X	X
31545	3P : D1 4-4-0 (1921)												
31743	3P : D1 4-4-0 (1921)												
31749	3P : D1 4-4-0 (1921)	X	X	X	X	X	X	X	X	X	Ex Redhill		
32100	3F : E2 0-6-0T (1913)												
32101	3F : E2 0-6-0T (1913)												
32102	3F : E2 0-6-0T (1913)												
32103	3F : E2 0-6-0T (1913)												
32104	3F : E2 0-6-0T (1913)												
32105	3F : E2 0-6-0T (1913)												
32106	3F : E2 0-6-0T (1913)												
32107	3F : E2 0-6-0T (1913)												
31315	2P : E 4-4-0 (1905)						To Redhill	X	X	X	X	X	X
41290	2MT 2-6-2T (1946)												
41291	2MT 2-6-2T (1946)												
41292	2MT 2-6-2T (1946)												
41294	2MT 2-6-2T (1946)												
41295	2MT 2-6-2T (1946)												
41296	2MT 2-6-2T (1946)												
31221	2F : C 0-6-0 (1900)	X	X	X	X	X	Ex Gillingham						
31461	2F : C 0-6-0 (1900)	X	Ex Faversham										
31573	2F : C 0-6-0 (1900)												
31575	2F : C 0-6-0 (1900)												
31576	2F : C 0-6-0 (1900)												
31578	2F : C 0-6-0 (1900)												
31579	2F : C 0-6-0 (1900)												
31581	2F : C 0-6-0 (1900)												
31582	2F : C 0-6-0 (1900)												
31583	2F : C 0-6-0 (1900)												
31584	2F : C 0-6-0 (1900)												
31718	2F : C 0-6-0 (1900)												
31719	2F : C 0-6-0 (1900)												
31005	1P : H 0-4-4T (1904)												
31158	1P : H 0-4-4T (1904)				To Gillingham	X	X	X	X	X	X	X	X
31261	1P : H 0-4-4T (1904)												
31263	1P : H 0-4-4T (1904)												
31265	1P : H 0-4-4T (1904)												
31266	1P : H 0-4-4T (1904)												
31269	1P : H 0-4-4T (1904)				To St L.	X	X	X	X	X	X	X	X
31320	1P : H 0-4-4T (1904)				To Brighton	X	X	X	X	X	X	X	X
31321	1P : H 0-4-4T (1904)												
31550	1P : H 0-4-4T (1904)	X	X	X	X	X	X	X	X	X	X	Ex Redhill	
31551	1P : H 0-4-4T (1904)	X	X	X	X	X	X	X	X	X	Ex Redhill		
31552	1P : H 0-4-4T (1904)	X	X	X	X	X	X	X	X	X	X	Ex Tonbridge	
31555	0F : P 0-6-0T (1909)												
31557	0F : P 0-6-0T (1909)												

sheds as far away as Thornton Junction and Glasgow (Eastfield).

As it transpired, the motive power emergency was over almost before it had started and it is not at all certain that all the proffered B1's actually reached the Southern.

By June the problems on both fronts had been resolved if not forgotten since the spectacle of B1 4-6-0's in Kent gave local enthusiasts a source of conversation that remained fresh for ten years whilst the matter of sea defences remained the hottest topic at the Herne Bay Chamber of Commerce for at least three decades.

The B1's disappeared as quickly as they had come and one wondered at the time if the generosity had not been a little overdone: there were, after all, only two Pacific turns - the 09.00 and 10.00 boat trains - worked from Victoria by Stewarts Lane engines whilst at the time of year in question there was no shortage of 2-6-0's and 4-4-0's available to take up the slack.

On the ordinary front nothing altered very much and Stewarts Lane went from 1953 into 1954 with only minor changes to its allocation which affected the small H 0-4-4 tanks as much as any other class. With 9 of the class on its books but only 6 in daily use - two of the four diagrams were too long to be covered by one engine each - the winter of 1953 saw three of the class sent away to Gillingham, St Leonards and Brighton and although they were replaced by the summer of 1954, it proved to be the start of a slow decline in the numbers of 0-4-4T's at Stewarts Lane.

A rather sad development in July 1953 was the withdrawal of C 0-6-0 31580 and although it was not the first of its class to go - five had been taken out of traffic between 1947 and 1951 - it was the first to go from Stewarts Lane and was an unsettling reminder that the old order was slowly being eroded. (As it happened, the C's proved too useful to be dispensed with completely and even after the 1959 electrification there were still over 60 of the class in traffic).

An interesting arrival in Spring 1953 was 31315, the last survivor of the E class 4-4-0's of 1906 which with the D class of 1901 had been responsible for much of the Chatham line's express work until the grouping. Eleven of the original E class had been rebuilt in 1920 to the E1 4-4-0 class and most of them survived until electrification, 31315, however, left Stewarts Lane for Redhill in January 1954 and was withdrawn a couple of months later.

1954/5

Loco	Class	Aug-54	Sep-54	Oct-54	Nov-54	Dec-54	Jan-55	Feb-55	Mar-55	Apr-55	May-55	Jun-55	Jul-55
												LOCOMOTIVE ALLOCATIONS & TRANSFERS : STEWARTS LANE (73A)	
35014	8P : MN 4-6-2 (1941)	X	X	X	X	X	X	X	X	X	X	Ex B'mouth	
35026	8P : MN 4-6-2 (1941)												
35027	8P : MN 4-6-2 (1941)											To B'mouth	X
35028	8P : MN 4-6-2 (1941)												
34017	7P : WC 4-6-2 (1945)												
34065	7P : WC 4-6-2 (1945)											To N. Elms	X
34066	7P : WC 4-6-2 (1945)												
34067	7P : WC 4-6-2 (1945)												
34068	7P : WC 4-6-2 (1945)												
34070	7P : WC 4-6-2 (1945)											To Dover	X
34071	7P : WC 4-6-2 (1945)											To Dover	X
34087	7P : WC 4-6-2 (1945)												
34088	7P : WC 4-6-2 (1945)												
34089	7P : WC 4-6-2 (1945)	X	X	Ex Ramsgate									
34090	7P : WC 4-6-2 (1945)												
34091	7P : WC 4-6-2 (1945)												
34092	7P : WC 4-6-2 (1945)												
34101	7P : WC 4-6-2 (1945)												
34102	7P : WC 4-6-2 (1945)												
34103	7P : WC 4-6-2 (1945)												
34104	7P : WC 4-6-2 (1945)												
70004	7MT 4-6-2 (1951)												
70014	7MT 4-6-2 (1951)												
31914	6F : W 2-6-4T (1931)												
31915	6F : W 2-6-4T (1931)												
31921	6F : W 2-6-4T (1931)	Ex H. Green											
30915	5P : V 4-4-0 (1930)												
30793	5P : N15 4-6-0 (1926)												
30794	5P : N15 4-6-0 (1926)												
30795	5P : N15 4-6-0 (1926)	Ex H. Green											
30763	5P : N15 4-6-0 (1925)												
30764	5P : N15 4-6-0 (1925)												
30765	5P : N15 4-6-0 (1925)												
30766	5P : N15 4-6-0 (1925)												
30767	5P : N15 4-6-0 (1925)												
30768	5P : N15 4-6-0 (1925)												
30769	5P : N15 4-6-0 (1925)												
30770	5P : N15 4-6-0 (1925)												
30771	5P : N15 4-6-0 (1925)												
30773	5P : N15 4-6-0 (1925)												
30774	5P : N15 4-6-0 (1925)												
30791	5P : N15 4-6-0 (1925)												
30792	5P : N15 4-6-0 (1925)												
73080	5MT 4-6-0 (1951)	X	X	X	X	X	X	X	X	X	X	NEW	
73081	5MT 4-6-0 (1951)	X	X	X	X	X	X	X	X	X	X	NEW	
73082	5MT 4-6-0 (1951)	X	X	X	X	X	X	X	X	X	X	NEW	
73083	5MT 4-6-0 (1951)	X	X	X	X	X	X	X	X	X	X	NEW	
33015	5F : Q1 0-6-0 (1942)	X	X	Ex Norwood			To N. Elms	X	X	X	X	X	X
33017	5F : Q1 0-6-0 (1942)	X	X	Ex Brighton			To N. Elms	X	X	X	X	X	X
33038	5F : Q1 0-6-0 (1942)	X	X	Ex Norwood			To N. Elms	X	X	X	X	X	X
31408	5F : N 2-6-0 (1917)	X	X	X	X	X	X	Ex B. Arms					
31409	5F : N 2-6-0 (1917)												
31410	5F : N 2-6-0 (1917)												
31411	5F : N 2-6-0 (1917)												
31412	5F : N 2-6-0 (1917)												
31413	5F : N 2-6-0 (1917)												
31414	5F : N 2-6-0 (1917)												
31810	5F : N 2-6-0 (1917)												
31811	5F : N 2-6-0 (1917)												
31812	5F : N 2-6-0 (1917)												
31894	4P : U1 2-6-0 (1925)	X	X	X	X	X	X	X	X	X	X	Ex Brighton	
31895	4P : U1 2-6-0 (1925)	X	X	X	X	X	X	X	X	X	X	Ex N'haven	
31896	4P : U1 2-6-0 (1925)	X	X	X	X	X	X	X	X	X	X	Ex Brighton	
31897	4P : U1 2-6-0 (1925)	X	X	X	X	X	X	X	X	X	X	Ex Redhill	
31898	4P : U1 2-6-0 (1925)	X	X	X	X	X	X	X	X	X	X	Ex Redhill	
31900	4P : U1 2-6-0 (1925)						To Brighton	X	X	X	X	X	X
31901	4P : U1 2-6-0 (1925)						To Brighton	X	X	X	X	X	X
31902	4P : U1 2-6-0 (1925)						To Brighton	X	X	X	X	X	X
31903	4P : U1 2-6-0 (1925)						To Brighton	X	X	X	X	X	X
31904	4P : U1 2-6-0 (1925)												
31905	4P : U1 2-6-0 (1925)												
31906	4P : U1 2-6-0 (1925)			To N. Elms	X	Ex N. Elms							
31907	4P : U1 2-6-0 (1925)			To N. Elms	X	Ex N. Elms							
31908	4P : U1 2-6-0 (1925)			To Ton	X	X	X	X	X	X	X	X	X

This proved to be the final season in which the King Arthur 4-6-0's held dominion on the Ramsgate expresses since a batch of new BR 5MT 4-6-0's arrived at the shed in June 1955 and brought to a close a reign that had lasted for twenty-three years. Many observers were surprised that the N15's had lasted as long as they had on the Ramsgate services and had it not been for the fact that the operating department had decreed them as class 5 rather than class 7 workings, the King Arthurs would probably have been ousted by light Pacifics some five years earlier.

In more humble areas, the growth in numbers of LMS 2MT 2-6-2T's was reversed with the transfer of 41295 to Barnstaple and 41296 to Exeter, thus reducing the allocation to four engines; a number consonant with the two daily diagrams. Two more H-class 0-4-4T's were despatched to Ashford and Redhill in June 1955, leaving only one engine to cover contingencies.

1955/6

By the end of the 1955 summer season the number of BR 5MT 4-6-0's at Stewarts Lane had risen to ten - enough for each Ramsgate working

One of the more memorable sights of Victoria was that of the 10.00 Continental express departing behind its Merchant Navy Pacific with the H 0-4-4T banker giving every impression of doing all the work. The H class were another SECR success story, the sixty-six strong class first appearing in 1904 for the heavy London suburban service. Made redundant by electrification between 1925 and 1938, the engines gravitated to rural work and carriage shunting with nearly sixty of the class remaining in traffic as late as 1959. Above, 31551 works the Stewarts Lane carriage pilot in June 1957. (L.G. Marshall)

with three engines spare for contingencies - while nine displaced King Arthurs departed for the London South Western; several going to Basingstoke where they replaced the N15X 4-6-0's which worked many of the outer-suburban stopping trains to and from Waterloo. One of the 'Arthurs' returned the following Spring and although the class continued to make appearances on the Ramsgate expresses from time to time, there was no question of an Arthurian renaissance of any kind.

Other changes saw the withdrawal of another class C 0-6-0, 31718 joining six others that were taken out of traffic during 1955. At the same time another of the class, 31583, was sent away to Tonbridge. This engine was one of a batch built at Longhedge works in 1903 and had thus had an unusually long and close association with the Stewarts Lane area. Of the remaining eleven engines, only 31461 was one of the Longhedge-built examples, the others being either Ashford or Glasgow built.

1956/7

With the scope for seasonal elasticity having been narrow by the reduction in N15 4-6-0's from sixteen in mid-1955 to eight a year later, matters were not improved by the loss of one of the new Standard 5MT's: 73087 being sent to Bath just as the summer season - when anything that could turn a wheel was needed - was

Loco	Class	Aug-54	Sep-54	Oct-54	Nov-54	Dec-54	Jan-55	Feb-55	Mar-55	Apr-55	May-55	Jun-55	Jul-55
						LOCOMOTIVE ALLOCATIONS & TRANSFERS : STEWARTS LANE (73A)							
42080	4MT 2-6-4T (1948)												
42081	4MT 2-6-4T (1948)												
42088	4MT 2-6-4T (1948)	X	X	X	X	Ex Brighton							
42089	4MT 2-6-4T (1948)												
42090	4MT 2-6-4T (1948)												
42091	4MT 2-6-4T (1948)												
30537	4F : Q 0-6-0 (1938)			To Norwood	X	X	X	X	X	X	X	X	X
30538	4F : Q 0-6-0 (1938)			To Norwood	X	X	X	X	X	X	X	X	X
31019	3P : E1 4-4-0 (1919)												
31067	3P : E1 4-4-0 (1919)												
31504	3P : E1 4-4-0 (1919)												
31506	3P : E1 4-4-0 (1919)												
31545	3P : D1 4-4-0 (1921)												
31743	3P : D1 4-4-0 (1921)												
31749	3P : D1 4-4-0 (1921)												
32100	3F : E2 0-6-0T (1913)												
32101	3F : E2 0-6-0T (1913)												
32102	3F : E2 0-6-0T (1913)												
32103	3F : E2 0-6-0T (1913)												
32104	3F : E2 0-6-0T (1913)												
32105	3F : E2 0-6-0T (1913)												
32106	3F : E2 0-6-0T (1913)												
32107	3F : E2 0-6-0T (1913)												
41290	2MT 2-6-2T (1946)												
41291	2MT 2-6-2T (1946)												
41292	2MT 2-6-2T (1946)												
41294	2MT 2-6-2T (1946)								To Ashford	X	X	X	X
41295	2MT 2-6-2T (1946)	To B'staple	X	X	X	X	X	X	X	X	X	X	X
41296	2MT 2-6-2T (1946)	To Ex Jcn	X	X	X	X	X	Ex Ex Jn					
32455	2F : E3 0-6-2T (1894)	Ex B. Arms											
31221	2F : C 0-6-0 (1900)			To Ashford	X	X	X	X	X	X	X	X	X
31253	2F : C 0-6-0 (1900)	X	X	X	X	X	X	X	X	Ex Guild			
31461	2F : C 0-6-0 (1900)												
31573	2F : C 0-6-0 (1900)												
31575	2F : C 0-6-0 (1900)												
31576	2F : C 0-6-0 (1900)												
31578	2F : C 0-6-0 (1900)												
31579	2F : C 0-6-0 (1900)												
31581	2F : C 0-6-0 (1900)												
31582	2F : C 0-6-0 (1900)												
31583	2F : C 0-6-0 (1900)												
31584	2F : C 0-6-0 (1900)												
31718	2F : C 0-6-0 (1900)												
31719	2F : C 0-6-0 (1900)												
31005	1P : H 0-4-4T (1904)											To Ashford	X
31261	1P : H 0-4-4T (1904)												
31263	1P : H 0-4-4T (1904)											To Redhill	X
31265	1P : H 0-4-4T (1904)												
31266	1P : H 0-4-4T (1904)												
31321	1P : H 0-4-4T (1904)												
31550	1P : H 0-4-4T (1904)												
31551	1P : H 0-4-4T (1904)												
31552	1P : H 0-4-4T (1904)												
31555	0F : P 0-6-0T (1909)							W/D	X	X	X	X	X
31557	0F : P 0-6-0T (1909)												
31558	0F : P 0-6-0T (1909)	X	X	X	X	X	X	X	X	X	X	Ex Brighton	

getting under way. Thank Heavens for the 4-4-0's and 2-6-0's! To ease the position, the loss of 73087 was balanced by making the 05.10 Victoria to Ramsgate and the 11.15 Ramsgate - Victoria a working for a West Country Pacific.

The burning issue of the day was the rebuilding of the Pacifics; a topic that had been stuff of speculation for more than ten years. The problem with the Pacifics was that their weak points outweighed their good - sometimes by a considerable margin. When the wind was blowing in the right direction the engines could put up performances that were second to none but the minute something went wrong, defects that on any other engine would be rectified in a shift or two put the 'Spams' out of consideration for a week. This was bad enough at Stewarts Lane where the pressure to put Pacifics into service was at its height for only two or three months in the year but at Ramsgate, where nine of the seventeen allocated to the shed had to be turned off shed in quick succession each morning, the position was so critical that all too often Schools 4-4-0's were having to cover the workings and whilst they were a superb engine in themselves, putting a class 5 engine into a class 7 diagram was an invitation to lose time. The situation eventually became so serious that Ramsgate were having to send some of their Pacifics to the London sheds for maintenance at weekends.

Rumours turned to fact in February 1956 when 35018 'British India Line' appeared from Eastleigh works with the appearance (and, as it turned out, the performance) of a conventional Pacifics and was put to work on the South Western main line. Several of the class were similarly rebuilt shortly afterwards but none were allocated to work on the South Eastern although when 35026 was called to Eastleigh for rebuilding in January 1957, it did for a moment seem as though Stewarts Lane's turn had come although in the event the replacement turned out to be unrebuilt 35001 from Exmouth Junction. In fact the shed had to wait until October 1958 until its first rebuilt Merchant Navy appeared.

With the Merchant Navy programme well under way, attention turned to the light Pacifics and the first of these, 34005 'Barnstaple', took to the road in June 1957, entering traffic at Stewarts Lane and being tried out for a time on the 10.00 Victoria - Dover boat train; a duty booked to one of the shed's Merchant Navy Pacifics.

Two light Pacifics were sent away to Dover at the end of the year and a third - in exchange for the rebuilt 34005 - was transferred to Nine Elms at the commencement of the 1957 summer season. The King Arthur reserve was further depleted by the loss of 30792 at Eastleigh and in exchange a pair of Schools 4-4-0's arrived from St Leonards after being made redundant by the introduction of express multiple units on the Charing Cross - Hastings service.

Matters were also changing at the lighter end of the scale. By mid-1957 Hither Green and Norwood sheds had received enough 350hp diesel shunters to make inroads into steam shunting on the LCDR whilst some LBSCR duties were transferred from Stewarts Lane to Bricklayers Arms. Other factors also played a part and the withdrawal of an E1 0-6-0T from Southampton shed towards the end of 1956 prompted the transfer of 32101 as a replacement; a move that broke up the long standing fellowship of E2 0-6-0T's at Stewarts Lane. Within six months three more of the class left for Bricklayers Arms resulting some of the work - such as the Victoria station pilot - formerly covered by E2's being handed over to H 0-4-4T's. 2MT 41296 which had spent some time at Exmouth Junction in 1954 returned in the West of England in November 1956 when it was transferred to Barnstaple. This time the move was permanent and the engine did not return.

To counter some of these losses four additional LMS 4MT tanks were received from Tunbridge Wells, Three Bridges and Ramsgate whilst the number of C 0-6-0's was increased from eleven to thirteen with the arrival of 31037 and 31317 from Ashford and Dover respectively. The greatest of surprises came in mid-1957 when a pair of O1 0-6-0's - 1903 rebuilds of an 1878 design - arrived from Ashford having been made redundant through the closure of

Loco	Class	Aug-55	Sep-55	Oct-55	Nov-55	Dec-55	Jan-56	Feb-56	Mar-56	Apr-56	May-56	Jun-56	Jul-56
35014	8P : MN 4-6-2 (1941)									To N. Elms	X	X	X
35015	8P : MN 4-6-2 (1941)		X	X	X	X	X	X	X	X	Ex N. Elms		
35026	8P : MN 4-6-2 (1941)												
35028	8P : MN 4-6-2 (1941)												
34017	7P : WC 4-6-2 (1945)												
34066	7P : WC 4-6-2 (1945)												
34067	7P : WC 4-6-2 (1945)												
34068	7P : WC 4-6-2 (1945)												
34087	7P : WC 4-6-2 (1945)												
34088	7P : WC 4-6-2 (1945)												
34089	7P : WC 4-6-2 (1945)												
34090	7P : WC 4-6-2 (1945)												
34091	7P : WC 4-6-2 (1945)												
34092	7P : WC 4-6-2 (1945)												
34101	7P : WC 4-6-2 (1945)												
34102	7P : WC 4-6-2 (1945)												
34103	7P : WC 4-6-2 (1945)												
34104	7P : WC 4-6-2 (1945)												
70004	7MT 4-6-2 (1951)												
70014	7MT 4-6-2 (1951)												
31914	6F : W 2-6-4T (1931)												
31915	6F : W 2-6-4T (1931)												
31921	6F : W 2-6-4T (1931)												
30915	5P : V 4-4-0 (1930)												
30793	5P : N15 4-6-0 (1926)												
30794	5P : N15 4-6-0 (1926)												
30795	5P : N15 4-6-0 (1926)		To E'leigh	X	X	X	X	X	X	X	Ex E'leigh		
30763	5P : N15 4-6-0 (1925)	To B'stoke	X	X	X	X	X	X	X	X	X	X	X
30764	5P : N15 4-6-0 (1925)	To B'mouth	X	X	X	X	X	X	X	X	X	X	X
30765	5P : N15 4-6-0 (1925)	To B'mouth	X	X	X	X	X	X	X	X	X	X	X
30766	5P : N15 4-6-0 (1925)												
30767	5P : N15 4-6-0 (1925)												
30768	5P : N15 4-6-0 (1925)												
30769	5P : N15 4-6-0 (1925)												
30770	5P : N15 4-6-0 (1925)	To B'stoke		X	X	X	X	X	X	X	X	X	X
30771	5P : N15 4-6-0 (1925)		To B'stoke	X	X	X	X	X	X	X	X	X	X
30773	5P : N15 4-6-0 (1925)		To N. Elms	X	X	X	X	X	X	X	X	X	X
30774	5P : N15 4-6-0 (1925)	To N. Elms	X	X	X	X	X	X	X	X	X	X	X
30791	5P : N15 4-6-0 (1925)		To E'leigh	X	X	X	X	X	X	X	X	X	X
30792	5P : N15 4-6-0 (1925)												
73080	5MT 4-6-0 (1951)												
73081	5MT 4-6-0 (1951)												
73082	5MT 4-6-0 (1951)												
73083	5MT 4-6-0 (1951)												
73084	5MT 4-6-0 (1951)		NEW										
73085	5MT 4-6-0 (1951)		NEW										
73086	5MT 4-6-0 (1951)		NEW										
73087	5MT 4-6-0 (1951)		NEW										
73088	5MT 4-6-0 (1951)		NEW										
73089	5MT 4-6-0 (1951)	X	NEW										
31408	5F : N 2-6-0 (1917)												
31409	5F : N 2-6-0 (1917)												
31410	5F : N 2-6-0 (1917)												
31411	5F : N 2-6-0 (1917)												
31412	5F : N 2-6-0 (1917)												
31413	5F : N 2-6-0 (1917)												
31414	5F : N 2-6-0 (1917)												
31810	5F : N 2-6-0 (1917)												
31811	5F : N 2-6-0 (1917)												
31812	5F : N 2-6-0 (1917)												
31894	4P : U1 2-6-0 (1925)												
31895	4P : U1 2-6-0 (1925)												
31896	4P : U1 2-6-0 (1925)												
31897	4P : U1 2-6-0 (1925)												
31898	4P : U1 2-6-0 (1925)												
31904	4P : U1 2-6-0 (1925)												
31905	4P : U1 2-6-0 (1925)												
31906	4P : U1 2-6-0 (1925)												
31907	4P : U1 2-6-0 (1925)												

Empty stock was brought into Victoria from either Stewarts Lane or Victoria carriage sidings and employed a wide engine of motive power which included some of the older express classes. On 22nd June 1957 D1 4-4-0 31743 of Stewarts Lane had the task of bringing in the empty stock of the down Night Ferry, part of a 3-day duty which alternated between Gillingham and Stewarts Lane sheds and covered several of the newspaper trains between London and the coast via Gravesend. For many years the workings had been in the hands of E1 4-4-0's with D1 4-4-0's taking over from early 1957. (L.G. Marshall)

the Kent & East Sussex. Since the last of the class had left the London area in mid-1951 for the quieter parts of East Kent, few thought they were ever likely to return or, in the unlikely event of their ever showing their faces West of the Medway, it would be to rot in store until the time came to meet the breakers torch. In fact the pair was put to permanent work on a turn that had previously been covered by a Norwood C2/X 0-6-0: the 07.56 Norwood to Gypsy Hill and the 12.20 Norwood to Mitcham and Hackbridge. A pair of O1's remained resident at Stewarts Lane until the electrification of June 1959.

With LBSCR engines going from Stewarts Lane to Southampton Docks and veteran LCDR 0-6-0's probing the darkest recesses of the Brighton suburban area, the times were indeed changing.

1957/8

By mid-1957 the situation referred to earlier concerning the Pacifics at Ramsgate became so serious that the running of four of the morning business trains from Ramsgate was handed over to Bricklayers Arms, the latter being given an allocation of Pacifics with which to cover the workings. This was a novel move since Bricklayers Arms had never been a shed associated with Pacifics and, with the exception of a single King Arthur 4-6-0, had had no express engines larger than a Schools 4-4-0. Under the new arrangement Bricklayers Arms Pacifics worked

Loco	Class	LOCOMOTIVE ALLOCATIONS & TRANSFERS : STEWARTS LANE (73A)											
		Aug-55	Sep-55	Oct-55	Nov-55	Dec-55	Jan-56	Feb-56	Mar-56	Apr-56	May-56	Jun-56	Jul-56
42080	4MT 2-6-4T (1948)												
42081	4MT 2-6-4T (1948)												
42088	4MT 2-6-4T (1948)												
42089	4MT 2-6-4T (1948)												
42090	4MT 2-6-4T (1948)												
42091	4MT 2-6-4T (1948)												
31019	3P : E1 4-4-0 (1919)												
31067	3P : E1 4-4-0 (1919)												
31504	3P : E1 4-4-0 (1919)												
31506	3P : E1 4-4-0 (1919)												
31545	3P : D1 4-4-0 (1921)												
31743	3P : D1 4-4-0 (1921)												
31749	3P : D1 4-4-0 (1921)												
32100	3F : E2 0-6-0T (1913)												
32101	3F : E2 0-6-0T (1913)												
32102	3F : E2 0-6-0T (1913)												
32103	3F : E2 0-6-0T (1913)												
32104	3F : E2 0-6-0T (1913)												
32105	3F : E2 0-6-0T (1913)												
32106	3F : E2 0-6-0T (1913)												
32107	3F : E2 0-6-0T (1913)												
41290	2MT 2-6-2T (1946)												
41291	2MT 2-6-2T (1946)												
41292	2MT 2-6-2T (1946)												
41296	2MT 2-6-2T (1946)												
32455	2F : E3 0-6-2T (1894)												
31253	2F : C 0-6-0 (1900)												
31461	2F : C 0-6-0 (1900)												
31573	2F : C 0-6-0 (1900)												
31575	2F : C 0-6-0 (1900)												
31576	2F : C 0-6-0 (1900)												
31578	2F : C 0-6-0 (1900)												
31579	2F : C 0-6-0 (1900)												
31581	2F : C 0-6-0 (1900)												
31582	2F : C 0-6-0 (1900)												
31583	2F : C 0-6-0 (1900)		To Ton	X	X	X	X	X	X	X	X	X	X
31584	2F : C 0-6-0 (1900)												
31718	2F : C 0-6-0 (1900)		W/D	X	X	X	X	X	X	X	X	X	X
31719	2F : C 0-6-0 (1900)												
31261	1P : H 0-4-4T (1904)												
31265	1P : H 0-4-4T (1904)												
31266	1P : H 0-4-4T (1904)												
31321	1P : H 0-4-4T (1904)												
31550	1P : H 0-4-4T (1904)												
31551	1P : H 0-4-4T (1904)												
31552	1P : H 0-4-4T (1904)												
31557	0F : P 0-6-0T (1909)												
31558	0F : P 0-6-0T (1909)												

down to the coast on evening trains from London and returned the following morning on Ramsgate business expresses. Amongst the contributions that provided Bricklayers Arms with its seven Pacifics was 34017 'Ilfracombe' of Stewarts Lane in October 1957 followed three months later by the recently rebuilt 34005. When the season-ticket holders of Herne Bay shouted, the echoes reverberated at Orpington and Waterloo!

In exchange for its lost light Pacifics Stewarts Lane received three Schools 4-4-0's from Bricklayers Arms plus a pair of King Arthur's from Ashford. The shed also saw some machinations with its Standard 5MT 4-6-0's just before the 1958 summer season: one going to Nine Elms and another to Bath, the deficit being made up by a pair of engines from, of all places, Holyhead. It was usually a feat of administration to effect locomotive exchanges between two divisions of the same region but to achieve it on an inter-regional level - especially when the London Midland appeared to be two engines down on the deal - seem to be the result of string-pulling par excellence.

However events a weeks later revealed the real reason for the arrival of 73041 and 73042 since they were to be the ransom for Stewarts Lane's two Britannia Pacifics - some exchange! - which in their seven year association with the Golden Arrow had become not only a talisman of Stewarts Lane but a hallmark of the entire region. A light Pacific took over the operation of the 'Arrow' but somehow it did not seem to be quite the same train. During the summer one boat train after another left Victoria behind a West Country Pacific and the Golden Arrow with its gleaming Britannia stood out from the rest.

The autumn of 1957 saw the departure of four of Stewarts Lane's thirteen C 0-6-0's, a pair going to Gillingham and Hither Green respectively. Early next year the complement was reduced to eight engines by the withdrawal of 31582 while at the same time the small band of O1 0-6-0's was halved. Having to cover five C diagrams with five engines did not leave much of a margin for failures and defects and the loss of three LMS 2-6-4T's and a pair of H 0-4-4T's did nothing to ease the position.

The continued presence - and activity - of inside cylinder 4-4-0's on the ex-LCDR was becoming something of a talking point, especially since the type was becoming more and more uncommon in the London area and as Compounds and Claud Hamiltons became apparent at St Pancras so attention switched to south of the Thames where pre-grouping 4-4-0's continued to run in their own right and not, as was the case elsewhere, as an occasional

substitute for something else. L and L1 engines had regular workings east of Tonbridge and Gillingham but it was mainly the restrictions at Holborn Viaduct that kept the D1 and E1 engines at work in the electrified area. The withdrawal pattern of the latter classes had been strange since three D1's and four E1's had been taken out of traffic between 1949 and 1951 yet no further withdrawals took place for another seven years. When scrapping eventually recommenced in February 1958, the first engine to go was one of Stewarts Lane's E1 4-4-0's, 31504 with another, 31506, following the following autumn.

The marginally newer D1 4-4-0's took over the Holborn Viaduct workings from 1958, the three engines concerned remaining intact until the electrification of June 1959.

There were some changes in the ranks of the small P 0-6-0T's which covered the Stewarts Lane carriage shunt. 31557 was withdrawn in October 1957 and was replaced by 31178,

formerly of Dover, which itself was sold to Bowaters' Paperworks of Sittingbourne seven months later. An H 0-4-4T took over the duties of the Stewarts lane carriage pilot from that time although 31558 - notable for retaining its SR livery and numbering for five years after nationalisation - remained spare at Stewarts Lane for some time afterwards and was not withdrawn until early 1960.

1958/59

The summer of 1958 was the last in which Stewarts Lane played its established role since the third-rail was extended to Ramsgate in June 1959 after which the shed's responsibilities shrank to covering the boat trains together with a diminishing amount of goods and LBSCR work. Ironically, 1958 proved to be the last of the exceptionally busy British summers - from 1960 the majority of holidaymakers were either using their cars or taking their holidays abroad - and main-line electrification never had to face

Loco	Class	Aug-56	Sep-56	Oct-56	Nov-56	Dec-56	Jan-57	Feb-57	Mar-57	Apr-57	May-57	Jun-57	Jul-57
	LOCOMOTIVE ALLOCATIONS & TRANSFERS : STEWARTS LANE (73A)												
35001	8P : MN 4-6-2 (1941)	X	X	X	X	X	Ex Ex Jcn						
35015	8P : MN 4-6-2 (1941)												
35026	8P : MN 4-6-2 (1941)						R/B	X	X	X	X	X	X
35028	8P : MN 4-6-2 (1941)												
34005	7P : WC/R (1957)	X	X	X	X	X	X	X	X	X		NEW	
34017	7P : WC 4-6-2 (1945)												
34066	7P : WC 4-6-2 (1945)												
34067	7P : WC 4-6-2 (1945)												
34068	7P : WC 4-6-2 (1945)												
34087	7P : WC 4-6-2 (1945)												
34088	7P : WC 4-6-2 (1945)												
34089	7P : WC 4-6-2 (1945)												
34090	7P : WC 4-6-2 (1945)											To N. Elms	X
34091	7P : WC 4-6-2 (1945)												
34092	7P : WC 4-6-2 (1945)												
34101	7P : WC 4-6-2 (1945)												
34102	7P : WC 4-6-2 (1945)												
34103	7P : WC 4-6-2 (1945)				To Dover	X	X	X	X	X	X	X	X
34104	7P : WC 4-6-2 (1945)				To Dover	X	X	X	X	X	X	X	X
70004	7MT 4-6-2 (1951)												
70014	7MT 4-6-2 (1951)												
31914	6F : W 2-6-4T (1931)												
31915	6F : W 2-6-4T (1931)												
31921	6F : W 2-6-4T (1931)												
30908	5P : V 4-4-0 (1930)	X	X	X	X	X	X	X	X	X	X	Ex St. L	
30909	5P : V 4-4-0 (1930)	X	X	X	X	X	X	X	X	X	X	Ex St. L	
30915	5P : V 4-4-0 (1930)			To Ramsgate	X	X	X	X	Ex Ramsgate				
30793	5P : N15 4-6-0 (1926)												
30794	5P : N15 4-6-0 (1926)												
30795	5P : N15 4-6-0 (1926)												
30766	5P : N15 4-6-0 (1925)												
30767	5P : N15 4-6-0 (1925)												
30768	5P : N15 4-6-0 (1925)												
30769	5P : N15 4-6-0 (1925)												
30792	5P : N15 4-6-0 (1925)											To E'leigh	X
73080	5MT 4-6-0 (1951)												
73081	5MT 4-6-0 (1951)												
73082	5MT 4-6-0 (1951)												
73083	5MT 4-6-0 (1951)												
73084	5MT 4-6-0 (1951)												
73085	5MT 4-6-0 (1951)												
73086	5MT 4-6-0 (1951)												
73087	5MT 4-6-0 (1951)	To Bath	X	X	X	X	X	X	X	X	X	X	X
73088	5MT 4-6-0 (1951)												
73089	5MT 4-6-0 (1951)												
31408	5F : N 2-6-0 (1917)												
31409	5F : N 2-6-0 (1917)												
31410	5F : N 2-6-0 (1917)												
31411	5F : N 2-6-0 (1917)												
31412	5F : N 2-6-0 (1917)												
31413	5F : N 2-6-0 (1917)												
31414	5F : N 2-6-0 (1917)												
31810	5F : N 2-6-0 (1917)												
31811	5F : N 2-6-0 (1917)												
31812	5F : N 2-6-0 (1917)												
31894	4P : U1 2-6-0 (1925)									To Ton	X	X	Ex Ton
31895	4P : U1 2-6-0 (1925)												
31896	4P : U1 2-6-0 (1925)									To Ton	X	X	X
31897	4P : U1 2-6-0 (1925)												
31898	4P : U1 2-6-0 (1925)												
31904	4P : U1 2-6-0 (1925)												
31905	4P : U1 2-6-0 (1925)												
31906	4P : U1 2-6-0 (1925)												
31907	4P : U1 2-6-0 (1925)												

Few engines had undergone the metamorphosis that befell the P class 0-6-0 tanks. Introduced in 1907 to operate local Push & Pull services on branch lines where a full train could not be justified. By the 1930's they had been superseded by 0-4-4T's made redundant by electrification but instead of being withdrawn were employed as shunting engines at locations barred to larger locomotives. All eight engines in the class were long-lived and the first withdrawal did not take place until February 1955. 31557 came to Stewarts Lane from Dover in December 1951 for shunting in Stewarts Lane carriage sidings. Although it was taken out of traffic in October 1957, other members of the class remained at Stewarts Lane until February 1960.(L.G. Marshall)

the challenges that the steam age had almost regarded as routine.

There was an irony in the fact that the Kent Coast electrification was not replacing anything - at least in the realms of motive power - that was particularly old. Most of the Ramsgate expresses were worked by engines that were barely four years old whilst few of the Pacifics had seen a decade's active service. It was not only the cynics who pointed out that the electrification might have had more point had the N15 4-6-0's been retained as the front-line engine so that the money spent on Pacifics and BR Standards between 1949 and 1959 been put to better use. On top of everything the

Loco	Class	LOCOMOTIVE ALLOCATIONS & TRANSFERS : STEWARTS LANE (73A)											
		Aug-56	Sep-56	Oct-56	Nov-56	Dec-56	Jan-57	Feb-57	Mar-57	Apr-57	May-57	Jun-57	Jul-57
42074	4MT 2-6-4T (1948)	X	X	X	X	X	X	X	X	X	X	Ex Ramsgate	
42080	4MT 2-6-4T (1948)												
42081	4MT 2-6-4T (1948)												
42086	4MT 2-6-4T (1948)	X	X	X	Ex T. Bges								
42087	4MT 2-6-4T (1948)	X	X	X	Ex T. Wells								
42088	4MT 2-6-4T (1948)												
42089	4MT 2-6-4T (1948)												
42090	4MT 2-6-4T (1948)												
42091	4MT 2-6-4T (1948)												
42106	4MT 2-6-4T (1948)	X	X	X	X	X	X	X	Ex T. Wells				
31019	3P : E1 4-4-0 (1919)												
31067	3P : E1 4-4-0 (1919)												
31504	3P : E1 4-4-0 (1919)												
31506	3P : E1 4-4-0 (1919)												
31545	3P : D1 4-4-0 (1921)												
31743	3P : D1 4-4-0 (1921)												
31749	3P : D1 4-4-0 (1921)												
32100	3F : E2 0-6-0T (1913)												
32101	3F : E2 0-6-0T (1913)						To Soton	X	X	X	X	X	X
32102	3F : E2 0-6-0T (1913)												
32103	3F : E2 0-6-0T (1913)												
32104	3F : E2 0-6-0T (1913)											To B. Arms	X
32105	3F : E2 0-6-0T (1913)											To B. Arms	X
32106	3F : E2 0-6-0T (1913)												
32107	3F : E2 0-6-0T (1913)											To B. Arms	X
41290	2MT 2-6-2T (1946)												
41291	2MT 2-6-2T (1946)												
41292	2MT 2-6-2T (1946)												
41296	2MT 2-6-2T (1946)				To B'staple	X	X	X	X	X	X	X	X
32455	2F : E3 0-6-2T (1894)												
32448	2F : C2X 0-6-0 (1908)	X	X	X	Ex Redhill		To Norwood	X	X	X	X	X	X
31037	2F : C 0-6-0 (1900)	X	X	X	X	X	X	X	X	X	X	Ex Ashford	
31253	2F : C 0-6-0 (1900)												
31317	2F : C 0-6-0 (1900)	X	X	X	X	X	X	X	X	X	X	Ex Dover	
31461	2F : C 0-6-0 (1900)								To B. Arms	X	X	X	X
31573	2F : C 0-6-0 (1900)												
31575	2F : C 0-6-0 (1900)												
31576	2F : C 0-6-0 (1900)												
31578	2F : C 0-6-0 (1900)												
31579	2F : C 0-6-0 (1900)												
31581	2F : C 0-6-0 (1900)												
31582	2F : C 0-6-0 (1900)												
31583	2F : C 0-6-0 (1900)	X	X	X	X	X	X	X	Ex Ton				
31584	2F : C 0-6-0 (1900)												
31719	2F : C 0-6-0 (1900)				To Norwood	X	Ex Norwood						
31048	2F : O1 0-6-0 (1903)	X	X	X	X	X	X	X	X	X	X	Ex Ashford	
31064	2F : O1 0-6-0 (1903)	X	X	X	X	X	X	X	X	X	X	Ex Ashford	
31261	1P : H 0-4-4T (1904)												
31265	1P : H 0-4-4T (1904)												
31266	1P : H 0-4-4T (1904)												
31321	1P : H 0-4-4T (1904)												
31550	1P : H 0-4-4T (1904)												
31551	1P : H 0-4-4T (1904)												
31552	1P : H 0-4-4T (1904)												
31557	0F : P 0-6-0T (1909)												
31558	0F : P 0-6-0T (1909)												

projected service of an hourly train between Victoria and Ramsgate was not seen as a tremendous improvement on the frequency of steam workings. The standard timing of one hour and fifty-four minutes to Ramsgate was an improvement on steam timings, most of which hovered around the two and a half hour mark but the element of the project that put it out of contention so far as most enthusiasts were concerned was the fact it was to be worked by multiple-units. It had been generally assumed that the service would be worked by locomotives of the type that handled the Newhaven boat train but now it seemed that the Granville express and Thanet Belle would be very little different from an ordinary Gillingham electric.

The first half of 1959 was a depressing period for Stewarts Lane - as indeed it was more the district as a whole - since all eyes were on the coming electrification whilst no-one had much interest in steam during its last few months of operation. The only event of note was the arrival of BR 4MT 4-6-0 75074 which arrived at Stewarts Lane from Basingstoke in March 1959 in an attempt to improve the punctuality of the 17.49 business express which had formerly been worked by an LMS 2-6-4T. As part of its diagram the engine also worked the 06.29 Victoria to Tunbridge Wells and the 13.47 and 21.20 departures from Tunbridge Wells to Victoria.

From March 1959 the first of the new electric locomotives started to arrive for trials and driver training runs between Victoria and Gillingham and from the 15th June all passenger services on the LCDR routes to Ramsgate and Dover were taken over by electric multiple units. Some steam workings remained - boat trains, parcels and goods - until a sufficiency of diesel or electric locomotives became available but the effect of electrification on Stewarts Lane was a decimation of the allocation with no less than 42 locomotives being transferred away almost overnight. (The receiving sheds were Nine Elms: 18 locomotives, Dover: 5, Eastleigh: 5, Tonbridge: 4, Ashford: 3, Guildford and Feltham: 2 each and one each to Brighton, Basingstoke and Bricklayers Arms).

1960 and after

One effect of the 1959 electrification was to reverse the situation whereby the LBSCR had been the minor steam operator since the remaining steam duties - other than the Dover and Folkestone Continental expresses - for which Stewarts Lane provided power were all concerned with Brighton line operations. Most of the workings were covered by the remaining N 2-6-0's which worked the 03.45 and 13.05 Battersea - Three Bridges goods and the 04.15 and 11.30 Battersea - Norwood services. The trio of W class 2-6-4 tanks also remained active with one being turned off shed each morning for a two-day cycle which commenced with the 11.30 Battersea - Norwood goods. Passenger bookings were in a minority and were limited to an LMS 2-6-4T for the Victoria station pilot and 75074 - later joined by 75069 - for its turn with the 06.29 Victoria - Tunbridge Wells.

The replacement for Chatham-road steam came in the form of 4-car CEP and BEP multiple units plus twenty-four E5000 class 2552hp electric locomotives. The latter were nominally based at Stewarts Lane but, in a radical departure from steam practice, were almost continually in traffic with most shed visits being made for maintenance purposes. The ability of electric locomotives to remain in traffic indefinitely created one of the greatest changes imaginable to shed activities since the booking-out of engines, previously an ulcerous task at the best of times, contracted to the extend that the only engines booked off Stewarts Lane for LCDR workings were for the 03.30 Victoria - Ramsgate news and - after the completion of the SER electrification - the empty stock for the Golden Arrow (which had reverted to its 10.00 departure) plus the Golden Arrow itself. In

LOCOMOTIVE ALLOCATIONS & TRANSFERS : STEWARTS LANE (73A)													
Loco	Class	Aug-57	Sep-57	Oct-57	Nov-57	Dec-57	Jan-58	Feb-58	Mar-58	Apr-58	May-58	Jun-58	Jul-58
35001	8P : MN 4-6-2 (1941)												
35015	8P : MN 4-6-2 (1941)												
35028	8P : MN 4-6-2 (1941)												
34005	7P : WC/R (1957)						To B. Arms	X	X	X	X	X	X
34017	7P : WC 4-6-2 (1945)			To B. Arms	X	X	X	X	X	X	X	X	X
34066	7P : WC 4-6-2 (1945)												
34067	7P : WC 4-6-2 (1945)												
34068	7P : WC 4-6-2 (1945)												
34077	7P : WC 4-6-2 (1945)	X	X	X	X	X	Ex Ramsgate						
34082	7P : WC 4-6-2 (1945)	X	X	X	X	X	Ex Ramsgate		To Dover	X		X	X
34085	7P : WC 4-6-2 (1945)	X	X	X	X	X	X	X	Ex Dover				
34086	7P : WC 4-6-2 (1945)	X	X	X	X	X	X		Ex Dover				
34087	7P : WC 4-6-2 (1945)												
34088	7P : WC 4-6-2 (1945)												
34089	7P : WC 4-6-2 (1945)												
34091	7P : WC 4-6-2 (1945)												
34092	7P : WC 4-6-2 (1945)												
34100	7P : WC 4-6-2 (1945)	X	X	X	X	X	X	Ex Ramsgate					
34101	7P : WC 4-6-2 (1945)												
34102	7P : WC 4-6-2 (1945)							To B'mouth	X	X	X	X	X
70004	7MT 4-6-2 (1951)												To T. Park
70014	7MT 4-6-2 (1951)												To T. Park
31914	6F : W 2-6-4T (1931)												
31915	6F : W 2-6-4T (1931)												
31921	6F : W 2-6-4T (1931)												
30908	5P : V 4-4-0 (1930)												
30909	5P : V 4-4-0 (1930)												
30915	5P : V 4-4-0 (1930)												
30937	5P : V 4-4-0 (1930)	X	X	X	X	X	X	X	X	X	Ex B. Arms		
30938	5P : V 4-4-0 (1930)	X	X	X	X	X	X	X	X	X	Ex B. Arms		
30939	5P : V 4-4-0 (1930)	X	X	X	X	X	X	X	X	X	Ex B. Arms		
30793	5P : N15 4-6-0 (1926)												
30794	5P : N15 4-6-0 (1926)												
30795	5P : N15 4-6-0 (1926)												
30802	5P : N15 4-6-0 (1926)	X	X	X	X	X	X	X	X	X	Ex Ashford		
30803	5P : N15 4-6-0 (1926)	X	X	X	X	X	X	X	X	X	Ex Ashford		
30766	5P : N15 4-6-0 (1925)												
30767	5P : N15 4-6-0 (1925)												
30768	5P : N15 4-6-0 (1925)												
30769	5P : N15 4-6-0 (1925)												
73041	5MT 4-6-0 (1951)	X	X	X	X	X	X	X	X	X	Ex Holyhead		
73042	5MT 4-6-0 (1951)	X	X	X	X	X	X	X	X	X	Ex Holyhead		
73080	5MT 4-6-0 (1951)												
73081	5MT 4-6-0 (1951)												
73082	5MT 4-6-0 (1951)												
73083	5MT 4-6-0 (1951)												
73084	5MT 4-6-0 (1951)												
73085	5MT 4-6-0 (1951)												
73086	5MT 4-6-0 (1951)												
73087	5MT 4-6-0 (1951)	X	X	Ex Bath								To Bath	X
73088	5MT 4-6-0 (1951)												
73089	5MT 4-6-0 (1951)										To N. Elms	X	X
31408	5F : N 2-6-0 (1917)												
31409	5F : N 2-6-0 (1917)												
31410	5F : N 2-6-0 (1917)												
31411	5F : N 2-6-0 (1917)												
31412	5F : N 2-6-0 (1917)												
31413	5F : N 2-6-0 (1917)												
31414	5F : N 2-6-0 (1917)												
31810	5F : N 2-6-0 (1917)												
31811	5F : N 2-6-0 (1917)												
31812	5F : N 2-6-0 (1917)												
31894	4P : U1 2-6-0 (1925)												
31895	4P : U1 2-6-0 (1925)												
31897	4P : U1 2-6-0 (1925)												
31898	4P : U1 2-6-0 (1925)												
31904	4P : U1 2-6-0 (1925)												
31905	4P : U1 2-6-0 (1925)												
31906	4P : U1 2-6-0 (1925)												
31907	4P : U1 2-6-0 (1925)												

BR Standard 73081 came new to Stewarts Lane in June 1955 to take over - with nine others of the class - the Kent Coast expresses from the N15 'King Arthur' 4-6-0's which had worked the service for more than twenty years. No such record of long service was possible for the newcomers and a mere four years - almost to the day - after its arrival, 73081, made redundant by electrification, was packed off to Nine Elms to spend its final half a dozen years of service on the London & South Western. (M. Bentley)

addition four of the E5000's were booked to be on shed at any one time for maintenance whilst a fifth acted as a spare engine for failures or special traffic requirements. The change from the old order was, to say the least, considerable.

The extension of the third-rail from Gillingham to Ramsgate was no more than a preliminary to the electrification of all main lines in Kent which was completed in 1962 and eliminated the final vestige of activity at Stewarts Lane. It was rather sobering to see that the Night Ferry - which earlier was so spectacularly double-headed - was worked by an engine which the day earlier had meandered through East Kent with a local goods between Ashford and Ramsgate.

This was a major characteristic of the new order in which specialisation in terms of passenger, goods or mixed traffic became meaningless overnight. Engine E5001 or one of its classmates left Stewarts Lane at 03.10 each morning to work the 03.40 Victoria - Ramsgate and then went through

| \multicolumn{13}{c}{LOCOMOTIVE ALLOCATIONS & TRANSFERS : STEWARTS LANE (73A)} |
Loco	Class	Aug-57	Sep-57	Oct-57	Nov-57	Dec-57	Jan-58	Feb-58	Mar-58	Apr-58	May-58	Jun-58	Jul-58
42074	4MT 2-6-4T (1948)								To T. Bges	X	X	X	X
42080	4MT 2-6-4T (1948)												
42081	4MT 2-6-4T (1948)												
42086	4MT 2-6-4T (1948)								To B. Arms	X	X	X	X
42087	4MT 2-6-4T (1948)												
42088	4MT 2-6-4T (1948)												
42089	4MT 2-6-4T (1948)												
42090	4MT 2-6-4T (1948)												
42091	4MT 2-6-4T (1948)												
42106	4MT 2-6-4T (1948)								To T. Wells	X	X	X	X
31019	3P : E1 4-4-0 (1919)												
31067	3P : E1 4-4-0 (1919)												
31504	3P : E1 4-4-0 (1919)							W/D	X	X	X	X	X
31506	3P : E1 4-4-0 (1919)												
31545	3P : D1 4-4-0 (1921)												
31743	3P : D1 4-4-0 (1921)												
31749	3P : D1 4-4-0 (1921)												
32100	3F : E2 0-6-0T (1913)												
32102	3F : E2 0-6-0T (1913)												
32103	3F : E2 0-6-0T (1913)												
32106	3F : E2 0-6-0T (1913)												
41290	2MT 2-6-2T (1946)												
41291	2MT 2-6-2T (1946)												
41292	2MT 2-6-2T (1946)												
32455	2F : E3 0-6-2T (1894)							W/D	X	X	X	X	X
31037	2F : C 0-6-0 (1900)		To Gill	X	X	X	X	X	X	X	X	X	X
31253	2F : C 0-6-0 (1900)		To H. Green	X	X	X	X	X	X	X	X	X	X
31317	2F : C 0-6-0 (1900)												
31573	2F : C 0-6-0 (1900)		To H. Green	X	X	X	X	X	X	X	X	X	X
31575	2F : C 0-6-0 (1900)												
31576	2F : C 0-6-0 (1900)		To Gill	X	X	X	X	X	X	X	X	X	X
31578	2F : C 0-6-0 (1900)												
31579	2F : C 0-6-0 (1900)												
31581	2F : C 0-6-0 (1900)												
31582	2F : C 0-6-0 (1900)										W/D	X	X
31583	2F : C 0-6-0 (1900)												
31584	2F : C 0-6-0 (1900)												
31719	2F : C 0-6-0 (1900)												
31048	2F : O1 0-6-0 (1903)												
31064	2F : O1 0-6-0 (1903)										W/D	X	X
31261	1P : H 0-4-4T (1904)												
31265	1P : H 0-4-4T (1904)												
31266	1P : H 0-4-4T (1904)										To Ton	X	X
31321	1P : H 0-4-4T (1904)						W/D	X	X	X	X	X	X
31550	1P : H 0-4-4T (1904)												
31551	1P : H 0-4-4T (1904)												
31552	1P : H 0-4-4T (1904)												
31178	0F : P 0-6-0T (1909)	X	X	Ex Dover							W/D	X	X
31557	0F : P 0-6-0T (1909)		W/D	X	X	X	X	X	X	X	X	X	X
31558	0F : P 0-6-0T (1909)												

a twenty-six day cycle which encompassed every locomotive-hauled LCDR service before arriving back in Stewarts Lane with a light engine run from Gillingham. As an example of efficiency, it may have been unsurpassed but it was also as operationally dull as it was possible to be.

Looking for interesting chinks in the armour of efficient uniformity was difficult but a few were there for the finding. The three SR locomotives (20001 - 3) had been transferred from their former base at Selhurst to Stewarts Lane in March 1959 from where they continued with their Brighton-line duties which included the Newhaven boat train. The use of the E5001's over the LBSCR was initially rather limited - one of the engines worked the 20.42 Bricklayers Arms - Horsham goods and the 03.00 Horsham - Norwood return but it was possible, after the electrification of the Sevenoaks - Dover section in 1962 - to find one of the older engines at work on the South-Eastern: a happening that was not widely known or advertised.

The train concerned was the Thursdays-only 20.45 Newcastle - Dover unadvertised overnight express which ran up the Great Central, the GC/GW joint and the West London extension with a change of engines at York and Kensington Olympia or Longhedge Junction. Since the imposition of a dated odd-day train threatened to make a nasty dent in the carefully planned cycle of E5001 electrics, one of the older SR electrics and a Hither Green crew was diagrammed to relieve the GC B1 4-6-0; the electric working the train to Dover Marine where it stabled until returning that night with the 21.25 Dover to Newcastle. This is believed to be the only regular appearance of the class off LBSCR metals.

Even after completion of the East Kent electrification in 1962 there still remained a considerable amount of work that could not be encompassed by electric locomotives and to fill the gap the South Eastern were presented with a fleet of Type 3 diesel electric engines which were divided into two types: one modified for working between Tonbridge and Hastings - which saw half a dozen goods trains in each direction daily - and the other for more general use. Like the electric locomotives, the diesels - with two exceptions - worked to lengthy cyclic diagrams, the Hastings engines having a twelve-day diagram whilst the conventional Type 3 workings took no less than twenty-one days to cover. (Whether any of the engines - diesel or electric - ever succeeded in working through the cycle without interruption is, to say the least, unlikely thanks to traffic fluctuations and engine failures).

The Hastings-gauge Type 3's (which the Southern designated the D6586 class) were based on Tonbridge and were not booked to appear in London to any great extent. One worked the 22.40 Tonbridge - Hither Green goods and returned south on the 05.40 London Bridge - Hastings, the only regular passenger service the class was booked to work out of London. Whilst in London the engine strayed onto the Chatham side with the 00.48 Hither Green to Swanley and the 02.30 Swanley - Hither Green goods. The only other passenger services booked to the Hastings Type 3's were the 06.45 Reading to Tonbridge and the 06.40 Paddock Wood to Reading.

The standard Type 3's allocated to the South Eastern saw even less passenger work than the Hastings version; the only services booked to them being some morning trains on the New Romney branch and an evening return trip

	LOCOMOTIVE ALLOCATIONS & TRANSFERS : STEWARTS LANE (73A)												
Loco	Class	Aug-58	Sep-58	Oct-58	Nov-58	Dec-58	Jan-59	Feb-59	Mar-59	Apr-59	May-59	Jun-59	Jul-59
5001	8P: 2550 ELECTRIC	X	X	X	X	X	X	X	NEW				
5002	8P: 2550 ELECTRIC	X	X	X	X	X	X	X	NEW				
5005	8P: 2550 ELECTRIC	X	X	X	X	X	X	X	X	X	X	NEW	
5006	8P: 2550 ELECTRIC	X	X	X	X	X	X	X	X	X	X	NEW	
5007	8P: 2550 ELECTRIC	X	X	X	X	X	X	X	X	X	X	X	NEW
35015	8P: MN/R (1956)	X	X	NEW								To N. Elms	X
35001	8P: MN 4-6-2 (1941)											To N. Elms	X
35015	8P: MN 4-6-2 (1941)			R/B	X	X	X	X	X	X	X	X	X
35028	8P: MN 4-6-2 (1941)											To N. Elms	X
20001	7P: Electric	X	X	X	X	X	X	X	Ex Selhurst				
20002	7P: Electric	X	X	X	X	X	X	X	Ex Selhurst				
20003	7P: Electric	X	X	X	X	X	X	X	Ex Selhurst				
34066	7P: WC 4-6-2 (1945)												
34067	7P: WC 4-6-2 (1945)												
34068	7P: WC 4-6-2 (1945)												
34077	7P: WC 4-6-2 (1945)												
34085	7P: WC 4-6-2 (1945)												
34086	7P: WC 4-6-2 (1945)												
34087	7P: WC 4-6-2 (1945)												
34088	7P: WC 4-6-2 (1945)												
34089	7P: WC 4-6-2 (1945)												
34091	7P: WC 4-6-2 (1945)												
34092	7P: WC 4-6-2 (1945)												
34100	7P: WC 4-6-2 (1945)												
34101	7P: WC 4-6-2 (1945)												
31914	6F: W 2-6-4T (1931)												
31915	6F: W 2-6-4T (1931)												
31921	6F: W 2-6-4T (1931)												
30908	5P: V 4-4-0 (1930)											To B'stoke	X
30909	5P: V 4-4-0 (1930)											To N. Elms	X
30915	5P: V 4-4-0 (1930)											To Brighton	X
30920	5P: V 4-4-0 (1930)	X	X	X	X	X	X	X	X	X	X	Ex Ramsgate	
30921	5P: V 4-4-0 (1930)	X	X	X	X	X	X	X	X	X	X	Ex Ramsgate	
30922	5P: V 4-4-0 (1930)	X	X	X	X	X	X	X	X	X	X	Ex Ramsgate	
30923	5P: V 4-4-0 (1930)	X	X	X	X	X	X	X	X	X	X	Ex B'stoke	
30937	5P: V 4-4-0 (1930)											To Ashford	X
30938	5P: V 4-4-0 (1930)											To Dover	X
30939	5P: V 4-4-0 (1930)											To Dover	X
30793	5P: N15 4-6-0 (1926)											To Feltham	X
30794	5P: N15 4-6-0 (1926)								To B'stoke	X	X	X	X
30795	5P: N15 4-6-0 (1926)											To Feltham	X
30802	5P: N15 4-6-0 (1926)											To E'leigh	X
30803	5P: N15 4-6-0 (1926)											To E'leigh	X
30766	5P: N15 4-6-0 (1925)								W/D	X	X	X	X
30767	5P: N15 4-6-0 (1925)											To E'leigh	X
30768	5P: N15 4-6-0 (1925)											To E'leigh	X
30769	5P: N15 4-6-0 (1925)											To E'leigh	X
73041	5MT 4-6-0 (1951)											To N. Elms	X
73042	5MT 4-6-0 (1951)											To N. Elms	X
73080	5MT 4-6-0 (1951)											To N. Elms	X
73081	5MT 4-6-0 (1951)											To N. Elms	X
73082	5MT 4-6-0 (1951)											To N. Elms	X
73083	5MT 4-6-0 (1951)											To N. Elms	X
73084	5MT 4-6-0 (1951)											To N. Elms	X
73085	5MT 4-6-0 (1951)											To N. Elms	X
73086	5MT 4-6-0 (1951)											To N. Elms	X
73088	5MT 4-6-0 (1951)			To N. Elms	X	X	X	X	X	X	X	X	X
31408	5F : N 2-6-0 (1917)											To Ashford	X
31409	5F : N 2-6-0 (1917)											To Ashford	X
31410	5F : N 2-6-0 (1917)												
31411	5F : N 2-6-0 (1917)												
31412	5F : N 2-6-0 (1917)												
31413	5F : N 2-6-0 (1917)											To Dover	X
31414	5F : N 2-6-0 (1917)											To Dover	X
31810	5F : N 2-6-0 (1917)											To Dover	X
31811	5F : N 2-6-0 (1917)											To Guild	X
31812	5F : N 2-6-0 (1917)											To Guild	X
31894	4P : U1 2-6-0 (1925)												
31895	4P : U1 2-6-0 (1925)												
31896	4P : U1 2-6-0 (1925)	X	X	X	X	X	X	X	X	X	X	Ex Ton	
31897	4P : U1 2-6-0 (1925)												
31898	4P : U1 2-6-0 (1925)												
31899	4P : U1 2-6-0 (1925)	X	X	X	X	X	X	X	X	X	X	Ex B. Arms	
31900	4P : U1 2-6-0 (1925)	X	X	X	X	X	X	X	X	X	X	Ex B. Arms	
31904	4P : U1 2-6-0 (1925)											To Ton	X
31905	4P : U1 2-6-0 (1925)											To Ton	X
31906	4P : U1 2-6-0 (1925)											To Ton	X
31907	4P : U1 2-6-0 (1925)											To Ton	X
75074	4MT 4-6-0 (1951)	X	X	X	X	X	X	X	Ex B'stoke				

between Ashford and Hastings. In order to ensure that the passenger trains were efficiently heated during the winter months, the passenger workings were collected into a single diagram which was - in theory - worked by the same engine day in, day out. Experience had shown that if they were not in regular use, train heating boilers - never especially reliable at the best of times - quickly became unserviceable. To the enthusiast the presence of a type 3 on a passenger train made a refreshing change from the near-universality of multiple units until one reflected, none too cheerfully, that only a few years before the Ashford - Hastings service had been booked to a St Leonards' Schools 4-4-0.

Another Type 3 was booked to spend each night working the empty stock of newspaper trains between Southwark and London Bridge, a duty for which a reliable boiler was needed. This working was also isolated from the cyclic diagrams in the hope that an engine

Kross	S pt-Al	S pt-A5	S pt-A6	S pt-A9	S pt-A	S pt-AA	S pt-AC	S pt-AD	S pt-AE	S pt-AG	S pt-Cl
8P: MN/R 4-6-2									1		
8P: MN 4-6-2	4	4	3	3	3	3	3	3	2		
7P: WC/R 4-6-2								1			
7P: WC 4-6-2	19	16	15	15	17	14	14	10	13	13	8
7MT 4-6-2	-	2	2	2	2	2	2	2			
6F: W 2-6-4T	3	2	2	2	3	3	3	3	3	3	3
5P: V 4-4-0			1	1	1	1	1	3	6	4	4
5P: N15 4-6-0	10	12	17	15	16	7	8	7	9		
5MT 4-6-0						10	9	10	9		
5F: Q1 0-6-0	-	3			3						
5F: N 2-6-0	16	12	11	11	9	10	10	10	10	3	5
4P: U1 2-6-0	8	10	11	6	6	9	9	8	8	7	7
4MT BR 2-6-4T											3
4MT 4-6-0										1	2
4MT 2-6-4T	-	5	6	5	5	6	6	0	7	6	
3P: L1 4-4-0	-	2	7								
3P: L 4-4-0	3										
3P: E1 4-4-0	5	4	4	4	4	4	4	4	2		2
3P: D1 4-4-0	4	2	2	3	3	3	3	3	4	1	
3F: E2 0-6-0T	8	8	8	8	8	8	8	4	4	4	4
2P: E 4-4-0				1							
2MT 2-6-2T		1	7	6	4	4	4	3	3	3	3
2F: E3 0-6-2T					1	1	1	1			
2F: E1 0-6-0T	1		-								
2F: C2X 0-6-0											1
2F: C 0-6-0	13	13	13	12	12	11	11	9	8	9	8
2F: O1 0-6-0								2	2		
1P: R 0-4-4T	1	1									
1P: H 0-4-4T	12	11	10	9	9	7	7	7	5	4	2
1F: '0756' 0-6-0T	1	1									
0F: P 0-6-0T	1	1	2	2	2	2	2	2	1	1	
TOTAL	109	110	122	105	116	105	105	102	97	59	52

with a serviceable boiler could be kept on the duty indefinitely.

Given that so much energy was expended in the movement of holiday crowds, it was surprising to find that the West London Extension (Clapham Junction to Kensington Olympia) was not included in either the 1959 or 1962 electrification schemes. Exactly why Kensington should have been excluded from the plan is unclear although a confusion of managements (most of the West London 'belonged' to the Western Region whilst many of the through trains ran to the Midland) may have had something to do with it. Another factor was the traditionally complicated method of working: trains from the LNWR changed engines at Mitre Bridge, Willesden, whilst services from other routes changed at Kensington. It may simply have been that the number of trains using the route even on the busiest summer Saturday was such a small proportion of the total Southern electrified train-mileage that the region was happy to use diesels.

On a summer Saturday there were normally eight services crossing into SR territory at Kensington, as shown in the accompanying table. Most of the incoming workings came off the Great Western (including several that originated on the Great Central) and changed engines at Olympia whilst the remainder ran up the London & North Western with the engine-change being effected at Mitre Bridge Junction near Willesden. The odd-man out was the

CROSS-LONDON HOLIDAY EXPRESSES : 1956 (Sats)
KENSINGTON (OLYMPIA)

Train	Route	Arr	Loco	Dep	Destination
01.00 Leicester Central)	Woodford and High Wycombe	03.39	U1 2-6-0 (S. Lane 19)	03.49	Ramsgate
23.35 Derby (Friargate)	Woodford and High Wycombe	04.15	U1 2-6-0 (S. Lane 20)	04.24	Ramsgate
23.45 Manchester (LR)	Bletchley and Willesden		LMS 5MT 4-6-0 (Longsight)	04/29	Hastings via Brighton
23.44 Sheffield (Central)	Woodford and High Wycombe	04.37	U1 2-6-0 (S. Lane 504)	04.47	Hastings via Brighton
07.28 Wolverhampton (GW)	Banbury and High Wycombe	10.46	N 2-6-0 (S. Lane 501)	10.56	Hastings via Brighton
10.10 Birmingham (GW)	Banbury and High Wycombe	12.45	U1 2-6-0 (S. Lane 21)	12.55	Margate
11.05 Walsall	Bletchley and Willesden		WC 4-6-2 (Brighton 733)	14/00	Hastings via Brighton
12.35 Leicester	Bletchley and Willesden		WC 4-6-2 (Brighton 734)	15/30	Hastings via Brighton

overnight service from Manchester, London Road, which was worked throughout by a Longsight 5MT 4-6-0.

One interesting by-product of the engine-changing at Mitre Bridge was the fact that SR light Pacifics could routinely be seen on Willesden loco between their northbound and southbound workings.

Compared to the volume of traffic taken to the coast by ordinary services from Victoria, the trains via Kensington were very small beer and of such small relative value that no pressing case was made urging electrification to Kensington or Willesden Junction. As it happened, this may have been fortuitous - prescient even - since the moment the electrification of Kent was completed, the Beeching report promptly placed a large question-mark over the future of many summer Saturday cross-country trains and for the few post-Beeching years that they continued to operate the Southern generally employed its Type 3's although wherever possible they preferred the originating region to diagram its engine through to destination. Such through working was nothing new and dated back to 1909 when the 'Sunny South Express' had been powered between Rugby and Brighton on alternate days by the LNWR and LBSCR. Engine-changing was resorted to from 1914 but through working was restored rather unexpectedly in 1950 with the 23.45 Manchester - Brighton in the presumption that other services would follow suit. This

Loco	Class	Aug-58	Sep-58	Oct-58	Nov-58	Dec-58	Jan-59	Feb-59	Mar-59	Apr-59	May-59	Jun-59	Jul-59
42080	4MT 2-6-4T (1948)												
42081	4MT 2-6-4T (1948)												
42087	4MT 2-6-4T (1948)											To T. Wells	
42088	4MT 2-6-4T (1948)												
42089	4MT 2-6-4T (1948)												
42090	4MT 2-6-4T (1948)												
42091	4MT 2-6-4T (1948)												
31019	3P: E1 4-4-0 (1919)											To N. Elms	X
31067	3P: E1 4-4-0 (1919)											To N. Elms	X
31506	3P: E1 4-4-0 (1919)			W/D	X	X	X	X	X	X	X	X	X
31145	3P: D1 4-4-0 (1921)	X	X	Ex B. Arms								To N. Elms	X
31545	3P: D1 4-4-0 (1921)											To N. Elms	X
31743	3P: D1 4-4-0 (1921)												
31749	3P: D1 4-4-0 (1921)											To B. Arms	X
32100	3F: E2 0-6-0T (1913)												
32102	3F: E2 0-6-0T (1913)												
32103	3F: E2 0-6-0T (1913)												
32106	3F: E2 0-6-0T (1913)												
41290	2MT 2-6-2T (1946)												
41291	2MT 2-6-2T (1946)												
41292	2MT 2-6-2T (1946)												
31317	2F: C 0-6-0 (1900)												
31575	2F: C 0-6-0 (1900)												
31578	2F: C 0-6-0 (1900)												
31579	2F: C 0-6-0 (1900)											To N. Elms	X
31581	2F: C 0-6-0 (1900)												
31583	2F: C 0-6-0 (1900)												
31584	2F: C 0-6-0 (1900)												
31714	2F: C 0-6-0 (1900)	X	X	X	X	X	X	X	X	X	X	Ex Fav	
31715	2F: C 0-6-0 (1900)	X	X	X	X	X	X	X	X	X	X	Ex Fav	
31719	2F: C 0-6-0 (1900)												
31048	2F: O1 0-6-0 (1903)											To N. Elms	X
31370	2F: O1 0-6-0 (1903)	X	X	Ex Ashford								To N. Elms	X
31261	1P: H 0-4-4T (1904)												
31265	1P: H 0-4-4T (1904)												
31550	1P: H 0-4-4T (1904)												
31551	1P: H 0-4-4T (1904)												
31552	1P: H 0-4-4T (1904)											To N. Elms	X
31558	0F: P 0-6-0T (1909)												

LOCOMOTIVE ALLOCATIONS & TRANSFERS : STEWARTS LANE (73A)

Loco	Class	Aug-59	Sep-59	Oct-59	Nov-59	Dec-59	Jan-60	Feb-60	Mar-60	Apr-60	May-60	Jun-60	Jul-60
5001	8P: 2550 ELECTRIC												
5002	8P: 2550 ELECTRIC												
5005	8P: 2550 ELECTRIC												
5006	8P: 2550 ELECTRIC												
5007	8P: 2550 ELECTRIC												
5008	8P: 2550 ELECTRIC	NEW											
5009	8P: 2550 ELECTRIC	NEW											
5010	8P: 2550 ELECTRIC	X	X	NEW									
5011	8P: 2550 ELECTRIC	X	X	NEW									
5012	8P: 2550 ELECTRIC	X	X	X	X	NEW							
5013	8P: 2550 ELECTRIC	X	X	X	X	NEW							
5014	8P: 2550 ELECTRIC	X	X	X	X	X	X	NEW					
5015	8P: 2550 ELECTRIC	X	X	X	X	X	X	NEW					
5016	8P: 2550 ELECTRIC	X	X	X	X	X	X	X	X	NEW			
5017	8P: 2550 ELECTRIC	X	X	X	X	X	X	NEW					
5018	8P: 2550 ELECTRIC	X	X	X	X	X	X	X	X	NEW			
5019	8P: 2550 ELECTRIC	X	X	X	X	X	X	X	X	X	X	X	NEW
5020	8P: 2550 ELECTRIC	X	X	X	X	X	X	X	X	X	X	X	NEW
20001	7P: Electric												
20002	7P: Electric												
20003	7P: Electric												
34085	7P : WC/R (1957)	X	X	X	X	X	X	X	X	X	X	X	NEW
34088	7P : WC/R (1957)	X	X	X	X	X	X	X	X	NEW			
34066	7P : WC 4-6-2 (1945)												
34067	7P : WC 4-6-2 (1945)												
34068	7P : WC 4-6-2 (1945)												
34077	7P : WC 4-6-2 (1945)												
34085	7P : WC 4-6-2 (1945)												R/B
34086	7P : WC 4-6-2 (1945)												
34087	7P : WC 4-6-2 (1945)												
34088	7P : WC 4-6-2 (1945)								R/B		X	X	X
34089	7P : WC 4-6-2 (1945)												
34091	7P : WC 4-6-2 (1945)												
34092	7P : WC 4-6-2 (1945)												
34100	7P : WC 4-6-2 (1945)												
34101	7P : WC 4-6-2 (1945)												
31914	6F : W 2-6-4T (1931)												
31915	6F : W 2-6-4T (1931)												
31921	6F : W 2-6-4T (1931)												
30920	5P : V 4-4-0 (1930)												
30921	5P : V 4-4-0 (1930)												
30922	5P : V 4-4-0 (1930)												
30923	5P : V 4-4-0 (1930)												
31410	5F : N 2-6-0 (1917)												
31411	5F : N 2-6-0 (1917)												
31412	5F : N 2-6-0 (1917)												
31823	5F : N 2-6-0 (1917)	X	X	X	X	X	X	X	X	X	X	X	Ex B. Arms
31824	5F : N 2-6-0 (1917)	X	X	X	X	X	X	X	X	X	X	X	Ex B. Arms
31894	4P : U1 2-6-0 (1925)												
31895	4P : U1 2-6-0 (1925)												
31896	4P : U1 2-6-0 (1925)												
31897	4P : U1 2-6-0 (1925)												
31898	4P : U1 2-6-0 (1925)												
31899	4P : U1 2-6-0 (1925)												
31900	4P : U1 2-6-0 (1925)												
75069	4MT 4-6-0 (1951)	X	X	X	X	Ex E'leigh							
75074	4MT 4-6-0 (1951)												
80066	4MT 2-6-4T (1951)	X	X	X	X	Ex Watford		To Ashford	X	X	X	X	X
80067	4MT 2-6-4T (1951)	X	X	X	X	Ex Watford							
80068	4MT 2-6-4T (1951)	X	X	X	X	Ex Watford							
80081	4MT 2-6-4T (1951)	X	X	X	X	Ex Willesden							
42080	4MT 2-6-4T (1948)					To Neasden	X	X	X	X	X	X	X
42081	4MT 2-6-4T (1948)					To Neasden	X	X	X	X	X	X	X
42088	4MT 2-6-4T (1948)					To Neasden	X	X	X	X	X	X	X
42089	4MT 2-6-4T (1948)					To Neasden	X	X	X	X	X	X	X
42090	4MT 2-6-4T (1948)					To Neasden	X	X	X	X	X	X	X
42091	4MT 2-6-4T (1948)					To Neasden	X	X	X	X	X	X	X
31019	3P : E1 4-4-0 (1919)	X	X	X	X	X	X	X	X	Ex Sarum			
31067	3P : E1 4-4-0 (1919)	X	X	X	X	X	X	X	X	Ex Sarum			
31743	3P : D1 4-4-0 (1921)							W/D	X	X	X	X	X
32100	3F : E2 0-6-0T (1913)												
32102	3F : E2 0-6-0T (1913)												
32103	3F : E2 0-6-0T (1913)												
32106	3F : E2 0-6-0T (1913)												
41290	2MT 2-6-2T (1946)												
41291	2MT 2-6-2T (1946)												
41292	2MT 2-6-2T (1946)												
31229	2F : C 0-6-0 (1900)	X	X	X	X	X	X	Ex N. Elms					To B. Arms
31317	2F : C 0-6-0 (1900)												
31575	2F : C 0-6-0 (1900)												
31578	2F : C 0-6-0 (1900)												
31581	2F : C 0-6-0 (1900)								W/D	X	X	X	X
31583	2F : C 0-6-0 (1900)												
31584	2F : C 0-6-0 (1900)												
31714	2F : C 0-6-0 (1900)												
31715	2F : C 0-6-0 (1900)												
31719	2F : C 0-6-0 (1900)												
31261	1P : H 0-4-4T (1904)												
31265	1P : H 0-4-4T (1904)												
31550	1P : H 0-4-4T (1904)												
31551	1P : H 0-4-4T (1904)												
31558	0F : P 0-6-0T (1909)							W/D	X	X	X	X	X

LOCOMOTIVE ALLOCATIONS & TRANSFERS : STEWARTS LANE (73A)

expectation did not materialise mainly because the number of trains involved and their seasonal nature did not engage the interest of either the Midland or Western Regions although in 1954 the latter was persuaded to spare a Hall 4-6-0 for rather inconclusive clearance trials between Clapham Junction and Kensington. From 1957 there was a tendency for day trips from the Midland to be worked through but the arrangement was marred by the spectre of trains turning up at Kensington with engines that had not been cleared for passage over the Southern and the matter was never satisfactorily resolved.

In the latter days of the through trains under dieselisation a clear policy was still absent and whils in one or two cases the Midland worked their trains through others continued to be re-engined by the Southern. The star turns in respect of the through workings included the 21.40(Sats) Newhaven - Glasgow which was worked throughout by a Willesden-based English Electric Type 4 and the 22.35 Dover - Manchester which was handled by a Cricklewood Sulzer type 2 and manned, most unusually, by drivers from both Hither Green and Cricklewood; the latter taking over as driver at Clapham Junction. Trains such as the 23.55 Derby - Ramsgate, the 07.32 Wolverhampton - Hastings and the 09.45 Wolverhampton - Margate continued to be re-engined at Kensington Olympia by the Southern using the region's SR D6500 type 3's.

By and large the constituent sections of the Southern kept to themselves even after nationalisation although exceptions could be found such as the LBSCR E2 0-6-0 tanks, two of which were used for goods shunting in Herne Hill yard while a third was used for empty stock workings into Victoria (E). The duties at Herne Hill included working trains to and from Camberwell and therefore called for a powerfully robust engine. For many years Stewarts Lane had an allocation of eight E2's which were also used for shunting duties at Battersea. 32106 - one of the batch with extended water tanks - is seen at Stewarts Lane in June 1957. (L.G. Marshall)

HERNE HILL

YARD WORKING : 1954/5

Train	Arrive	Engine	Shed	Pilot	Shed	Depart	Destination
23.45 Bromley South	00.13	C 0-6-0	H. Green 200				
23.48 Blackfriars	00.17	C 0-6-0	S. Lane 72				
		C 0-6-0	H. Green 200			00.23	Light to S. Lane loco
Light ex S. Lane loco	00.42	N 2-6-0	S. Lane 61				(For 01.35)
22.25 Faversham	00.58	BR5 4-6-0	S. Lane 15				
		BR5 4-6-0	S. Lane 15			01.10	Light to S. Lane loco
		C 0-6-0	S. Lane 72			01.10	Blackfriars
23.55 Ferme Park	01.10	J50 0-6-0T	Hornsey 115				
		N 2-6-0	S. Lane 61			01.35	Faversham
00.05 Brent	01.37	3F 0-6-0T	Cwd 3				
		C 0-6-0	S. Lane 74			01.40	Light to Camberwell
		3F 0-6-0T	W'den 62			01.45	Willesden
		J50 0-6-0T	Hornsey 115			02.00	Ferme Park
00.10 Hoo Jcn	02.05	C 0-6-0	H. Green 187	C 0-6-0	S. Lane 74		
00.50 Ferme Park	02.10	J50 0-6-0T	Hornsey 4				
Light ex S. Lane loco	02.15	C 0-6-0	S. Lane 70				
		C 0-6-0	H. Green 187			02.25	Light to S. Lane loco
		C 0-6-0	S. Lane 70			02.32	Gillingham
Light ex Blackfriars	02.35	C 0-6-0	S. Lane 72				(For 02.50)
00.55 Brent	02.32	3F 0-6-0T	Cwd 6				
		C 0-6-0	S. Lane 72			02.50	Bromley South
		3F 0-6-0T	Cwd 3			02.50	Brent
23.55 Gillingham	03.05	C 0-6-0	S. Lane 70				
		J50 0-6-0T	Hornsey 4			03.15	Ferme Park
		C 0-6-0	S. Lane 70			03.20	Light to S. Lane loco
		3F 0-6-0T	Cwd 6			03.30	Brent
03.05 Ferme Park	04.05	J50 0-6-0T	Hornsey 15				
01.05 Sittingbourne	04.08	E1 4-4-0	S. Lane 47				
Light ex S. Lane loco	04.52	N 2-6-0	S. Lane 62				(For 05.23)
Light ex S. Lane loco	05.05	E2 0-6-0T	S. Lane 76				(For Yard Pilot)
		E1 4-4-0	S. Lane 47			05.12	Light to Ewer St loco
03.25 Sevenoaks	05.15	N 2-6-0	S. Lane 64				
03.25 Brent	05.20	3F 0-6-0T	Cwd 21				
		N 2-6-0	S. Lane 62			05.23	Dover Town
		J50 0-6-0T	Hornsey 15			05.23	Ferme Park
		N 2-6-0	S. Lane 64			05.55	Light to S. Lane loco
		C 0-6-0	S. Lane 74			06.12	Wandsworth Road
		3F 0-6-0T	Cwd 21			06.45	Brent
Light ex S. Lane loco	10.35	N 2-6-0	S. Lane 64				(For 10.54)
Light ex Bickley	10.38	C 0-6-0	H. Green 199				(For 10.53)
		C 0-6-0	H. Green 199			10.53	Blackfriars
		N 2-6-0	S. Lane 64			10.54	Ashford
		E2 0-6-0T	S. Lane 75			11.20	Light to Camberwell
10.52 Hither Green	11.47	C 0-6-0	H. Green	E2 0-6-0T	S. Lane 75		
10.40 Ferme Park	12.11	J50 0-6-0T	Hornsey 51				
10.55 Brent	12.18	3F 0-6-0T	Cwd 52				
		C 0-6-0	H. Green	E2 0-6-0T	S. Lane 75	12.55	Hither Green
12.40 Wandsworth Road	13.08	C 0-6-0	H. Green 194				
		J50 0-6-0T	Hornsey 51			13.32	Ferme Park
12.30 Brent	14.05	3F 0-6-0T	Cwd 60				
		3F 0-6-0T	Cwd 52			14.10	Brent
Light ex S. Lane loco	14.31	C 0-6-0	S. Lane 72				(For 14.55)
		C 0-6-0	S. Lane 72	C 0-6-0	H. Green 194	14.55	Brockley Lane
		3F 0-6-0T	Cwd 60			15.06	Brent
Light ex Camberwell	15.15	C 0-6-0	H. Green 194				
		C 0-6-0	H. Green 194			15.25	Stewarts Lane
		E2 0-6-0T	S. Lane 76			19.22	Light to Camberwell
19.23 Brockley Lane	19.57	C 0-6-0	S. Lane 72	E2 0-6-0T	S. Lane 76		
		C 0-6-0	S. Lane 72			20.05	Light to Camberwell
19.50 Wandsworth Road	20.22	C 0-6-0	S. Lane 74	C 0-6-0	S. Lane 72		
		C 0-6-0	S. Lane 72			20.40	Light to S. Lane loco
		C 0-6-0	S. Lane 74			20.45	Light to Camberwell
19.23 Brent	21.08	3F 0-6-0T	Cwd 93				
20.50 Ferme Park	21.56	J50 0-6-0T	Hornsey 97				
Light ex S. Lane loco	22.05	E2 0-6-0T	S. Lane 75				(For Yard Pilot)
21.16 Hither Green	22.20	C 0-6-0	S. Lane 71	C 0-6-0	S. Lane 74		
		C 0-6-0	S. Lane 71			22.25	Light to Blackfriars
		3F 0-6-0T	Cwd 93			22.40	Brent
		J50 0-6-0T	Hornsey 97			22.52	Ferme Park
		E2 0-6-0T	S. Lane 76			22.54	Stewarts Lane
Light ex H. Green Loco	23.22	C 0-6-0	Gill 240				(For 23.40)
		C 0-6-0	S. Lane 74			23.25	Light to Camberwell
22.00 Willesden	23.25	3F 0-6-0T	W'den 62				
		C 0-6-0	Gill 240			23.40	Chatham
22.28 Erith (North End)	23.45	C 0-6-0	H. Green 191	C 0-6-0	S. Lane 74		
		C 0-6-0	H. Green 191			23.50	Light to H. Green loco

To most observers Herne Hill had been the station at which incoming Ramsgate expresses divided into Victoria and Holborn Viaduct sections but which, since the termination of such activities in 1914, had simply been one of a hundred similar suburban stations. To the operator, on the other hand, Herne Hill was the focal point of most operating activity since it was the location of the LCDR's largest marshalling yard where inward traffic (principally from the Great Northern and the Midland) was received and sorted into services serving local (eight departures) and long distance LCDR destinations.

The yard was located to the North of the passenger station on the branch to Holborn Viaduct and while this was suitable for receiving trains from the widened lines and passing the traffic forward to the Chatham main line, the position could not have been worse so far as traffic for the Kent Coast was concerned since there was no direct access to the line that ran from Brixton to Peckham Rye and gave connections towards the Dartford area. Trains for the Dartford area therefore had to leave the yard and travel towards Holborn Viaduct, stopping at Camberwell to change direction and then gaining access to the Brixton - Peckham line via the spur between Loughborough Junction and Cambria Junction. Propelling the mile between Herne Hill and Camberwell was forbidden and therefore trains had start out of the yard with an engine at either end; the train engine trailing as far as Camberwell. A similar procedure applied for incoming trains and great care to be taken to ensure that pilot engines were standing by at Camberwell in good time.

Access to the yard was similarly awkward for trains arriving on the up main line from the Brixton direction - services from Willesden were a case in point - but for these a concession was given allowing them to reverse into the yard without having to have a second engine. Trains leaving Herne Hill for the Brixton direction also reversed from the yard onto the down main at the Bromley end of the passenger station where they changed direction and proceeded normally.

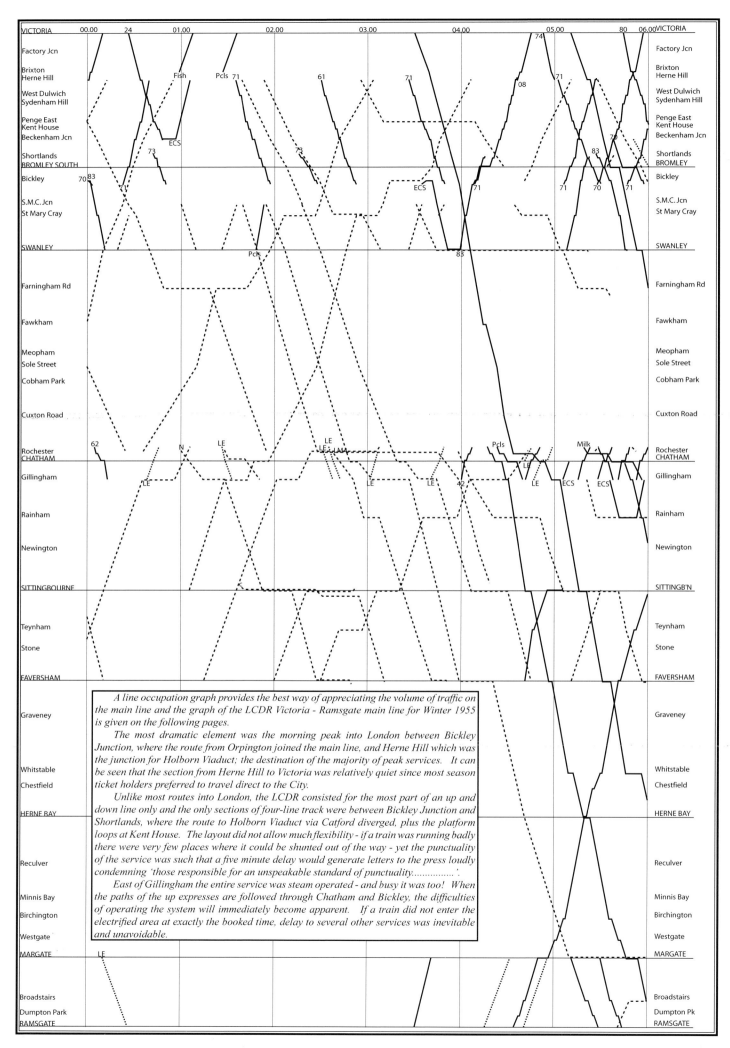

A line occupation graph provides the best way of appreciating the volume of traffic on the main line and the graph of the LCDR Victoria - Ramsgate main line for Winter 1955 is given on the following pages.

The most dramatic element was the morning peak into London between Bickley Junction, where the route from Orpington joined the main line, and Herne Hill which was the junction for Holborn Viaduct; the destination of the majority of peak services. It can be seen that the section from Herne Hill to Victoria was relatively quiet since most season ticket holders preferred to travel direct to the City.

Unlike most routes into London, the LCDR consisted for the most part of an up and down line only and the only sections of four-line track were between Bickley Junction and Shortlands, where the route to Holborn Viaduct via Catford diverged, plus the platform loops at Kent House. The layout did not allow much flexibility - if a train was running badly there were very few places where it could be shunted out of the way - yet the punctuality of the service was such that a five minute delay would generate letters to the press loudly condemning 'those responsible for an unspeakable standard of punctuality................'.

East of Gillingham the entire service was steam operated - and busy it was too! When the paths of the up expresses are followed through Chatham and Bickley, the difficulties of operating the system will immediately become apparent. If a train did not enter the electrified area at exactly the booked time, delay to several other services was inevitable and unavoidable.

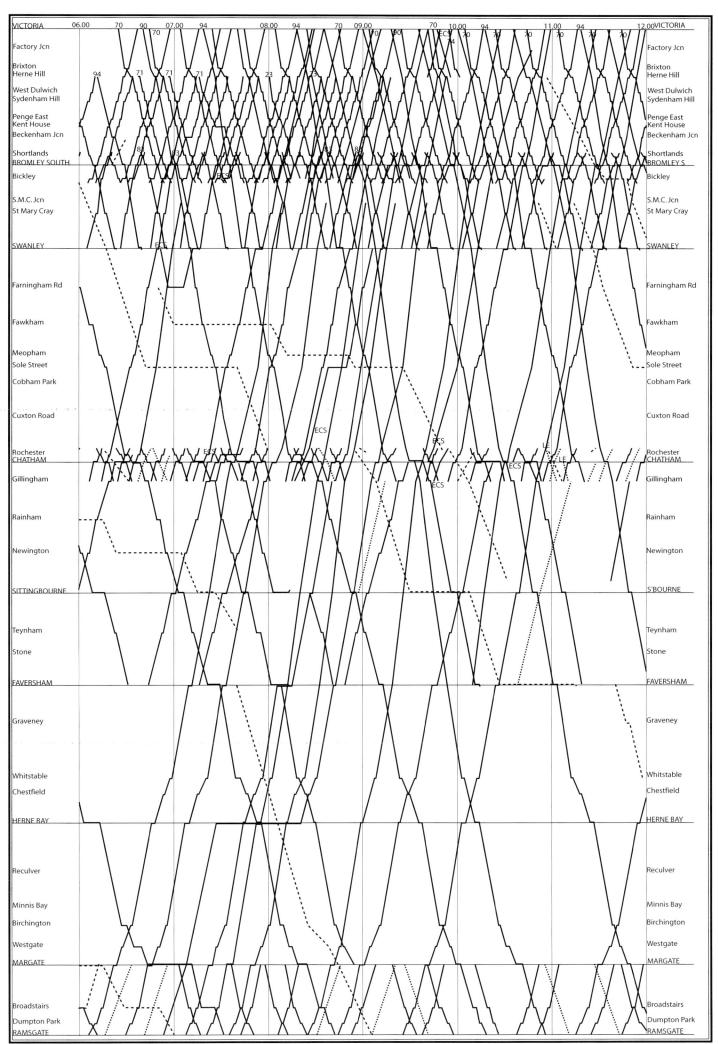

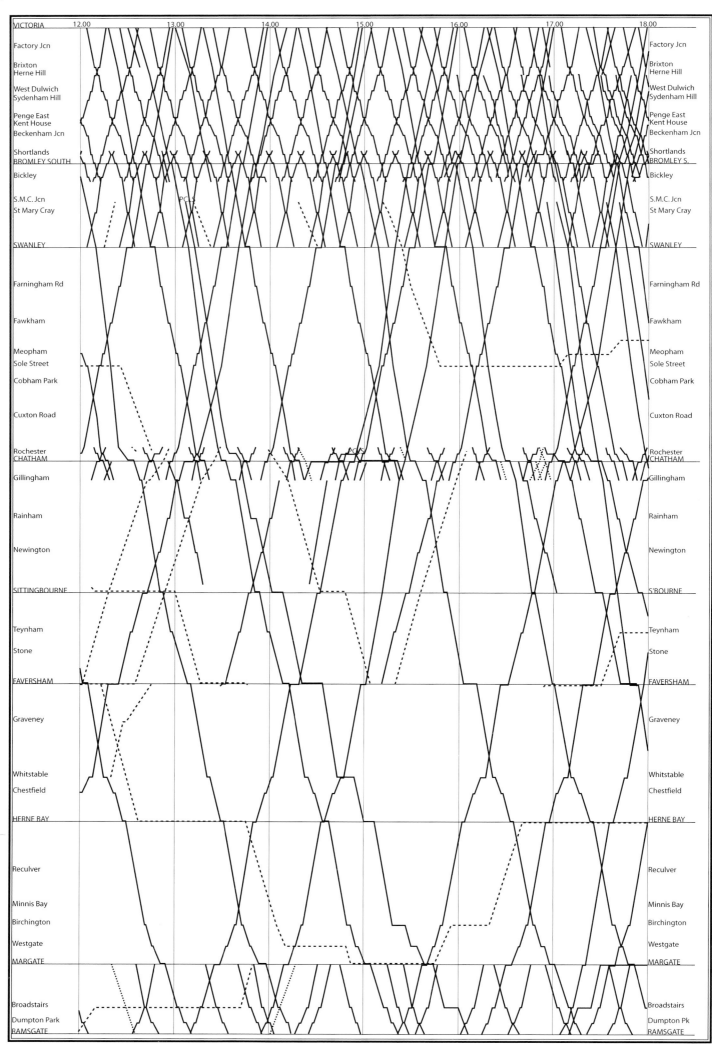

VICTORIA
Factory Jcn
Brixton
Herne Hill
West Dulwich
Sydenham Hill
Penge East
Kent House
Beckenham Jcn
Shortlands
BROMLEY SOUTH
Bickley
S.M.C. Jcn
St Mary Cray
SWANLEY
Farningham Rd
Fawkham
Meopham
Sole Street
Cobham Park
Cuxton Road
Rochester
CHATHAM
Gillingham
Rainham
Newington
SITTINGBOURNE
Teynham
Stone
FAVERSHAM
Graveney
Whitstable
Chestfield
HERNE BAY
Reculver
Minnis Bay
Birchington
Westgate
MARGATE
Broadstairs
Dumpton Park
RAMSGATE

12.00 13.00 14.00 15.00 16.00 17.00 18.00

PCS

PCS

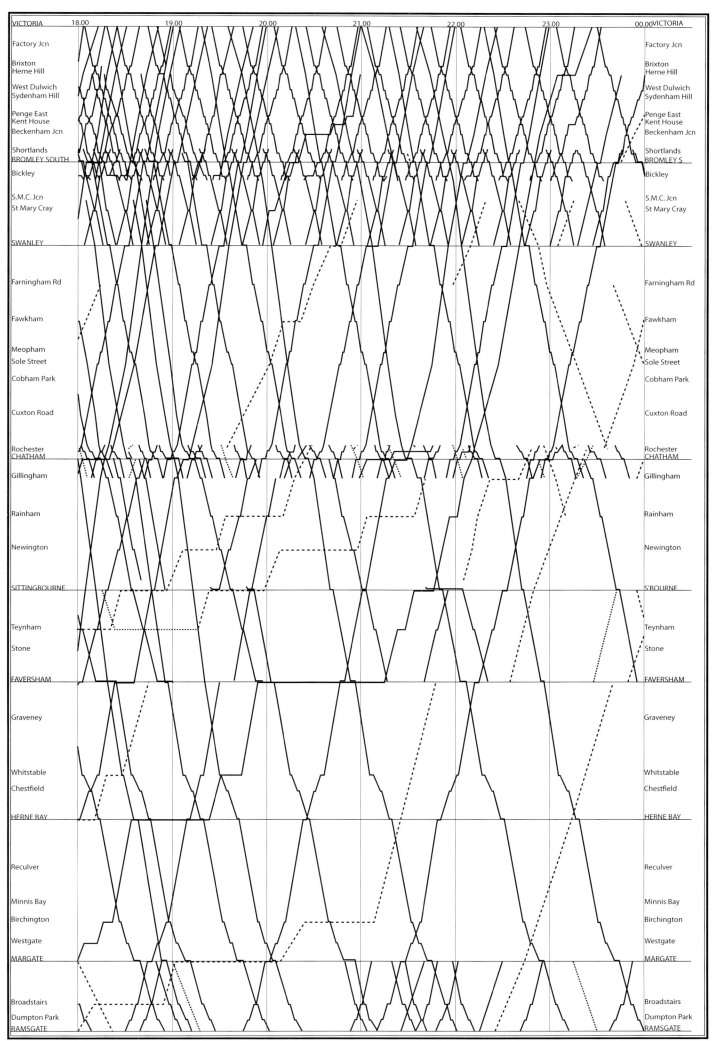

VICTORIA

Factory Jcn

Brixton
Herne Hill

West Dulwich
Sydenham Hill

Penge East
Kent House
Beckenham Jcn

Shortlands
BROMLEY SOUTH

Bickley

S.M.C. Jcn
St Mary Cray

SWANLEY

Farningham Rd

Fawkham

Meopham
Sole Street

Cobham Park

Cuxton Road

Rochester
CHATHAM

Gillingham

Rainham

Newington

SITTINGBOURNE

Teynham

Stone

FAVERSHAM

Graveney

Whitstable
Chestfield

HERNE BAY

Reculver

Minnis Bay
Birchington

Westgate

MARGATE

Broadstairs
Dumpton Park
RAMSGATE

18.00   19.00   20.00   21.00   22.00   23.00   00.00 VICTORIA

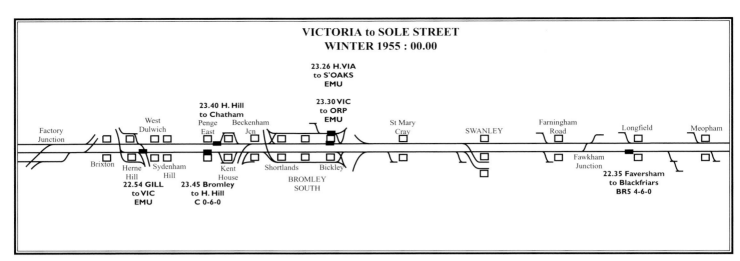

VICTORIA to SOLE STREET
WINTER 1955 : 00.00

23.26 H.VIA to S'OAKS EMU

23.40 H. Hill to Chatham

23.30 VIC to ORP EMU

Factory Junction · West Dulwich · Penge East · Beckenham Jcn · St Mary Cray · SWANLEY · Farningham Road · Longfield · Meopham

Brixton · Herne Hill · Sydenham Hill · Kent House · Shortlands · Bickley · Fawkham Junction

22.54 GILL to VIC EMU

23.45 Bromley to H. Hill C 0-6-0

BROMLEY SOUTH

22.35 Faversham to Blackfriars BR5 4-6-0

CONTROLLER'S LOG: The Chatham is not a railway that understands moderation - either the line is running to the very limits of its capacity or else it is all but moribund. At the moment the latter state applies and even the normally frenetic inner-suburban area is very quiet. The lull in traffic gives an opportunity to reflect on the nature of the route and to marvel, perhaps, at the fact that the traffic conveyed by

the Holborn Viaduct route via Bellingham, rejoining the main line at Shortlands Junction. Since traffic can be as heavy from Holborn Viaduct as it is from Victoria - and is of an all-stations nature - diverting services in this way is very much a last resort. For obvious reasons the volume of goods traffic west of St Mary Cray is low and most goods traffic from the coast either leaves the main line for Hither

Beyond the London area three London-bound goods services with fruits, hops and general goods take advantage of the lull in passenger traffic as they rattle through Longfield, Rochester and Teynham. In the opposite direction a Dover-based 2-6-0 shakes a few windows as it gets hold of its train of empties for Shepherdswell Colliery.

Steam-hauled passenger services are almost

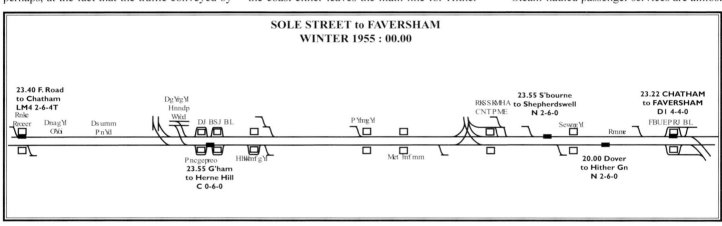

SOLE STREET to FAVERSHAM
WINTER 1955 : 00.00

23.40 F. Road to Chatham LM4 2-6-4T

23.55 S'bourne to Shepherdswell N 2-6-0

23.22 CHATHAM to FAVERSHAM D1 4-4-0

23.55 G'ham to Herne Hill C 0-6-0

20.00 Dover to Hither Gn N 2-6-0

one of London's busiest routes is done so with virtually no help from quadrupling - indeed the only four-tracked section is the two and a quarter mile length between Shortlands and Bickley Junction. All other traffic has to be conducted over an up and down line - no mean feat when one considers that a wide range of traffic from all-stations locals to boat trains and Ramsgate expresses has to be worked over the same track. At extremely difficult times a handful of expresses are booked to take the branch at Brixton - the Catford loop - and use

Green at St Mary Cray Junction or runs via Hoo Junction and Dartford.

The two down trains at Bickley demonstrate very clearly one of the advantages of the four-line section; the 23.26 Holborn Viaduct having run down the slow line from Shortlands, leaving the main line clear for the 23.30 from Victoria. Both trains are able to receive a clear run as far as Bickley Junction where the Victoria service will diverge for Orpington, the 23.26 continuing down the main line for Swanley and the Maidstone branch.

non-existent and those that can be seen have all completed their journeys. Of particular interest is the last of the Victoria trains which is just running into Ramsgate behind a light Pacific which is finishing a working that has taken the engine to no less than three London termini. The engine started the day with the 07.20 Ramsgate to Cannon Street via Chatham but - unusually - returned via Ashford with the 11.15 from Charing Cross. Later in the day it worked to Victoria with the 17.05 Pullman, returning after a quick turn-round with the 21.35.

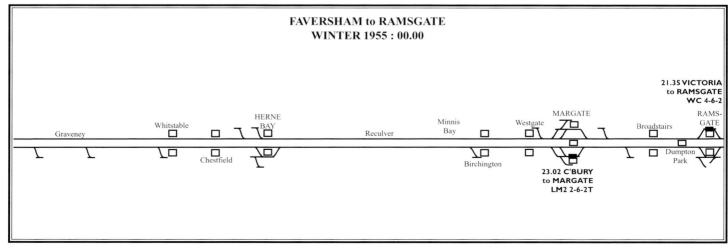

FAVERSHAM to RAMSGATE
WINTER 1955 : 00.00

21.35 VICTORIA to RAMSGATE WC 4-6-2

Graveney · Whitstable · HERNE BAY · Reculver · Minnis Bay · Westgate · MARGATE · Broadstairs · RAMSGATE

Chestfield · Birchington · Dumpton Park

23.02 C'BURY to MARGATE LM2 2-6-2T

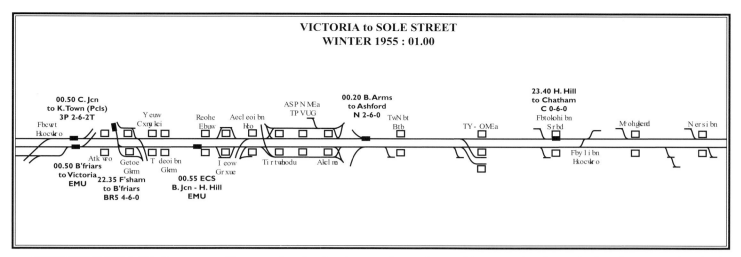

VICTORIA to SOLE STREET
WINTER 1955 : 01.00

00.50 C. Jcn
to K. Town (Pcls)
3P 2-6-2T

23.40 H. Hill
to Chatham
C 0-6-0

00.20 B. Arms
to Ashford
N 2-6-0

00.50 B'friars
to Victoria
EMU

22.35 F'sham
to B'friars
BR5 4-6-0

00.55 ECS
B. Jcn - H. Hill
EMU

CONTROLLER'S LOG: Passenger traffic has now ceased altogether and the only reminder to be seen is a train of empty stock on its way to berth at Herne Hill after working the 00.25 Victoria to Beckenham Junction. Thereafter and until the morning peak starts, the only passenger services to be seen will be an hourly standing by for about an hour after working the 23.48 goods trip from Blackfriars while the 4-6-0 will run light to Stewarts Lane yard and work the 01.55 milk to Victoria and, after a visit to Stewarts Lane loco, the 03.30 Victoria to Ramsgate News.

This is not the only engine-change that has

Another train that changes engines is the 18.50 Dover to Hoo Junction which is on the point of leaving Faversham. The Dover N 2-6-0 will work as far as Gillingham where it will be replaced by a Gillingham-based engine of the same class. The Dover 2-6-0 will turn on Gillingham loco and return east with the 03.58

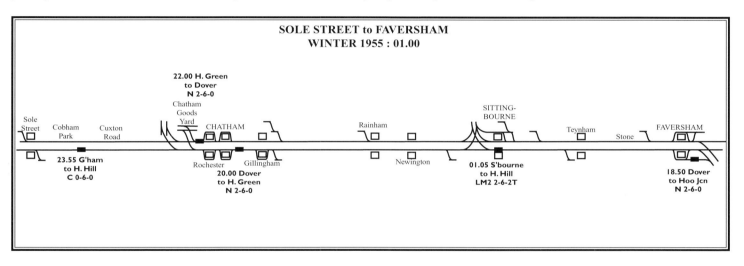

SOLE STREET to FAVERSHAM
WINTER 1955 : 01.00

22.00 H. Green
to Dover
N 2-6-0

Chatham
Goods
Yard

CHATHAM

SITTING-
BOURNE

Sole
Street

Cobham
Park

Cuxton
Road

Rainham

Teynham

FAVERSHAM

Stone

23.55 G'ham
to H. Hill
C 0-6-0

Rochester

20.00 Dover
to H. Green
N 2-6-0

Gillingham

Newington

01.05 S'bourne
to H. Hill
LM2 2-6-2T

18.50 Dover
to Hoo Jcn
N 2-6-0

departure in the down direction only between Holborn Viaduct or Blackfriars and Orpington. Victoria is very quiet and no movement of any consequence will take place until the departure of the 03.30 Ramsgate news.

There are quiet a few goods trains on the run and one that has to be watched fairly closely is the 22.35 ex Faversham to Blackfriars (actually a continuation of the 18.00 from Ramsgate) which is arriving at Herne Hill where its 5MT 4-6-0 gives way to a C 0-6-0. The latter has been

to be monitored and within half an hour an E1 4-4-0 engine will ring off Gillingham loco to take over the 01.05 Sittingbourne - Herne Hill goods which is about to start its journey and is worked by an LMS 2MT 2-6-2T for the first ten miles of its journey. Both are unusual engines to find on a main-line goods service and the 4-4-0 especially so. The latter is based at Stewarts Lane and spent the day on East Kent passenger trains after arriving in the area with the 05.50 Cannon Street - Dover Priory.

Chatham - Deal via Ramsgate.

Although N class 2-6-0's are the favoured engines for most express goods work, the older C 0-6-0's continue to turn the clock back. The 23.40 Herne Hill to Chatham, now shunting at Farningham Road, is booked for one of the class while the 23.55 Gillingham to Herne Hill is booked to another. The trains are not related however since the up service is worked by a Stewarts Lane engine, a Gillingham 0-6-0 working the down.

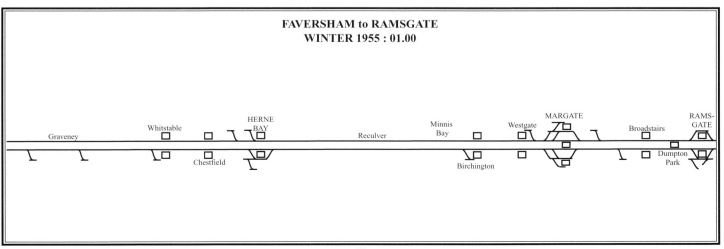

FAVERSHAM to RAMSGATE
WINTER 1955 : 01.00

Graveney

Whitstable

HERNE
BAY

Reculver

Minnis
Bay

Westgate

MARGATE

Broadstairs

RAMS-
GATE

Chestfield

Birchington

Dumpton
Park

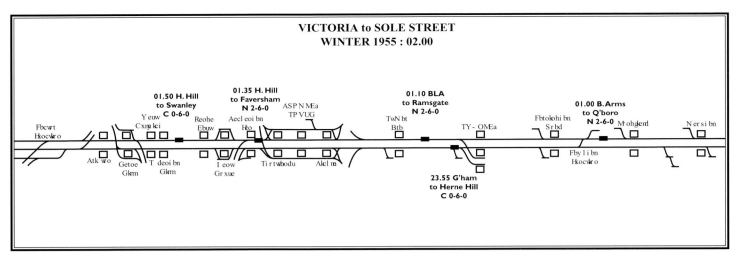

VICTORIA to SOLE STREET
WINTER 1955 : 02.00

CONTROLLER'S LOG: For a moment the main line has quite an Edwardian atmosphere to it, especially in the Rochester area as a class C 0-6-0 wheels the 23.40 Herne Hill goods into the yard whilst an E1 4-4-0 trundles the 01.05 ex Sittingbourne over the Medway bridge and prepares for the seven mile climb at 1 in 142 to the North Down summit at Sole Street. Further

the train at both Queenborough and Sheerness Dockyard before working the 07.55 passenger to Sittingbourne. (This for up road passengers is rather a timeless journey with the branch train being worked by a C 0-6-0 while the main line connection is booked to an L 4-4-0).

The more modern face of the Chatham is represented by the N class 2-6-0's, a trio of

trains are worked by Bricklayers Arms' engines, neither of which works through to destination. The Queenborough train will be re-engined at Chatham and taken over by a C 0-6-0 whilst the N 2-6-0 of the Ramsgate service will be replaced at Faversham by a U1 2-6-0.

Two other N 2-6-0's can be seen at work on the up road: one getting ready to leave

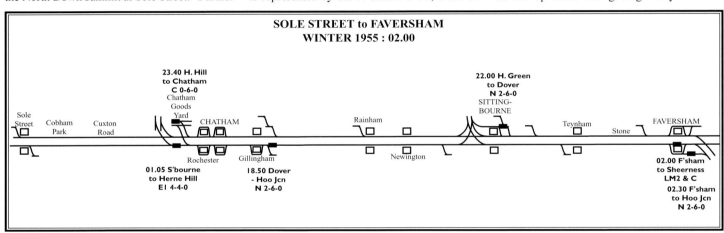

SOLE STREET to FAVERSHAM
WINTER 1955 : 02.00

south two more class C's are at work; one near Swanley with the 23.55 Gillingham to Herne Hill - a service which returns empty milk churns to the West via London - and the other with the 01.50 Herne Hill to Swanley and Chatham.

At Faversham, the curious combination of a Class C 0-6-0 and an LMS 2MT 2-6-2T gets the Sheerness goods away from the yard and on the move. The 0-6-0 is the train engine but the 2-6-2 will assist as far as Queenborough after which it will return light to Sittingbourne for the 05.05 Sheerness passenger. The 0-6-0 will shunt

which are romping through the outer suburbs with trains for Queenborough, Ramsgate and Faversham. Neither of the leading pair of trains have originated on the section but have come from Bricklayers Arms via the SER main line, joining the Chatham at St Mary Cray. Both are the nearest the Southern comes to an express goods train - the SR system of goods train operation is much less complex than that of other parts of BR - having a fitted head of three and six wagons respectively. The 2-6-0's concerned are comparative strangers since both

Faversham for Hoo Junction, Gravesend whilst the other is slowing up for Gillingham where the incoming Dover-based 2-6-0 will be exchanged for another from Gillingham shed.

Hoo Junction is a fairly large marshalling Yard five miles from Chatham on the North Kent line and is the focal point for traffic to the heavily industrialised area between Gravesend and London and for the LSWR and GWR via Maidstone, Paddock Wood, Tonbridge and Redhill. Much of the work at Hoo Junction was covered by Gillingham engines and men.

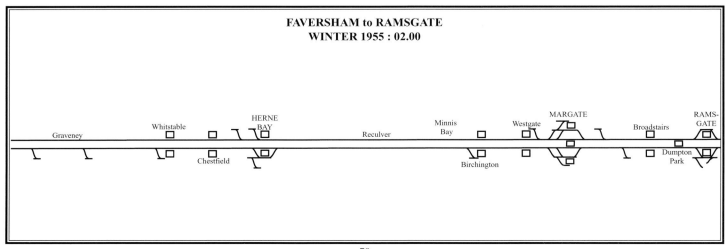

FAVERSHAM to RAMSGATE
WINTER 1955 : 02.00

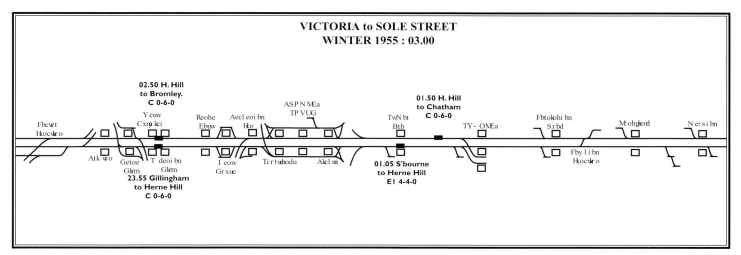

VICTORIA to SOLE STREET
WINTER 1955 : 03.00

CONTROLLER'S LOG: If the SECR atmosphere was strong an hour ago, it is now almost complete, at least in the suburban area where traffic is being conducted by a trio of class C 0-6-0 and an E1 4-4-0. The latter re-engined the 01.05 Sittingbourne to Herne Hill goods at Gillingham, taking the train over from an LMS 2MT 2-6-2T. It is not the type of service that a 4-4-0 would be expected to work but the train is light and consists for the most part of vans from Gillingham containing empty milk churns. The engine is one of four allocated to Stewarts Lane and used on diagrams that operate on the heavily restricted lines at Holborn Viaduct. Their passenger work is largely confined to early morning services from Cannon Street to Ramsgate via Dartford and stopping trains east of Faversham but on Saturdays it is possible to have a run behind a member of the class

over the LCDR main line; the engine that on weekdays would work the 01.05 Sittingbourne goods returning to London on the 14.02 Dover to Victoria express.

Outside the suburban area, the SECR influence is less marked and a high proportion of the very respectable number of goods trains at work are handled by N 2-6-0's, the odd-men-out being a class C and an LM 4MT 2-6-4T.

Five of the LMS 2-6-4 tanks are based at Dover and are used mainly on the Ramsgate - Deal - Dover - Maidstone axis. Some work between Dover and Faversham but the example seen above is the only instance of the class working up the main line. The engine worked in with the 17.09 Dover Priory to Chatham stopping passenger before running light to Farningham Road for the 23.40 goods to Chatham. Its last duty before returning to Dover was to re-engine

the 00.40 Snodland - Snowdown at Strood; an unusual task for a passenger tank but not, since the train consisted of mineral empties, unduly onerous.

In addition to monitoring the progress of these services and liaising as necessary with the yards, the most important duty at this time of morning is to ensure that all the booked multiple units are in place at stations such as Swanley and Gillingham. More often than not many of the final services of the day terminate with four instead of eight coaches - thanks to the vagaries of the day - and the highest priority is given to running empty units to make good the shortfall and ensure that services commence their workings with the correct formations. At this time of night therefore it is quite normal to see unscheduled empty carriage movements being moved at high speed around the district.

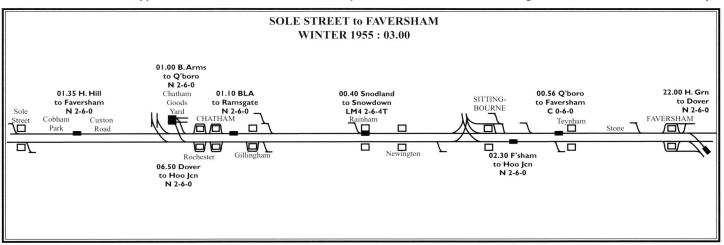

SOLE STREET to FAVERSHAM
WINTER 1955 : 03.00

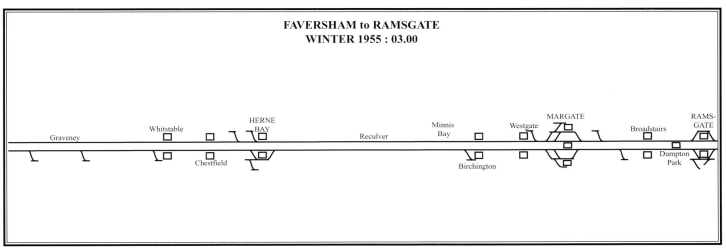

FAVERSHAM to RAMSGATE
WINTER 1955 : 03.00

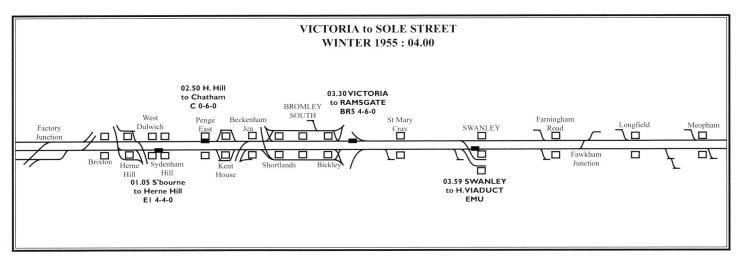

VICTORIA to SOLE STREET
WINTER 1955 : 04.00

CONTROLLER'S LOG: For the first time for some hours there are stirrings in Thanet as an L 4-4-0 works between Ramsgate and Margate with the 23.50 from London Bridge via Canterbury West - the nearest thing to a overnight train in these parts. It is an interesting service worth losing a night's sleep for since it uses the old route via Redhill and Edenbridge before joining the SECR main line at Tonbridge. Motive power for the greater part of the journey

it continues to act as an overlap between the SER and the LCDR. The latter's trains from Victoria terminate at Ramsgate while South Eastern services from Charing Cross via both Canterbury West and Dover continue forward to Margate giving Thanet the benefit of two main lines and an extraordinary variety of both trains and engines.

The first of the near-hourly Victoria - Ramsgate trains can be seen speeding through

no more than the 160 miles of a return trip to Ramsgate plus a modicum of empty stock work between Victoria and Stewarts Lane. Of the remaining two engines, one works a night goods between Battersea and Three Bridges - a rare instance of a LCDR engine covering an LBSCR duty - whilst the other does a double trip to Ramsgate, working the 03.30 and 15.35 departures from Ramsgate. Not infrequently, however, an eight engine is sent out for the

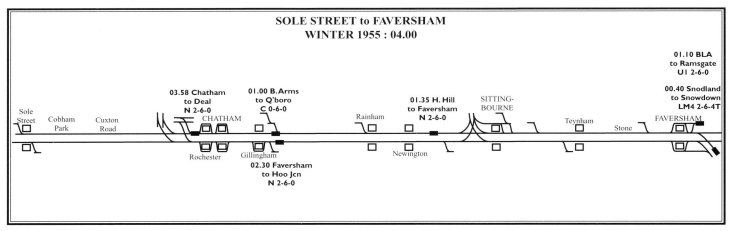

SOLE STREET to FAVERSHAM
WINTER 1955 : 04.00

is provided by an Ashford King Arthur 4-6-0 but at Ashford the train divides, the main portion and its N15 running to Deal via Folkestone and Dover while the Thanet section is worked forward by an Ashford 4-4-0. On reaching Margate the 4-4-0 spends several hours as the station pilot before working home with the 07.58 Margate to Hastings.

One of the more interesting points about the line between Ramsgate and Margate is that

the outer suburbs behind one of the new BR Standard 5MT 4-6-0's that have recently taken over from the King Arthur N15's. Stewarts Lane loco has the responsibility for covering most of the Victoria - Ramsgate services and is required to turn out seven 4-6-0's for the workings. It would be pleasing to report that the cost of the new engines has been repaid by an increase in engine miles but the sad truth is that the daily work of five of the seven engines amounts to

second part of the diagram. Criticisms concerning apparently poor mileages have to be balanced by the reflection that spare capacity has to be built in to the diagrams in order to allow for the special traffic requirements of the summer months. The volume of this additional traffic can be gauged from the fact that Stewarts Lane has an allocation of nineteen West Country light Pacifics - none of which has any regular winter work!

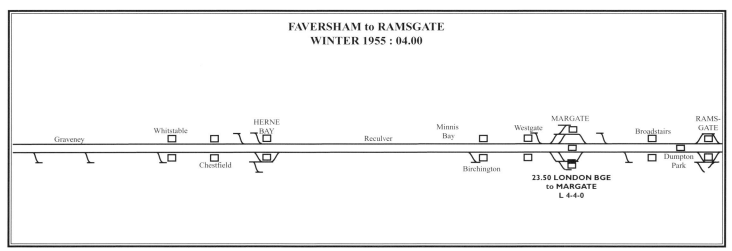

FAVERSHAM to RAMSGATE
WINTER 1955 : 04.00

London services fell into two categories: one being the (roughly) hourly service between Victoria and Ramsgate and the other being the business expresses which operated between Ramsgate and Cannon Street and left the LCDR at St Mary Cray Junction to complete their journeys over the South Eastern main line. The latter service, which operated during the peak only, was based upon Ramsgate and was dominated by West Country Pacifics whilst the Victoria service, based on London, was handled for the most part by the BR Standard 5MT 4-6-0's that had replaced the King Arthur 4-6-0's from 1955. The utilisation of the Stewarts Lane 4-6-0's was not high and few of the engines involved achieved much more than a 160-mile return trip to Ramsgate. This low daily mileage did however ensure that the engines were available for additional work during the summer peak. Under normal circumstances the BR 5MT engines did not work between Faversham and Dover but 73089 of Stewarts Lane was seen at the Dover coaling stage prior to returning to London with an additional boat train. (L.G. Marshall)

Dieselisation of the Charing Cross - Hastings resulted in a number of Bricklayers Arms Schools 4-4-0's being dispersed to other sheds in the South-East; one of the engines effected being 30938 'St Olave's' which moved to Stewarts Lane in May 1958 and is seen entering Whitstable with the 12.35 Victoria to Ramsgate on Monday 18th August 1958. This service was normally covered by a BR Standard 5MT 4-6-0 and was an unusual duty for a 4-4-0 since the return working was on the evening Ramsgate - Blackfriars goods service. The goods loading permitted for a Schools 4-4-0 was less than that of the booked 4-6-0. (N.K. Harrop)

Stewarts Lane and Ramsgate sheds were given significant numbers of Pacifics; the former for working the Continental Boat trains during the summer and the latter the business trains between Ramsgate and London via Chatham together with the SER expresses from Margate to Charing Cross via Deal. To describe the years in which unrebuilt Pacifics were allocated to Ramsgate as a difficult time would be an understatement and by the late 1950's matters had reached such a low point that half the Ramsgate allocation had to be transferred to Bricklayers Arms in order to make inroads into the arrears of maintenance whilst the remaining locomotives were exchanged for rebuilds. Above, One of the first rebuilt Light Pacifics to operate from Bricklayers Arms was 34003 'Plymouth', seen arriving at Gillingham in June 1959 with a Victoria to Ramsgate express. Below, Two months after being rebuilt, the original modified Light Pacific, 34005 'Barnstaple' runs through Sittingbourne with a Dover to Victoria express in August 1957. (L.G. Marshall)

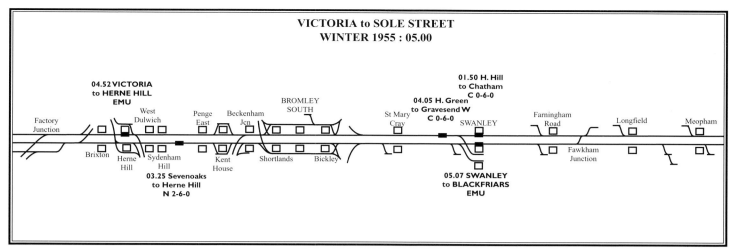

VICTORIA to SOLE STREET
WINTER 1955 : 05.00

CONTROLLER'S LOG: Having got the stock in the correct places for the commencement of the peak, now comes the nail-biting time of waiting for drivers and guards to sign on punctually. In theory there are sufficient spare crews to cover any eventualities but in practice the spare turns can often be reduced by leave, vacancies and sickness making life very difficult if someone fails to take duty. In the absence of a spare man, crews will be 'moved up' - ie persuaded to work the train that precedes theirs - the process continuing until a spare man can be found who can be slotted into the working. Such off-the-cuff manoeuvres are not too difficult (with a little practice) at places such as Gillingham where there is a large compliment of men but at smaller locations such as Swanley, which has three starting turns, it requires some presence of mind if an attack of last-minute sickness is not to be translated into a late-running service.

There are some interesting trains to be seen in East Kent, not the least of which is the service that has just pulled away from Faversham. This is one of the few services between London and the coast diagrammed to a pre-grouping 4-4-0, the engine - rather confusingly - being a Stewarts Lane E1 4-4-0, outbased at Gillingham. D, D1, E and E1 4-4-0's were permitted into Holborn Viaduct but the L1 4-4-0's, the only 4-4-0's allocated to Gillingham at the time, were not and thus it arose that a Gillingham diagram came to be worked by a Stewarts Lane engine. The E1 concerned works the 20.59 Gillingham - Cannon Street Parcels, the 03.00 Holborn Viaduct to Ramsgate and the 08.44 Ramsgate to Chatham, the engine being changed by Stewarts Lane at the weekends.

The first LCDR service to leave Thanet can be seen approaching Birchington and this too is a 4-4-0 duty, worked by a Ramsgate L 4-4-0 and known, familiarly if irreverently by passengers and staff the length and breadth of the system as the 'Jew's Express' since the commercial travellers who used it could get a reduced rate fare to London.

Since the arrival of the third-rail in the Medway in 1938, 0-4-4 tanks have rather faded from the main line although one engine spends some time during the morning working in stages between Chatham and Sittingbourne - a pleasant reminder of days past. The engine concerned has arrived in Gillingham with the News from Strood and, having exchange its stock for a push and pull set, is waiting to go forward with the 05.35 empty passenger to Rainham to form the 05.52 back to Gillingham..

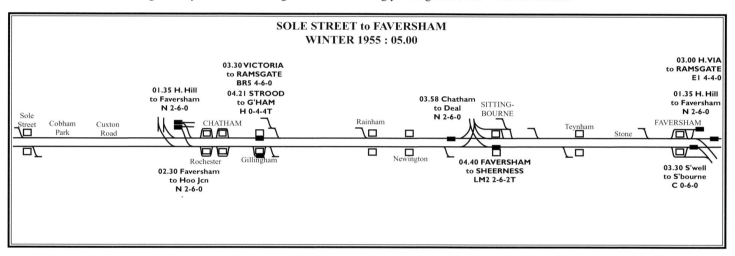

SOLE STREET to FAVERSHAM
WINTER 1955 : 05.00

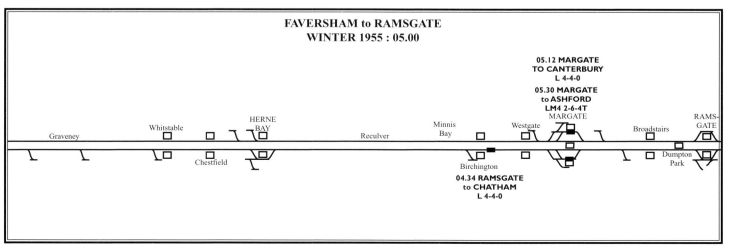

FAVERSHAM to RAMSGATE
WINTER 1955 : 05.00

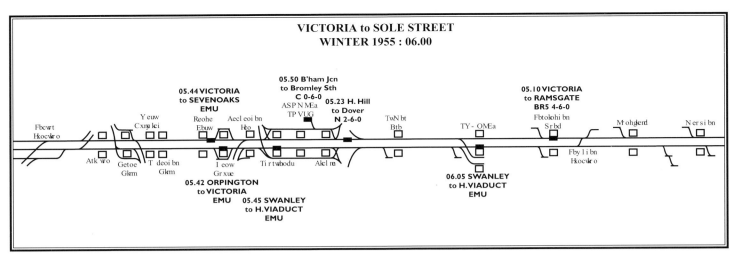

VICTORIA to SOLE STREET
WINTER 1955 : 06.00

05.44 VICTORIA to SEVENOAKS EMU

05.50 B'ham Jcn to Bromley Sth C 0-6-0

05.23 H. Hill to Dover N 2-6-0

05.10 VICTORIA to RAMSGATE BR5 4-6-0

ASP N MEa TP VUG

05.42 ORPINGTON to VICTORIA EMU

05.45 SWANLEY to H.VIADUCT EMU

06.05 SWANLEY to H.VIADUCT EMU

CONTROLLER'S LOG: With the morning peak about to erupt, having made sure that all the component parts are in their proper places, a check has to be made to ensure that any lagging goods trains are placed out of harms way - which usually means sticking the train in the nearest yard or siding and sending the engine and crew to wherever they need to be for their next working. On a good day, all

Attention must be turned to Ramsgate which has woken from its slumbers and is now like a coiled spring, straining to unwind. In the next hour and a half no less than five business expresses for Cannon Street will be despatched plus one stopping train for Gillingham. The users of these services include the wealthier and more vociferous element of the season ticket

to Deal and Ashford. We have to make sure that the stock is in the right place and that the engines are ringing off shed at the booked times. Two Pacifics and their Cannon Street expresses are lined in the up side platforms while the 03.00 ex Holborn Viaduct, with its E1 4-4-0, passes the Ashford - Margate goods at Broadstairs. The latter should just about clear the line at Margate as the 06.06 Ramsgate to Cannon Street reaches

---

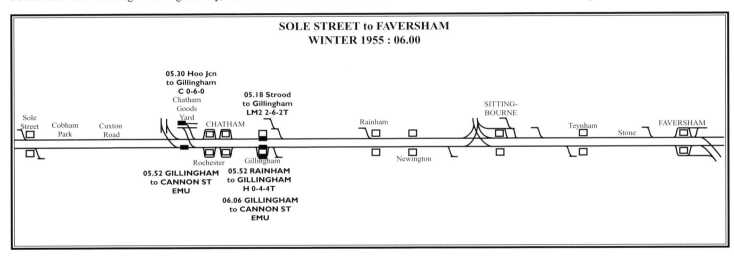

SOLE STREET to FAVERSHAM
WINTER 1955 : 06.00

05.30 Hoo Jcn to Gillingham C 0-6-0

Chatham Goods Yard

05.18 Strood to Gillingham LM2 2-6-2T

Sole Street — Cobham Park — Cuxton Road — CHATHAM — Rochester — Gillingham — Rainham — Newington — SITTING-BOURNE — Teynham — Stone — FAVERSHAM

05.52 GILLINGHAM to CANNON ST EMU

05.52 RAINHAM to GILLINGHAM H 0-4-4T

06.06 GILLINGHAM to CANNON ST EMU

---

the up trains should all be home and dried by six - the whipper-in being a train of Sittingbourne coal from Snowdown colliery - leaving just a few on the down road to keep an eye on. The 05.23 Herne Hill to Ramsgate is following the 05.10 Victoria - Ramsgate express and will go inside at Sole Street. A C 0-6-0 is shunting at Farningham Road and will emerge in just under an hour with the 06.50 stopping goods to Gillingham. Neither should give much cause for concern.

milieu and it is fair to assume that some of them carry some influence in high places. It does not do, therefore, to mess around with their trains. The engines used for these trains are varied and while West Country Pacifics work the bulk of the Cannon Street trains, one (which runs empty to Herne Bay) is diagrammed to a Schools 4-4-0 while the Gillingham stopper is given an L 4-4-0. On top of this is all the SECR traffic moving the other way from Margate through Ramsgate

Dumpton Park.

Ancient and modern rub shoulders in the Medway area as an H 0-4-4T tank runs into Gillingham with the 05.52 push and pull from Rainham and connects with a Cannon Street electric. Similarly at Teynham and Sittingbourne, ultra-modern LMS 2-6-2 tanks keep company with a pair of C 0-6-0's and the L 4-4-0 of the 04.34 ex Ramsgate. How would the now-defunct Leader have fitted into all this?

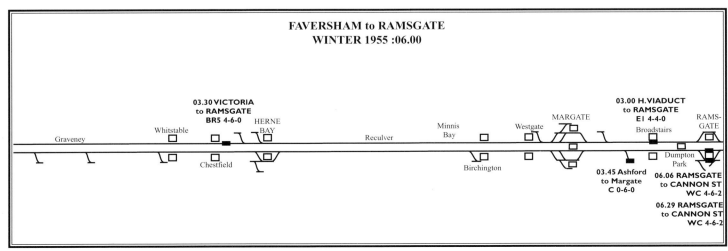

FAVERSHAM to RAMSGATE
WINTER 1955 :06.00

03.30 VICTORIA to RAMSGATE BR5 4-6-0

03.00 H.VIADUCT to RAMSGATE E1 4-4-0

Graveney — Whitstable — Chestfield — HERNE BAY — Reculver — Minnis Bay — Birchington — Westgate — MARGATE — Broadstairs — Dumpton Park — RAMS-GATE

03.45 Ashford to Margate C 0-6-0

06.06 RAMSGATE to CANNON ST WC 4-6-2

06.29 RAMSGATE to CANNON ST WC 4-6-2

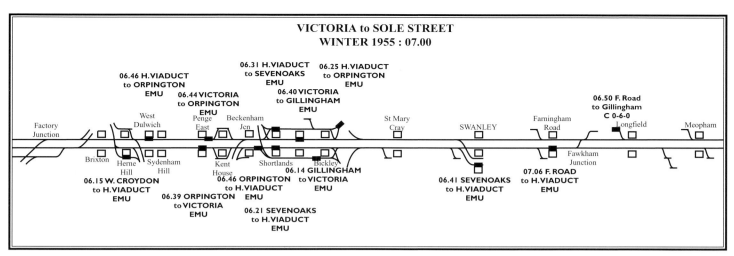

VICTORIA to SOLE STREET
WINTER 1955 : 07.00

06.46 H.VIADUCT to ORPINGTON EMU
06.31 H.VIADUCT to SEVENOAKS EMU
06.25 H.VIADUCT to ORPINGTON EMU
06.44 VICTORIA to ORPINGTON EMU
06.40 VICTORIA to GILLINGHAM EMU
06.50 F. Road to Gillingham C 0-6-0

Factory Junction · West Dulwich · Penge East · Beckenham Jcn · St Mary Cray · SWANLEY · Farningham Road · Longfield · Meopham

Brixton · Herne Hill · Sydenham Hill · Kent House · Shortlands · Bickley · Fawkham Junction

06.15 W. CROYDON to H.VIADUCT EMU
06.14 GILLINGHAM to VICTORIA EMU
06.46 ORPINGTON to H.VIADUCT EMU
06.41 SEVENOAKS to H.VIADUCT EMU
07.06 F. ROAD to H.VIADUCT EMU
06.39 ORPINGTON to VICTORIA EMU
06.21 SEVENOAKS to H.VIADUCT EMU

CONTROLLER'S LOG: As is clearly visible in the suburban area, the floodgates have opened with trains running thick and fast towards London and even though it is only seven in the morning, the frequency of the service is such that the slightest delay to one will almost certainly be felt by several others. One aspect of the peak working that might surprise many unfamiliar with the LCDR is that Victoria plays

49 in Holborn Viaduct. In pregrouping days many of the Ramsgate - Victoria expresses used to detach through coaches for Holborn Viaduct at Herne Hill and since the practice ceased, Holborn Viaduct has tended to disappear from public view.

The concentration of trains is not much less in the Thanet area where everything is steam-worked. Three Cannon Street expresses are on

pair of platform loops, where it can be shunted clear of the up main line. The point is made by the 04.34 ex Ramsgate which terminated in Chatham at 06.22 and had to be run empty to Rochester in order to clear the main line for the stream of electrics leaving Gillingham for the North Kent lines. Rochester is a much quieter location than Chatham and on reaching the slow line, the L 4-4-0 is able to shunt its stock without

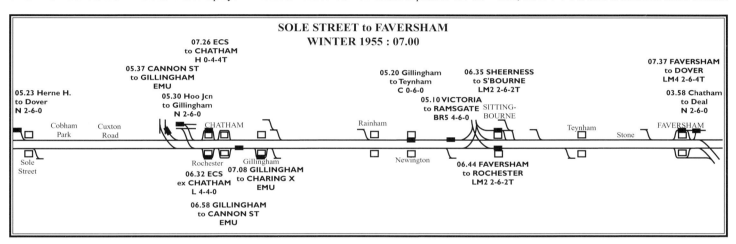

SOLE STREET to FAVERSHAM
WINTER 1955 : 07.00

07.26 ECS to CHATHAM H 0-4-4T
05.37 CANNON ST to GILLINGHAM EMU
05.30 Hoo Jcn to Gillingham N 2-6-0
05.20 Gillingham to Teynham C 0-6-0
06.35 SHEERNESS to S'BOURNE LM2 2-6-2T
07.37 FAVERSHAM to DOVER LM4 2-6-4T
05.23 Herne H. to Dover N 2-6-0
05.10 VICTORIA to RAMSGATE BR5 4-6-0
03.58 Chatham to Deal N 2-6-0

Cobham Park · Cuxton Road · CHATHAM · Rainham · SITTINGBOURNE · Teynham · Stone · FAVERSHAM

Sole Street · Rochester · Gillingham · Newington

06.32 ECS ex CHATHAM L 4-4-0
07.08 GILLINGHAM to CHARING X EMU
06.44 FAVERSHAM to ROCHESTER LM2 2-6-2T
06.58 GILLINGHAM to CANNON ST EMU

a relatively minor role in the rush hour, the bulk of the traffic being directed to Holborn Viaduct which is the line's City Terminus. In fact Blackfriars stations receives almost as many trains as Victoria whilst those from Ramsgate leave the main line at St Mary Cray Junction and run via the South Eastern to Cannon Street. The number of trains arriving in LCDR London termini between 06.00 and 10.00 is eighty-eight (including one express: the Night Ferry) with 19 terminating at Blackfriars, 20 in Victoria and

the move between Ramsgate and Faversham - one runs as empty stock to Herne Bay - while two more wait to depart from Ramsgate station. On the up side at Margate a pair of expresses get ready to leave for London via Ashford.

Although Chatham has a pair of platform loops, the layout is barely sufficient for the service especially since several local trains from the Sittingbourne direction terminate there and the general procedure is for the stock to be worked to Rochester, which also has a

fear of delaying on the main line. The 4-4-0 will eventually run light to Gillingham loco, turn and return east with the Dover portion of the 08.35 Victoria to Ramsgate. The converse also applies and an H class 0-4-4T waits in the down platform loop with the empty stock for the 07.40 Chatham to Sheerness: a curious working in which the 0-4-4T has to run round its train at Sittingbourne.

Ideally, Chatham could do with another platform.

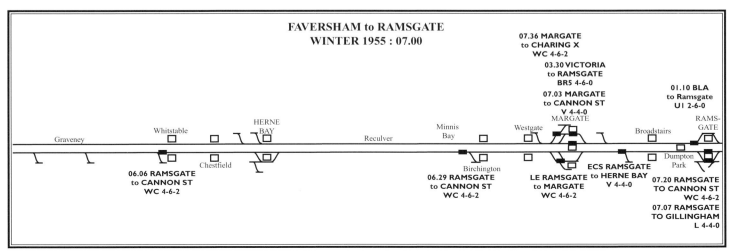

FAVERSHAM to RAMSGATE
WINTER 1955 : 07.00

07.36 MARGATE to CHARING X WC 4-6-2
03.30 VICTORIA to RAMSGATE BR5 4-6-0
07.03 MARGATE to CANNON ST V 4-4-0
01.10 BLA to Ramsgate U1 2-6-0

Graveney · Whitstable · HERNE BAY · Reculver · Minnis Bay · Westgate · MARGATE · Broadstairs · RAMSGATE

Chestfield · Birchington · Dumpton Park

06.06 RAMSGATE to CANNON ST WC 4-6-2
06.29 RAMSGATE to CANNON ST WC 4-6-2
LE RAMSGATE to MARGATE WC 4-6-2
ECS RAMSGATE to HERNE BAY V 4-4-0
07.20 RAMSGATE TO CANNON ST WC 4-6-2
07.07 RAMSGATE TO GILLINGHAM L 4-4-0

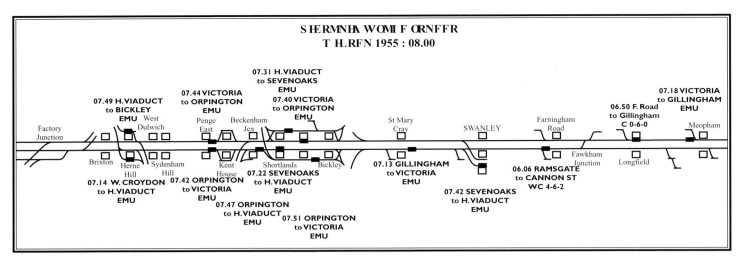

CONTROLLER'S LOG: With so many trains approaching from (and going to) so many points of the compass, it may be wondered how an effective control can be maintained over the service. The simple answer is that most of the control is done before the service gets under way and it is in this respect that the Southern - and the Chatham in particular - differs from most of the other lines entering London. On parts of the jigsaw are in place before the peak commences. Once this has been achieved, a figurative trigger is pulled and for better or worse, trains start running with much depending on the excellent reliability of the multiple units, signalling, driving and the discipline of the passengers themselves. The last mentioned is not to be underestimated since the speed with which passengers join trains and close doors passengers are prepared for the alteration.

Generally, however, if a major fault develops, there is not always a great deal that can be done and one simply has to put up with the frustration of watching the rogue train filtering its way up the line, hoping that the reaction will be minimal. That is the price that has to be paid for running a highly intensive service over a thirty-five mile bottleneck!

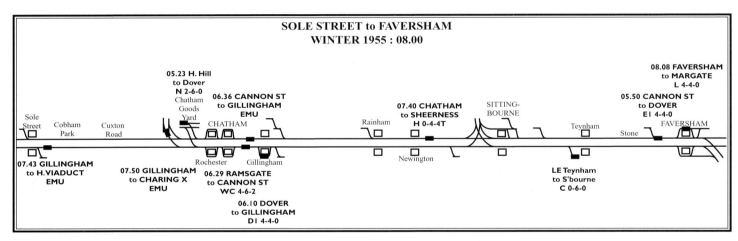

the Great Northern, for example, there are long stretches of four track running with enough time between trains to allow decisions to be taken and implemented yet on the Chatham the density of service - not to mention the paucity of slow lines - simply does not permit the luxury of improvisation. 90% of the success of the Chatham's peak service depends upon everything and everyone being in its correct place before trains start running and it is one of the Controller's function to ensure that all the behind them contributes a great deal to the successful operation of the service. To assist with communications and decision-making, the Peak is watched from each signalbox by an Assistant Station Master who is able not only to use his authority in making instant changes to the service but can communicate the effects locally. If, for example, it is necessary to run a stopping train over the local line instead of the fast between Bickley and Shortlands, he can be left to advise the stations concerned so that

Some help is given by the timetabling which runs trains in flights so that an occasional spare path, very useful for out of course running, exists every fifteen minutes or so.

One train that requires especial monitoring is the 07.20 from Ramsgate which, after leaving Margate, calls only at Herne Bay and Whitstable before running non-stop to Cannon Street. This is the principal express for the commuting *prominenci* of the Kent Coast and a thorn in the side of the Operating Superintendents Office.

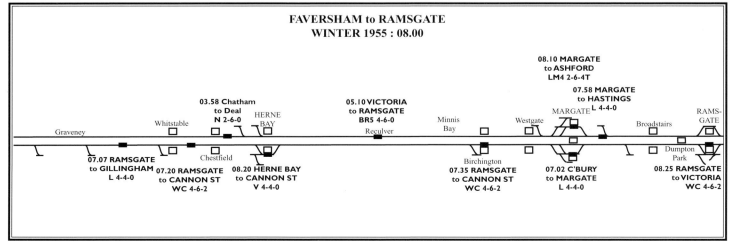

On normal weekdays passenger workings by N 2-6-0's were few and far between with most members of the class being occupied on main line goods services. During the Summer and at weekends especially the picture changed dramatically since the sheer volume of passenger traffic was such that almost anything that could turn a wheel was chalked up for passenger work. Above, 31403 of Ashford - and therefore quite a stranger - approaches Sittingbourne with a Victoria to Ramsgate excursion in August 1957. Below, On the same day 31408 of Stewarts Lane calls with another special; the fireman taking the opportunity to pull some coal forward before the right-away is given. (L.G. Marshall)

The Kent Coast summer was not guaranteed to produce blue skies and sunshine and on a not untypical day of heavy cloud and threatening rain in August 1958, U1 2-6-0 31890 of Bricklayers Arms restarts the 08.58 Blackheath - Ramsgate from Whitstable. 31890 was the prototype 3-cylinder 2-6-4 express tank, A890 'River Frome', built in 1925 but rebuilt as a conventional 2-6-0 in 1928. In its new form 890 was followed by twenty new 3-cylinder U1 2-6-0's (N.K. Harrop)

Although one of the Faversham U1 2-6-0's was booked to work a Cannon Street - Dover business expresses, most 2-6-0 express work came during the summer holidays when traffic was at its heaviest and engines at a premium. U1 2-6-0 31901 (Bricklayers Arms) lifts its valves as it slows to the 30 mph speed restriction at Faversham with an excursion for the Kent Coast in June 1959. (L.G. Marshall)

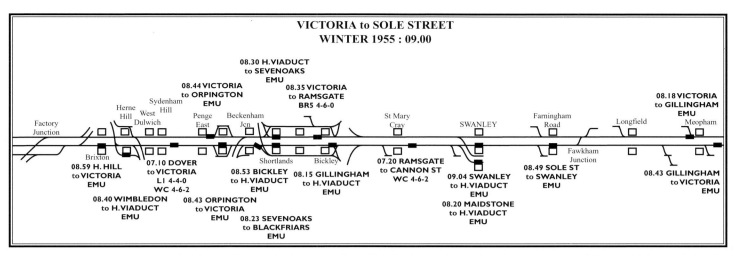

VICTORIA to SOLE STREET
WINTER 1955 : 09.00

08.30 H. VIADUCT to SEVENOAKS EMU
08.44 VICTORIA to ORPINGTON EMU
08.35 VICTORIA to RAMSGATE BR5 4-6-0
08.18 VICTORIA to GILLINGHAM EMU

Factory Junction — Herne Hill — Sydenham Hill — West Dulwich — Penge East — Beckenham Jcn — St Mary Cray — SWANLEY — Farningham Road — Longfield — Meopham

Brixton — Shortlands — Bickley — Fawkham Junction

08.59 H. Hill to VICTORIA EMU
07.10 DOVER to VICTORIA L1 4-4-0 WC 4-6-2
08.53 BICKLEY to H. VIADUCT EMU
08.15 GILLINGHAM to H. VIADUCT EMU
07.20 RAMSGATE to CANNON ST WC 4-6-2
09.04 SWANLEY to H. VIADUCT EMU
08.49 SOLE ST to SWANLEY EMU
08.43 GILLINGHAM to VICTORIA EMU
08.40 WIMBLEDON to H. VIADUCT EMU
08.43 ORPINGTON to VICTORIA EMU
08.23 SEVENOAKS to BLACKFRIARS EMU
08.20 MAIDSTONE to H. VIADUCT EMU

CONTROLLER'S LOG: The focus of attention lies with the up Night Ferry which should be approaching Sydenham Hill and is not the most welcome of visitors to the inner suburban area since the running of the morning peak is challenge enough without the added complication of a steam express being admitted the Catford route from Shortlands Junction and rejoining the main line at Brixton four minutes after the passage of the Ferry. In the event of the Ferry running more than a few minutes behind time at Orpington, priority is usually given to the electric service with the express being held on the branch at Bickley Junction to the Ramsgate trains run fairly regularly, the 08.35 is unique in that the split between the Ramsgate and Dover portions takes place at Chatham, rather than Faversham, with the latter being worked forward by an L class 4-4-0. The provision of through Dover coaches is something of a luxury and in the majority of

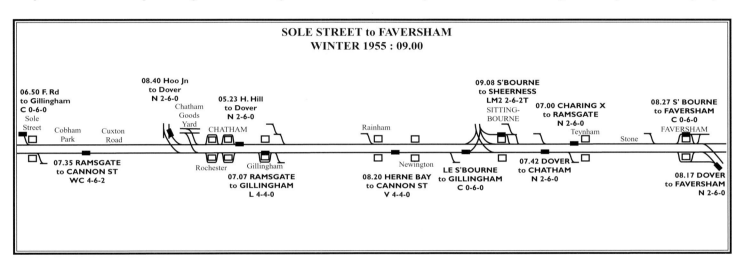

SOLE STREET to FAVERSHAM
WINTER 1955 : 09.00

06.50 F. Rd to Gillingham C 0-6-0
08.40 Hoo Jn to Dover N 2-6-0
05.23 H. Hill to Dover N 2-6-0
09.08 S'BOURNE to SHEERNESS LM2 2-6-2T
07.00 CHARING X to RAMSGATE N 2-6-0
08.27 S' BOURNE to FAVERSHAM C 0-6-0

Sole Street — Cobham Park — Cuxton Road — Chatham Goods Yard — CHATHAM — Rainham — SITTING-BOURNE — Teynham — Stone — FAVERSHAM

Rochester — Gillingham — Newington

07.35 RAMSGATE to CANNON ST WC 4-6-2
07.07 RAMSGATE to GILLINGHAM L 4-4-0
08.20 HERNE BAY to CANNON ST V 4-4-0
LE S'BOURNE to GILLINGHAM C 0-6-0
07.42 DOVER to CHATHAM N 2-6-0
08.17 DOVER to FAVERSHAM N 2-6-0

during the busiest time. To the observer the Night Ferry makes a splendid sight as the unfamiliar blue Wagon-Lits vehicles make their way through South London behind the strange combination of a light Pacific and an L1 4-4-0. The operator takes a more cynical view since the Ferry has to join the route precisely at 08.44 (and a half!) or cause a great deal of delay to the suburban service. As it is, it has a devious path to follow since it takes the slow line from Bickley in order to run neck and neck with the 07.54 Maidstone to Victoria, the latter taking

follow the 08.23 Sevenoaks - Blackfriars. The other up steam express in the area - the 07.20 ex Ramsgate - is less of a problem since it will leave the Chatham main line in a few minutes time when it reaches St Mary Cray Junction. The remainder of its journey will be made over the South Eastern route via Hither Green.

Matters are rather less fraught in the down direction where the first of the Ramsgate day expresses - the 08.35 from Victoria - is climbing away from its call at Bromley South and has a clear run for quite a distance ahead. Although

cases a change at Faversham is required. It is pleasing to see that one of the older 4-4-0's can still be entrusted with express passenger duties.

A small number of Merchant Navy Pacifics - the largest engines on the Southern - have been allocated to the South Eastern for the heavy 09.00 and 10.00 Dover boat trains and the first of these is now pulling away from Victoria, its large Pacific treading rather warily on the 1 in 60 climb to Grosvenor Bridge, happy to let the ex-LBSCR E2 0-6-0T banker at the rear of the train to do the lion's share of the work.

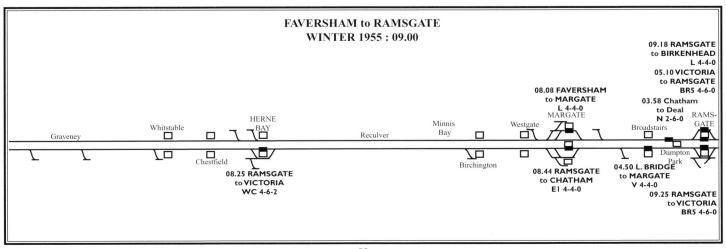

FAVERSHAM to RAMSGATE
WINTER 1955 : 09.00

09.18 RAMSGATE to BIRKENHEAD L 4-4-0
05.10 VICTORIA to RAMSGATE BR5 4-6-0
08.08 FAVERSHAM to MARGATE L 4-4-0
03.58 Chatham to Deal N 2-6-0

Graveney — Whitstable — HERNE BAY — Reculver — Minnis Bay — Westgate — MARGATE — Broadstairs — RAMS-GATE

Chestfield — Birchington — Dumpton Park

08.25 RAMSGATE to VICTORIA WC 4-6-2
08.44 RAMSGATE to CHATHAM E1 4-4-0
04.50 L. BRIDGE to MARGATE V 4-4-0
09.25 RAMSGATE to VICTORIA BR5 4-6-0

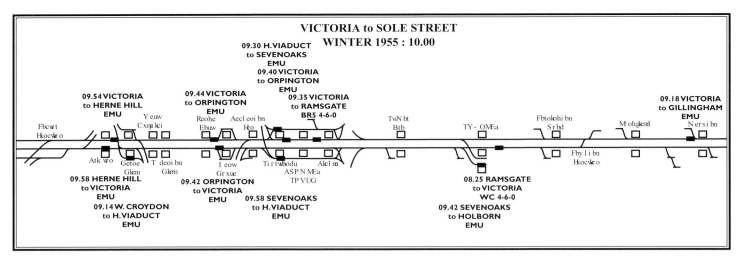

VICTORIA to SOLE STREET
WINTER 1955 : 10.00

09.30 H.VIADUCT to SEVENOAKS EMU
09.40 VICTORIA to ORPINGTON EMU
09.54 VICTORIA to HERNE HILL EMU
09.44 VICTORIA to ORPINGTON EMU
09.35 VICTORIA to RAMSGATE BR5 4-6-0
09.18 VICTORIA to GILLINGHAM EMU
09.58 HERNE HILL to VICTORIA EMU
09.42 ORPINGTON to VICTORIA EMU
09.14 W. CROYDON to H.VIADUCT EMU
09.58 SEVENOAKS to H.VIADUCT EMU
08.25 RAMSGATE to VICTORIA WC 4-6-0
09.42 SEVENOAKS to HOLBORN EMU

CONTROLLER'S LOG: With the morning peak subsiding and being replaced by the basic pattern of service, goods trains can start to run again and a number make an almost tentative appearance in the Medway area. A C class 0-6-0 rattles towards Chatham with a goods for the Sheerness branch while a judgement is made whether or not to let the N 2-6-0-hauled Gillingham to Hoo Junction

even that design dates back to 1917.

The most important trains on the 'screen' at the moment are the 08.25 and 09.20 expresses from Ramsgate and Dover respectively. These are the first off-peak services - reduced rate tickets being barred from the Cannon Street trains - and are exceptionally well used. The Ramsgate train - now approaching Swanley, runs non-stop between Whitstable and Victoria

Both trains are booked to light Pacifics yet the train loads are relatively light: the Dover train consisting of nine coaches and the Ramsgate only seven. (The chances of a light Pacific actually working the 09.20 ex Dover are only even since the service is generally used for any unbalanced engine at Dover and five consecutive days can see five different classes - anything from a Schools to a Merchant Navy

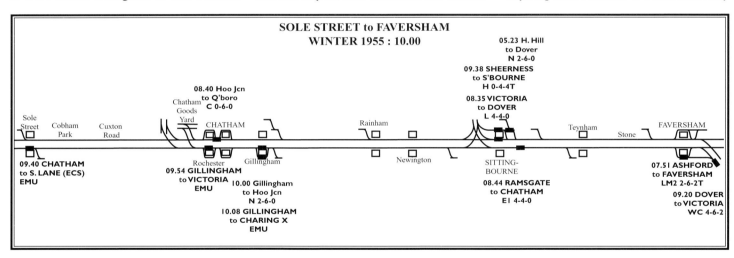

SOLE STREET to FAVERSHAM
WINTER 1955 : 10.00

05.23 H. Hill to Dover N 2-6-0
09.38 SHEERNESS to S'BOURNE H 0-4-4T
08.35 VICTORIA to DOVER L 4-4-0
08.40 Hoo Jcn to Q'boro C 0-6-0
Chatham Goods Yard
Sole Street / Cobham Park / Cuxton Road / CHATHAM / Rainham / Teynham / Stone / FAVERSHAM
09.40 CHATHAM to S. LANE (ECS) EMU
Rochester / 09.54 GILLINGHAM to VICTORIA EMU / Gillingham / 10.00 Gillingham to Hoo Jcn N 2-6-0 / 10.08 GILLINGHAM to CHARING X EMU
Newington
SITTINGBOURNE
08.44 RAMSGATE to CHATHAM E1 4-4-0
07.51 ASHFORD to FAVERSHAM LM2 2-6-2T
09.20 DOVER to VICTORIA WC 4-6-2

Goods down to Chatham goods yard ahead of the 10.08 Charing Cross electric. Looking ten miles to the east one might well wonder whether the grouping, let alone nationalisation, actually happened! The Dover section of the 08.35 from Victoria is standing in Sittingbourne behind an L 4-4-0 and is about to be passed by an E1 4-4-0 on an up stopping train while the Sheerness connection is being worked by an 0-4-4T. All this conspires to make the N 2-6-0 on the down Dover goods seem positively modern although

whilst the 09.20 ex Dover calls at Chatham and Bromley South. Why a stop should be made in the Medway is a mystery since the queue for tickets at Canterbury East often extends 200 yards or more from the booking office and the chance of anyone boarding at Chatham getting more than a small slice of a corridor is remote. To make matters worse Faversham and Sittingbourne passengers brought in by the 08.44 Ramsgate stopping train add to the melee at Chatham.

- on the train).

In the down direction the 09.35 Victoria to Ramsgate leads a pack of electrics as its BR 5MT climbs away from Bromley. The punctual working of this group if trains is more than usually important since the 10.00 Boat express (MN Pacific on the front and an H 0-4-4T on the rear) is on the point of pulling away from Victoria and any delay will not only be felt as far afield as Paris but will affect the 10.04 Victoria to Orpington electric.

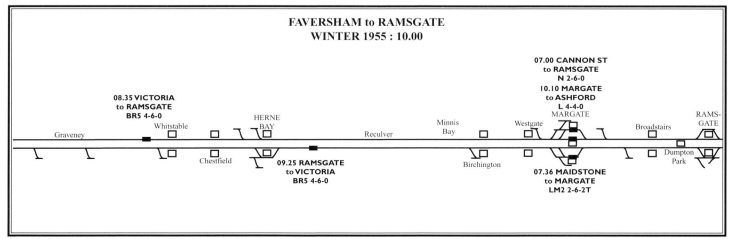

FAVERSHAM to RAMSGATE
WINTER 1955 : 10.00

07.00 CANNON ST to RAMSGATE N 2-6-0
10.10 MARGATE to ASHFORD L 4-4-0
08.35 VICTORIA to RAMSGATE BR5 4-6-0
Graveney / Whitstable / HERNE BAY / Reculver / Minnis Bay / Westgate / MARGATE / Broadstairs / RAMSGATE
Chestfield / 09.25 RAMSGATE to VICTORIA BR5 4-6-0 / Birchington / 07.36 MAIDSTONE to MARGATE LM2 2-6-2T / Dumpton Park

90

The table of traffic arrivals and departures at Chatham Goods Yard, below, gives a good idea of the ubiquity of the C class 0-6-0; almost half the movements being made by members of the class. Not all the trains worked by C 0-6-0's were local and many of the Gillingham engines made their way to London as a matter of routine. These visits were usually via Hoo Junction and a series of local goods services but an exception was made for the 23.40 Herne Hill to Chatham which ran via Sole Street and was booked to a C 0-6-0. 31227 of Gillingham approaches Sittingbourne on 11th August 1957. (L.G. Marshall)

Chatham goods yard was situated close to Rochester station and was approached by a spur that trailed from the London direction; down trains reversing to get onto the headshunt and then changing direction again to get into the goods yard. In addition to dealing with terminating traffic for what was quite an industrialised area, Chatham goods received six daily arrivals via Sole Street from yards in London and four from Hoo Junction; a good proportion of these trains going forward to East Kent stations after remarshalling. Traffic en route to local yards and stations was handled by six local workings which served both the Isle of Sheppey and stations as far as Faversham.

Most trains were handled by the ubiquitous C 0-6-0 or N 2-6-0, the chief exceptions being a Dover-based LMS 2-6-4 tank which brought in the 23.40 from Farningham Road and a Stewarts Lane BR 5MT 4-6-0 which handled the evening Ramsgate - Blackfriars express goods.

CHATHAM GOODS
Yard Working 1954/5

Train	Arrive	Engine	Shed	Depart	Destination
23.55 Gillingham	00.06	C 0-6-0	S. Lane 70		
23.40 Farningham Road	00.24	LM4 2-6-4T	Dover 450		
		LM4 2-6-4T	Dover 450	00.30	Light to Gillingham loco
		C 0-6-0	S. Lane 70	00.35	Herne Hill
(22.00 H. Green)		N 2-6-0	H. Green 17	01.00	Dover Town
Light ex Hoo Junction	01.10	C 0-6-0	Gill 239		(For 01.25)
(21.54 Northfleet)		C 0-6-0	Gill 239	01.25	Gillingham
23.40 Herne Hill	01.55	C 0-6-0	Gill 240		
18.50 Dover Town	02.23	N 2-6-0	Gill 236		(Fwd at 03.05)
01.00 Bricklayers Arms	02.28	N 2-6-0	BLA 125		(Fwd at 03.45)
		C 0-6-0	Gill 240	02.30	Light to Gillingham loco
		N 2-6-0	BLA 125	03.00	Light to Hoo Junction
(18.50 Dover T.)		N 2-6-0	Gill 236	03.05	Hoo Junction
Light ex Gillingham loco	03.08	C 0-6-0	Gill 237		(For 03.45)
Light ex Gillingham loco	03.15	N 2-6-0	Dover 452		(For 03.58)
(01.00 B. Arms)		C 0-6-0	Gill 237	03.45	Queenborough
		N 2-6-0	Dover 452	03.58	Deal via Ramsgate
02.30 Faversham	04.45	N 2-6-0	Fav 277	05.25	Hoo Junction
05.30 Hoo Junction	05.50	C 0-6-0	Gill 243		(Fwd at 07.16)
		C 0-6-0	Gill 243	06.00	Light to Gillingham loco
Light ex Northfleet	06.05	N 2-6-0	Gill 236		
(05.30 Hoo Jcn)		N 2-6-0	Gill 236	07.16	Gillingham
05.23 Herne Hill	08.00	N 2-6-0	S. Lane 62	08.55	Dover Town
08.40 Hoo Junction	09.02	N 2-6-0	Fav 277		
Light ex Gillingham loco	09.20	C 0-6-0	Gill 242		(For 09.55)
		N 2-6-0	Fav 277	09.30	Light to Gillingham loco
02.32 Herne Hill	09.50	C 0-6-0	S. Lane 70		(Fwd at 10.55)
		C 0-6-0	Gill 242	09.55	Queenborough
10.00 Gillingham	10.10	C 0-6-0	Ton 323		(Fwd at 11.24)
		C 0-6-0	Ton 323	10.27	Light to Hoo Junction
Light ex Gillingham loco	10.36	N 2-6-0	Gill 236		(For 11.24)
(02.32 Herne Hill)		C 0-6-0	S. Lane 70	10.55	Gillingham
(10.00 Gillingham)		N 2-6-0	Gill 236	11.24	Hoo Junction
12.15 Hoo Junction	12.35	C 0-6-0	Fav 280		
10.50 Hither Green	12.45	N 2-6-0	BLA 125		(Fwd at 13.59)
		N 2-6-0	BLA 125	13.18	Light to Gillingham loco
(10.50 H. Green)		C 0-6-0	Fav 280	13.59	Faversham
13.55 Snowdown	16.05	N 2-6-0	S. Lane 61		(Fwd at 19.35)
		N 2-6-0	S. Lane 61	16.35	Light to Gillingham loco
Light ex Gillingham loco	19.03	N 2-6-0	S. Lane 61		
(13.55 Snowdown)		N 2-6-0	S. Lane 61	19.35	Fawkham
Light ex Gillingham loco	20.06	C 0-6-0	Gill 237		
		C 0-6-0	Gill 237	20.55	Hoo Junction
21.05 Hoo Junction	21.37	C 0-6-0	S. Lane 70		
		C 0-6-0	S. Lane 70	21.44	Light to Gillingham loco
21.42 Queenborough	22.48	N 2-6-0	BLA 126		(Fwd at 23.15)
21.54 Northfleet	23.05	N 2-6-0	Gill 236		(Fwd at 01.25)
(21.42 ex Q'borough)		N 2-6-0	BLA 126	23.15	Bricklayers Arms
22.35 Faversham	23.21	BR5 4-6-0	S. Lane 15	23.35	Blackfriars
		N 2-6-0	Gill 236	23.35	Light to Gillingham loco
22.00 Hither Green	23.37	N 2-6-0	H. Green 176		(Fwd at 01.00)

GILLINGHAM (KENT)

GILLINGHAM STATION WORKING (1954/5)

Train	Arrive	Engine	Shed	Dep	Destination	Train	Arrive	Engine	Shed	Dep	Destination
23.55 Gillingham Yard		C 0-6-0	S. Lane 70	00/01	Herne Hill	11.00 Shepherdswell	12.42	N 2-6-0	H. Green 172	12.44	Hoo Junction
20.00 Dover Town		N 2-6-0	S. Lane 62	00/57	Hither Green	12.56 Chatham	13.00	LM2 2-6-2T	Fav 269	13.01	Sittingbourne
22.00 Hither Green		N 2-6-0	H. Green 176	01/12	Dover Town	11.15 Ramsgate	13.01	BR5 4-6-0	S. Lane 12	13.02	Victoria
01.05 Sittingbourne		E1 4-4-0	S. Lane 47	01/45	Herne Hill	10.00 Dover Town		N 2-6-0	H. Green 176	13/17	Hoo Junction
21.54 Northfleet		C 0-6-0	Gill 239	01/48	Gillingham Yard	12.35 Victoria	13.36	BR5 4-6-0	S. Lane 15	13.38	Ramsgate
18.50 Dover Town	02.02	N 2-6-0	Gill 236	02.15	Hoo Junction	11.00 H. Viaduct (Pcls)		E1 4-4-0	BLA 91	13/43	Ramsgate
00.40 Snodland		LM4 2-6-4T	Dover 450	02/50	Snowdown	12.37 Dover Priory	14.06	E1 4-4-0	S. Lane 46		
01.10 Bricklayers Arms		N 2-6-0	BLA 121	03/00	Ramsgate			E1 4-4-0	S. Lane 46	14.10	Light to Loco
01.35 Herne Hill		N 2-6-0	S. Lane 61	03/30	Faversham	10.50 Hither Green		C 0-6-0	Fav 280	14/11	Faversham
01.00 Bricklayers Arms		C 0-6-0	Gill 237	03/58	Queenborough	14.08 Sheerness	14.36	LM2 2-6-2T	Fav 270		
03.58 Chatham Goods		N 2-6-0	Dover 452	04/10	Deal			LM2 2-6-2T	Fav 270	14.40	Light to Loco
03.00 H. Viaduct	04.29	E1 4-4-0	S. Lane 45	04.30	Ramsgate	Light ex Loco	14.40	D1 4-4-0	Dover 444		(For 14.57)
02.30 Faversham		N 2-6-0	Fav 277	04/32	Hoo Junction	13.10 Ramsgate	14.44	BR5 4-6-0	S. Lane 13	14.46	Victoria
04.21 Strood	04.39	H 0-4-4T	Gill 231					D1 4-4-0	Dover 444	14.57	Chatham (ECS)
03.30 Victoria	04.58	BR5 4-6-0	S. Lane 16	05.03	Ramsgate	13.55 Ramsgate		V 4-4-0	Ram 481	15/22	Victoria
		C 0-6-0	Gill 245	05.20	Teynham Goods	14.54 Rochester (Pcls)	15.24	C 0-6-0	S. Lane 70		
		H 0-4-4T	Gill 231	05.35	Rainham ECS			C 0-6-0	S. Lane 70	15.30	Light to Loco
05.45 Chatham	05.49	LM2 2-6-2T	Fav 272	05.50	Faversham	14.35 Victoria	15.36	WC 4-6-2	Dover 431	15.38	Dover Priory
05.52 Rainham (P&P)	05.57	H 0-4-4T	Gill 231			15.11 Faversham	15.46	LM2 2-6-2T	Fav 271	15.47	Chatham
04.34 Ramsgate	06.17	L 4-4-0	Ram 489	06.18	Chatham	13.55 Snowdown		N 2-6-0	S. Lane 61	15/58	Fawkham
05.10 Victoria	06.42	BR5 4-6-0	S. Lane 12	06.44	Ramsgate			C 0-6-0	S. Lane 70	16/32	Light to Gravesend
		H 0-4-4T	Gill 231	06.50	Light to Rochester	15.35 Victoria		BR5 4-6-0	S. Lane 16	16/35	Ramsgate
06.44 Faversham	07.20	LM2 2-6-2T	Fav 269	07.22	Rochester	16.37 Chatham	16.41	LM2 2-6-2T	Fav 271	16.43	Sittingbourne
05.50 Cannon St	07.23	E1 4-4-0	S. Lane 46	07.25	Ramsgate	15.22 Ramsgate	17.01	BR5 4-6-0	S. Lane 14	17.02	Victoria
05.30 Hoo Jcn		N 2-6-0	Gill 236	07/30		16.55 Strood	17.10	D1 4-4-0	Dover 444	17.11	Dover Priory
06.06 Ramsgate		WC 4-6-2	Ram 466	07/33	Cannon Street	16.45 Cannon Street		WC 4-6-2	Ram 471	17/31	Ramsgate
07.40 Chatham	07.44	H 0-4-4T	Gill 231	07.46	Sittingbourne	16.32 Cannon Street	17.34	L1 4-4-0	BLA 88	17.35	Ramsgate
06.10 Dover Priory	07.53	D1 4-4-0	Dover 444			16.15 Ramsgate	17.57	BR5 4-6-0	S. Lane 10	17.59	Victoria
06.29 Ramsgate	07.58	WC 4-6-2	Ram 467	07.59	Cannon Street	17.15 Cannon Street		WC 4-6-2	Ram 467	18/02	Ramsgate
		D1 4-4-0	Dover 444	08.00	Light to Loco	17.05 Ramsgate (Pullman)		WC 4-6-2	Ram 470	18/14	Victoria
07.20 Ramsgate		WC 4-6-2	Ram 470	08/31	Cannon Street	17.21 Cannon Street	18.18	U1 2-6-0	Fav 260	18.18	Dover Priory
07.00 Cannon Street	08.32	N 2-6-0	S. Lane 63	08.34	Ramsgate	18.21 Chatham	18.25	LM2 2-6-2T	Fav 270	18.26	Sheerness
07.07 Ramsgate	08.41	L 4-4-0	Ram 490			17.45 Cannon Street		WC 4-6-2	Ram 466	18/36	Ramsgate
		L 4-4-0	Ram 490	08.45	Light to Loco	17.09 Dover Priory	18.37	LM4 2-6-4T	Dover 450	18.38	Chatham
07.35 Ramsgate		WC 4-6-2	Ram 471	08/49	Cannon Street	18.38 Chatham	18.42	C 0-6-0	Gill 237	18.43	Sittingbourne
08.20 Herne Bay		V 4-4-0	Ram 478	09/05	Cannon Street	17.40 Dover Priory	19.01	BR5 4-6-0	S. Lane 11	19.03	Victoria
05.23 Herne Hill		N 2-6-0	S. Lane 62	09/08	Dover Town	18.16 Cannon Street		V 4-4-0	Ram 478	19/04	Ramsgate
07.42 Dover Priory	09.23	N 2-6-0	Fav 260	09.23	Chatham	18.23 Cannon Street	19.18	V 4-4-0	BLA 81	19.19	Dover Priory
Light ex Loco	09.30	L 4-4-0 & C 0-6-0	Ram 490/Gill 243			19.05 Sheerness	19.48	C & LM2	237/271	19.49	Chatham
08.25 Ramsgate		WC 4-6-2	Ram 473	09/34	Victoria	19.39 Faversham	20.06	D1 4-4-0	Fav 262		
08.35 Victoria		BR5 4-6-0	S. Lane 13	09/35	Ramsgate			D1 4-4-0	Fav 262	20.11	Chatham (ECS)
09.38 Chatham	09.42	L 4-4-0	Ram 489	09.43	Dover Priory	16.20 Canterbury East		N 2-6-0	BLA 121	20/18	Blackfriars
		L 4-4-0 & C 0-6-0	Ram 490/Gill 243	09.45	Strood ECS	19.35 Victoria		WC 4-6-2	Ram 473	20/29	Ramsgate
10.00 Gillingham Yard		C 0-6-0	Ton 323	10/02	Hoo Junction	20.38 Chatham	20.42	LM2 2-6-2T	Fav 271	20.43	Faversham
08.40 Hoo Junction		C 0-6-0	Gill 242	10/07	Queenborough	19.45 Ramsgate	21.16	BR5 4-6-0	S. lane 16	21.18	Victoria
08.44 Ramsgate	10.17	E1 4-4-0	S. Lane 45	10.18	Chatham	20.35 Victoria	21.36	V 4-4-0	Ram 481	21.38	Ramsgate
09.20 Dover Priory		WC 4-6-2	Dover 431	10/27	Victoria	19.17 Teynham (Goods)	21.40	C 0-6-0	Gill 242		(Yard pilot to 01.00)
09.35 Victoria	10.35	BR5 4-6-0	S. Lane 14	10.36	Ramsgate	17.10 Ramsgate (Pcls)		N 2-6-0	S. Lane 63	22/07	Victoria
09.25 Ramsgate		BR5 4-6-0	S. Lane 16	10/50	Victoria	21.35 Victoria		WC 4-6-2	Ram 470	22/31	Ramsgate
10.46 Chatham	10.50	L 4-4-0	Ram 490	10.51	Faversham	21.42 Queenborough		N 2-6-0	BLA 126	22/42	Bricklayers Arms
02.32 Herne Hill		C 0-6-0	S. Lane 70	11/05	Gillingham Yard	21.10 Ramsgate	22.48	L1 4-4-0	BLA 88	22.49	Charing Cross
10.35 Victoria		BR5 4-6-0	S. Lane 10	11/38	Ramsgate	22.36 Hoo Junction		C 0-6-0	Gill 237	23/04	Rainham
11.18 Sheerness	11.49	H 0-4-4T	Gill 231			22.35 Faversham		BR5 4-6-0	S. Lane 15	23/16	Blackfriars
		H 0-4-4T	Gill 231	12.00	Light to Loco	23.22 Chatham	23.26	D1 4-4-0	Fav 262	23.27	Faversham
11.35 Victoria (Pullman)	12.37	BR5 4-6-0	S. Lane 11	12.38	Ramsgate						

The Medway towns of Rochester, Chatham and Gillingham embraced a population of 160,000 within an area no more than two miles in length and it was to the credit of the Southern (and its predecessors) that each of the towns had its own station since most other railway companies would have made a central station suffice for all three. Although Chatham had the smallest static population of the trio, the nearby Royal Naval establishment made it the most commercially important yet the station, hemmed in by tunnels and a rock cutting, could not be expanded to anything approaching a desirable size and had to remain, like Rochester, a pair of island platforms.

What scope there was for enlargement at Rochester was taken up by Chatham goods yard (and, in pre-grouping times, the SER Chatham Central branch) and since there was no room

to spare at Chatham LCDR, almost all the Medway's operating facilities had to be located at Gillingham where a goods yard, motive power depot and electric carriage sheds were constructed just to the east of the three-platform station. Thus the topography determined the extent of the outer suburban service with trains starting from and termination at Gillingham; a pattern that was perpetuated after the 1938 electrification.

Although a number of passenger steam services to East Kent, Sheppey and beyond started from the Medways station, most were divided between Faversham and Ramsgate sheds and Gillingham's share came to no more than a pair of Sheppey trains for which a C 0-6-0 and an H 0-4-4T were provided respectively. Perhaps the most interesting duty Gillingham had to provide an engine for was an L1 4-4-0

diagram in which the engine ran light to Strood for the 04.33 passenger to Maidstone West. It next appeared over twenty-two hours later when it arrived back at Strood with the midnight goods from Maidstone and banked the 00.40 Snodland to Snowdown - a 2-6-4T working - up the bank to Rochester Bridge Junction. During its absence the 4-4-0 had worked as far east as it was possible to do on SECR metals, eventually getting as far as Reading with the 09.08 from Tunbridge Wells West. The only large engine on Gillingham's books was a class N which looked after some of the heavier workings to and from Hoo Junction.

The remainder of Gillingham's turns were prosaic by comparison: a pair of H 0-4-4T's on the Allhallows branch, a little work on the Isle of Sheppey and seven C 0-6-0 daily goods duties based on Hoo Junction.

HOO JUNCTION MARSHALLING YARD
YARD WORKING : 1954/5

Train	Arrive	Engine	Shed	Dep	Destination
		C 0-6-0	HG 187	00.10	Herne Hill
Light ex Gillingham loco	00.10	C 0-6-0	Fav 280		Pilot to 06.18
(21.42 Queenborough)		N 2-6-0	BLA 126	00.30	Bricklayers Arms
		N 2-6-0	HG 172	00.30	Redhill
23.42 Littlebrook	00.35	C 0-6-0	Gill 239		
Light ex Strood	00.45	N 2-6-0	HG 180		(To work 01.15)
		C 0-6-0	Gill 239	00.50	Light to Gillingham loco
		N 2-6-0	HG 180	01.15	Redhill
23.00 Angerstein Wharf	01.36	N 2-6-0	BLA 124		(Fwd at 02.15)
		C 0-6-0	Gill 243	01.55	Dartford
23.26 Tonbridge	02.00	N 2-6-0	HG 177		(Fwd at 02.25)
01.15 Greenhithe	02.08	C 0-6-0	Gill 245		
(23.00 Angerstein Wharf)		N 2-6-0	BLA 124	02.15	Reading (GW)
(23.26 Tonbridge)		N 2-6-0	HG 177	02.25	Angerstein Wharf
		C 0-6-0	Gill 245	02.50	Light to Gillingham loco
Light ex Chatham	03.00	C 0-6-0	Gill 238		(To work 03.10)
22.24 Mottingham	03.01	C 0-6-0	Gill 238		(Stale)
		C 0-6-0	Gill 238	03.10	Hither Green
Light ex Chatham	03.12	N 2-6-0	BLA 125		(To work 04.22)
		C 0-6-0	Gill 238	03.15	Light to Gillingham loco
18.50 Dover Town	03.25	N 2-6-0	Gill 236		
		N 2-6-0	Gill 236	03.45	Northfleet
Light ex Gillingham loco	04.00	C 0-6-0	Gill 240		(To work 04.40)
		N 2-6-0	BLA 125	04.22	Hither Green
00.10 Tonbridge	04.30	C 0-6-0	Ton 323		
		C 0-6-0	Gill 240	04.40	Allhallows
		C 0-6-0	Ton 323	04.40	Light to Rochester
04.00 Dartford	04.55	C 0-6-0	Gill 243		
03.55 Hither Green	05.08	N 2-6-0	HG 170		
		C 0-6-0	Gill 243	05.30	Gillingham
02.30 Faversham	05.43	N 2-6-0	Fav 277		
		C 0-6-0	Fav 280	06.18	Light to Higham
Light ex Higham	06.35	C 0-6-0	Fav 280		(Pilot to 12.15)
		N 2-6-0	HG 170	07.45	Strood
		N 2-6-0	Fav 277	08.40	Dover Town
08.46 Strood	09.40	N 2-6-0	HG 170		
		N 2-6-0	HG 170	10.05	Tonbridge
08.38 Paddock Wood	10.18	N 2-6-0	HG 171		
Light ex Strood	10.10	C 0-6-0	Gill 243		(To work 10.46)
Light ex Chatham	10.40	C 0-6-0	Ton 323		
		C 0-6-0	Gill 243	10.46	Crayford
		C 0-6-0	Ton 323	11.08	Halling
03.58 Woking	11.17	N 2-6-0	HG 180		(Fwd at 12.40)
		N 2-6-0	HG 171	11.40	Hither Green
10.00 Gillingham	11.42	N 2-6-0	Gill 236		
		C 0-6-0	Fav 280	12.15	Chatham
Light ex Strood	12.15	C 0-6-0	Gill 239		(To work 15.34)
09.00 Paddock Wood	12.24	N 2-6-0	HG 173		
(03.58 Woking)		N 2-6-0	HG 180	12.40	Angerstein Wharf
		N 2-6-0	Gill 236	12.50	Grain
		N 2-6-0	HG 173	13.08	Light to Gillingham loco
11.00 Shepherdswell	13.10	N 2-6-0	HG 172		
		N 2-6-0	HG 172	13.40	Light to Gillingham loco
10.00 Dover	13.45	N 2-6-0	HG 176		
12.25 Halling	13.48	C 0-6-0	Ton 323		
		C 0-6-0	Ton 323	14.08	Brookgate
		N 2-6-0	HG 176	15.05	Hither Green
14.10 Crayford	15.22	C 0-6-0	Gill 243		(Pilot to 01.55)
		C 0-6-0	Gill 239	15.34	Aylesford
15.24 Tonbridge	16.46	C 0-6-0	BLA 123		
14.34 Maidstone West	17.14	N 2-6-0	BLA 119		
		N 2-6-0	BLA 123	17.16	Light to Strood
		N 2-6-0	BLA 119	18.12	Strood
18.57 Strood	19.20	N 2-6-0	BLA 119		
Light ex Strood	19.38	N 2-6-0	BLA 123		(To work 20.35)
15.50 Grain	19.38	N 2-6-0	Gill 236		
		N 2-6-0	Gill 236	20.02	Light to Northfleet
		N 2-6-0	BLA 119	20.03	Paddock Wood
17.50 Paddock Wood	20.17	N1 2-6-0	HG 185		
18.35 Allhallows	20.34	C 0-6-0	S. Lane 70		
		N 2-6-0	BLA 123	20.35	North End
16.20 Canterbury East	20.45	N 2-6-0	BLA 121	21.05	Blackfriars
		C 0-6-0	S. Lane 70	21.05	Chatham
20.55 Chatham	21.13	C 0-6-0	Gill 237		
20.10 Hither Green	21.15	C 0-6-0	HG 187		
20.05 Aylesford	21.23	C 0-6-0	Gill 239		
21.54 Northfleet	22.09	N 2-6-0	Gill 236		(Fwd at 22.45)
		N1 2-6-0	HG 185	22.25	Hither Green
		C 0-6-0	Gill 237	22.36	Rainham
(21.54 Northfleet)		N 2-6-0	Gill 236	22.45	Gillingham
		C 0-6-0	Gill 239	22.45	Littlebrook
Light ex Gillingham	22.50	C 0-6-0	Gill 245		(To work 23.30)
		C 0-6-0	Gill 245	23.30	Northfleet
21.42 Queenborough	23.37	N 2-6-0	BLA 126		(Fwd at 00.30)
Light ex Gillingham loco	23.38	N 2-6-0	HG 172		(To work 00.30)

Hoo Junction was not a London, Chatham & Dover location but it was near enough - four miles from Rochester on the North Kent line to Gravesend - to have a close bearing on Chatham line affairs and it was essentially a gathering point for traffic destined for the heavily industrialised area between Gravesend and London; an area that was difficult to reach from the west because of the density of passenger services and the difficulty of threading slow and lengthy goods trains through the London area. Much of the traffic from the North and West was therefore directed around London, via Redhill, Tonbridge and Paddock Wood, to be fed into the area via Maidstone West and Strood for remarshalling at Hoo Junction. One can see from the map of the North Kent lines - the three parallel routes that ran from London to Dartford via Woolwich, Welling and Sidcup - that only the route via Sidcup was directly accessible from the South Eastern's main yard at Hither Green whilst in addition direct access to the Angerstein branch at Charlton and its many yards and sidings could only be achieved from the East. A few essential trains ran from Bricklayers Arms to Angerstein Wharf but since they had to reverse at Charlton - blocking a very busy suburban main line in the process - the Southern cannot be blamed for routing as much traffic as possible around London and through Hoo Junction.

While the majority of trains into Hoo Junction came over the ex-South Eastern line from the Maidstone direction, a significant number were through workings from the LCDR loaded with coal from the collieries in the Dover area. There was also a fairly regular service between Hoo Junction and Chatham Goods Yard.

The number of trains dealt with belies the fact that the Southern was solely a passenger railway and also illustrates what the region did with its fleet of N 2-6-0 and C 0-6-0 locomotives - in fact all the services dealt with at the yard were worked by these two classes. Surprisingly, given that on average there was an arrival or departure every seventeen minutes, there was no motive power depot attached to the yard and trains therefore had to be worked either by the return workings of inward services or by ferrying engines to and from Gillingham shed; a six mile trip which included having to run the gauntlet of the congested area between Rochester Bridge Junction and Gillingham station.

With a throughput of about 650 wagons per shift, shunting was a continuous process employing a pair of class C 0-6-0's and, during the early 1950's, Z class 0-8-0T 30951. Much to the regret of local enthusiasts in March 1953 the latter was transferred to Three Bridges and replaced by a Hither Green-based 0-6-0 diesel shunter.

31510 was a long-term resident of Gillingham and is pictured on the shed in June 1959. The engine to the right is D1 4-4-0 31509 of Faversham. Although the C class were goods engines, they were diagrammed to more passenger work than might be expected. Their star turn was with the 18.38 Chatham to Sittingbourne, a three coach birdcage set which connected with the 17.45 Cannon Street to Ramsgate but had to arrive in Sittingbourne well clear of the 18.16 express from Cannon Street. The 18.38 was booked non-stop from Gillingham and if the 17.45 was late from Chatham, one would be treated to the sight of an 0-6-0 reaching speeds that might have surprised its designer. (L.G. Marshall)

GILLINGHAM MPD : ENGINE MOVEMENTS

Inward Working	On Shed	Engine	Diagram	Off Shed	To Work
		N 2-6-0	HG 180	00.05	01.15 Gds Hoo Jcn - Redhill
23.40 Gds Farningham Rd - Chatham	00.30	LM4 2-6-4T	Dvr 450		(For 01.45)
Gillingham Pilot	01.10	C 0-6-0	Gill 242		(For 04.45)
		E1 4-4-0	S. Lane 47	01.25	01.42 Goods to Herne Hill
01.05 Gds Sittingbourne - Gillingham	01.28	LM2 2-6-2T	Fav 269		(For 05.00)
		LM4 2-6-4T	Dvr 450	01.45	02.28 Gds Strood - Snowdown
		C 0-6-0	Gill 238	01.50	03.10 Gds Hoo Jcn - Hither Green
		N 2-6-0	Gill 236	01.55	02.15 Gds Gillingham - Hoo Jcn
01.25 Gds Chatham - Gillingham	02.00	C 0-6-0	Gill 239		(For 05.20)
18.50 Gds Dover - Gillingham	02.10	N 2-6-0	Dvr 452		(For 03.55)
23.40 Gds Herne Hill - Chatham	02.40	C 0-6-0	Gill 240		(For 03.40)
		C 0-6-0	Gill 237	03.00	03.47 Gds Chatham - Queenborough
00.01 Maidstone - Strood Gds	03.00	L1 4-4-0	Gill 230		(For 03.40)
01.15 Gds Greenhithe - Hoo Jcn	03.12	C 0-6-0	Gill 245		(For 04.55)
22.24 Gds Mottingham - Hoo Jcn	03.37	C 0-6-0	Gill 238		(For 01.50)
		C 0-6-0	Gill 240	03.40	04.38 Gds Hoo Jcn - Allhallows
		L1 4-4-0	Gill 230	03.40	04.33 Strood - Maidstone
		H 0-4-4T	Gill 231	03.40	04.22 Strood - Gillingham
		N 2-6-0	Dvr 452	03.55	04.48 Gds Chatham - Deal
		H 0-4-4T	Gill 232	04.25	04.41 Gravesend
		C 0-6-0	Gill 242	04.45	Chatham Pilot
		C 0-6-0	Gill 245	04.55	05.28 Gds to Teynham
		LM2 2-6-2T	Fav 272	05.00	05.45 Chatham - Sittingbourne
		C 0-6-0	Gill 239	05.20	Strood Pilot
06.32 Chatham - Rochester ECS	06.45	L 4-4-0	Ram 489		(For 08.50)
Gillingham Pilot	07.00	C 0-6-0	Gill 243		(For 09.30)
05.11 Rochester - Gravesend Milk	07.00	C 0-6-0	Ton 323		(For 09.50)
07.16 Gds ex Chatham	07.45	N 2-6-0	Gill 236		(For 10.28)
07.42 Rochester - Strood ECS	08.00	LM2 2-6-2T	Fav 269		(For 11.55)
06.10 Dover - Gillingham	08.00	D1 4-4-0	Dvr 444		(For 14.35)
Light ex Queenborough	08.14	C 0-6-0	Gill 237		(For 14.00)
		L 4-4-0	Ram 489	08.50	09.38 Chatham - Dover
07.07 Ramsgate - Gillingham	08.50	L 4-4-0	Ram 490		(For 09.25)
08.40 Gds Hoo Jcn - Chatham	09.02	N 2-6-0	Fav 277		(For 11.43)
		L 4-4-0	Ram 490	09.25	09.45 Strood ECS (Pilot)
		C 0-6-0	Gill 243	09.25	09.45 Strood ECS
07.42 Dover - Chatham	09.46	U1 2-6-0	Fav 260		(For 13.30)
		C 0-6-0	Ton 323	09.50	11.10 Gds Gillingham - Chatham
		N 2-6-0	Gill 236	10.28	11.24 Gds Chatham - Hoo Jcn
10.35 ECS Chatham - Strood	10.50	E1 4-4-0	S. Lane 45		(For 19.00)
02.32 Gds Herne Hill - Gillingham	11.25	C 0-6-0	S. Lane 70		(For 14.33)
		LM2 2-6-2T	Fav 269	11.55	12.15 ECS Gillingham - Chatham
11.36 Sittingbourne	11.55	H 0-4-4T	Gill 231		(For 13.30)
10.50 Gds Hither Green - Chatham	13.25	N 2-6-0	BLA 125		(For 22.10)
09.00 Gds Paddock Wood - Hoo Jn	13.29	N 2-6-0	HG 173		(For 00.05)
		U1 2-6-0	Fav 260	13.30	Light to Ewer St/17.21 C. St - Dover
		H 0-4-4T	Gill 231	13.30	14.33 Gravesend - Allhallows
Light ex Maidstone West	13.54	C 0-6-0	HG 201		(For 16.42)
10.40 Gds Shepherdswell - Hoo Jcn	14.00	N 2-6-0	HG 172		(For 23.15)
		C 0-6-0	Gill 237	14.00	14.22 Strood ECS
12.35 Dover - Gillingham	14.10	E1 4-4-0	S. Lane 46		(For 01.25)
		C 0-6-0	S. Lane 70	14.33	14.54 Pcls Rochester - Gillingham
		D1 4-4-0	Dvr 444	14.35	14.57 Chatham ECS
14.08 Sheerness - Gillingham	14.45	LM2 2-6-2T	Fav 270		(For 17.45)
14.54 Pcls Rochester - Gillingham	15.30	C 0-6-0	S. Lane 70		(For 16.30)
14.58 Gravesend - Chatham Milk	15.30	H 0-4-4T	Gill 232		(For 16.42)
		C 0-6-0	S. Lane 70	16.30	17.39 Gravesend - Allhallows
		H 0-4-4T	Gill 232	16.42	18.08 Gravesend - Allhallows
		N 2-6-0	HG 201	16.42	Dartford Pilot
13.55 Gds Snowdown - Chatham	16.45	N 2-6-0	S. Lane 61		(For 18.55)
Gillingham Pilot	17.35	C 0-6-0	Gill 245		(For 22.28)
		LM2 2-6-2T	Fav 270	17.45	18.21 Chatham - Sheerness
		N 2-6-0	S. Lane 61	18.55	19.35 Gds Chatham - Fawkham
		E1 4-4-0	S. Lane 45	19.00	20.59 (Pcls) Cannon St
17.09 Dover - Chatham	19.45	LM4 2-6-4T	Dvr 450		(For 22.25)
21.33 Chatham Sdgs - Chatham Milk	21.45	D1 4-4-0	Fav 262		(For 22.20)
21.05 Gds Hoo Jcn - Chatham	21.52	C 0-6-0	S. Lane 70		(For 23.50)
20.52 Allhallows - Gravesend	22.09	H 0-4-4T	Gill 231		(For 23.40)
		N 2-6-0	BLA 125	22.10	22.40 Gds Gillingham - B. Arms
		D1 4-4-0	Fav 262	22.20	23.22 Chatham - Faversham
		LM4 2-6-4T	Dvr 450	22.25	Light to Farningham Rd
		C 0-6-0	Gill 245	22.28	23.30 Gds Hoo Jcn - Greenhithe
21.42 Gds Queenborough - Gillingham	22.30	C 0-6-0	Fav 278		(For 23.45)
		N 2-6-0	HG 172	23.15	00.30 Gds Hoo Jcn - Tonbridge
22.36 Gds Hoo Jcn - Rainham	23.30	C 0-6-0	Gill 237		(For 03.00)
23.07 Gravesend	23.36	H 0-4-4T	Gill 232		(For 04.25)
		C 0-6-0	S. Lane 70	23.40	23.50 Gds Gillingham - Herne Hill
		C 0-6-0	Fav 280	23.45	Hoo Jcn Pilot
21.54 Gds Northfleet - Chatham	23.45	N 2-6-0	Gill 236		(For 01.55)

* A pair of diesel pilots alternated weekly between the Hoo Junction and Chatham Yard pilots. The change was made on Sundays

Having been stripped of most of its passenger work by the 1939 electrification, Gillingham loco spent the last twenty years of its existence as a predominately freight-only establishment and therefore something of a rarity in Southern circles. This, however, was not to suggest that the shed's activities lacked interest and in fact operations at Gillingham shed were very often more nail-biting than those of very much larger establishments.

The reason for this lay in the goods traffic for which the shed was almost solely responsible and the consequent unpredictability with which engines would return to Gillingham. The shed had an allocation (in 1955) of twelve class C 0-6-0's - the backbone of the shed's allocation - with which to cover nine daily diagrams, one of which called for two engines since it was of more than twenty-four hours duration.

Thus there were only two engines left to cover failures and maintenance and while this alone would be enough to cause headaches, predicting the time at which engines would return from one diagram and be ready to go out on another was an all but impossible task.

A typical example was that of the engine which rang off shed at 03.40 to work the 04.38 goods from Hoo Junction to Allhallows. Ringing-off times were always carefully

LOCOMOTIVE ALLOCATIONS & TRANSFERS : GILLINGHAM (73D)

Loco	Class	Aug-50	Sep-50	Oct-50	Nov-50	Dec-50	Jan-51	Feb-51	Mar-51	Apr-51	May-51	Jun-51	Jul-51
30951	6F : Z 0-8-0T (1929)												
33026	5F : Q1 0-6-0 (1942)	X	X	X	Ex Ton								
33027	5F : Q1 0-6-0 (1942)	X	X	X	Ex Ton								
33028	5F : Q1 0-6-0 (1942)	X	X	X	Ex Ton								
31492	3P : D1 4-4-0 (1921)								To Fav	X	X	X	X
31494	3P : D1 4-4-0 (1921)					To Fav	X	X	X	X	X	X	X
31735	3P : D1 4-4-0 (1921)	X	X	X	X	Ex Dover				To Ton	X	X	X
31516	2P : E 4-4-0 (1905)					To Ashford	X	X	X	X	X	X	X
31092	2P : D 4-4-0 (1901)											W/D	X
31488	2P : D 4-4-0 (1901)	X	X	X	X	X	X	X	X	X	X	Ex B. Arms	
31586	2P : D 4-4-0 (1901)	X	X	X	X	X	X	X	X	X	X	Ex Fav	To Redhill
31729	2P : D 4-4-0 (1901)												
31086	2F : C 0-6-0 (1900)						To B. Arms	X	X	X	X	X	X
31090	2F : C 0-6-0 (1900)						To B. Arms	X	X	X	X	X	X
31112	2F : C 0-6-0 (1900)												
31221	2F : C 0-6-0 (1900)												
31223	2F : C 0-6-0 (1900)												
31225	2F : C 0-6-0 (1900)												
31227	2F : C 0-6-0 (1900)	X	X	X	X	X	Ex B. Arms						
31229	2F : C 0-6-0 (1900)	X	X	X	X	X	X	X	Ex Fav				
31234	2F : C 0-6-0 (1900)	X	X	X	X	X	Ex S. Lane						
31242	2F : C 0-6-0 (1900)	X	X	X	X	X	X	X	Ex Fav				
31255	2F : C 0-6-0 (1900)								To Fav	X	X	X	X
31256	2F : C 0-6-0 (1900)								To Fav	X	X	X	X
31267	2F : C 0-6-0 (1900)								To Fav	X	X	X	X
31287	2F : C 0-6-0 (1900)						To B. Arms		X	X	X	X	X
31317	2F : C 0-6-0 (1900)								To Fav	X	X	X	X
31495	2F : C 0-6-0 (1900)	X	X	X	X	X	X	X	Ex Fav				
31498	2F : C 0-6-0 (1900)												
31508	2F : C 0-6-0 (1900)	X	X	X	X	X	Ex B. Arms						
31510	2F : C 0-6-0 (1900)												
31573	2F : C 0-6-0 (1900)						To S. Lane	X	X	X	X	X	X
31579	2F : C 0-6-0 (1900)						To S. Lane	X	X	X	X	X	X
31583	2F : C 0-6-0 (1900)												To S. Lane
31585	2F : C 0-6-0 (1900)												
31588	2F : C 0-6-0 (1900)												
31681	2F : C 0-6-0 (1900)	X	X	X	X	X	Ex S. Lane						
31682	2F : C 0-6-0 (1900)												
31683	2F : C 0-6-0 (1900)	X	X	X	X	X	Ex S. Lane						
31688	2F : C 0-6-0 (1900)											To H. Green	X
31693	2F : C 0-6-0 (1900)								To Fav	X	X	X	X
31712	2F : C 0-6-0 (1900)												
31713	2F : C 0-6-0 (1900)												
31724	2F : C 0-6-0 (1900)						To B. Arms	X	X	X	X	X	X
31697	1P : R1 0-4-4T (1900)												
31658	1P : R 0-4-4T (1891)												
31659	1P : R 0-4-4T (1891)												
31662	1P : R 0-4-4T (1891)												
31663	1P : R 0-4-4T (1891)												
31665	1P : R 0-4-4T (1891)											To Ton	X
31666	1P : R 0-4-4T (1891)						To Ton	X	X	X	X	X	X
31306	1P : H 0-4-4T (1904)	X	X	X	X	X	X	X	X	X	X	Ex Dover	
31307	1P : H 0-4-4T (1904)	X	X	X	X	X	Ex S. Lane						
31308	1P : H 0-4-4T (1904)												

LOCOMOTIVE ALLOCATIONS & TRANSFERS : GILLINGHAM (73D)

Loco	Class	Aug-51	Sep-51	Oct-51	Nov-51	Dec-51	Jan-52	Feb-52	Mar-52	Apr-52	May-52	Jun-52	Jul-52
30951	6F : Z 0-8-0T (1929)												
33026	5F : Q1 0-6-0 (1942)		To Ton	X	X	X	X	X	X	X	X	X	X
33027	5F : Q1 0-6-0 (1942)		To Ton	X	X	X	X	X	X	X	X	X	X
33028	5F : Q1 0-6-0 (1942)		To Ton	X	X	X	X	X	X	X	X	X	X
31815	5F : N 2-6-0 (1917)	X	X	X	X	Ex S. Lane							
31816	5F : N 2-6-0 (1917)	X	Ex S. Lane										
31509	3P : D1 4-4-0 (1921)	X	X	X	X	Ex Fav							
31545	3P : D1 4-4-0 (1921)	X	X	X	X	Ex Fav							
31488	2P : D 4-4-0 (1901)					To Reading	X	X	X	X	X	X	X
31501	2P : D 4-4-0 (1901)	X	X	X	X	X	Ex H. Green						
31729	2P : D 4-4-0 (1901)												
31112	2F : C 0-6-0 (1900)												
31221	2F : C 0-6-0 (1900)												
31223	2F : C 0-6-0 (1900)												
31225	2F : C 0-6-0 (1900)		To H. Green	X	X	X	X	X	X	X	X	Ex H. Green	
31227	2F : C 0-6-0 (1900)												
31229	2F : C 0-6-0 (1900)												
31234	2F : C 0-6-0 (1900)												
31242	2F : C 0-6-0 (1900)												
31495	2F : C 0-6-0 (1900)												
31498	2F : C 0-6-0 (1900)												
31508	2F : C 0-6-0 (1900)												
31510	2F : C 0-6-0 (1900)												
31585	2F : C 0-6-0 (1900)		To Ton	X	X	X	X	X	X	X	X	X	X
31588	2F : C 0-6-0 (1900)		To Ton	X	X	X	X	X	X	X	X	X	X
31593	2F : C 0-6-0 (1900)	X	Ex Ton										
31681	2F : C 0-6-0 (1900)												
31682	2F : C 0-6-0 (1900)												
31683	2F : C 0-6-0 (1900)												
31684	2F : C 0-6-0 (1900)	X	Ex Ton										
31686	2F : C 0-6-0 (1900)	X	Ex Ton									To H. Green	X
31712	2F : C 0-6-0 (1900)												
31713	2F : C 0-6-0 (1900)												
31697	1P : R1 0-4-4T (1900)												
31658	1P : R 0-4-4T (1891)												
31659	1P : R 0-4-4T (1891)		W/D	X	X	X	X	X	X	X	X	X	X
31660	1P : R 0-4-4T (1891)	X	X	X	X	Ex S. Lane							
31662	1P : R 0-4-4T (1891)												
31663	1P : R 0-4-4T (1891)												
31295	1P : H 0-4-4T (1904)	X	X	X	X	X	X	X	X	X	X	Ex Fav	
31305	1P : H 0-4-4T (1904)	X	X	X	X	X	X	X	X	X	X	Ex Fav	
31306	1P : H 0-4-4T (1904)												
31307	1P : H 0-4-4T (1904)												
31308	1P : H 0-4-4T (1904)												

watched since late starts were invariably the starting point of considerable - and usually one-sided - correspondence whilst the 03.40 departure was monitored even more closely than usual since after arriving at Allhallows with the goods from Hoo Junction, the engine had no more than nineteen minutes with which to turn round and work the 07.14 passenger to Gravesend. It was always diagramming folly to book an engine to a passenger service from a goods but to do so in the space of only nineteen minutes was asking for trouble. Matters were not helped by the fact that the 0-6-0 left Gillingham shed coupled to an L1 4-4-0 (for the 04.33 Strood - Maidstone passenger) and an H 0-4-4T which worked the 04.22 Strood - Gillingham newspapers.

The possibilities for delay were already great - although very often the engines were sent out separately - but were augmented by the fact that the 0-6-0 only arrived on the shed - if it was on time - from its previous working (the 23.40 Herne Hill - Chatham goods) an hour before setting off again and the shed therefore did not have very much time to decide whether to keep the engine in the working or to use another. The latter option meant either using one of the very small reservoir of 'spare' engines or stepping-up engines that were already in steam. On top of everything, if the decision was taken to use the booked engine, the possibility always remained that it would be found to have a fault when it arrived back on shed.

If these problems were multiplied by every turn that Gillingham had to provide engines for, it can be seen that, for all its size, the shed's problems were of no small magnitude.

Although well stricken in years, no concessions were made for the C class 0-6-0's whose hours in traffic bordered on the excessive. The engine referred to above spend twenty-three hours in traffic whilst another, the engine which came off shed at 01.50 to work the 03.10 Hoo Junction - Hither Green did not return to base for nearly twenty-six hours. One could even guarantee that the engine would even come back since it - and its shedmates - were completely at the mercy of the traffic department and the requirements of goods traffic. One engine, for example, was due on shed after working the 16.16 Hither Green to Mottingham and the 22.24 Mottingham - Hoo Junction but the controller might decide to move the traffic from Mottingham on another service and use the Gillingham 0-6-0 on a special from Hither Green to Tonbridge in which case several days might pass before the engine saw the light of day over its home shed. In the meantime Gillingham shed would be expected to turn out engines punctually as though nothing had happened.

There was also the law of distorted equality to be taken into account. If Stewarts Lane, for example, was short of power and used a Gillingham engine to cover one of its turns, nothing would be said but if Gillingham - without an engine to scratch its backside with, as the saying went - used a foreign engine for one of its turns, the shed would never hear the end of it!

1950/1

The shed's proximity to Chatham and its war-time naval needs had seen an increase in its allocation and the early 1950's saw the backlog being reduced as operating conditions returned to a more normal state of affairs. The mainstay of the shed, as ever, was it fleet of C class 0-6-0's which were clearly being overstretched in some quarters. To assist a trio of Q1 0-6-0's arrived from Tonbridge in November 1950 whilst the number of C 0-6-0's was gradually reduced - not without considerable exchanges involving Bricklayers Arms and Faversham - from twenty-four to nineteen.

Local passenger traffic - chiefly the Allhallows branch - was handled by half a dozen elderly R 0-4-4 tanks whose longevity almost certainly owed much to the war. Withdrawals of the eighteen-strong class had actually started in 1940 and one of the Gillingham engines had been replaced by one of the later R1 engines. In contrast to the position with the C class 0-6-0's, Gillingham was provided with quite a handsome reserve of 0-4-4T's for its daily needs which amounted to two diagrams on weekdays and four on Saturdays when a Gillingham engine was used on the Swanley - Gravesned West service. The diagrams were, however, long - of around nineteen hours each - and some insurance was evidently needed against the age of the engines concerned. The presence of H 0-4-4T 31308 and the subsequent arrival of two more of the class suggested that the reign of the LCDR tanks was finally drawing to a close.

The shed was similarly well provided for with 4-4-0 passenger engines even though there was only a single diagram to be covered. This duty - variously covered by D, D1 and E class 4-4-0's - was of interest in that much of its work lay well away from the Medway region, the engine working initially to Maidstone West and then to Redhill and Reading South. The final part of the working was on a goods from Maidstone to Strood; the engine returning to shed after banking a 2-6-4T-worked goods up the spur from Strood to Rochester. The diagram, which kept the engine in traffic for almost twenty-four hours, was usually worked by two engines which alternated daily.

1951/2

In August 1951 the trio of Q1 engines were returned to Tonbridge in exchange for three class C 0-6-0's whilst the heavier work for which the Q1's had been used was taken over by N 2-6-0's, a pair of which arrived from Stewarts Lane in September and December respectively. The survival of the R and R1 0-4-4T's seemed less

Loco	Class	Aug-52	Sep-52	Oct-52	Nov-52	Dec-52	Jan-53	Feb-53	Mar-53	Apr-53	May-53	Jun-53	Jul-53
	LOCOMOTIVE ALLOCATIONS & TRANSFERS : GILLINGHAM (73D)												
30951	6F : Z 0-8-0T (1929)								To T. Bges	X	X	X	X
31815	5F : N 2-6-0 (1917)												
31816	5F : N 2-6-0 (1917)												
31758	3P : L1 4-4-0 (1926)	X	X	X	X	X	X	X	X	X	Ex S. Lane		
31759	3P : L1 4-4-0 (1926)	X	X	X	X	X	X	X	X	X	Ex S. Lane		
31509	3P : D1 4-4-0 (1921)									To S. Lane	X	X	X
31545	3P : D1 4-4-0 (1921)									To S. Lane	X	X	X
31501	2P : D 4-4-0 (1901)								W/D	X	X	X	X
31729	2P : D 4-4-0 (1901)												
31112	2F : C 0-6-0 (1900)												
31221	2F : C 0-6-0 (1900)												
31223	2F : C 0-6-0 (1900)												
31225	2F : C 0-6-0 (1900)												
31227	2F : C 0-6-0 (1900)												
31229	2F : C 0-6-0 (1900)												
31234	2F : C 0-6-0 (1900)												W/D
31242	2F : C 0-6-0 (1900)												
31495	2F : C 0-6-0 (1900)												
31498	2F : C 0-6-0 (1900)												
31508	2F : C 0-6-0 (1900)												
31510	2F : C 0-6-0 (1900)												
31593	2F : C 0-6-0 (1900)												
31681	2F : C 0-6-0 (1900)												
31682	2F : C 0-6-0 (1900)												
31683	2F : C 0-6-0 (1900)												
31684	2F : C 0-6-0 (1900)												
31712	2F : C 0-6-0 (1900)												
31713	2F : C 0-6-0 (1900)												
31697	1P : R1 0-4-4T (1900)								W/D	X	X	X	X
31658	1P : R 0-4-4T (1891)					W/D	X	X	X	X	X	X	X
31660	1P : R 0-4-4T (1891)									To Fav	X	X	X
31662	1P : R 0-4-4T (1891)												
31663	1P : R 0-4-4T (1891)									To Fav	X	Ex Fav	W/D
31161	1P : H 0-4-4T (1904)	X	X	X	X	X	X	X	Ex Ashford				
31295	1P : H 0-4-4T (1904)												To St L.
31305	1P : H 0-4-4T (1904)												
31306	1P : H 0-4-4T (1904)												
31307	1P : H 0-4-4T (1904)												
31308	1P : H 0-4-4T (1904)												
31518	1P : H 0-4-4T (1904)	X	X	X	X	X	X	X	Ex St L.				

Loco	Class	Aug-53	Sep-53	Oct-53	Nov-53	Dec-53	Jan-54	Feb-54	Mar-54	Apr-54	May-54	Jun-54	Jul-54
	LOCOMOTIVE ALLOCATIONS & TRANSFERS : GILLINGHAM (73D)												
31815	5F : N 2-6-0 (1917)		To S. Lane	X	X	X	X	X	X	X	Ex S. Lane		
31816	5F : N 2-6-0 (1917)		To S. Lane	X	X	X	X	X	X	X	Ex S. Lane		
31758	3P : L1 4-4-0 (1926)		To Ashford	X	X	X	X	X	X	X	X	X	X
31759	3P : L1 4-4-0 (1926)		To Ashford	X	X	X	X	X	X	X	X	X	X
31505	3P : D1 4-4-0 (1921)	X	X	X	X	X	X	X	X	X	X	Ex Fav	
31509	3P : D1 4-4-0 (1921)	X	X	X	X	X	Ex S. Lane						
31729	2P : D 4-4-0 (1901)								W/D	X	X		
31112	2F : C 0-6-0 (1900)												
31221	2F : C 0-6-0 (1900)						To S. Lane	X	X	X	X	X	X
31223	2F : C 0-6-0 (1900)						To Ashford	X	X	X	X	X	X
31225	2F : C 0-6-0 (1900)						To B. Arms	X	X	X	X	X	X
31227	2F : C 0-6-0 (1900)												
31229	2F : C 0-6-0 (1900)												
31242	2F : C 0-6-0 (1900)						To B. Arms	X	Ex B. Arms				
31495	2F : C 0-6-0 (1900)												
31498	2F : C 0-6-0 (1900)						To H. Green	X	X	X	X	X	X
31508	2F : C 0-6-0 (1900)						To Fav	X	Ex Fav				
31510	2F : C 0-6-0 (1900)												
31593	2F : C 0-6-0 (1900)												
31681	2F : C 0-6-0 (1900)												
31682	2F : C 0-6-0 (1900)												
31683	2F : C 0-6-0 (1900)												
31684	2F : C 0-6-0 (1900)												
31711	2F : C 0-6-0 (1900)	X	X	X	X	X	Ex Ashford						
31712	2F : C 0-6-0 (1900)												
31713	2F : C 0-6-0 (1900)												
31660	1P : R 0-4-4T (1891)	X	Ex Fav		W/D	X	X	X	X	X	X	X	X
31662	1P : R 0-4-4T (1891)		W/D	X	X	X	X	X	X	X	X	X	X
31158	1P : H 0-4-4T (1904)	X	X	X	Ex S. Lane								
31161	1P : H 0-4-4T (1904)												
31305	1P : H 0-4-4T (1904)												
31306	1P : H 0-4-4T (1904)												
31307	1P : H 0-4-4T (1904)												
31308	1P : H 0-4-4T (1904)												
31518	1P : H 0-4-4T (1904)												

Class	Oct-50	Oct-51	Oct-52	Oct-53	Oct-54	Oct-55	Oct-56	Oct-57	Oct-58	May-59
SUMMARY OF MOTIVE POWER : GILLINGHAM - 73D (1950 - 60)										
6F : Z 0-8-0T (1929)	1	1	1							
5F : N 2-6-0 (1917)		1	2		2	2	2	2	2	2
3P : L1 4-4-0 (1926)					3	3	3	3	3	
3P : D1 4-4-0 (1921)	2		2		2					
2P : E 4-4-0 (1905)	1									
2P : D 4-4-0 (1901)	2	2	2	1						
2F : C 0-6-0 (1900)	24	19	19	18	15	12	12	12	12	11
1P : R1 0-4-4T (1900)	1	1	1							
1P : R 0-4-4T (1891)	6	3	4	1						
1P : H 0-4-4T (1904)	1	3	5	6	7	6	5	5	6	6

assured with the arrival of two more H 0-4-4T's in June 1952. Rumours at the time suggested that the H class engines would not be retained for long since their replacement by LMS 2-6-2T's of the type recently introduced at Stewarts Lane and Faversham was thought to be imminent. (In the event the new engines were never allocated to Gillingham which soldiered on with its 0-4-4T's until the depot's closure in 1959).

1952/3

Early 1953 saw diesel locomotives introduced to the area with three 350hp engines - nominally allocated to Hither Green - being based at Chatham Sidings, Maidstone West and Hoo Junction for continuous shunting duties. One result of this development was the loss of Z 0-8-0T, 30951, which moved from Hoo Junction to Three Bridges in March 1953.

The R 0-4-4T's, under threat from the H 0-4-4T's, received a reprieve in Spring 1953 when 31660 and 31663 were transferred to Faversham to operate the emergency shuttle service to and from Herne Bay in connection with the line being washed away between Reculver and Birchington. The loss of the pair was compensated for by H 0-4-4T's 31161 and 31518 - bringing the allocation to seven - which arrived from Ashford and St Leonards.

May 1953 saw the shed's two D1 4-4-0's being exchanged for a pair of Stewarts Lane L1 4-4-0's; the latter having an extra reserve of power for the Tonbridge - Redhill - Reading service (not to mention the goods element of the diagram) whilst the D1 engines had a wider route availability and were suited for operations based upon Holborn Viaduct.

1953/4

The use of L1 4-4-0's proved to be short-lived since they - plus the two N 2-6-0's - were transferred away at the close of the 1953 summer season, leaving Gillingham to soldier on, as best it could, with a solitary D 4-4-0 for its Reading job and with C 0-6-0's for the 2-6-0 diagram. The N 2-6-0's were replaced in May 1954 whilst the 4-4-0 position was eased with the return of D1 31509 from Stewarts Lane in January 1954. In June 1954 a second D1 came to the shed as replacement for the withdrawal of 31729.

In September 1953 R 0-4-4T 31662 was taken out of traffic and replaced by 31660 from Faversham which was itself withdrawn two months later leaving the shed, for the first time in many years, without a representative of the class.

The reduction in C class 0-6-0's allocated to Gillingham was accelerated in January 1954 when no less than five of the shed's eighteen engines were transferred away. Two

were returned after an absence of a few weeks but the total of fifteen engines was nine less than it had been only four years earlier. An interesting move occured at the end of 1954 when a C class 0-6-0 was transferred to Guildford.

1954/5

For two months during the Autumn of 1954 Gillingham once again had an R 0-4-4T on its books; 31671 arriving from Faversham in August before being taken out of traffic in

Loco	Class	Aug-54	Sep-54	Oct-54	Nov-54	Dec-54	Jan-55	Feb-55	Mar-55	Apr-55	May-55	Jun-55	Jul-55
31815	5F : N 2-6-0 (1917)												
31816	5F : N 2-6-0 (1917)												
31785	3P : L1 4-4-0 (1926)	X	X	X	X	X	X	X	X	X	X	Ex B. Arms	
31786	3P : L1 4-4-0 (1926)	X	X	X	X	X	X	X	X	X	X	Ex B. Arms	
31787	3P : L1 4-4-0 (1926)	X	X	X	X	X	X	X	X	X	X	Ex B. Arms	
31505	3P : D1 4-4-0 (1921)											To Fav	X
31509	3P : D1 4-4-0 (1921)											To Fav	X
31112	2F : C 0-6-0 (1900)												
31227	2F : C 0-6-0 (1900)												
31229	2F : C 0-6-0 (1900)												
31242	2F : C 0-6-0 (1900)											To Fav	X
31495	2F : C 0-6-0 (1900)												
31508	2F : C 0-6-0 (1900)												
31510	2F : C 0-6-0 (1900)												
31593	2F : C 0-6-0 (1900)						To Guild	X	X	X	X	X	X
31681	2F : C 0-6-0 (1900)												
31682	2F : C 0-6-0 (1900)												
31683	2F : C 0-6-0 (1900)												
31684	2F : C 0-6-0 (1900)												
31711	2F : C 0-6-0 (1900)												
31712	2F : C 0-6-0 (1900)												
31713	2F : C 0-6-0 (1900)									W/D	X	X	X
31671	1P : R 0-4-4T (1891)	Ex Fav		W/D	X	X	X	X	X	X	X	X	X
31158	1P : H 0-4-4T (1904)									W/D	X	X	X
31161	1P : H 0-4-4T (1904)												
31305	1P : H 0-4-4T (1904)					To Fav	X	X	X	X	X	X	X
31306	1P : H 0-4-4T (1904)					To B. Arms	X	X	X	X	X	X	X
31307	1P : H 0-4-4T (1904)												
31308	1P : H 0-4-4T (1904)												
31320	1P : H 0-4-4T (1904)	X	X	X	X	X	X	X	X	X	Ex Brighton		
31322	1P : H 0-4-4T (1904)	X	X	X	X	X	X	X	X	X	Ex T. Wells		
31518	1P : H 0-4-4T (1904)												

LOCOMOTIVE ALLOCATIONS & TRANSFERS : GILLINGHAM (73D)

Loco	Class	Aug-55	Sep-55	Oct-55	Nov-55	Dec-55	Jan-56	Feb-56	Mar-56	Apr-56	May-56	Jun-56	Jul-56
31815	5F : N 2-6-0 (1917)												
31816	5F : N 2-6-0 (1917)												
31785	3P : L1 4-4-0 (1926)												
31786	3P : L1 4-4-0 (1926)												
31787	3P : L1 4-4-0 (1926)												
31112	2F : C 0-6-0 (1900)												
31227	2F : C 0-6-0 (1900)												
31229	2F : C 0-6-0 (1900)												
31495	2F : C 0-6-0 (1900)												
31508	2F : C 0-6-0 (1900)												
31510	2F : C 0-6-0 (1900)												
31681	2F : C 0-6-0 (1900)												
31682	2F : C 0-6-0 (1900)												
31683	2F : C 0-6-0 (1900)												
31684	2F : C 0-6-0 (1900)												
31711	2F : C 0-6-0 (1900)												
31712	2F : C 0-6-0 (1900)												
31161	1P : H 0-4-4T (1904)												
31307	1P : H 0-4-4T (1904)					To Ashford	X	X	X	X	X	X	X
31308	1P : H 0-4-4T (1904)												
31320	1P : H 0-4-4T (1904)						W/D	X	X	X	X	X	X
31322	1P : H 0-4-4T (1904)												
31512	1P : H 0-4-4T (1904)	X	X	X	X	Ex Ashford							
31518	1P : H 0-4-4T (1904)												

LOCOMOTIVE ALLOCATIONS & TRANSFERS : GILLINGHAM (73D)

Loco	Class	Aug-56	Sep-56	Oct-56	Nov-56	Dec-56	Jan-57	Feb-57	Mar-57	Apr-57	May-57	Jun-57	Jul-57
31815	5F : N 2-6-0 (1917)												
31816	5F : N 2-6-0 (1917)												
31785	3P : L1 4-4-0 (1926)												
31786	3P : L1 4-4-0 (1926)												
31787	3P : L1 4-4-0 (1926)												
31112	2F : C 0-6-0 (1900)												
31227	2F : C 0-6-0 (1900)												
31229	2F : C 0-6-0 (1900)												
31297	2F : C 0-6-0 (1900)	X	X	X	X	X	X	X	X	X	X	Ex B. Arms	
31495	2F : C 0-6-0 (1900)												
31508	2F : C 0-6-0 (1900)												
31510	2F : C 0-6-0 (1900)												
31681	2F : C 0-6-0 (1900)												
31682	2F : C 0-6-0 (1900)												
31683	2F : C 0-6-0 (1900)												
31684	2F : C 0-6-0 (1900)												
31711	2F : C 0-6-0 (1900)					W/D	X	X	X	X	X	X	X
31712	2F : C 0-6-0 (1900)						W/D	X	X	X	X	X	X
31161	1P : H 0-4-4T (1904)												
31308	1P : H 0-4-4T (1904)												
31322	1P : H 0-4-4T (1904)												
31512	1P : H 0-4-4T (1904)												
31518	1P : H 0-4-4T (1904)												

Apart from emergencies such as the flooding between Reculver and Minnis Bay in 1953 when several members of the class were drafted in to assist with ballast trains, the distinctive Q1 0-6-0's were not much seen on the Chatham section and how 33039 of Hither Green came to be working a Faversham to Dover train in June 1959 is an illustration of how distorted engine workings could become on summer Saturdays. The only regular appearance by the class was at Swanley where one of the Tonbridge allocation worked 05.46 goods from Sevenoaks and shunted the yard before returning. (L.G. Marshall)

October. The main event of the period came in June 1955 when three L1 4-4-0's arrived from Bricklayers Arms to replace the two D1 4-4-0's which were sent to Favershan for work on the Canterbury East/Dover line. The L1's - relatively modern engines given Gillingham's penchant for collecting locomotives of antiquarian qualities - proved to be permenent residents and remained at the shed until closure in June 1959.

1955 - 60

From mid-1955 onwards changes to the Gillingham allocation were minimal and for the most part were concerned with the replacement of the odd 0-6-0 and 0-4-4T that was taken out of traffic, with the complement of engines remaining constant at just over twenty until the closure of the shed in June 1959 when the twenty-two remaining engines were dispersed to Nine Elms (14), Tonbridge (3), Brighton (2), Guildford (2) amd Three Bridges (1).

After the 1959 electrification locomotive activity at Gillingham shrank to almost nothing and although Chatham Goods and Hoo Junction remained active, diesel and electric engines were able to turn in the yards and with three exceptions there was no need for them to venture as far East as Gillingham. The exceptions, all E5001 electric locomotives which came to Gillingham for crew relief, left the shed at 08.30 for the 09.50 Hoo Junction to Hither Green, 17.45 for the 18.45 Gillingham - Sittingbourne Goods and 23.25 for the 01.00 Hoo Junction to Hither Green.

LOCOMOTIVE ALLOCATIONS & TRANSFERS : GILLINGHAM (73D)													
Loco	Class	Aug-57	Sep-57	Oct-57	Nov-57	Dec-57	Jan-58	Feb-58	Mar-58	Apr-58	May-58	Jun-58	Jul-58
31815	5F : N 2-6-0 (1917)												
31816	5F : N 2-6-0 (1917)												
31785	3P : L1 4-4-0 (1926)												
31786	3P : L1 4-4-0 (1926)												
31787	3P : L1 4-4-0 (1926)												
31037	2F : C 0-6-0 (1900)	X	X	Ex S. Lane									
31112	2F : C 0-6-0 (1900)												
31227	2F : C 0-6-0 (1900)												
31229	2F : C 0-6-0 (1900)												
31297	2F : C 0-6-0 (1900)												
31495	2F : C 0-6-0 (1900)												
31508	2F : C 0-6-0 (1900)			W/D	X	X	X	X	X	X	X	X	X
31510	2F : C 0-6-0 (1900)												
31576	2F : C 0-6-0 (1900)	X	X	Ex S. Lane									
31681	2F : C 0-6-0 (1900)												
31682	2F : C 0-6-0 (1900)												
31683	2F : C 0-6-0 (1900)												
31684	2F : C 0-6-0 (1900)												
31161	1P : H 0-4-4T (1904)												
31308	1P : H 0-4-4T (1904)												
31322	1P : H 0-4-4T (1904)												
31512	1P : H 0-4-4T (1904)												
31518	1P : H 0-4-4T (1904)												
31548	1P : H 0-4-4T (1904)	X	X	X	X	X	X	X	X	X	Ex Ton		

LOCOMOTIVE ALLOCATIONS & TRANSFERS : GILLINGHAM (73D)													
Loco	Class	Aug-58	Sep-58	Oct-58	Nov-58	Dec-58	Jan-59	Feb-59	Mar-59	Apr-59	May-59	Jun-59	Jul-59
31815	5F : N 2-6-0 (1917)											To Guild	X
31816	5F : N 2-6-0 (1917)											To Guild	X
31785	3P : L1 4-4-0 (1926)											To N. Elms	X
31786	3P : L1 4-4-0 (1926)											To N. Elms	X
31787	3P : L1 4-4-0 (1926)											To N. Elms	X
31037	2F : C 0-6-0 (1900)											To N. Elms	X
31112	2F : C 0-6-0 (1900)											To N. Elms	X
31227	2F : C 0-6-0 (1900)											To N. Elms	X
31229	2F : C 0-6-0 (1900)											To N. Elms	X
31297	2F : C 0-6-0 (1900)											To N. Elms	X
31495	2F : C 0-6-0 (1900)											To N. Elms	X
31510	2F : C 0-6-0 (1900)											To N. Elms	X
31576	2F : C 0-6-0 (1900)											To N. Elms	X
31681	2F : C 0-6-0 (1900)								W/D	X	X	X	X
31682	2F : C 0-6-0 (1900)											To N. Elms	X
31683	2F : C 0-6-0 (1900)											To N. Elms	X
31684	2F : C 0-6-0 (1900)											To N. Elms	X
31161	1P : H 0-4-4T (1904)											To T. Bges	X
31308	1P : H 0-4-4T (1904)											To Brighton	X
31322	1P : H 0-4-4T (1904)											To Ton	X
31512	1P : H 0-4-4T (1904)											To Ton	X
31518	1P : H 0-4-4T (1904)											To Ton	X
31548	1P : H 0-4-4T (1904)											To Brighton	X

In spite of the 140 Pacifics that the Southern came to acquire in its latter days, for the most part LCDR expresses remained in the hands of 4-6-0's. For many years from 1927 the N15 King Arthur 4-6-0's dominated both the Ramsgate - Cannon Street and the Victoria - Ramsgate expresses and the class remained unchallenged until the late 1940's when the Ramsgate allocation was displaced by a batch of new light Pacifics for working the Cannon Street diagrams. The Stewarts Lane engines were not affected by this development and remained in charge of the Victoria - Ramsgate expresses until the summer of 1955 when their duties started to be taken over by BR 5MT 4-6-0's. By the end of the year the new engines had officially taken over all the N15 workings at Stewarts Lane but in fact the King Arthurs remained active by standing in for BR 5MT engines and assisting with the exceptionally heavy seasonal traffic between London and Thanet.

30797 'Sir Blamor de Ganis' is prepared at its home shed of Dover to work a special to Charing Cross via Tonbridge in September 1957. Although Dover had an allocation of nine N15's, most were kept in reserve for relief trains - of which there were a great many - and there were only two regular diagrams for the class: an overnight express goods to Southwark and the 06.50 business train from Dover Priory to Cannon Street. (L.G. Marshall)

King Arthur 30794 'Sir Ector de Maris' of Stewarts Lane on Ramsgate loco in September 1957. Once the BR Standard 4-6-0's had bedded down on the Victoria services in 1955, the number of visits by King Arthur's at Ramsgate diminished to the point where the only booked workings were on the 10.12 Tonbridge - Ramsgate and the 16.55 Margate - Charing Cross. However the ratio of engines to diagrams for the Stewarts Lane Standard 4-6-0's was sufficiently tight to ensure that the instances of N15 substitution occurred on a regular basis and the class remained a regular feature of Kent Coast life until the end of steam working in June 1959. (L.G. Marshall)

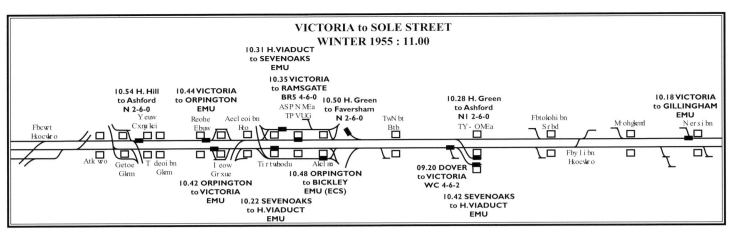

VICTORIA to SOLE STREET
WINTER 1955 : 11.00

(Diagram labels include:)

10.31 H.VIADUCT to SEVENOAKS EMU

10.35 VICTORIA to RAMSGATE BR5 4-6-0

10.54 H. Hill to Ashford N 2-6-0

10.44 VICTORIA to ORPINGTON EMU

10.50 H. Green to Faversham N 2-6-0

10.28 H. Green to Ashford N1 2-6-0

10.18 VICTORIA to GILLINGHAM EMU

10.42 ORPINGTON to VICTORIA EMU

10.48 ORPINGTON to BICKLEY EMU (ECS)

09.20 DOVER to VICTORIA WC 4-6-2

10.22 SEVENOAKS to H.VIADUCT EMU

10.42 SEVENOAKS to H.VIADUCT EMU

CONTROLLER'S LOG: Although Herne Hill is the principal LCDR marshalling yard in London, it is not the only London terminal for LCDR traffic and in fact goods traffic joins the main line by (at least) three different routes. One is via Herne Hill but this is largely limited to cross London traffic from the Great Northern and Midland lines and traffic from other parts of the system comes via the relatively new (1933) yard at Hither Green and is run in through

wide range of traffic that varies from industrial and household coal to miscellaneous goods and empty wagons for the fruit industry east of the Medway. Quite a number of SER workings avoid the congested South Eastern route by using the connection between the two main lines at St Mary Cray and one of these, the 10.28 Hither Green to Ashford, can be seen taking the Maidstone branch at Swanley - an interesting example of a train running more than 90% of

the C 0-6-0 handling much of the local traffic. Occasionally the roles are reversed as is the case with the mid-day Faversham - Whitstable and Faversham - Margate trips where the former, a fourteen mile round trip, is booked to a 2-6-0 whilst the Thanet service has an 0-6-0.

While a high degree of standardisation has been achieved in goods motive power circles - the N1 2-6-0 at Swanley is rather exceptional - the same cannot be said for passenger trains

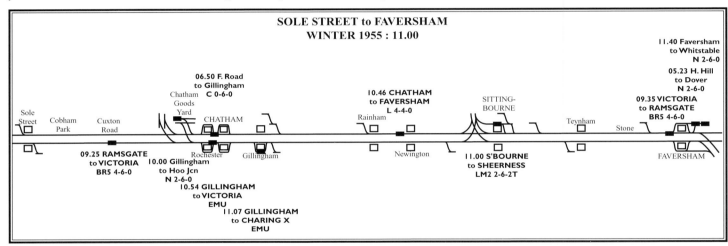

SOLE STREET to FAVERSHAM
WINTER 1955 : 11.00

(Diagram labels include:)

11.40 Faversham to Whitstable N 2-6-0

05.23 H. Hill to Dover N 2-6-0

06.50 F. Road to Gillingham C 0-6-0

10.46 CHATHAM to FAVERSHAM L 4-4-0

09.35 VICTORIA to RAMSGATE BR5 4-6-0

09.25 RAMSGATE to VICTORIA BR5 4-6-0

10.00 Gillingham to Hoo Jcn N 2-6-0

11.00 S'BOURNE to SHEERNESS LM2 2-6-2T

10.54 GILLINGHAM to VICTORIA EMU

11.07 GILLINGHAM to CHARING X EMU

(Stations: Sole Street, Cobham Park, Cuxton Road, Chatham Goods Yard, CHATHAM, Rochester, Gillingham, Rainham, Newington, SITTINGBOURNE, Teynham, Stone, FAVERSHAM)

---

trains to LCDR destinations via Mary Cray Junction. A significant tonnage of traffic also arrives in the Medway area from Hoo Junction which serves the heavily industrialised North Kent coast between Gravesend and London. Unlike many of the other railways radiating from London, the LCDR does not have any particular pattern of goods flows - there is no hourly procession of trains from Herne Hill to Faversham, for example - and trains therefore appear to run rather haphazardly, conveying a

its journey on 'foreign' metals. Following the 10.28 is a Hither Green to Faversham service while a Herne Hill - Ashford goods is making its way through the inner suburbs and will take the Maidstone branch at Swanley. To find a 'pure' LCDR goods service, it is necessary to look east to Faversham where the 05.23 Herne Hill to Dover is in the process of detaching traffic for the Thanet road before carrying on to Canterbury and Dover. The standard goods engine for most long distance trains is the N 2-6-0 with

where the recent introduction of LMS and BR Standard engines has simply increased the level of variety. Nowhere is this more apparent than in Thanet where the SECR and LCDR overlap. The two Victoria trains standing in Ramsgate sport a pair of 4-6-0's whilst one of the highly efficient LMS 2-6-4 tanks accelerates away from Broadstairs with a stopping train from Ashford via Canterbury West. Ahead of it in Margate is the 06.56 ex Holborn Viaduct with its E1 4-4-0 - you can't get much more varied than that!

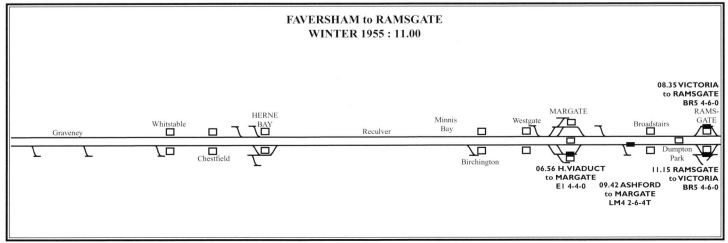

FAVERSHAM to RAMSGATE
WINTER 1955 : 11.00

(Diagram labels include:)

08.35 VICTORIA to RAMSGATE BR5 4-6-0

06.56 H.VIADUCT to MARGATE E1 4-4-0

09.42 ASHFORD to MARGATE LM4 2-6-4T

11.15 RAMSGATE to VICTORIA BR5 4-6-0

(Stations: Graveney, Whitstable, Chestfield, HERNE BAY, Reculver, Minnis Bay, Birchington, Westgate, MARGATE, Broadstairs, Dumpton Park, RAMSGATE)

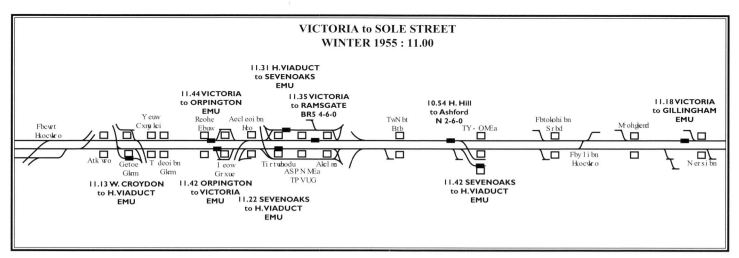

VICTORIA to SOLE STREET
WINTER 1955 : 11.00

11.44 VICTORIA to ORPINGTON EMU

11.31 H. VIADUCT to SEVENOAKS EMU

11.35 VICTORIA to RAMSGATE BR5 4-6-0

10.54 H. Hill to Ashford N 2-6-0

11.18 VICTORIA to GILLINGHAM EMU

11.13 W. CROYDON to H. VIADUCT EMU

11.42 ORPINGTON to VICTORIA EMU

11.22 SEVENOAKS to H. VIADUCT EMU

11.42 SEVENOAKS to H. VIADUCT EMU

CONTROLLER'S LOG: If the Thanet area was varied an hour ago, take another look for there are now - between Faversham and Ramsgate - no less than twelve trains and seven classes of engine; a situation that makes an extraordinary contrast with the London end of the line where the great majority of services are

Introduced in 1904 for the London suburban service, the 1925 electrification to Orpington and its 1938 extension to Gillingham all but eliminated them from the London area whilst post-war developments have seen many of their duties being handed over to LMS 2MT 2-6-2T's. The latter are very modern, comfortable

been taken over by 2-6-2T's.

One of the most remarkable things about East Kent is the presence of its coalfield - more than one hundred miles from its nearest neighbour - and the Welsh-speaking communities who man the pits at Tilmanstone and Snowdown. Other Kentish mines exist at Sturry, Sandwich and

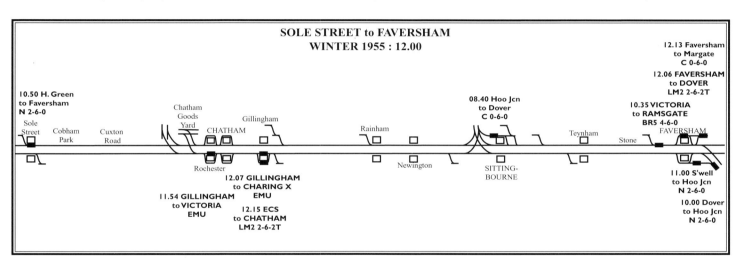

SOLE STREET to FAVERSHAM
WINTER 1955 : 12.00

12.13 Faversham to Margate C 0-6-0

12.06 FAVERSHAM to DOVER LM2 2-6-2T

10.50 H. Green to Faversham N 2-6-0

08.40 Hoo Jcn to Dover C 0-6-0

10.35 VICTORIA to RAMSGATE BR5 4-6-0

12.07 GILLINGHAM to CHARING X EMU

11.54 GILLINGHAM to VICTORIA EMU

12.15 ECS to CHATHAM LM2 2-6-2T

11.00 S'well to Hoo Jcn N 2-6-0

10.00 Dover to Hoo Jcn N 2-6-0

worked by an efficient if rather dull monotony of electric multiple units. Further colour is added at Gillingham where the H 0-4-4T that has arrived with the 11.11 ex Sheerness is relieved by an LMS 2-6-2T, the latter taking the stock to Chatham to form the 12.56 to Sittingbourne. The 0-4-4T goes to the shed for coal and water prior to running light to Gravesend Central to work the afternoon turn on the Allhallows branch and the sight of the engine prompts one to wonder what the future holds for the class.

and efficient machines but one would be hard-pressed to say that any difference could be noticed in the operation of the service: the trains are neither heavier nor faster than they were twenty years ago. Gillingham shed now has work for only two 0-4-4T's; one of which spends all day - 04.25 until 23.36 - on the Allhallows branch while the other joins it in the afternoon after spending the morning at Sheerness. The work formerly covered by the class on the Sittingbourne - Sheerness branch has largely

Deal.

Output from Snowdown and Tilmanstone is served by four daily departures each, two of which can be seen with their N 2-6-0's at Faversham en route to Hoo Junction marshalling yard.

As always with collieries, the provision of empty wagons is always a problem but some easement is given by the 08.40 Hoo Junction to Dover which is routed via the Isle of Sheppey to scavenge for any empties that may be hiding.

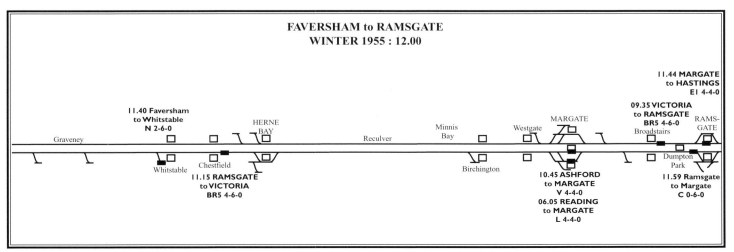

FAVERSHAM to RAMSGATE
WINTER 1955 : 12.00

11.44 MARGATE to HASTINGS E1 4-4-0

09.35 VICTORIA to RAMSGATE BR5 4-6-0

11.40 Faversham to Whitstable N 2-6-0

11.15 RAMSGATE to VICTORIA BR5 4-6-0

10.45 ASHFORD to MARGATE V 4-4-0

06.05 READING to MARGATE L 4-4-0

11.59 Ramsgate to Margate C 0-6-0

SITTINGBOURNE

SITTINGBOURNE
STATION WORKING (1954/5)

Train	Arrive	Engine	Shed	Dep	Destination
20.00 Dover Town		N 2-6-0	S. Lane 62	00/10	Hither Green
(Ex Goods Yard)		LM2 2-6-2T	Fav 269	01.05	Herne Hill
18.50 Dover Town		N 2-6-0	Dover 452	01/35	Hoo Junction
00.56 Queenborough	01.40	C 0-6-0	Fav 280		(Fwd at 02.26)
22.00 Hither Green	01.52	N 2-6-0	H. Green 176	02.11	Dover Town
02.00 Faversham	02.20	C 0-6-0 & LM2 2-6-2T	Fav 269 & Fav 279		(Fwd at 02.50)
(00.56 Queenborough)		C 0-6-0	Fav 280	02.26	Faversham
(02.00 Faversham)		C 0-6-0 & LM2 2-6-2T	Fav 269 & Fav 279	02.50	Sheerness
02.30 Faversham	03.05	N 2-6-0	Fav 277	03.20	Hoo Junction
00.40 Snodland		LM4 2-6-4T	Dover 450	03/25	Snowdown
01.10 Bricklayers Arms		N 2-6-0	BLA 121	03/45	Ramsgate
01.35 Herne Hill	04.06	N 2-6-0	S. Lane 61	04.30	Faversham
03.00 Victoria	04.42	E1 4-4-0	S. Lane 45	04.45	Ramsgate
04.40 Faversham	04.55	2 x LM2 2-6-2T	Fav 269 & Fav 270		(Forms 05.05)
(Detach pilot)		LM2 2-6-2T	Fav 269	05.05	Sheerness
03.58 Chatham Yard	05.05	N 2-6-0	Dover 452		(Fwd at 05.40)
03.30 Victoria	05.16	BR5 4-6-0	S. Lane 16	05.20	Ramsgate
03.30 Shepherdswell	05.30		Fav 278		(Yard Pilot)
(03.58 Chatham Yard)		N 2-6-0	Dover 452	05.40	Deal via Ramsgate
		LM2 2-6-2T	Fav 270	05.51	Sheerness
05.31 Sheerness	05.54	LM2 2-6-2T	Fav 269		
04.34 Ramsgate	05.58	L 4-4-0	Ram 489	05.59	Chatham
05.45 Chatham	06.08	LM2 2-6-2T	Fav 272		(Fwd at 06.16)
		LM2 2-6-2T	Fav 271	06.11	Sheerness
(Attach pilot)		2 x LM2 2-6-2T	Fav 272/Fav 269	06.16	Faversham
06.35 Sheerness	06.55	LM2 2-6-2T	Fav 270		
06.44 Faversham	06.59	LM2 2-6-2T	Fav 269	07.01	Rochester
05.10 Victoria	07.03	BR5 4-6-0	S. Lane 12	07.06	Ramsgate
		LM2 2-6-2T	Fav 270	07.10	Sheerness
05.20 Gillingham	07.15	C 0-6-0	Gill 245		(Fwd at 07.25)
06.06 Ramsgate		WC 4-6-2	Ram 466	07/22	Cannon Street
(05.20 Gillingham)		C 0-6-0	Gill 245	07.25	Teynham
06.10 Dover Priory	07.31	D1 4-4-0	Dover 444	07.33	Gillingham
07.22 Sheerness	07.39	LM2 2-6-2T	Fav 271		
06.29 Ramsgate	07.44	WC 4-6-2	Ram 467	07.45	Cannon Street
05.50 Cannon Street	07.43	E1 4-4-0	S. Lane 46	07.46	Dover Priory
		LM2 2-6-2T	Fav 271	07.48	Sheerness
07.40 Chatham	08.04	H 0-4-4T	Gill 231		(Forms 08.13)
Light ex Teynham		C 0-6-0	Gill 245		
		H 0-4-4T	Gill 231	08.13	Sheerness
07.55 Sheerness	08.15	C 0-6-0	Fav 279		
07.20 Ramsgate		WC 4-6-2	Ram 470	08/20	Cannon Street
07.07 Ramsgate	08.26	L 4-4-0	Ram 490	08.27	Gillingham
		C 0-6-0	Fav 279	08.27	Faversham
07.35 Ramsgate		WC 4-6-2	Ram 471	08/40	Cannon Street
08.22 Sheerness	08.42	LM2 2-6-2T	Fav 270		
08.20 Herne Bay	08.53	V 4-4-0	Ram 478	08.54	Cannon Street
07.00 Cannon Street	08.52	N 2-6-0	S. Lane 63	08.55	Ramsgate
		C 0-6-0	Gill 245	08.57	Light to Gillingham loco
07.42 Dover Priory	09.03	N 2-6-0	Fav 260	09.05	Chatham
		LM2 2-6-2T	Fav 270	09.08	Sheerness
08.25 Ramsgate		WC 4-6-2	Ram 473	09/25	Victoria
05.23 Herne Hill	09.30	N 2-6-0	S. Lane 62		(Fwd at 10.07)
08.35 Victoria		BR5 4-6-0	S. Lane 13	09/45	Ramsgate
09.38 Chatham	09.55	L 4-4-0	Rams 489		(Forms 10.00)
09.38 Sheerness	09.58	H 0-4-4T	Gill 231		
(09.38 Chatham)		L 4-4-0	Rams 489	10.00	Dover Priory
08.44 Ramsgate	10.02	E1 4-4-0	S. Lane 45	10.03	Chatham
(05.23 Herne Hill)		N 2-6-0	S. Lane 62	10.07	Dover Town
09.20 Dover Priory		WC 4-6-2	Dover 431	10/17	Victoria
		H 0-4-4T	Gill 231	10.19	Sheerness
10.10 Sheerness	10.31	LM2 2-6-2T	Fav 270		
09.25 Ramsgate	10.37	BR5 4-6-0	S. Lane 16	10.39	Victoria
09.35 Victoria	10.48	BR5 4-6-0	S. Lane 14	10.50	Ramsgate
		LM2 2-6-2T	Fav 270	11.00	Sheerness
10.46 Chatham	11.06	L 4-4-0	Ram 490	11.08	Faversham
10.35 Victoria	11.49	BR5 4-6-0	S. Lane 10	11.51	Ramsgate
(Ex Yard Pilot)		C 0-6-0	Fav 278	11.53	Sheerness
Light ex Gillingham loco	12.00	N 2-6-0	Fav 277		(For 13.00 Dover)
08.40 Hoo Jcn via Q'boro	12.09	C 0-6-0	Gill 242		(Engine Change)
11.00 Shepherdswell		N 2-6-0	H. Green 172	12/18	Hoo Junction
12.18 Sheerness	12.38	LM2 2-6-2T	Fav 270		
11.15 Ramsgate	12.39	BR5 4-6-0	S. Lane 12	12.42	Victoria
11.35 Victoria (Pullman)	12.50	BR5 4-6-0	S. Lane 11	12.52	Ramsgate
10.00 Dover Town		N 2-6-0	H. Green 176	12/53	Hoo Junction
		LM2 2-6-2T	Fav 270	12.56	Sheerness

Train	Arrive	Engine	Shed	Dep	Destination
(08.40 Hoo Jcn via Q'boro)		N 2-6-0	Fav 277	13.00	Dover Town
12.56 Chatham	13.20	LM2 2-6-2T	Fav 269		(Forms 13.26)
		LM2 2-6-2T	Fav 269	13.26	Sheerness
13.20 Sheerness	13.41	C 0-6-0	Fav 278		
12.37 Dover Priory	13.47	E1 4-4-0	S. Lane 46	13.48	Gillingham
12.35 Victoria	13.50		S. Lane 15	13.53	Ramsgate
		C 0-6-0	Gill 242	13.55	Sheerness
11.00 H. Viaduct (Pcls)	14.01	E1 4-4-0	BLA 91	14.08	Ramsgate
13.10 Ramsgate	14.30	BR5 4-6-0	S. Lane 13	14.32	Victoria
10.50 Hither Green	14.32	C 0-6-0	Fav 280		(Fwd at 14.48)
Light ex Faversham loco	14.40	LM2 2-6-2T	Fav 272		(For 16.00 Sheerness)
		C 0-6-0	Fav 278	14.43	Sheerness
		C 0-6-0	Fav 280	14/48	Faversham
13.55 Ramsgate		V 4-4-0	Ram 481	15/11	Victoria
15.11 Faversham	15.26	LM2 2-6-2T	Fav 271	15.28	Chatham
13.55 Snowdown		N 2-6-0	S. Lane 61	15/36	Fawkham
15.20 Sheerness	15.41	C 0-6-0	Gill 242		(Yard Pilot to 19.58)
14.35 Victoria	15.50	WC 4-6-2	Dover 431	15.52	Dover Priory
		LM2 2-6-2T	Fav 272	16.00	Sheerness
16.15 Sheerness	16.36	LM2 2-6-2T	Fav 269		
15.22 Ramsgate	16.46	BR5 4-6-0	S. Lane 14	16.48	Victoria
15.35 Victoria	16.46	BR5 4-6-0	S. Lane 16	16.48	Ramsgate
		LM2 2-6-2T	Fav 269	16.56	Sheerness
16.37 Chatham	17.02	LM2 2-6-2T	Fav 271		
16.55 Strood	17.26	D1 4-4-0	Dover 444		(Fwd at 17.31)
		LM2 2-6-2T	Fav 271	17.29	Sheerness
17.10 Sheerness	17.29	LM2 2-6-2T	Fav 272		
(16.55 Strood)		D1 4-4-0	Dover 444	17.31	Dover Priory
16.15 Ramsgate	17.36	BR5 4-6-0	S. Lane 10	17.38	Victoria
16.45 Cannon Street		WC 4-6-2	Ram 471	17/40	Ramsgate
16.32 Cannon Street	17.53	L1 4-4-0	BLA 88	17.56	Ramsgate
		LM2 2-6-2T	Fav 272	17.57	Sheerness
17.40 Sheerness	18.00	LM2 2-6-2T	Fav 269		
17.05 Ramsgate (Pullman)		WC 4-6-2	Ram 470	18/05	Victoria
17.15 Cannon Street		WC 4-6-2	Ram 467	18/11	Ramsgate
		LM2 2-6-2T	Fav 269	18.15	Light to Teynham
17.09 Dover Priory	18.18	LM4 2-6-4T	Dover 450	18.19	Chatham
18.06 Sheerness	18.26	LM2 2-6-2T	Fav 271		
16.20 Canterbury East	18.27	N 2-6-0	BLA 121		(Fwd at 18.56)
17.21 Cannon Street	18.34	U1 2-6-0	Fav 260	18.35	Dover Priory
17.45 Cannon Street		WC 4-6-2	Ram 466	18/47	Ramsgate
17.40 Dover Priory	18.47	BR5 4-6-0	S. Lane 11	18.49	Ramsgate
18.38 Chatham	18.55	C 0-6-0	Gill 237		(Couple to 19.30 Chatham)
(16.20 Canterbury East)		N 2-6-0	BLA 121	18.56	Blackfriars
18.16 Cannon Street		V 4-4-0	Ram 478	19/13	Ramsgate
19.17 Teynham	19.23	LM2 2-6-2T	Fav 269		(Change engines)
19.05 Sheerness	19.25	LM2 2-6-2T	Fav 272		(Forms 19.30)
		C 0-6-0 & LM2 2-6-2T	Gill 237 & Fav 271	19.30	Chatham
18.23 Cannon Street	19.37	V 4-4-0	BLA 81	19.38	Dover Priory
		LM2 2-6-2T	Fav 271	19.45	Sheerness
19.39 Faversham	19.50	D1 4-4-0	Fav 262	19.51	Gillingham
19.28 Sheerness	19.48	LM2 2-6-2T	Fav 270	19.52	Faversham
(19.17 Teynham)		C 0-6-0	Gill 242	19.58	Gillingham Goods
20.17 Sheerness	20.35	LM2 2-6-2T	Fav 272		
19.35 Victoria	20.40	WC 4-6-2	Ram 473	20.42	Ramsgate
		LM2 2-6-2T	Fav 272	20.51	Sheerness
19.45 Ramsgate	21.01	BR5 4-6-0	S. Lane 16	21.03	Victoria
20.38 Chatham	21.01	LM2 2-6-2T	Fav 271	21.03	Faversham
Light ex Faversham loco	21.08	N 2-6-0	Dover 451		(Yard pilot to 23.55)
		LM2 2-6-2T	Fav 269	21.10	Sheerness
17.10 Ramsgate (Pcls)	21.34	N 2-6-0	S. Lane 63		(Fwd at 21.46)
21.22 Sheerness	21.42	LM2 2-6-2T	Fav 272		(Forms 22.05)
(17.10 Ramsgate Pcls)		N 2-6-0	S. Lane 63	21.46	Victoria
20.35 Victoria	21.50	V 4-4-0	Ram 481	21.52	Ramsgate
21.40 Faversham	21.55	C 0-6-0	Fav 280	22.00	Sheerness
		LM2 2-6-2T	Fav 272	22.05	Faversham
22.11 Sheerness	22.32	LM2 2-6-2T	Fav 269		
21.10 Ramsgate	22.30	L1 4-4-0	BLA 88	22.33	Charing Cross
		LM2 2-6-2T	Fav 269	22.45	Sheerness
21.35 Victoria	22.42	WC 4-6-2	Ram 470	22.43	Ramsgate
22.35 Faversham		BR5 4-6-0	S. Lane 15	22/50	Blackfriars
23.13 Sheerness	23.31	C 0-6-0 & LM2 2-6-2T	Fav 280 & Fav 269		(269 to Yard Pilot)
23.22 Chatham	23.42	D1 4-4-0	Fav 262	23.44	Faversham
		C 0-6-0	Fav 280	23.52	Sheerness
		N 2-6-0	Dover 451	23.55	Shepherdswell

Choosing the most interesting LCDR station from which to watch trains would not be an easy matter but there can be no doubt that Sittingbourne would be high in the list of contenders. The number of venerable inside cylinder 4-4-0's to be seen did not match that of Faversham where they powered a considerable proportion of the Dover line trains, but there was a frequent service of branch trains to Sheerness and although the majority were handled by Faversham-based LMS 2-6-2T's, some produced a variety of interesting engines. Unlike Faversham where trains had to come down to 30 mph, non-stop trains could pass through Sittingbourne at as near 85 mph as they could get and the sight of a few evening business trains streaking through on their way to Ramsgate was enough to dispel from the mind of a visitor any delusions he might have had of the Chatham being a backwater line. Nowhere was LCDR variety more apparent than at Sittingbourne as the hour of ten in the morning - the time when most observers would present themselves at the end of the down platform - typified. An L 4-4-0 would run in with the 08.35 Victoria - Ramsgate and be followed a few minutes later by an H 0-4-4T with the Sheerness branch train. While the 0-4-4T was running round its train to form the 10.19 back to Sheppey, an E1 4-4-0 would call with an up main line stopping train, passing as it pulled away, an N 2-6-0 with a London to Dover goods. As whistles blew and doors slammed on the Sheerness branch train, the modern age thrust itself into the scene with a shattering noise as a light Pacific and nine corridors crashed through on the up main with the 09.20 Dover - Victoria express. In a mere nineteen minutes, five trains with five different classes of engine had passed through. Railways did not come much more varied than that.

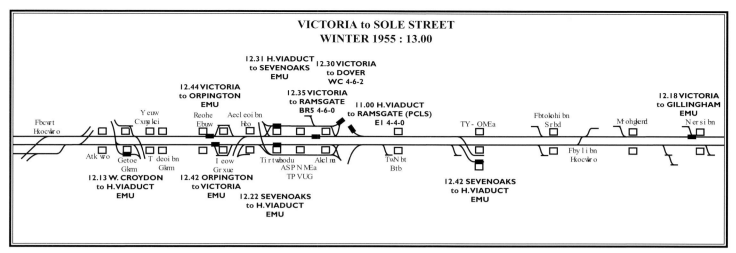

VICTORIA to SOLE STREET
WINTER 1955 : 13.00

CONTROLLER'S LOG: Mention earlier of the disappearing H class begs the question whether the LCDR could have followed the example of the Great Eastern and operated an electric-type suburban service with steam. The the rest of the infrastructure.

The difference electrification made to the service was staggering. In 1922 only ten trains from Orpington arrived in LCDR London between 07.00 and 10.00: an average all station to Swanley where it combines with a train from Maidstone. By contrast the SER electric services to Charing Cross via the densely populated areas of Gravesend and Dartford are much more energetically run.

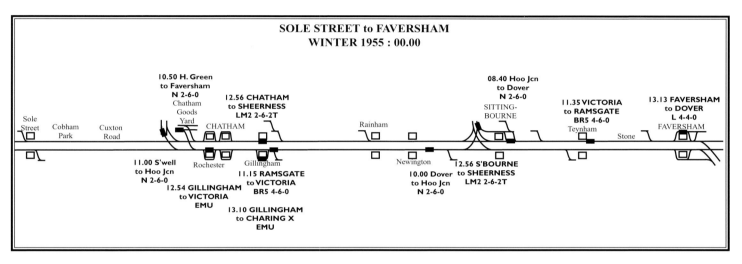

SOLE STREET to FAVERSHAM
WINTER 1955 : 00.00

answer is probably not since the key ingredient at Liverpool Street were the engine release bays which enabled trains to turn-round in about four minutes with the minimum of conflicting light engine movements. The facilities at Victoria were much more basic and did not diminish light engine and stock movements to the point where an intensive steam operation could be introduced and progress had to wait for the electric multiple unit which had no extraneous movements. In addition the third-rail system allowed the service to be revolutionised without significant expenditure having to be made on of one every 18 minutes. By 1930 the ten trains had grown to seventeen - a train every ten minutes - and remained at that level for the next twenty-five years: a level of intensity that it is difficult to see sustained by locomotives and hauled stock. In 1938, the third rail reached Gillingham yet the service via Farningham Road never attracted the level of growth - the war may have had a bearing on matters - that usually followed electrification schemes and in fact the service over the outer suburban remains rather half-hearted, consisting of an hourly stopping train from Gillingham which calls at Given that almost half the mileage between London and Thanet was electrified in 1938, it is perhaps surprising that no electric locomotives, similar to those of the Metropolitan Railway, have been produced to work the expresses between Victoria and Gillingham. The stumbling block has been the number of electric engines needed - over a dozen - would not make an appreciable saving in the number of steam engines used whilst a minimum of two crews per train would be needed. The prospect of summer Saturday chaos at Gillingham as every train changes engines is not a happy one!

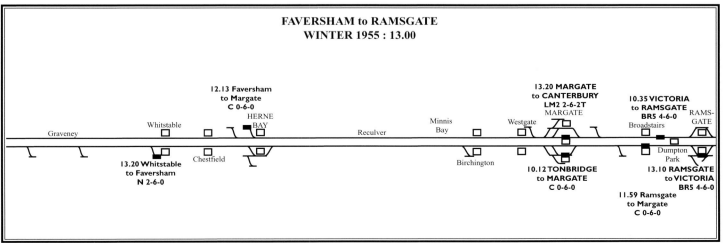

FAVERSHAM to RAMSGATE
WINTER 1955 : 13.00

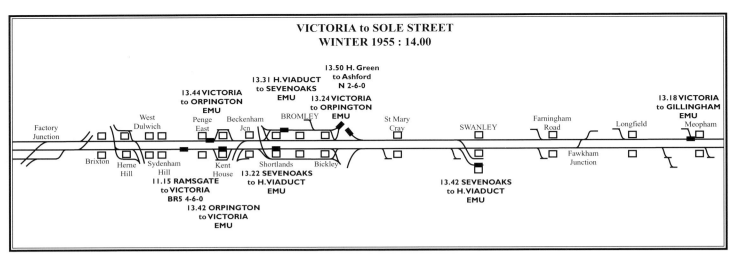

VICTORIA to SOLE STREET
WINTER 1955 : 14.00

CONTROLLER'S LOG: As a Schools 4-4-0 pulls away from Ramsgate with the 13.55 express for Victoria, one is reminded that the monopoly of Standard 5MT 4-6-0's on the Ramsgate expresses is not complete! In fact their gasp on the down service - which has been total since the 03.30 ex Victoria - is also about to be loosened since the 14.35 from Victoria - an odd-man-out in several senses - is booked

The sight of two expresses on the up road between Ramsgate and Whitstable reminds one that the discipline of the thirty-five minute departures of the down trains does not apply in the opposite direction and departures from Ramsgate tend to be rather haphazard at times. Until a short time ago, the last express to leave Ramsgate was the 09.25 leaving a gap of almost four hours until the next. (The 11.15

have some interesting engines on show; the former having a pair of E1 4-4-0's on the up and down main lines whilst a C 0-6-0 goods engine takes a turn with the Sheerness branch train.

At Faversham a German L 4-4-0 runs in with a stopping train from Dover and joins company with a D1 4-4-0 which is waiting to connect with the 12.35 Victoria - Ramsgate. The L 4-4-0 will have to be released from its train fairly

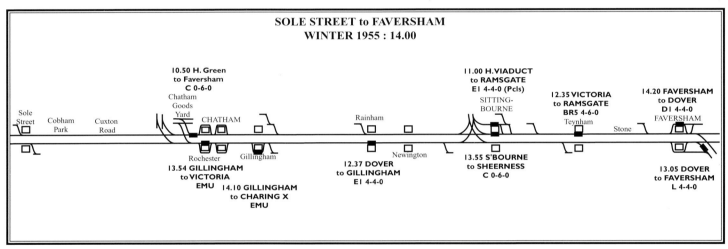

SOLE STREET to FAVERSHAM
WINTER 1955 : 14.00

to be worked by a WC Pacific which works the leading four coaches through to Dover whilst the five-coach Ramsgate section is worked forward from Faversham by an L class 4-4-0. There is something rather timeless about boarding the train at Whitstable and Herne Bay to find it being worked by the same engine that worked it forty years earlier and it is difficult to think of anywhere else on British Railways where one might do the same.

ex Ramsgate, now approaching Sydenham Hill, can be discounted since it calls at every station to Rochester - hardly the hallmark of an express - and takes almost three hours to complete its journey). Two expresses then follow within the space of three quarters of an hour after which a wait of over three hours elapses until the next. The SR penchant for interval timings is by no means universally applied!

The Sittingbourne and Faversham areas

smartly since it has to turn and be made ready for the Ramsgate portion of the 14.35 Victoria to Dover. Another C 0-6-0 on a passenger train can be seen at Dumpton Park where a Ramsgate member of the class pauses with a train to Maidstone via Dover. The 0-6-0 works only as far as Ramsgate, however, where the Redhill BR 4MT 2-6-0 which worked in with the 04.43 Tonbridge - Deal and the 07.33 Deal - Ramsgate will take over.

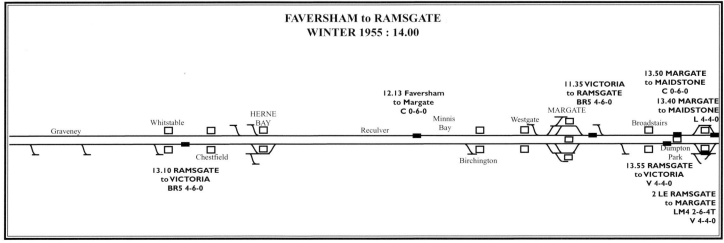

FAVERSHAM to RAMSGATE
WINTER 1955 : 14.00

FAVERSHAM

FAVERSHAM
STATION WORKING (1954/5)

Train	Arrive	Engine	Shed	Dep	Destination	Train	Arrive	Engine	Shed	Dep	Destination
23.55 Sittingbourne Goods		N 2-6-0	Dover 451	00/10	Shepherdswell	11.15 Ramsgate	12.18	BR5 4-6-0	S. Lane 12	12.24	Victoria
01.15 Faversham Yard		N 2-6-0	Dover 452	01/20	Hoo Junction	10.00 Dover Town		N 2-6-0	HG 176	12/37	Hoo Junction
02.00 Faversham Yard		LM2 & C 0-6-0	Fav 269 & 279	02/05	Sheerness	11.35 Victoria (Pullman)	13.07	BR5 4-6-0	S. Lane 11	13.10	Ramsgate
22.00 Hither Green		N 2-6-0	HG 176	02/25	Dover Town			L 4-4-0	Ram 490	13.13	Dover Priory
02.30 Faversham Yard		N 2-6-0	Fav 277	02/35	Hoo Junction	08.40 Hoo Junction		N 2-6-0	Fav 277	13/14	Dover Town
00.56 Queenborough		C 0-6-0	Fav 280	03/08	Faversham Yard	12.37 Dover Priory	13.30	E1 4-4-0	S. Lane 46	13.32	Gillingham
00.40 Snodland		LM4 2-6-4T	Dover 450	03/38	Snowdown	13.05 Dover Priory	14.02	L 4-4-0	Ram 489		
01.10 Bricklayers Arms		N 2-6-0	BLA 121	03/57	Ramsgate	12.35 Victoria	14.08	BR5 4-6-0	S. Lane 15	14.12	Ramsgate
		LM2 2-6-2T	Fav 270	04.40	Sheerness	13.10 Ramsgate	14.13	BR5 4-6-0	S. Lane 13	14.19	Victoria
01.35 Herne Hill		N 2-6-0	S. Lane 61	04/43	Faversham Yard			D1 4-4-0	Fav 262	14.20	Dover Priory
03.00 H. Viaduct	04.56	E1 4-4-0	S. Lane 45	04.59	Ramsgate	11.00 H. Viaduct (Pcls)	14.20	E1 4-4-0	BLA 91	14.33	Ramsgate
03.30 Shepherdswell	05.00	N 2-6-0	Dover 453		(Change engines)	13.55 Ramsgate	14.57	V 4-4-0	Ram 481	15.01	Victoria
		U1 2-6-0	Fav 260	05.05	Dover Priory	10.50 Hither Green		C 0-6-0	Fav 280	15/04	Faversham Yard
(03.30 Shepherdswell)		C 0-6-0	Fav 278	05.10	(Change engines)			LM2 2-6-2T	Fav 271	15.11	Chatham
03.30 Victoria	05.31	BR5 4-6-0	S. Lane 16		(Fwd at 05.36)	13.55 Snowdown		N 2-6-0	S. Lane 61	15/25	Fawkham
04.42 Dover Priory	05.34	LM4 2-6-4T	Ash 354			14.35 Victoria	16.03	WC 4-6-2	Dover 431	16.06	Dover Priory
(03.30 Victoria)		BR5 4-6-0	S. Lane 16	05.36	Ramsgate			L 4-4-0	Ram 489	16.11	Ramsgate
04.34 Ramsgate	05.41	L 4-4-0	Ram 489	05.43	Chatham	15.28 Dover Priory	16.23	LM2 2-6-2T	Ash 360		
03.58 Chatham Goods		N 2-6-0	Dover 452	05/53	Deal via Ramsgate	15.22 Ramsgate	16.26	BR5 4-6-0	S. Lane 14	16.31	Victoria
		N 2-6-0	BLA 121	06.14	Dover Priory	15.35 Victoria	16.59	BR5 4-6-0	S. Lane 16	17.01	Ramsgate
05.45 Chatham	06.31	2 x LM2 2-6-2T	Fav 272/269					LM2 2-6-2T	Ash 360	17.12	Dover Priory
		LM2 2-6-2T	Fav 272	06.36	Canterbury East (ECS)	16.18 Dover Priory	17.16	L 4-4-0	Ram 490		
		LM2 2-6-2T	Fav 269	06.44	Rochester	16.15 Ramsgate	17.19	BR5 4-6-0	S. Lane 10	17.25	Victoria
06.10 Dover Priory	07.07	D1 4-4-0	Dover 444		(Fwd at 07.16)	16.20 Canterbury East		N 2-6-0	BLA 121	17/35	Blackfriars
06.06 Ramsgate	07.09	WC 4-6-2	Ram 466	07.11	Cannon Street	16.55 Strood	17.42	D1 4-4-0	Dover 444	17.52	Dover Priory
(06.10 Dover Priory)		D1 4-4-0	Dover 444	07.16	Gillingham	16.45 Cannon Street	17.49	WC 4-6-2	Ram 471	17.53	Ramsgate
05.10 Victoria	07.21	BR5 4-6-0	S. Lane 12	07.29	Ramsgate	17.05 Ramsgate (Pullman)		WC 4-6-2	Ram 470	17/57	Victoria
07.10 Canterbury East	07.29	LM2 2-6-2T	Fav 272			17.09 Dover Priory	18.01	LM4 2-6-4T	Dover 450	18.03	Chatham
06.29 Ramsgate	07.31	WC 4-6-2	Ram 467	07.33	Cannon Street	16.32 Cannon Street	18.11	L1 4-4-0	BLA 88		(Fwd at 18.24)
		LM2 2-6-2T	Fav 272	07.40	Light to Loco	17.15 Cannon Street		WC 4-6-2	Ram 467	18/19	Ramsgate
		LM4 2-6-4T	Ash 354	07.37	Dover Priory	17.22 Ramsgate	18.23	BR5 4-6-0	S. Lane 11		(Fwd at 18.36)
05.50 Cannon St	08.02	E1 4-4-0	S. Lane 46		(Fwd at 08.13)	(16.32 Cannon Street)		L1 4-4-0	BLA 88	18.24	Ramsgate
07.07 Ramsgate	08.06	L 4-4-0	Ram 490		(Fwd at 08.15)	17.40 Dover Priory	18.30	D1 4-4-0	Fav 262		(Fwd at 18.36)
		L 4-4-0	Fav 264	08.08	Margate			BR5 4-6-0	S. Lane 11	18.36	Victoria
(05.50 Cannon St)		E1 4-4-0	S. Lane 46	08.13	Dover Priory	17.21 Cannon Street	18.50	U1 2-6-0	Fav 260		(Fwd at 19.00)
07.20 Ramsgate		WC 4-6-2	Ram 470	08/12	Cannon Street	17.45 Cannon Street	18.55	WC 4-6-2	Ram 466	18.57	Ramsgate
(07.07 Ramsgate)		L 4-4-0	Ram 490	08.15	Gillingham	(17.21 Cannon Street)		U1 2-6-0	Fav 260	19.00	Dover Priory
07.35 Ramsgate		WC 4-6-2	Ram 471	08/33	Cannon Street	18.16 Cannon Street		V 4-4-0	Ram 478	19/21	Ramsgate
07.42 Dover Priory	08.39	U1 2-6-0	Fav 260		(Fwd at 08.48)	17.32 Ashford via Dover	19.27	LM4 2-6-4T	Ash 355		
08.20 Herne Bay	08.41	V 4-4-0	Ram 478	08.42	Cannon Street	16.12 Tonbridge via Ramsgate	19.30	L 4-4-0	Fav 264		
08.27 Sittingbourne	08.42	C 0-6-0	Fav 279					D1 4-4-0	Fav 262	19.39	Gillingham
		C 0-6-0	Fav 279	08.45	Light to Loco	17.10 Ramsgate (Pcls)	19.54	N 2-6-0	S. Lane 63		(Fwd at 21.15)
(07.42 Dover Priory)		U1 2-6-0	Fav 260	08.48	Chatham	18.23 Cannon Street	19.53	V 4-4-0	BLA 81	19.57	Dover Priory
08.17 Dover Priory	09.10	N 2-6-0	BLA 121		(Wks carriage pilot)	19.28 Sheerness	20.03	LM2 2-6-2T	Fav 270		
07.00 Cannon Street	09.10	N 2-6-0	S. Lane 63	09.13	Ramsgate			L 4-4-0	Ram 490	20.05	Ramsgate
08.25 Ramsgate		WC 4-6-2	Ram 473	09/17	Victoria	19.45 Ramsgate	20.47	BR5 4-6-0	S. Lane 16	20.50	Victoria
		D1 4-4-0	Fav 262	09.18	Dover Priory	19.35 Victoria	20.53	WC 4-6-2	Ram 473	20.56	Ramsgate
07.51 Ashford via Dover	09.41	LM2 2-6-2T	Ash 360					LM4 2-6-4T	Ash 355	21.01	Dover Priory
08.44 Ramsgate	09.44	E1 4-4-0	S. Lane 45	09.47	Chatham	(17.10 Ramsgate (Pcls))		N 2-6-0	S. Lane 63	21.15	Victoria
08.35 Victoria		BR5 4-6-0	S. Lane 13	09/53	Ramsgate	20.38 Chatham	21.17	LM2 2-6-2T	Fav 271		
		LM2 2-6-2T	Ash 360	09.55	Light to Loco			C 0-6-0	Fav 280	21.40	Sheerness
09.20 Dover Priory		WC 4-6-2	Dover 431	10/09	Victoria	20.35 Victoria	22.03	V 4-4-0	Ram 481	22.07	Ramsgate
09.38 Chatham	10.11	L 4-4-0	Ram 489	10.14	Dover Priory	21.10 Ramsgate	22.12	L1 4-4-0	BLA 88	22.15	Charing Cross
05.23 Herne Hill Yard		N 2-6-0	S. Lane 62	10/25	Dover Town	21.22 Sheerness	22.20	LM2 2-6-2T	Fav 272		
09.25 Ramsgate	10.24	BR5 4-6-0	S. Lane 16	10.26	Victoria	22.35 Faversham Yard		BR5 4-6-0	S. Lane 15	22/40	Blackfriars
09.35 Victoria	11.01	BR5 4-6-0	S. Lane 14	11.03	Ramsgate	21.35 Victoria	22.54	WC 4-6-2	Ram 470	22.56	Ramsgate
10.46 Chatham	11.19	L 4-4-0	Ram 490					LM4 2-6-4T	Dover 448	22.57	Dover Priory
11.00 Shepherdswell		N 2-6-0	HG 172	12/04	Hoo Junction	22.47 Dover Priory	23.38	U1 2-6-0	Fav 260		
10.35 Victoria	12.02	BR5 4-6-0	S. Lane 10	12.05	Ramsgate	23.22 Chatham	23.55	D1 4-4-0	Fav 262		
		LM2 2-6-2T	Ash 360	12.06	Dover Priory	20.00 Dover Town		N 2-6-0	S. Lane 62	23/55	Hither Green
11.19 Dover Priory	12.16	D1 4-4-0	Fav 262								

With so much of interest to be seen on the ex-London, Chatham and Dover, selecting a location that had more to offer than the rest was no easy task but Faversham would certainly have been well up in the list of finalists. The Junction for the routes to Ramsgate and Dover, almost all expresses from Victoria to Thanet paused to make a connection with Canterbury East and Dover; the three or four coach connection often being worked by engines that had been elderly when George V came to the Throne. One could strike an unhappy hour when a Dover connection was worked by LMS tank from Dover or Ashford but with six of the fifteen services booked to inside cyliner 4-4-0's and most of the remainder to pre-Bulleid designs, the changes of a disappointment were not great. For some reason an idea had grown up that all the Victoria - Ramsgate services conveyed through coaches to Dover and it came as a surprise to visitors, especially those travelling to Canterbury or Dover, that this was very much the exception to the rule. In fact only two of the ten expresses from Victoria to Ramsgate ran with combined portions and of these, the 08.35 divided at Chatham whilst the 14.35 had Dover as its principal destination, the Thanet portion being worked from Faversham by an L 4-4-0. There were a few miscellaneous and peak service trains that ran through between London and Dover but these tended to be of a stopping or semi-fast nature.

The position was slightly more civilised in the up direction where the 11.15, 13.10 and 17.22 Ramsgate - Victoria expresses attached through coaches from Dover at Faversham: an awkward operation since the Dover coaches had to be draw back by the station pilot and then propelled onto the rear of the Ramsgate section. In addition there was the 09.20 Dover to Victoria which ran non-stop through Faversham and gave passengers from the Canterbury direction a rare opportunity to use a London express. There was no corresponding down train from Victoria.

In many respects Faversham shed was the complement to Gillingham and whereas the latter dealt mainly with goods traffic based upon Hoo Junction and Chatham, Faversham was heavily involved with passenger work over the main line to Dover and on the Sittingbourne - Sheerness branch. Faversham also had a significant element of goods work - a third of its allocation consisted of C class 0-6-0's - most of which involved the servicing of local yards and stations between the Medway/Sheerness and Margate. The duties of the C 0-6-0's were not wholly limited to goods traffic and a surprisingly high number of passenger trains, especially over the Sheerness branch, were worked by the class.

Through trains between Victoria and Dover were few in number and connections were provided with the Victoria - Ramsgate express: a working shared by so many sheds that it produced one of the most colourful ranges of engines to be seen on any route in the country. Excluding the handful of through trains from London, the ten daily departures from Faversham to Canterbury East and Dover were worked by no less than seven different classes of engines with no single type predominating.

A notable feature of the Faversham - Dover workings was that little cognisance was taken of the boundary between the SER and LCDR. Several services over the line were worked by engines from Ashford shed and by way of reciprocation two of Faversham's 4-4-0's worked deep into South Eastern country with a two-day cycle with commenced with the 08.08 Faversham - Margate and continued on with passenger workings to Ashford, Hastings, Tonbridge and Edenbridge before working back the next day with the 16.12 Tonbridge to Faversham via Deal and Ramsgate. The intervening night was spent on St Leonards loco, Hastings.

A Faversham engine also had the distinction of taking part in the evening peak from London when one of the shed's U1 2-6-0's was booked to work the 17.21 Cannon Street to Dover. This was a curious (and often uncertain) working since the engine concerned spent much of the day on Gillingham shed before being taken light to London by a set of Gillingham men and of course if one of the London sheds had an unbalanced engine on hand, the latter was often put into the working. In later years the working became even more speculative when the U1 was given the 11.40 Hoo Junction - Hither Green goods and a Lewisham to Blackfriars parcels train before being expected to turn up punctually at Cannon Street.

1950/1

In common with many second division sheds Faversham entered the 1950's with more than its share of the venerable and chief amongst these were the R and R1 0-4-4 tanks, used on the Sheerness branch, and an O1 0-6-0 which was generally employed on the Faversham Creek shunt. In addition there was an interesting miscellany of 4-4-0 types. Also of interest were a pair of U 2-6-0's which had started life as River class 2-6-4T's and which might, had it not been for a misfortune of history, have been working the Victoria - Ramsgate services.

The first signs of reinvigoration came in late 1950 when a pair of H 0-4-4T's arrived from Ramsgate as successors to the R and R1 engines. At first the move seemed to suggest a false start as one of the engines was withdrawn after four months work at Faversham whilst the other was transferred away to Tonbridge. Shortly afterwards, however, five other members of the class arrived from various parts of the region and for a while it appeared as that the H engines would spend some years on the Sheerness locals. At the end of the period and after a considerable interchange of C 0-6-0's with Gillingham, Faversham lost its sole O1 0-6-0 when it departed for Dover for work between Tilmanstone colliery and the exchange sidings at Snowdown.

1951/2

For some time there had been an expectation that the traditional branch 0-4-4T's were to be replaced by something as progressive as the Pacifics on the main line and even though H 0-4-4T's were taking over the Sheerness duties from the R and R1 engines, current rumours anticipated an allocation of the revolutionary Leader class to Faversham. Trials with the new design had been held between Eastleigh and Basingstoke and although the test had seen 50 mph sustained with loads of nearly 500 tons, technical problems plagued the issue and by mid-1951 the venture was abandoned in favour of LMS 2MT 2-6-2T's, five of which reached Faversham at the end of 1951 for duties between Sittingbourne and Sheerness.

It is fascinating to consider how the local services would have looked had the Leaders (and

LOCOMOTIVE ALLOCATIONS & TRANSFERS : FAVERSHAM (73E)

Loco	Class	Aug-50	Sep-50	Oct-50	Nov-50	Dec-50	Jan-51	Feb-51	Mar-51	Apr-51	May-51	Jun-51	Jul-51
31850	5F : N 2-6-0 (1917)												
31854	5F : N 2-6-0 (1917)												
31868	5F : N 2-6-0 (1917)									To Redhill	X	X	X
31803	4P : U 2-6-0 (R/B 2-6-4T) 1928	X	X	X	X	X	Ex Guild						
31804	4P : U 2-6-0 (R/B 2-6-4T) 1928	X	X	X	X	X	Ex Guild						
31806	4P : U 2-6-0 (R/B 2-6-4T) 1928												
31808	4P : U 2-6-0 (R/B 2-6-4T) 1928												
31638	4P : U 2-6-0 (1928)												To Redhill
31487	3P : D1 4-4-0 (1921)	X	X	X	X	Ex S. Lane							
31489	3P : D1 4-4-0 (1921)												
31492	3P : D1 4-4-0 (1921)	X	X	X	X	X	X	X	X	Ex Gill			
31494	3P : D1 4-4-0 (1921)	X	X	X	X	Ex Gill							
31502	3P : D1 4-4-0 (1921)								W/D	X	X	X	X
31505	3P : D1 4-4-0 (1921)											To Ashford	X
31509	3P : D1 4-4-0 (1921)	X	X	X	X	X	X	X	X	Ex Ton			
31545	3P : D1 4-4-0 (1921)	X	X	X	X	X	X	X	X	Ex Ton			
31727	3P : D1 4-4-0 (1921)									To Ton	X	X	X
31739	3P : D1 4-4-0 (1921)												
31741	3P : D1 4-4-0 (1921)					To B. Arms	X	X	X	X	X	X	X
31157	2P : E 4-4-0 (1905)								W/D	X	X	X	X
31501	2P : D 4-4-0 (1901)												
31586	2P : D 4-4-0 (1901)											To Gill	X
31591	2P : D 4-4-0 (1901)	X	X	X	X	X	X	X	X	Ex B. Arms	X	To Redhill	
31734	2P : D 4-4-0 (1901)					To Ton	X	X	X	X	X	X	X
31748	2P : D 4-4-0 (1901)	X	X	X	X	Ex Rams			W/D	X	X	X	X
31229	2F : C 0-6-0 (1900)								To Gill	X	X	X	X
31242	2F : C 0-6-0 (1900)								To Gill	X	X	X	X
31253	2F : C 0-6-0 (1900)	X	X	X	X	X	X	X	X	X	X	Ex B. Arms	
31255	2F : C 0-6-0 (1900)	X	X	X	X	X	X	X	X	Ex Gill			
31256	2F : C 0-6-0 (1900)	X	X	X	X	X	X	X	X	Ex Gill			
31267	2F : C 0-6-0 (1900)	X	X	X	X	X	X	X	X	Ex Gill			
31268	2F : C 0-6-0 (1900)												
31317	2F : C 0-6-0 (1900)	X	X	X	X	X	X	X	X	X	X	To Dover	X
31461	2F : C 0-6-0 (1900)	X	X	X	X	X	X	X	X	X	X	X	Ex Ton
31481	2F : C 0-6-0 (1900)												
31495	2F : C 0-6-0 (1900)									To Gill	X	X	X
31691	2F : C 0-6-0 (1900)												To H. Green
31692	2F : C 0-6-0 (1900)												To H. Green
31693	2F : C 0-6-0 (1900)	X	X	X	X	X	X	X	X	Ex Gill	X	X	To H. Green
31714	2F : C 0-6-0 (1900)	X	X	X	X	X	X	X	X	X	X	X	Ex S. Lane
31715	2F : C 0-6-0 (1900)												
31369	2F : O1 0-6-0 (1903)												To Dover
31696	1P : R1 0-4-4T (1900)								W/D	X	X	X	X
31698	1P : R1 0-4-4T (1900)												
31704	1P : R1 0-4-4T (1900)	X	X	X	X	X	X	X	X	Ex Ton			
31705	1P : R1 0-4-4T (1900)										W/D	X	X
31708	1P : R1 0-4-4T (1900)	X	X	X	X	X	X	X	X	Ex Dover			
31661	1P : R 0-4-4T (1891)												
31674	1P : R 0-4-4T (1891)												
31162	1P : H 0-4-4T (1904)	X	X	X	X	X	X	X	X	X	X	X	Ex B. Arms
31259	1P : H 0-4-4T (1904)	X	X	X	Ex Ramsgate				To Ton	X	X	X	X
31295	1P : H 0-4-4T (1904)	X	X	X	X	X	X	X	X	X	X	X	Ex S. Lane
31305	1P : H 0-4-4T (1904)	X	X	X	X	X	X	X	X	X	Ex Ashford		
31326	1P : H 0-4-4T (1904)	X	X	X	X	X	X	X	X	X	X	Ex B. Arms	
31327	1P : H 0-4-4T (1904)	X	X	X	X	X	X	X	X	X	X	X	Ex Ton
31532	1P : H 0-4-4T (1904)	X	X	X	Ex Ramsgate				W/D	X	X	X	X

The first new engines to go to Faversham for as long as anyone could remember, the LMS 2MT 2-6-2T's had a very narrow sphere of activity, their working limits being defined by Strood, Sheerness and Faversham with the greater part of their work being performed on the Sittingbourne - Sheerness branch. 41311 stands on Faversham shed in June 1959 in the company of H 0-4-4T 31503. The latter acted as the stand-by in the event of their being insufficient 2-6-2T's available for the shed's four diagrams. (L.G. Marshall)

their incombustible firemen) taken to the road but few doubted the wisdom of opting for the LMS locomotives which were both efficient and popular. Their arrival made a considerable dent in the use made of the various 0-4-4T's and although the H class pottered about the area right up to the end of steam, their reign at Faversham was very short-lived.

The period also saw a degree of uniformity in the 4-4-0's used by Faversham and by mid-1952 most work was in the hands of the shed's five D1 4-4-0's with a pair of E engines kept in reserve.

1952/3

The Spring of 1953 saw some interesting arrivals at Faversham when the line was severed for several weeks between Herne Bay and Birchington with expresses being rerouted to Ramsgate via Canterbury and the wartime connection between the LCDR and the SER. Whitstable, Chestfield and Herne Bay were served by a connecting push and pull service which initially prompted a return of some motor-fitted R class 0-4-4T's. Since the emergency service was formed by two

Loco	Class	Aug-51	Sep-51	Oct-51	Nov-51	Dec-51	Jan-52	Feb-52	Mar-52	Apr-52	May-52	Jun-52	Jul-52
	LOCOMOTIVE ALLOCATIONS & TRANSFERS : FAVERSHAM (73E)												
31850	5F : N 2-6-0 (1917)												
31854	5F : N 2-6-0 (1917)												
31803	4P : U 2-6-0 (R/B 2-6-4T) 1928												
31804	4P : U 2-6-0 (R/B 2-6-4T) 1928												
31806	4P : U 2-6-0 (R/B 2-6-4T) 1928												
31808	4P : U 2-6-0 (R/B 2-6-4T) 1928								To E'leigh	X	X	X	X
31637	4P : U 2-6-0 (1928)	X	X	X	X	X	X	X	X	X	X	Ex N. Elms	
31487	3P : D1 4-4-0 (1921)												
31489	3P : D1 4-4-0 (1921)												
31492	3P : D1 4-4-0 (1921)												
31494	3P : D1 4-4-0 (1921)												
31505	3P : D1 4-4-0 (1921)	X	X	X	X	X	X	X	X	X	X	Ex B. Arms	
31509	3P : D1 4-4-0 (1921)					To Gill	X	X	X	X	X	X	X
31545	3P : D1 4-4-0 (1921)					To Gill	X	X	X	X	X	X	X
31739	3P : D1 4-4-0 (1921)		To Ton	X	X	X	X	X	X	X	X	X	X
31166	2P : E 4-4-0 (1905)	X	X	X	X	X	X	X	Ex B. Arms				
31315	2P : E 4-4-0 (1905)	X	X	X	X	X	X	X	Ex B. Arms				
31501	2P : D 4-4-0 (1901)					To H. Green	X	X	X	X	X	X	X
41308	2MT 2-6-2T (1946)	X	X	X	X	NEW							
41309	2MT 2-6-2T (1946)	X	X	X	X	NEW							
41310	2MT 2-6-2T (1946)	X	X	X	X	NEW							
41311	2MT 2-6-2T (1946)	X	X	X	X	NEW							
41312	2MT 2-6-2T (1946)	X	X	X	X	NEW							
31253	2F : C 0-6-0 (1900)												
31255	2F : C 0-6-0 (1900)												
31256	2F : C 0-6-0 (1900)												
31260	2F : C 0-6-0 (1900)	X	Ex Ton										
31267	2F : C 0-6-0 (1900)												
31268	2F : C 0-6-0 (1900)												
31461	2F : C 0-6-0 (1900)												
31481	2F : C 0-6-0 (1900)												
31714	2F : C 0-6-0 (1900)												
31715	2F : C 0-6-0 (1900)												
31698	1P : R1 0-4-4T (1900)												
31704	1P : R1 0-4-4T (1900)												
31708	1P : R1 0-4-4T (1900)												
31661	1P : R 0-4-4T (1891)												
31674	1P : R 0-4-4T (1891)											W/D	X
31162	1P : H 0-4-4T (1904)												
31295	1P : H 0-4-4T (1904)											To Gill	X
31305	1P : H 0-4-4T (1904)											To Gill	X
31324	1P : H 0-4-4T (1904)	X	X	X	X	Ex B. Arms						To Rams	X
31326	1P : H 0-4-4T (1904)											To Rams	X
31327	1P : H 0-4-4T (1904)						To Ashford	X	X	X	X	X	X
31329	1P : H 0-4-4T (1904)	X	X	X	X	Ex S. Lane							
31500	1P : H 0-4-4T (1904)	X	X	X	X	Ex B. Arms							
31503	1P : H 0-4-4T (1904)	X	X	X	X	Ex B. Arms							

push and pull units either side of the engine, it was decided that something more powerful than an R or H was required and three LSWR M7 0-4-4T's were therefore commandeered from Portsmouth and Yeovil. Unfortunately the additional power of the engines was negated by the fact the majority of drivers at Faversham could not (or would not) adjust to the M7's and after a week or two they were sent packing to Brighton; the R's being reinstated for the remainder of the emergency period.

The M7's were not the only strangers at that time for two months Faversham was host to a trio of Q1 0-6-0's - not a class of engine often associated with the Chatham road. Their purpose was to work the many special ballast trains that were needed for the rebuilding of the main line.

1953/4

The resumption of normal working between Herne Bay and Birchington seemed to give impetus to the pruning of the older classes. Almost all the 0-4-4T's disappeared while the transfer of 31166 left the D1 class as the only 4-4-0's working from the shed. N 2-6-0 31852 which had arrived from Fratton to assist with the Herne Bay crisis was retained and in its place U 2-6-0 31637 was sent to Portsmouth which resulted in Faversham having a complete set of ex-River U locomotives.

At Faversham the difference between the N 2-6-0 and the U1 was of significance and while both types were identical so far as passenger work was concerned, the N class was a far more powerful goods engine - 5F as opposed to 3F - and indispensable therefore for heavy hauls of coal over the difficult line through Canterbury East from Snowdown and on to Hoo Junction. The U1 engines were retained mainly for passenger work and although the railway made no distinction between the U1 rebuilds and the U1 proper, the historian derived some satisfaction from knowing that the Faversham workings - and the 17.21 Cannon Street to Dover in particular - were

Loco	Class	Aug-52	Sep-52	Oct-52	Nov-52	Dec-52	Jan-53	Feb-53	Mar-53	Apr-53	May-53	Jun-53	Jul-53
		LOCOMOTIVE ALLOCATIONS & TRANSFERS : FAVERSHAM (73E)											
33004	5F : Q1 0-6-0 (1942)	X	X	X	X	X	X	X	Ex Guild		To Guild	X	X
33005	5F : Q1 0-6-0 (1942)	X	X	X	X	X	X	X	Ex Guild		To Guild	X	X
33016	5F : Q1 0-6-0 (1942)	X	X	X	X	X	X	X	Ex E'leigh		To E'leigh	X	X
31850	5F : N 2-6-0 (1917)												
31852	5F : N 2-6-0 (1917)	X	X	X	X	X	X	X	Ex Fratton				
31854	5F : N 2-6-0 (1917)												
31803	4P : U 2-6-0 (R/B 2-6-4T) 1928												
31804	4P : U 2-6-0 (R/B 2-6-4T) 1928												
31806	4P : U 2-6-0 (R/B 2-6-4T) 1928												
31637	4P : U 2-6-0 (1928)												
31247	3P : D1 4-4-0 (1921)	X	X	X	X	Ex Dover							
31487	3P : D1 4-4-0 (1921)												
31489	3P : D1 4-4-0 (1921)												
31492	3P : D1 4-4-0 (1921)												
31494	3P : D1 4-4-0 (1921)												
31505	3P : D1 4-4-0 (1921)												
30052	2P : M7 0-4-4T (1897)	X	X	X	X	X	X	X	Ex Fratton	To Brighton	X	X	X
30053	2P : M7 0-4-4T (1897)	X	X	X	X	X	X	X	Ex Fratton	To Brighton	X	X	X
30129	2P : M7 0-4-4T (1897)	X	X	X	X	X	X	X	Ex Yeovil	To Brighton	X	X	X
31166	2P : E 4-4-0 (1905)												
31315	2P : E 4-4-0 (1905)										To S. Lane	X	X
41303	2MT 2-6-2T (1946)	X	X	X	X	X	X	X	Ex B. Arms				
41308	2MT 2-6-2T (1946)												
41309	2MT 2-6-2T (1946)												
41310	2MT 2-6-2T (1946)												
41311	2MT 2-6-2T (1946)												
41312	2MT 2-6-2T (1946)												
31037	2F : C 0-6-0 (1900)	X	X	X	X	Ex St L.							
31253	2F : C 0-6-0 (1900)												
31255	2F : C 0-6-0 (1900)												
31256	2F : C 0-6-0 (1900)												
31260	2F : C 0-6-0 (1900)										W/D	X	X
31267	2F : C 0-6-0 (1900)												
31268	2F : C 0-6-0 (1900)												
31461	2F : C 0-6-0 (1900)												
31481	2F : C 0-6-0 (1900)												
31714	2F : C 0-6-0 (1900)												
31715	2F : C 0-6-0 (1900)												
31698	1P : R1 0-4-4T (1900)								To Ton	X	X	X	X
31708	1P : R1 0-4-4T (1900)		W/D	X	X	X	X	X	X	X	X	X	X
31660	1P : R 0-4-4T (1891)	X	X	X	X	X	X	X	Ex Gill				
31661	1P : R 0-4-4T (1891)								To Ashford	X	X	X	X
31663	1P : R 0-4-4T (1891)	X	X	X	X	X	X	X	Ex Gill		To Gill	X	X
31671	1P : R 0-4-4T (1891)	X	X	X	X	X	X	X	Ex Ton				
31162	1P : H 0-4-4T (1904)								To St L.	X	X	X	
31329	1P : H 0-4-4T (1904)												
31500	1P : H 0-4-4T (1904)								To Ashford	X	X	X	
31503	1P : H 0-4-4T (1904)												
31519	1P : H 0-4-4T (1904)	X	X	X	X	X	X	X	Ex St L.				To St L.

Loco	Class	Aug-53	Sep-53	Oct-53	Nov-53	Dec-53	Jan-54	Feb-54	Mar-54	Apr-54	May-54	Jun-54	Jul-54
		LOCOMOTIVE ALLOCATIONS & TRANSFERS : FAVERSHAM (73E)											
31850	5F : N 2-6-0 (1917)												
31852	5F : N 2-6-0 (1917)												
31854	5F : N 2-6-0 (1917)												
31802	4P : U 2-6-0 (R/B 2-6-4T) 1928	X	X	X	X	X	X	X	X	X	Ex Guild		
31803	4P : U 2-6-0 (R/B 2-6-4T) 1928												
31804	4P : U 2-6-0 (R/B 2-6-4T) 1928												
31806	4P : U 2-6-0 (R/B 2-6-4T) 1928												
31637	4P : U 2-6-0 (1928)		To Fratton	X	X	X	X	X	X	X	X	X	X
31247	3P : D1 4-4-0 (1921)												
31470	3P : D1 4-4-0 (1921)	X	Ex Dover										
31487	3P : D1 4-4-0 (1921)												
31489	3P : D1 4-4-0 (1921)												
31492	3P : D1 4-4-0 (1921)												
31494	3P : D1 4-4-0 (1921)												
31505	3P : D1 4-4-0 (1921)											To Gill	X
31166	2P : E 4-4-0 (1905)				To Ton	X	X	X	X	X	X	X	X
41303	2MT 2-6-2T (1946)												
41308	2MT 2-6-2T (1946)												
41309	2MT 2-6-2T (1946)												
41310	2MT 2-6-2T (1946)												
41311	2MT 2-6-2T (1946)												
41312	2MT 2-6-2T (1946)												
31037	2F : C 0-6-0 (1900)						To Ashford	X	X	X	X	X	X
31253	2F : C 0-6-0 (1900)												
31255	2F : C 0-6-0 (1900)												
31256	2F : C 0-6-0 (1900)												
31267	2F : C 0-6-0 (1900)						To B. Arms	X	X	X	X	X	X
31268	2F : C 0-6-0 (1900)												
31461	2F : C 0-6-0 (1900)		To S. Lane	X	X	X	X	X	X	X	X	X	X
31481	2F : C 0-6-0 (1900)												
31508	2F : C 0-6-0 (1900)	X	X	X	X	X	Ex Gill		To Gill	X	X	X	X
31714	2F : C 0-6-0 (1900)												
31715	2F : C 0-6-0 (1900)												
31720	2F : C 0-6-0 (1900)	X	X	X	X	X	Ex H. Green						
31660	1P : R 0-4-4T (1891)		To Gill	X	X	X	X	X	X	X	X	X	X
31671	1P : R 0-4-4T (1891)												
31503	1P : H 0-4-4T (1904)												

SUMMARY OF MOTIVE POWER : FAVERSHAM - 73E (1950 - 60)										
Class	Oct-50	Oct-51	Oct-52	Oct-53	Oct-54	Oct-55	Oct-56	Oct-57	Oct-58	May-59
5F : N 2-6-0 (1917)	3	2	2	3	2	2	2	2	2	2
4P : U1 2-6-0 (1925)						3	3	3	3	3
4P : U 2-6-0 (R/B 2-6-4T) 1928	2	4	3	3	3					
4P : U 2-6-0 (1928)	1		1							
3P : L 4-4-0 (1914)							4	4	4	3
3P : D1 4-4-0 (1921)	6	6	5	7	5	6	3	3	3	3
2P : E 4-4-0 (1905)	1		2	1						
2P : D 4-4-0 (1901)	3	1								
2MT 2-6-2T (1946)			5	6	6	6	6	6	6	6
2F : C 0-6-0 (1900)	8	10	10	9	8	8	8	9	9	9
2F : 01 0-6-0 (1903)	1									
1P : R1 0-4-4T (1900)	3	3	1							
1P : R 0-4-4T (1891)	2	2	1	1						
1P : H 0-4-4T (1904)		5	4	1	1	1	1	1	1	1
TOTAL	30	33	34	31	25	26	27	28	28	27

LOCOMOTIVE ALLOCATIONS & TRANSFERS : FAVERSHAM (73E)													
Loco	Class	Aug-54	Sep-54	Oct-54	Nov-54	Dec-54	Jan-55	Feb-55	Mar-55	Apr-55	May-55	Jun-55	Jul-55
31850	5F : N 2-6-0 (1917)												
31852	5F : N 2-6-0 (1917)												
31854	5F : N 2-6-0 (1917)			To H. Green	X	X	X	X	X	X	X	X	X
31892	4P : U1 2-6-0 (1925)	X	X	X	X	X	X	X	X	X	X	X	Ex H. Green
31893	4P : U1 2-6-0 (1925)	X	X	X	X	X	X	X	X	X	X	X	Ex H. Green
31903	4P : U1 2-6-0 (1925)	X	X	X	X	X	X	X	X	X	X	X	Ex Brighton
31802	4P : U 2-6-0 (R/B 2-6-4T) 1928												To E'liegh
31803	4P : U 2-6-0 (R/B 2-6-4T) 1928												To E'liegh
31804	4P : U 2-6-0 (R/B 2-6-4T) 1928												To E'liegh
31806	4P : U 2-6-0 (R/B 2-6-4T) 1928			To N. Elms	X	X	X	X	X	X	X	X	X
31247	3P : D1 4-4-0 (1921)			To Dover	X	X	X	X	X	X	X	X	X
31470	3P : D1 4-4-0 (1921)												
31487	3P : D1 4-4-0 (1921)												
31489	3P : D1 4-4-0 (1921)												
31492	3P : D1 4-4-0 (1921)												
31494	3P : D1 4-4-0 (1921)												
31505	3P : D1 4-4-0 (1921)	X	X	X	X	X	X	X	X	X	X	Ex Gill	
31509	3P : D1 4-4-0 (1921)	X	X	X	X	X	X	X	X	X	X	Ex Gill	
41303	2MT 2-6-2T (1946)							To Ashford	X	X	X	X	X
41308	2MT 2-6-2T (1946)												
41309	2MT 2-6-2T (1946)												
41310	2MT 2-6-2T (1946)												
41311	2MT 2-6-2T (1946)												
41312	2MT 2-6-2T (1946)												
41313	2MT 2-6-2T (1946)	X	X	X	X	X	X	X	X	X	X	Ex T. Bges	
31242	2F : C 0-6-0 (1900)	X	X	X	X	X	X	X	X	X	X	Ex Gill	
31253	2F : C 0-6-0 (1900)					To Guild	X	X	X	X	X	X	X
31255	2F : C 0-6-0 (1900)												
31256	2F : C 0-6-0 (1900)												
31268	2F : C 0-6-0 (1900)												
31481	2F : C 0-6-0 (1900)												
31714	2F : C 0-6-0 (1900)												
31715	2F : C 0-6-0 (1900)												
31720	2F : C 0-6-0 (1900)												
31671	1P : R 0-4-4T (1891)	To Gill	X	X	X	X	X	X	X	X	X	X	X
31305	1P : H 0-4-4T (1904)	X	X	X	X	Ex Gill							
31503	1P : H 0-4-4T (1904)												

LOCOMOTIVE ALLOCATIONS & TRANSFERS : FAVERSHAM (73E)													
Loco	Class	Aug-55	Sep-55	Oct-55	Nov-55	Dec-55	Jan-56	Feb-56	Mar-56	Apr-56	May-56	Jun-56	Jul-56
31850	5F : N 2-6-0 (1917)												
31852	5F : N 2-6-0 (1917)												
31892	4P : U1 2-6-0 (1925)												
31893	4P : U1 2-6-0 (1925)												
31903	4P : U1 2-6-0 (1925)												
31765	3P : L 4-4-0 (1914)	X	X	X	X	Ex Ton							
31766	3P : L 4-4-0 (1914)	X	X	X	X	Ex Ton							
31767	3P : L 4-4-0 (1914)	X	X	X	X	Ex St L.							
31768	3P : L 4-4-0 (1914)	X	X	X	X	Ex St L.							
31470	3P : D1 4-4-0 (1921)					To Ton	X	X	X	X	X	X	X
31487	3P : D1 4-4-0 (1921)					To Ton	X	X	X	X	X	X	X
31489	3P : D1 4-4-0 (1921)					To Ton	X	X	X	X	X	X	X
31492	3P : D1 4-4-0 (1921)					To Ton	X	X	X	X	X	X	X
31494	3P : D1 4-4-0 (1921)												
31505	3P : D1 4-4-0 (1921)		Ashford	X	X	Ex Ashford							
31509	3P : D1 4-4-0 (1921)												
41308	2MT 2-6-2T (1946)												
41309	2MT 2-6-2T (1946)												
41310	2MT 2-6-2T (1946)												
41311	2MT 2-6-2T (1946)												
41312	2MT 2-6-2T (1946)												
41313	2MT 2-6-2T (1946)												
31242	2F : C 0-6-0 (1900)												
31255	2F : C 0-6-0 (1900)												
31256	2F : C 0-6-0 (1900)												
31268	2F : C 0-6-0 (1900)												
31481	2F : C 0-6-0 (1900)												
31714	2F : C 0-6-0 (1900)												
31715	2F : C 0-6-0 (1900)												
31720	2F : C 0-6-0 (1900)												
31305	1P : H 0-4-4T (1904)		To B. Arms	X	X	X	X	X	X	X	X	X	X
31503	1P : H 0-4-4T (1904)												

worked by direct descendants of the ill-fated 2-6-4 express tanks.

1954/5

August 1954 saw the departure of the last of the shed's R class 0-4-4T's; 31671 being sent to Gillingham in exchange for 31305 which left Faversham with two 0-4-4 tanks as stand-by engines for the Ivatt 2-6-2T's. Towards the end of the period all three ex-River class engines were transferred to the South Western and replaced by U1 2-6-0's.

1955-60

After a decade in which many engines had come and gone, by mid-1955 Faversham's locomotive position had stabilised and the only change of note occurred in December of that year when four D1 4-4-0's were transferred to Tonbridge to work the through services to Brighton. Their replacements were a quartet of L 4-4-0's which were deemed better suited to Faversham's two-day diagram which involved work in the Hastings area where the L class had done a great deal of work over the years. The three remaining D1 engines were retained to cover for L's when problems arose.

In September 1955 H 0-4-4T 31305 was transferred to Bricklayers Arms, leaving Faversham with only one 0-4-4T on its books: 31503 which remained at the shed until closure in June 1959.

Apart from L 31767 which was taken out of traffic in March 1959, the shed's allocation remained intact up to the point of closure in June 1959 when the twenty-seven engines were dispersed to Nine Elms (12), Ashford (8), Exmouth Junction, Feltham and Stewarts Lane (2 apiece) and Tonbridge (1). In their place Faversham - which had become a diesel maintenance depot - received a small (nominal) allocation of diesel shunters only one of which actually spent any time at its home station. The remaining engines were actually based at Gillingham, Chatham, Margate, Shepherdswell,

Sittingbourne and Ramsgate. All were 350hp 0-6-0's apart from the last two which were 204hp Drewry locomotives.

All passenger traffic was handled by multiple-units and although the first half of the 1960's saw the retention of most goods trains, little of the activity affected what remained of Faversham loco. E5001 and E6001 electric locomotives ran in light from places such as Queenborough and Margate but they were usually directed straight into the yard where, after being relieved, they would depart with their trains. Typical of the new order was the E5001 engine which arrived in the yard at 04.20 with the 01.53 goods from Hither Green. The incoming Faversham men ran the engine from the yard to the station where they attached it to the 05.03 Dover Parcels and handed over to a set of Dover men who worked the train away. To complete the ubiquity of the situation, two hours later the engine was speeding towards London with the up Night Ferry. It was all very modern and efficient but, ye Gods, unbelievably dull.

LOCOMOTIVE ALLOCATIONS & TRANSFERS : FAVERSHAM (73E)

Loco	Class	Aug-56	Sep-56	Oct-56	Nov-56	Dec-56	Jan-57	Feb-57	Mar-57	Apr-57	May-57	Jun-57	Jul-57
31850	5F : N 2-6-0 (1917)												
31852	5F : N 2-6-0 (1917)												
31892	4P : U1 2-6-0 (1925)												
31893	4P : U1 2-6-0 (1925)												
31903	4P : U1 2-6-0 (1925)												
31765	3P : L 4-4-0 (1914)												
31766	3P : L 4-4-0 (1914)												
31767	3P : L 4-4-0 (1914)												
31768	3P : L 4-4-0 (1914)												
31494	3P : D1 4-4-0 (1921)												
31505	3P : D1 4-4-0 (1921)												
31509	3P : D1 4-4-0 (1921)												
41308	2MT 2-6-2T (1946)												
41309	2MT 2-6-2T (1946)												
41310	2MT 2-6-2T (1946)												
41311	2MT 2-6-2T (1946)												
41312	2MT 2-6-2T (1946)												
41313	2MT 2-6-2T (1946)												
31242	2F : C 0-6-0 (1900)												
31255	2F : C 0-6-0 (1900)												
31256	2F : C 0-6-0 (1900)												
31268	2F : C 0-6-0 (1900)												
31298	2F : C 0-6-0 (1900)	X	X	X	X	X	X	X	X	X		Ex Rams	
31481	2F : C 0-6-0 (1900)												
31714	2F : C 0-6-0 (1900)												
31715	2F : C 0-6-0 (1900)												
31720	2F : C 0-6-0 (1900)												
31503	1P : H 0-4-4T (1904)												

LOCOMOTIVE ALLOCATIONS & TRANSFERS : FAVERSHAM (73E)

Loco	Class	Aug-57	Sep-57	Oct-57	Nov-57	Dec-57	Jan-58	Feb-58	Mar-58	Apr-58	May-58	Jun-58	Jul-58
31850	5F : N 2-6-0 (1917)												
31852	5F : N 2-6-0 (1917)												
31892	4P : U1 2-6-0 (1925)												
31893	4P : U1 2-6-0 (1925)												
31903	4P : U1 2-6-0 (1925)												
31765	3P : L 4-4-0 (1914)												
31766	3P : L 4-4-0 (1914)												
31767	3P : L 4-4-0 (1914)												
31768	3P : L 4-4-0 (1914)												
31494	3P : D1 4-4-0 (1921)												
31505	3P : D1 4-4-0 (1921)												
31509	3P : D1 4-4-0 (1921)												
41308	2MT 2-6-2T (1946)												
41309	2MT 2-6-2T (1946)												
41310	2MT 2-6-2T (1946)												
41311	2MT 2-6-2T (1946)												
41312	2MT 2-6-2T (1946)												
41313	2MT 2-6-2T (1946)												
31242	2F : C 0-6-0 (1900)												
31255	2F : C 0-6-0 (1900)												
31256	2F : C 0-6-0 (1900)												
31268	2F : C 0-6-0 (1900)												
31298	2F : C 0-6-0 (1900)												
31481	2F : C 0-6-0 (1900)												
31714	2F : C 0-6-0 (1900)												
31715	2F : C 0-6-0 (1900)												
31720	2F : C 0-6-0 (1900)												
31503	1P : H 0-4-4T (1904)												

LOCOMOTIVE ALLOCATIONS & TRANSFERS : FAVERSHAM (73E)

Loco	Class	Aug-58	Sep-58	Oct-58	Nov-58	Dec-58	Jan-59	Feb-59	Mar-59	Apr-59	May-59	Jun-59	Jul-59
31850	5F : N 2-6-0 (1917)											To Ex Jn	X
31852	5F : N 2-6-0 (1917)											To Ex Jn	X
31892	4P : U1 2-6-0 (1925)											To Feltham	X
31893	4P : U1 2-6-0 (1925)											To Feltham	X
31903	4P : U1 2-6-0 (1925)											To Ton	X
31765	3P : L 4-4-0 (1914)											To N. Elms	X
31766	3P : L 4-4-0 (1914)											To N. Elms	X
31767	3P : L 4-4-0 (1914)								W/D	X	X	X	X
31768	3P : L 4-4-0 (1914)											To N. Elms	X
31494	3P : D1 4-4-0 (1921)											To N. Elms	X
31505	3P : D1 4-4-0 (1921)											To N. Elms	X
31509	3P : D1 4-4-0 (1921)											To N. Elms	X
41308	2MT 2-6-2T (1946)											To Ashford	X
41309	2MT 2-6-2T (1946)											To Ashford	X
41310	2MT 2-6-2T (1946)											To Ashford	X
41311	2MT 2-6-2T (1946)											To Ashford	X
41312	2MT 2-6-2T (1946)											To Ashford	X
41313	2MT 2-6-2T (1946)											To Ashford	X
31242	2F : C 0-6-0 (1900)											To N. Elms	X
31255	2F : C 0-6-0 (1900)											To Ashford	X
31256	2F : C 0-6-0 (1900)											To Ashford	X
31268	2F : C 0-6-0 (1900)											To N. Elms	X
31298	2F : C 0-6-0 (1900)											To N. Elms	X
31481	2F : C 0-6-0 (1900)											To N. Elms	X
31714	2F : C 0-6-0 (1900)											To S. Lane	X
31715	2F : C 0-6-0 (1900)											To S. Lane	X
31720	2F : C 0-6-0 (1900)											To N. Elms	X
31503	1P : H 0-4-4T (1904)											To N. Elms	X

Said by many footplatemen to be the best engine for the line, it is a matter for regret that the Schools 4-4-0's did not play a greater part in the running of Kent Coast expresses. A 4-6-0 disguised as a 4-4-0, the class seemed to be especially well adapted to the curves and undulations of the Chatham main line yet they were forced to yield first and second place to the light Pacifics of Ramsgate and the King Arthur 4-6-0's which handled the bulk of the Kent Coast traffic. To guarantee a run behind one of the class, it was necessary to leave London in the evening since the only Chatham-line services booked to Schools engines were the 18.16 and 18.23 from Cannon Street and the 20.35 from Victoria. Their use was similarly limited on the SER route to Ramsgate but the class dominated - with complete success - the service between Charing Cross and Hastings. In the upper view 30938 'St Olave's' blows off as it gets away from Gillingham with an express for the Coast during the Spring of 1959. Below, 30937 'Epsom' accelerates a down Thanet express away from Faversham on Saturday 13 June 1959. (L.G. Marshall)

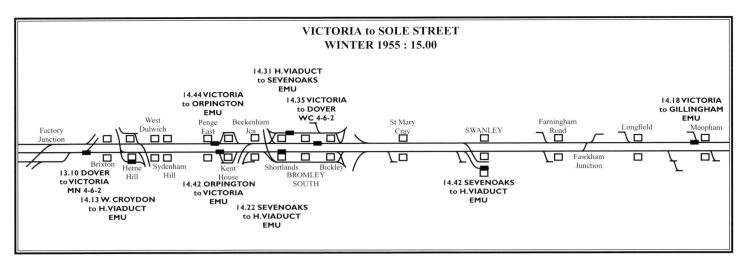

VICTORIA to SOLE STREET
WINTER 1955 : 15.00

CONTROLLER'S LOG: The time has now arrived when checks have to be made to see that every coach, guard and driver involved in the evening peak is in his place and ready for the exodus which will start in a about an hours time. This can sometimes be a frenetically active time as units are moved empty to Victoria or Holborn Viaduct to make good any shortages that may

embargo on steam is not possible and several long distance arrivals have to be dealt with. Amongst these is the Golden Arrow and its subsidiary whose arrival as thousands of office-workers stream in the opposite direction, is not entirely welcome. Fortunately Victoria plays second fiddle to Holborn Viaduct and of the 68 departures that make up the evening peak only

Stewarts Lane Merchant Navy.

There is an interesting selection of services for London at Margate and for those tired of the LCDR route there is a choice between the 14.45 and 15.25 South Eastern expresses. Care must be exercised before boarding however since the first of the two departures - undoubtedly the more interesting of the pair in the eyes of

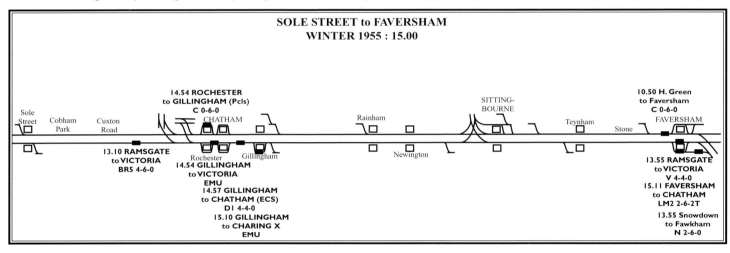

SOLE STREET to FAVERSHAM
WINTER 1955 : 15.00

have cropped up earlier in the day and there is a rise in tension that is almost visible between three and four each afternoon. The travelling public who use the peak service are not known for their qualities of forgiveness.

Steam is largely absent on departures from Victoria during the peak and the 15.35 Ramsgate express will be the last for four hours although during that time seven steam workings will leave Cannon Street for the Kent Coast, joining the main line at St Mary Cray Junction. A total

18 depart from Victoria. The bulk of the service operates from Holborn Viaduct where 39 trains leave between 16.00 and 19.00. The 11 trains making up the balance depart from Blackfriars.

Bullied Pacifics have not played an especially prominent part in the London area so far yet there are two examples to be seen now: one being the 14.35 Victoria - Dover which is the return working of the 09.20 ex Dover and the other being the Ostend and Calais boat train which is approaching the Thames behind a

the enthusiast - calls at all stations via Dover to Ashford before running via Edenbridge, Redhill and the LBSCR main line to London Bridge and Cannon Street. The second of the two trains is also routed via Deal and Dover but runs non-stop between Ashford and Waterloo to reach London a good forty minutes ahead of its rival. There is little advantage to be had in catching the 15.22 Ramsgate - Victoria since it makes innumerable stops and reaches London only eight minutes ahead of the 15.25 ex Margate.

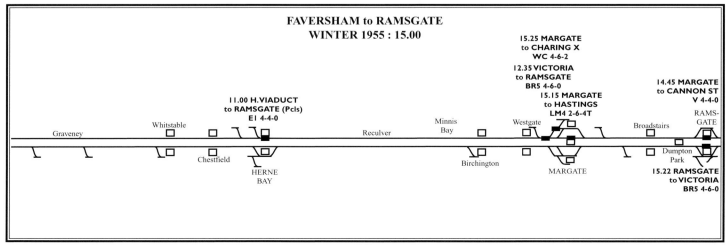

FAVERSHAM to RAMSGATE
WINTER 1955 : 15.00

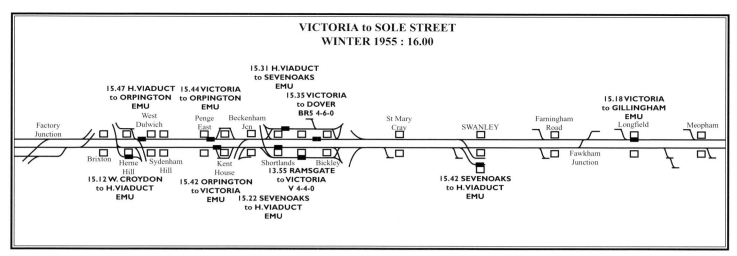

VICTORIA to SOLE STREET
WINTER 1955 : 16.00

CONTROLLER'S LOG: The rush - which will continue for three hours - has started and already trains are running between Bickley and Herne Hill like flies round a jampot! Up road services are just as dense - and just as important - as those on the down since the peak service can only operate by being fed with incoming trains. The majority of trains in the suburban area are electrics but the 15.35 Victoria to Ramsgate - the 'Granville' of yore

two return trips in a day. The 15.35 is also the last down express to be worked by a 5MT 4-6-0; subsequent trains being handled by a Schools 4-4-0 and a light Pacific.

As the 'Granville' storms away from Bromley South it passes the 13.55 Ramsgate - Victoria which is notable because it is worked by a Schools 4-4-0 instead of the more familiar 4-6-0 and it is run up the local line instead of the main as is usually the case with expresses.

since they more than any other class might have been tailor-made for the line. The new 5MT engines and the 'King Arthur's' are very popular but by common consent, the Schools 4-4-0 is the engine par excellence.

Goods traffic is *non gratia* at this time of day and most has been banished until later in the evening. One of the few stragglers is the 13.55 from Snowdown Colliery to Fawkham (for Gravesend West) which is presently sandwiched

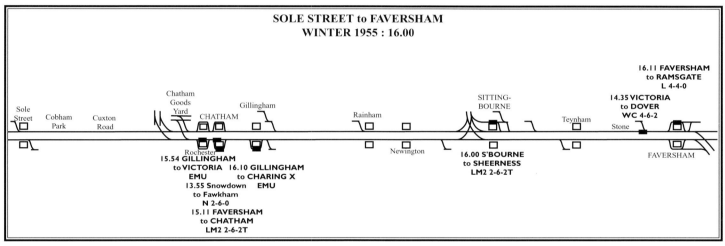

SOLE STREET to FAVERSHAM
WINTER 1955 : 16.00

and one of the fastest trains of the day in prewar years - is accelerating away from Bromley South with sixteen miles of hard work ahead before reaching the summit of the North Downs at Sole Street. This is the most arduous of all the Stewarts Lane passenger duties since it involves the same engine that earlier worked the 03.30 Victoria to Ramsgate and the 09.25 return and is the only engine booked to cover

The reason for this apparent derogation is to give both the express and the 15.22 Sevenoaks - Holborn Viaduct a clear run to Shortlands without fear of conflict. At the junction the Sevenoaks trains will take the Catford branch while the express has an unimpeded run to Kent House and beyond.

It is a matter of regret that only one of the Ramsgate expresses is booked to a Schools

between pair of electrics at Rochester. As soon as the road clears it will shunt clear of the main line at Chatham goods yard and remain there until the peak is over. It's N 2-6-0 will run light to Gillingham loco and remain on shed until the train is ready to move again. The only other goods on the move is the Margate - Faversham trip which is collecting fruit traffic to connect with the 22.35 Faversham - Blackfriars.

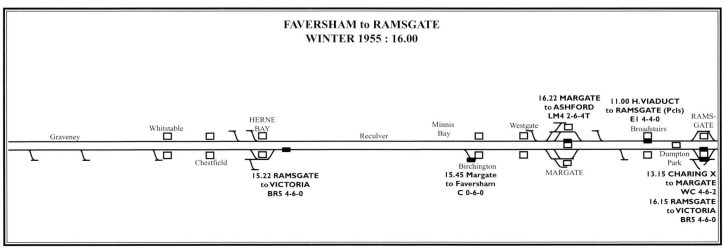

FAVERSHAM to RAMSGATE
WINTER 1955 : 16.00

MARGATE STATION WORKING : 1954/5

Train	Arrive	Engine		Dep	Destination
		LM2 2-6-2T	Ash 362	00.10	Ramsgate loco
02.30 Ashford	03.40	L 4-4-0	Ash 345		
Light ex Ramsgate loco	04.32	L 4-4-0	Rams 488		(For 05.12)
04.34 Ramsgate	04.48	L 4-4-0	Rams 489		(Fwd at 04.57)
Light ex Ramsgate loco	04.57	LM4 2-6-4T	Rams 492		(For 05.30)
(04.34 Rams)		L 4-4-0	Rams 489	04.57	Chatham
		L 4-4-0	Rams 488	05.12	Canterbury West
		LM4 2-6-4T	Rams 492	05.30	Ashford
03.00 H. Viaduct	05.47	E1 4-4-0	S. Lane 45	05.54	Ramsgate
01.10 Bricklayers Arms	06.11	U1 2-6-0	Fav 276	06.15	Ramsgate Goods
06.06 Ramsgate	06.21	WC 4-6-2	Rams 466	06.23	Cannon Street
03.45 Ashford Goods	06.28	C 0-6-0	Rams 499		
Light ex Ramsgate loco	06.33	V 4-4-0	Rams 477		(For 07.03)
Light ex Ramsgate loco	06.40	LM4 2-6-4T	Rams 494		(For 08.10)
03.30 Victoria	06.43	BR5 4-6-0	S. Lane 16		(Fwd at 07.10)
06.29 Ramsgate	06.43	WC 4-6-2	Rams 467	06.46	Cannon Street
Light ex Ramsgate loco	06.56	WC 4-6-2	Rams 469		(For 07.36)
		V 4-4-0	Rams 477	07.03	Cannon Street
ECS ex Ramsgate		V 4-4-0	Rams 478	07.07	Herne Bay
(03.30 Vic)		BR5 4-6-0	S. Lane 16	07.10	Ramsgate
07.07 Ramsgate	07.21	L 4-4-0	Rams 490	07.23	Gillingham
		WC 4-6-2	Rams 469	07.36	Charing X
07.20 Ramsgate	07.34	WC 4-6-2	Rams 470	07.37	Cannon Street
07.35 Ramsgate	07.49	WC 4-6-2	Rams 471	07.51	Cannon Street
07.02 Canterbury W.	07.56	L 4-4-0	Ash 346		
		L 4-4-0	Ash 345	07.58	Hastings
		LM4 2-6-4T	Rams 494	08.10	Ashford
07.08 Dover	08.19	BR4 2-6-0	Redhill 628		
05.10 Victoria	08.19	BR5 4-6-0	S. Lane 12	08.24	Ramsgate
08.25 Ramsgate	08.39	WC 4-6-2	Rams 473	08.41	Victoria
Light ex Ramsgate loco	08.46	WC 4-6-2	Rams 472		(For 09.40)
08.08 Faversham	08.54	L 4-4-0	Fav 264		
08.44 Ramsgate	08.58	E1 4-4-0	S. Lane 45	09.01	Chatham
03.58 Chatham Goods		N 2-6-0	Dover 452	09/05	Deal
04.50 London Bridge	09.07	V 4-4-0	BLA 81		
		L 4-4-0	Ash 346	09.18	Birkenhead
		V 4-4-0	BLA 81	09.25	Ramsgate loco
		WC 4-6-2	Rams 472	09.40	Charing X
09.25 Ramsgate	09.39	BR5 4-6-0	S. Lane 16	09.42	Victoria
07.36 Maidstone East	09.51	LM2 2-6-2T	Ash 362		(Works pilot)
07.00 Cannon St	09.59	N 2-6-0	S. Lane 63	10.02	Ramsgate
		L 4-4-0	Fav 264	10.10	Ashford
		BR4 2-6-0	Redhill 628	10.18	Ramsgate loco
08.35 Victoria	10.37	BR5 4-6-0	S. Lane 13	10.40	Ramsgate
		C 0-6-0	Rams 499	10.50	Ramsgate loco
06.56 H. Viaduct	10.51	E1 4-4-0	BLA 90		
09.42 Ashford	11.04	LM4 2-6-4T	Rams 492		
		LM4 2-6-4T	Rams 492	11.27	Ramsgate loco
11.15 Ramsgate	11.29	BR5 4-6-0	S. Lane 12	11.32	Victoria
06.05 Reading South	11.39	L 4-4-0	Ton 290		
		E1 4-4-0	BLA 90	11.44	Hastings
09.35 Victoria	11.48	BR5 4-6-0	S. Lane 14	11.50	Ramsgate
10.45 Ashford	11.58	V 4-4-0	BLA 81		
		V 4-4-0	BLA 81	12.36	Charing X
10.12 Tonbridge	12.48	C 0-6-0	Rams 497		
10.35 Victoria	12.51	BR5 4-6-0	S. Lane 10	12.54	Ramsgate
(Ex Pilot)		LM2 2-6-2T	Ash 362	13.20	Canterbury West
13.10 Ramsgate	13.25	BR5 4-6-0	S. Lane 13	13.29	Victoria
		L 4-4-0	Ton 290	13.40	Maidstone East
		C 0-6-0	Rams 497	13.50	Maidstone East
11.35 Victoria (Pullman)	13.53	BR5 4-6-0	S. Lane 11	13.58	Ramsgate
11.59 Ramsgate Goods	13.58	C 0-6-0	Rams 499		

Train	Arrive	Engine		Dep	Destination
13.55 Ramsgate	14.09	V 4-4-0	Rams 481	14.12	Victoria
Light ex Ramsgate loco	14.17	LM4 2-6-4T	Ash 492		(Wks 15.15)
Light ex Ramsgate loco	14.17	V 4-4-0	BLA 83		(Wks 14.45)
11.15 Charing X	14.31	WC 4-6-2	Rams 474		
12.28 Maidstone East	14.39	LM2 2-6-2T	Ash 362		(Works Pilot)
		V 4-4-0	BLA 83	14.45	Cannon Street
12.13 Faversham Goods	14.55	C 0-6-0	Fav 279		
12.35 Victoria	15.01	BR5 4-6-0	S. Lane 15	15.05	Ramsgate
		LM4 2-6-4T	Ash 492	15.15	Hastings
		WC 4-6-2	Rams 474	15.25	Charing X
15.22 Ramsgate	15.37	BR5 4-6-0	S. Lane 14	15.40	Victoria
11.00 H. Viaduct (Pcls)	15.38	E1 4-4-0	BLA 91	15.44	Ramsgate
		C 0-6-0	Fav 279	15.45	Faversham Goods
15.00 Canterbury West	15.47	LM4 2-6-4T	Ash 356		
13.15 Charing X	16.16	WC 4-6-2	Rams 469		
		LM4 2-6-4T	Ash 356	16.22	Ashford
16.15 Ramsgate	16.30	BR5 4-6-0	S. Lane 10	16.34	Victoria
07.35 Birkenhead	16.46	V 4-4-0	Rams 485		
		WC 4-6-2	Rams 469	16.55	Charing X
Light ex Ramsgate loco	16.55	U1 2-6-0	Fav 276		(Wks 17.35)
14.35 Victoria	16.58	L 4-4-0	Rams 489	17.01	Ramsgate
17.05 Ramsgate (Pullman)	17.19	WC 4-6-2	Rams 470	17.21	Victoria
17.10 Ramsgate (Pcls)	17.30	N 2-6-0	S. Lane 63		(Fwd at 18.00)
		U1 2-6-0	Fav 276	17.35	Dover
17.22 Ramsgate	17.36	BR5 4-6-0	S. Lane 11	17.39	Victoria
15.36 Maidstone East	17.49	LM4 2-6-4T	Ash 354		
15.35 Victoria	17.48	BR5 4-6-0	S. Lane 16	17.51	Ramsgate
		C 0-6-0	Rams 499	17.55	Ashford Goods
(17.10 Ramsgate Pcls)		N 2-6-0	S. Lane 63	18.00	Victoria
		LM4 2-6-4T	Ash 354	18.15	Ramsgate loco
16.45 Cannon Street	18.36	WC 4-6-2	Rams 471	18.39	Ramsgate
16.12 Tonbridge	18.44	L 4-4-0	Fav 264	18.47	Faversham
		V 4-4-0	Rams 485	18.50	Charing X
16.15 Charing X	18.53	WC 4-6-2	Dover 434		
17.15 Cannon Street	18.53	WC 4-6-2	Rams 467	18.56	Ramsgate
18.00 Ramsgate Goods	19.02	BR5 4-6-0	S. Lane 15		(Fwd at 20.08)
16.32 Cannon Street	19.08	L1 4-4-0	BLA 88	19.11	Ramsgate
17.45 Cannon Street	19.42	WC 4-6-2	Rams 466	19.45	Ramsgate
19.45 Ramsgate	19.59	BR5 4-6-0	S. Lane 16	20.02	Victoria
18.16 Cannon Street	20.04	V 4-4-0	Rams 478	20.06	Ramsgate
17.58 Maidstone East	20.07	LM4 2-6-4T	Rams 494		
(18.00 Ramsgate Goods)		BR5 4-6-0	S. Lane 15	20.08	Blackfriars Goods
		LM4 2-6-4T	Rams 494	20.20	Ramsgate loco
20.05 Faversham	20.49	L 4-4-0	Rams 490	20.56	Ramsgate
(Ex pilot)		LM2 2-6-2T	Ash 362	21.20	Canterbury West
21.10 Ramsgate	21.25	L1 4-4-0	BLA 88	21.28	Charing X
		WC 4-6-2	Dover 434	21.28	Cannon Street
Light ex Ramsgate loco	21.33	LM4 2-6-4T	Ash 354		(For 21.45)
21.25 Ramsgate (ECS)	21.40	V 4-4-0	Rams 477		
19.35 Victoria	21.42	WC 4-6-2	Rams 473	21.45	Ramsgate
19.12 Tonbridge	21.49	L 4-4-0	Rams 488		
		LM4 2-6-4T	Ash 354	21.58	Ashford
		V 4-4-0	Rams 477	22.00	Ramsgate loco
19.15 Charing X	22.02	WC 4-6-2	Rams 468		
		L 4-4-0	Rams 488	22.25	Ramsgate loco
		WC 4-6-2	Rams 468	22.25	Ramsgate loco
18.50 Dover Goods		N 2-6-0	Dover 452	22/44	Hoo Junction
21.36 Ashford	22.55	L 4-4-0	Rams 489		
20.35 Victoria	22.53	V 4-4-0	Rams 481	22.56	Ramsgate
		L 4-4-0	Rams 489	23.15	Ramsgate loco
21.35 Victoria	23.41	WC 4-6-2	Rams 470	23.44	Ramsgate
23.03 Canterbury West	23.53	LM2 2-6-2T	Ash 362		

Famous to millions as one of England's holiday playgrounds, there was nothing that the beach or the pier could offer that compared in any way with the show the railway put on as a matter of routine every day of the year, thanks to the fact that Margate was both a through station on the LCDR and the terminus of SER services from Charing Cross and Ashford via both Deal and Canterbury West.

This overlap of the two railways was curious and instead of making an end-on connection at Ramsgate, the South Eastern continued to use Margate as its terminus with the result that Thanet enjoyed the competing services of two main lines. Head Office at Waterloo justified the duality as being necessary to meet the heavy local demand between Margate, Broadstairs and Ramsgate whilst to visiting enthusiasts Thanet was about as close as one could get to heaven without actually dying.

With a significant number of terminating services, Margate must have been one of the busiest passenger locations not to have a fully-fledged locomotive depot and although it had a handful of sidings and a 60' turntable, most SER engines had to run the six miles to Ramsgate for servicing and this resulted in a large number of light engine movements. Occasional trains changed engines at Ramsgate to allow the principal engine more time to prepare for the return journey: a strategy more freely resorted to when down trains were running late.

The variety of trains and engines to be seen at Margate is shown above and calls for no comment beyond remarking that for all the high degree of activity, the table represents an ordinary winter's day. Saturdays at the height of the holiday season with trains queuing all the way from Chatham was another story!

RAMSGATE STATION WORKING (1954/5)

Train	Arrive	Engine	Shed	Dep	Destination
02.30 Ashford via Canterbury	03.20	L 4-4-0	Ash 345	03.31	Margate
		L 4-4-0	Ram 489	04.34	Chatham
03.45 Ashford (Goods)	05.20	N 2-6-0	Ash 371		(Fwd at 05.40)
05.12 Margate	05.29	L 4-4-0	Ram 488		(Fwd at 05.37)
		WC 4-6-2	Ram 456	05.31	Charing Cross via Deal
(05.12 Margate)		L 4-4-0	Ram 488	05.37	Canterbury West
(03.45 Ashford (Goods))		C 0-6-0	Ram 499	05.40	Margate (Goods)
05.30 Margate	05.44	LM4 2-6-4T	Ram 492	05.47	Ashford via Canterbury
		WC 4-6-2	Ram 466	06.06	Cannon St via Chatham
03.00 Holborn V via Chatham	06.10	E1 4-4-0	S. Lane 45		
		WC 4-6-2	Ram 467	06.29	Cannon St via Chatham
		WC 4-6-2	Ram 468	06.44	Cannon St via Deal
		V 4-4-0	Ram 478	06.53	Herne Bay (ECS)
01.10 Bricklayers Arms	07.00	U1 2-6-0	Fav 276		
		L 4-4-0	Ram 490	07.07	Gillingham
07.03 Margate	07.17	V 4-4-0	Ram 477	07.19	Cannon St via Canterbury
		WC 4-6-2	Ram 470	07.20	Cannon St via Chatham
03.30 Victoria	07.31	BR5 4-6-0	S. Lane 16		
		WC 4-6-2	Ram 471	07.35	Cannon St via Chatham
07.02 Canterbury West	07.37	L 4-4-0	Ash 346	07.42	Margate
07.36 Margate	07.50	WC 4-6-2	Ram 469	07.53	Charing Cross via Deal
07.08 Dover via Deal	08.03	BR4 2-6-0	Red 628	08.05	Margate
03.40 London Bge via Deal	08.08	LM4 2-6-4T	Dover 450		
07.58 Margate	08.12	L 4-4-0	Ash 345	08.14	Hastings via Canterbury
		WC 4-6-2	Ram 473	08.25	Victoria via Chatham
08.10 Margate	08.24	LM4 2-6-4T	Ram 494	08.29	Ashford via Canterbury
05.10 Victoria	08.42	BR5 4-6-0	S. Lane 12		
		E1 4-4-0	S. Lane 45	08.44	Gillingham
04.50 London Bge via Redhill/C'bury	08.48	V 4-4-0	BLA 81	08.52	Margate
		V 4-4-0	Ram 485	08.56	Birkenhead via Deal
03.58 Chatham (Goods)		N 2-6-0	Dover 452	09/05	Deal
		N 2-6-0	Ash 372	09.19	Ashford (Goods)
		BR5 4-6-0	S. Lane 16	09.25	Victoria via Chatham
09.18 Margate	09.34	L 4-4-0	Ash 346	09.36	Ashford via Canterbury
07.36 Maidstone	09.35	LM2 2-6-2T	Ash 362	09.37	Margate
09.40 Margate	09.57	WC 4-6-2	Ram 472	09.59	Charing Cross via Deal
07.00 Cannon St via Chatham	10.18	N 2-6-0	S. Lane 63		
10.10 Margate	10.26	L 4-4-0	Fav 264	10.29	Charing Cross via Canterbury
06.56 H. Viaduct via Deal	10.34	E1 4-4-0	BLA 90	10.37	Margate
09.42 Ashford via Canterbury	10.48	LM4 2-6-4T	Ram 492	10.50	Margate
08.35 Victoria	10.56	BR5 4-6-0	S. Lane 13		
		BR5 4-6-0	S. Lane 12	11.15	Victoria via Chatham
06.05 Reading via Deal	11.20	L 4-4-0	Ton 290	11.25	Margate
		L 4-4-0	Ash 347	11.30	Charing Cross via Deal
10.45 Ashford via Canterbury	11.41	LM4 2-6-4T	Ash 356		(Engine change)
(10.45 Ashford via Canterbury)		V 4-4-0	BLA 81	11.44	Margate
		C 0-6-0	Ram 499	11.59	Margate (Goods)
11.44 Margate	11.59	E1 4-4-0	BLA 90	12.02	Hastings via Canterbury
09.35 Victoria	12.06	BR5 4-6-0	S. Lane 14		
09.15 Charing Cross via Deal	12.12	V 4-4-0	BLA 83		
10.12 Tonbridge via Canterbury	12.28	N15 4-6-0	Ash 341		(Engine change)
(10.12 Tonbridge via Canterbury)		C 0-6-0	Ram 497	12.34	(Engine change)
12.36 Margate	12.50	V 4-4-0	BLA 81	12.53	Charing Cross via Deal
		BR5 4-6-0	S. Lane 13	13.10	Victoria via Chatham
10.35 Victoria	13.10	BR5 4-6-0	S. Lane 10		
13.20 Margate	13.35	LM2 2-6-2T	Ash 362		(Change engines)
(13.20 Margate)		LM4 2-6-4T	Ash 356	13.40	Canterbury West
		V 4-4-0	Ram 481	13.55	Victoria via Chatham
13.40 Margate	13.56	L 4-4-0	Ton 290	13.57	Maidstone via Canterbury
13.50 Margate	14.04	C 0-6-0	Ram 497		(Change engines)
(13.50 Margate)		BR4 2-6-0	Red 628	14.09	Maidstone via Deal
11.15 Charing Cross via Deal	14.12	WC 4-6-2	Ram 470		(Engine change)
11.35 Victoria (Pullman)	14.14	BR5 4-6-0	S. Lane 11		
(11.15 Charing Cross via Deal)		WC 4-6-2	Ram 474	14.17	Margate
12.28 Maidstone via Canterbury	14.20	LM4 2-6-4T	Ram 493		(Engine change)

Train	Arrive	Engine	Shed	Dep	Destination
(12.28 Maidstone via Canterbury)		LM2 2-6-2T	Ash 362	14.25	Margate
14.45 Margate	14.59	V 4-4-0	BLA 83	15.02	Cannon St via Deal
		BR5 4-6-0	S. Lane 14	15.22	Victoria via Chatham
12.35 Victoria	15.22	BR5 4-6-0	S. Lane 15		
15.15 Margate	15.29	LM4 2-6-4T	Ram 492	15.31	Hastings via Canterbury
15.00 Canterbury	15.31	LM4 2-6-4T	Ash 356	15.33	Margate
15.25 Margate	15.39	WC 4-6-2	Ram 474	15.41	Charing Cross via Deal
14.37 Ashford via C'bury	15.41	N15 4-6-0	Ash 340		
13.15 Charing Cross via Deal	15.58	WC 4-6-2	Ram 469	16.02	Margate
11.00 Holborn V. (Pcls)	16.06	E1 4-4-0	BLA 91		
		BR5 4-6-0	S. Lane 10	16.15	Victoria via Chatham
07.35 Birkenhead via C'bury	16.29	V 4-4-0	Ram 485	16.32	Margate
16.22 Margate	16.38	LM4 2-6-4T	Ash 356	16.41	Ashford via Canterbury
12.50 Ashford (Goods)	16.50	N 2-6-0	Ash 370		
(Pullman)		WC 4-6-2	Ram 470	17.05	Victoria via Chatham
(Parcels)		N 2-6-0	S. Lane 63	17.10	Victoria via Chatham
07.35 Birkenhead via Deal	17.10	L 4-4-0	Ash 345		
16.55 Margate	17.11	WC 4-6-2	Ram 469		(Change engines)
(16.55 Margate)	17.11	N15 4-6-0	Ash 340	17.17	Charing Cross via Deal
14.35 Victoria	17.18	L 4-4-0	Ram 489		
		BR5 4-6-0	S. Lane 11	17.22	Victoria via Chatham
15.36 Maidstone via C'bury	17.33	LM4 2-6-4T	Ash 354	17.35	Margate
		L 4-4-0	Ram 489	17.36	Ashford via Canterbury
17.35 Margate	17.50	U1 2-6-0	Fav 276	17.52	Dover via Deal
		BR5 4-6-0	S. Lane 15	18.00	Faversham (Goods)
15.35 Victoria	18.08	BR5 4-6-0	S. Lane 16		
16.12 Tonbridge via C'bury	18.14	L 4-4-0	Fav 264		(Fwd at 18.30)
15.15 Charing Cross via Deal	18.22	WC 4-6-2	Ram 472		
17.55 Margate (Goods)	18.22	C 0-6-0	Ram 499		(Forward at 18.55)
(16.12 Tonbridge via C'bury)		L 4-4-0	Fav 264	18.30	Faversham
16.15 Charing Cross via Deal	18.37	WC 4-6-2	Dover 434	18.39	Margate
(17.55 Margate (Goods))		N 2-6-0	Ash 370	18.55	Ashford (Goods)
16.45 Cannon St	18.55	WC 4-6-2	Ram 471		
18.50 Margate	19.06	V 4-4-0	Ram 485	19.10	Charing Cross via Deal
17.15 Cannon St	19.12	WC 4-6-2	Ram 467		
18.39 Deal	19.13	LM4 2-6-4T	Dover 449		
		L 4-4-0	Ash 345	19.18	Ashford via Canterbury
16.32 Cannon St	19.27	L1 4-4-0	BLA 88		
		E1 4-4-0	BLA 91	19.35	H. Viaduct via Ashford
17.00 Cannon St via Deal	19.36	WC 4-6-2	Ram 465		
		BR5 4-6-0	S. Lane 16	19.45	Victoria via Chatham
17.58 Maidstone via C'bury	19.48	LM4 2-6-4T	Ram 494	19.53	Margate
17.45 Cannon St	20.02	WC 4-6-2	Ram 466		
		N 2-6-0	Ash 374	20.10	Deal (Goods)
18.16 Cannon St	20.22	V 4-4-0	Ram 478		
18.18 Cannon St via Deal	21.09	V 4-4-0	Ram 477		
		L1 4-4-0	BLA 88	21.10	Charing Cross via Chatham
20.05 Faversham	21.10	L 4-4-0	Ram 490		
		LM4 2-6-4T	Dover 449	21.17	Folkestone via Deal
		V 4-4-0	Ram 477	21.25	Margate (ECS)
19.12 Tonbridge via C'bury	21.32	L 4-4-0	Ram 488	21.35	Margate
21.20 Margate	21.35	LM2 2-6-2T	Ash 362	21.36	Canterbury West
21.28 Margate	21.42	WC 4-6-2	Dover 434	21.44	Cannon St via Deal/Redhill
19.15 Charing Cross via Deal	21.46	WC 4-6-2	Ram 468	21.48	Margate
19.35 Victoria	22.01	WC 4-6-2	Ram 473		
18.50 Dover (Goods)	22.08	N 2-6-0	Dover 452		(Fwd at 22.20)
21.58 Margate	22.12	LM4 2-6-4T	Ash 354	22.14	Ashford via Canterbury
(18.50 Dover (Goods))		N 2-6-0	Dover 452	22.20	Hoo Junction
21.36 Ashford via C'bury	22.39	L 4-4-0	Ram 489	22.41	
19.34 Charing Cross via Deal	23.12	V 4-4-0	Ram 485		
20.35 Victoria	23.12	V 4-4-0	Ram 481		
23.02 Canterbury	23.36	LM2 2-6-2T	Ash 362	23.38	Margate
21.35 Victoria	00.00	WC 4-6-2	Ram 470		
21.15 Charing Cross via Deal	00.20	WC 4-6-2	Ram 474		

Of all the motive power locations on the ex-LCDR none perhaps was so critical to operations as Ramsgate. Stewarts Lane carried a heavy burden with its responsibility of the Kent Coast expresses and the Continental services but these took second place to the series of business expresses which conveyed the season ticket holders of Thanet and East Kent to London and brought them back in the evening. A bad run by a boat train might upset a number of passengers who made the journey twice a year or less but a late arrival in Cannon Street by a business express from Ramsgate affected several hundred people who not only paid large sums of money for their season tickets but had (or seemed to have) a direct line to the District Operating Manager. In addition to vociferous complaints, if the 07.20 Ramsgate to Cannon Street lost time then so did half a dozen other services on the approaches to London. The Gods who ordered such things generally guaranteed that any delay on the outskirts of Cannon Street would involved three newspaper editors, two Whitehall Mandarins and a Cabinet Minister.

Ramsgate's chief responsibility therefore was the running of the Kent Coast business service which comprised five Cannon Street expresses (one of which ran empty to Herne Bay before starting its journey) and one to Victoria. These trains generally called at all or most stations to Whitstable before running fast to London and were therefore accompanied by a number of stopping trains which connected with the electric service at Gillingham.

Up to the time of the grouping the South Eastern and London, Chatham & Dover had had entirely separate routes in Thanet; Victoria (LCDR) trains running to the terminus at Ramsgate Harbour while South Eastern trains terminated in their own station at Margate. The 1899 merger of the two systems made such duplication unnecessary but it was left to the Southern Railway to effect the change by closing Ramsgate Harbour station and - in addition to many other works which included replacing all the Thanet stations - building a spur connecting the two main lines near Dumpton Park.

One result of the alterations was to make Ramsgate a 'joint' station whose motive power facilities were shared by both the LCDR and the SER who, in spite of the events of 1899 and 1923 (to say nothing of 1948) kept to their own sections of Kent with very little overlapping. Thus, in addition to the all-important business expresses to Cannon Street via Chatham, Ramsgate also had to provide power for the SER route to Charing Cross via Ashford and in fact the latter accounted for about 60% of Ramsgate's working.

The SER duties were more complicated than those of the LCDR since almost all the workings of the former started and terminated at Margate which resulted in a considerable mileage of light running between Ramsgate and Margate. To reduce line occupation some trains changed engines whilst calling at Ramsgate, a procedure that gave rise to some interesting sights such as that of the 13.50 Margate to Maidstone via Deal which exchanged a class C 0-6-0 for a Redhill-based Standard 4MT 2-6-0.

Most of the more important express workings handled by Ramsgate engines were diagrammed to Light Pacifics, sixteen of which had replaced the tried, tested and trusted N15 King Arthur

N15 4-6-0 30803 'Sir Harry de Fise Lake' of Stewarts Lane passes Gillingham with an express for the Kent Coast in June 1959. (L.G. Marshall)

Amongst the strangest Chatham section engine diagrams was a Gillingham L1 4-4-0 which in a twenty-three hour spell of duty, did not work a single train on home metals. Instead the 4-4-0 worked the 04.33 Strood - Maidstone Newspapers, 07.17 Maidstone - Redhill and the 10.16 Redhill to Reading; taking the latter - the 07.33 ex Eastbourne - over from a Tunbridge Wells LM4 2-6-4T. Having got as far West as it was possible to go without trespassing on the Great Western, the L1 returned East with the 13.50 Reading (South) to Redhill, the 17.39 Reading to Tonbridge from Redhill, the 21.35 Tonbridge - Paddock Wood (which during the winter had to run hard to keep clear of the down Night Ferry) and the 22.24 Paddock Wood to Maidstone West. To round off the day the 4-4-0 switched to goods working by working the midnight coal empties from Maidstone to Snowdown; a curious service which reversed at Snodland and Aylesford after doubling back on itself. The L1 came off at Strood and was replaced by a Dover LM4 2-6-4T which the 4-4-0 then banked up the climb from Strood to Rochester. Because of the hours involved, the working was deemed to be too much for one engine and Gillingham shed was therefore awarded a trip of L1 4-4-0's, 31785 to 31787, for the duty. Above, 31785 sits on Gillingham loco on 17th August 1958. (L.G. Marshall)

Inward Working	On Shed	Engine	Diagram	Off Shed	To Work
21.35 Victoria	00.18	WC 4-6-2	RAM 470		(For 07.00)
21.15 Charing X via Dover	00.30	WC 4-6-2	RAM 474		(For 14.00)
Light ex Margate	00.35	LM2 2-6-2T	Ash 362		(For 02.10)
		LM2 2-6-2T	Ash 361	02.10	Light to Canterbury W.
		L 4-4-0	RAM 488	04.13	Light to Margate
		L 4-4-0	RAM 489	04.15	04.34 Chatham
		LM4 2-6-4T	RAM 492	04.40	Light to Margate
		C 0-6-0	RAM 499	05.00	05.40 Goods to Margate
		WC 4-6-2	RAM 465	05.05	05.31 Charing X via Dover
		H 0-4-4T	RAM 496	05.15	Carriage pilot
00.20 B. Arms via Ashford	05.30	N 2-6-0	ASH 371		(For 06.50)
		WC 4-6-2	RAM 466	05.50	06.06 Cannon St via Chatham
		WC 4-6-2	RAM 467	06.10	06.29 Cannon St via Chatham
		V 4-4-0	RAM 477	06.15	Light to Margate
		WC 4-6-2	RAM 468	06.24	06.46 Cannon St via Dover
03.00 Holborn V via Chatham	06.25	E1 4-4-0	S. Lane 45		(For 08.25)
		V 4-4-0	RAM 478	06.35	06.53 Herne Bay/Cannon St
		WC 4-6-2	RAM 469	06.40	Light to Margate
01.10 Gds ex B. Arms	06.45	Fav 276	U1 2-6-0		(For 16.40)
		L 4-4-0	RAM 490	06.50	07.07 Gillingham
		C 0-6-0	RAM 497	06.50	Yard Pilot
		N 2-6-0	ASH 371	06.50	Light to Minster
		WC 4-6-2	RAM 470	07.00	07.20 Cannon St via Chatham
03.30 Victoria	07.15	BR5 4-6-0	SL 16		(For 09.10)
		WC 4-6-2	RAM 471	07.20	07.35 Cannon St via Chatham
		WC 4-6-2	RAM 473	08.10	08.25 Victoria
		E1 4-4-0	S. Lane 45	08.25	08.44 Ramsgate - Chatham
07.08 Dover (P)	08.25	LM4 2-6-4T	Dvr 450		(For 10.15)
		WC 4-6-2	RAM 472	08.30	Light to Margate
		V 4-4-0	RAM 485	08.36	08.56 Redhill (Birkenhead)
05.10 Victoria	09.00	BR5 4-6-0	SL 12		(For 11.00)
		BR5 4-6-0	SL 16	09.10	09.25 Victoria
Light ex Margate	09.43	V 4-4-0	BLA 81		(For 11.30)
Light ex Minster	10.00	L 4-4-0	Ash 347		(For 11.10)
		LM4 2-6-4T	Dvr 450	10.15	Light to Minster
07.00 Cannon St via Chatham	10.30	N 2-6-0	SL 63		(For 16.55)
08.35 Victoria	11.08	BR5 4-6-0	SL 12		(For 12.55)
Light ex Margate	11.09	C 0-6-0	RAM 499		(For 11.30)
		L 4-4-0	Ash 347	11.10	11.30 Tonbridge via Dover
Light ex Margate	11.15	LM4 2-6-4T	RAM 492		(For 14.00)
		V 4-4-0	BLA 81	11.30	11.46 Margate
		C 0-6-0	RAM 499	11.30	11.59 Goods to Margate
10.45 Ashford	11.55	LM4 2-6-4T	Ash 356		(For 13.20)
09.35 Victoria	12.15	BR5 4-6-0	SL 14		(For 15.00)
09.15 Charing X via Deal	12.40	V 4-4-0	BLA 83		(For 14.00)
10.12 Tonbridge	12.45	N15 4-6-0	Ash 341		(For 13.45)
		BR5 4-6-0	SL 13	12.55	13.10 Victoria
		LM4 2-6-4T	Ash 356	13.20	13.40 Canterbury West
10.35 Victoria	13.20	BR5 4-6-0	SL 10		(For 16.00)
		V 4-4-0	RAM 481	13.40	13.55 Victoria
		N15 4-6-0	Ash 341	13.45	Light to Minster
13.20 Margate	13.45	LM2 2-6-2T	Ash 362		(For 14.05)
		V 4-4-0	BLA 83	14.00	Light to Margate
		WC 4-6-2	RAM 474	14.00	14.17 Margate
		LM4 2-6-4T	RAM 492	14.00	Light to Margate
		LM2 2-6-2T	Ash 362	14.05	14.25 Margate
13.50 Margate	14.10	C 0-6-0	RAM 497		(For 14.50)
11.15 Charing X via Dover	14.25	WC 4-6-2	RAM 470		(For 16.50)
12.28 Maidstone East	14.30	LM4 2-6-4T	RAM 493		(For 04.40)
11.35 Victoria (Pullman)	14.40	BR5 4-6-0	SL 11		(For 17.05)
		C 0-6-0	RAM 497	14.50	Yard Pilot
		BR5 4-6-0	SL 14	15.00	15.22 Victoria
12.35 Victoria	15.40	BR5 4-6-0	SL 15		(For 18.50)
		BR5 4-6-0	SL 10	16.00	16.15 Victoria
11.44 Charing Corss via Ashford	16.00	N15 4-6-0	Ash 340		(For 17.00)
11.41 (Pcls) Cannon St via Chatham	16.15	E1 4-4-0	BLA 91		(For 19.10)
16.05 Gds ex Minster	16.28	N 2-6-0	Ash 370		(For 18.30)
		Fav 276	U1 2-6-0	16.40	Light to Margate
		WC 4-6-2	RAM 470	16.50	17.05 Victoria Pullman
		N 2-6-0	SL 63	16.55	17.10 (Pcls) Victoria
		N15 4-6-0	Ash 340	17.00	17.17 Charing Cross via Dover
15.48 Ashford	17.20	BR5 4-6-0	SL 11	17.05	17.22 Victoria
		L 4-4-0	Ash 345		(For 18.50)
		BR5 4-6-0	SL 15	17.30	18.00 Blackfriars Goods
16.55 Margate - Ramsgate	17.30	WC 4-6-2	RAM 469		(For 06.40)
15.35 Victoria	18.20	BR5 4-6-0	SL 16		(For 19.30)
		N 2-6-0	Ash 370	18.30	18.55 Ashford
17.55 Goods ex Margate	18.30	C 0-6-0	RAM 499		(For 05.00)
Light ex Margate	18.33	LM4 2-6-4T	Ash 354		(For 21.16)
		L 4-4-0	Ash 345	18.50	19.18 Ashford
		E1 4-4-0	BLA 91	19.10	19.35 Holborn V via Dover
16.45 Cannon St via Chatham	19.13	WC 4-6-2	RAM 471		(For 07.20)
18.39 Deal	19.20	LM4 2-6-4T	Dvr 449		(For 20.50)
		BR5 4-6-0	SL 16	19.30	19.45 Victoria
17.15 Cannon St via Chatham	19.30	WC 4-6-2	RAM 467		(For 06.10)
16.32 Cannon St via Chatham	19.40	L1 4-4-0	BLA 88		(For 20.55)
Light ex Margate	19.44	WC 4-6-2	Dvr 434		(For 20.30)
Light ex Margate	19.44	WC 4-6-2	RAM 472		(For 08.30)
17.00 Cannon St via Dover	19.55	WC 4-6-2	RAM 465		(For 05.05)
17.45 Cannon St via Chatham	20.20	WC 4-6-2	RAM 466		(For 05.50)
		WC 4-6-2	Dvr 434	20.30	Light to Margate
Carriage pilot	20.30	H 0-4-4T	RAM 496		(For 05.15)
18.16 Cannon St via Chatham	20.40	V 4-4-0	RAM 478		(For 06.35)
		LM4 2-6-4T	Dvr 449	20.50	21.17 Folkestone Junction
		L1 4-4-0	BLA 88	20.55	21.10 Charing X via Chatham
		LM4 2-6-4T	Ash 354	21.16	Light to Margate
20.05 Faversham	21.23	L 4-4-0	RAM 490		(For 06.50)
Yard Pilot	22.10	C 0-6-0	RAM 497		(For 06.50)
19.35 Victoria	22.13	WC 4-6-2	RAM 473		(For 08.10)
Light ex Margate	22.15	V 4-4-0	RAM 477		(For 06.15)
Light ex Margate	22.40	WC 4-6-2	RAM 468		(For 06.24)
Light ex Margate	22.40	L 4-4-0	RAM 488		(For 04.13)
19.34 Charing X via Deal	23.20	V 4-4-0	RAM 485		(For 08.36)
20.35 Victoria	23.30	V 4-4-0	RAM 481		(For 13.40)
Light ex Margate	23.33	L 4-4-0	RAM 489		(For 04.15)

4-6-0's shortly after the war and introduced a decade of uncertainty in the running of the service which hitherto had operated almost as clockwork. At the time of replacement the Ramsgate N15's had been in a very run-down condition - so much so that a batch of Light Pacifics earmarked for the West Country had rapidly been reallocated to Ramsgate for fear that the Cannon Street service might collapse completely. With hindsight it might have been better had the N15's been brought up to scratch and allowed to continue in service and one has a suspicion that had this been allowed to happen, the service would not have fallen so far from grace as it occasionally did. Not all the fault lay with the new Pacifics and to browse - as the author once did - through the list of disciplinary charges aimed at firemen circa 1950 is enough to make one's hair stand on end. Ramsgate lay in an area of high employment and since the railway found itself unable to compete effectively with local firms for rates of pay or conditions of service, the calibre of staff was not always as high as might have been wished. However the Pacifics seemed suited for long non-stop runs and the fact that some of the business expresses made seven or eight stops in the twenty miles between Ramsgate and Whitstable simply gave rein to their uncertainty in getting a train on the move. Compounding the state of affairs was the time taken to effect repairs and a defect that might be put right in a shift on a King Arthur often took several

days with a Pacific - a problem that eventually resulted in some of Ramsgate's Pacifics being transferred to Bricklayers Arms.

Between the grumbles of season-ticket holders and the form 2's that kept the Shedmaster's clerical staff busy, the sight of so many Pacifics with their imposing 'air-smoothed' covers in one location was a magnet for the enthusiasts of the area although one had to pick one's time carefully in order to see the best of them. Between five and half-past eight in the morning there was a continuous succession of Pacifics ringing off shed, some working to Cannon Street via Chatham, others to London via Deal and Ashford with a couple running light to Margate to start off a pair of South astern services from that point. It was difficult to think of another location where so many large engines could be seen in such a short space of time - it was certainly worth sacrificing some sleep for - yet once the 09.40 Margate to Charing Cross via Deal had gone through, no other Pacific was seen for four and a quarter hours. At Ramsgate it was either a flood or a drought and in the evening the deluge of Pacifics reappeared with nine arrivals between the 15.15 ex Charing Cross via Deal and the 19.35 from Victoria via Chatham.

Strangely, foreign Pacifics were rather an uncommon sight in Thanet and the only booked instance came with the 16.15 Charing Cross - Deal - Dover which was booked to a Dover Pacific. The engine returned with the 21.28

Margate - Cannon Street mail which it worked as far as Dover Priory where it was relieved by a Bricklayers Arms Schools 4-4-0 for the continuation via Tonbridge and Redhill.

As with the Stewarts Lane engines, daily mileages were not high; most engines achieving little more than a single round trip to London: 160 miles via Chatham or 200 to Charing Cross via Deal and Dover. Rather curiously the one exception to the rule concerned two of the most important trains of the day - the 07.20 Ramsgate to Cannon Street via Chatham and the 17.05 'Thanet Belle' to Victoria - which were diagrammed to the same Pacific. The Pacific was booked to work up to Cannon Street with the 07.20 and return with the 11.15 Charing Cross to Margate via Deal, an unusual instance of an engine working to London via the LCDR and returning via the SER. The engine was relieved by another Pacific at Ramsgate and then turned out two and a half hours later for the 17.05 Pullman to Victoria. The final leg of the working was with the 21.35 Victoria to Ramsgate via Chatham. Whether the engine actually worked both legs of the working depended upon its condition when arriving back with the 11.15 ex Charing Cross and the availability of engines at Ramsgate but the mileage of 341 miles was uncommonly high for the South Eastern.

Backing up the Ramsgate Pacifics were eight Schools class 4-4-0's; an engine that in the eyes of many Ramsgate footplatemen were far better suited to the Chatham route than the

The introduction of LMS 2-6-2 and 2-6-4 tanks almost eradicated the H 0-4-4T's from main line work in East Kent, leaving only a handful at Ramsgate and Dover to carry out station pilot duties. 31542 shunts carriage stock at Dover Priory in September 1957. (L.G. Marshall)

LOCOMOTIVE ALLOCATIONS & TRANSFERS : RAMSGATE(74B)

Loco	Class	Aug-50	Sep-50	Oct-50	Nov-50	Dec-50	Jan-51	Feb-51	Mar-51	Apr-51	May-51	Jun-51	Jul-51
34077	7P : WC 4-6-2 (1945)												
34078	7P : WC 4-6-2 (1945)												
34079	7P : WC 4-6-2 (1945)												
34080	7P : WC 4-6-2 (1945)												
34081	7P : WC 4-6-2 (1945)												
34082	7P : WC 4-6-2 (1945)												
34083	7P : WC 4-6-2 (1945)	X	X	X	X	X	X	X	Ex S. Lane				
34084	7P : WC 4-6-2 (1945)	X	X	X	X	X	X	X	Ex S. Lane				
34085	7P : WC 4-6-2 (1945)	X	X	X	X	X	X	X	Ex S. Lane				
34086	7P : WC 4-6-2 (1945)												
34087	7P : WC 4-6-2 (1945)								To S. Lane	X	X	X	X
34088	7P : WC 4-6-2 (1945)								To S. Lane	X	X	X	X
34089	7P : WC 4-6-2 (1945)												
34090	7P : WC 4-6-2 (1945)								To S. Lane	X	X	X	X
34096	7P : WC 4-6-2 (1945)												
34097	7P : WC 4-6-2 (1945)												
34098	7P : WC 4-6-2 (1945)												
34099	7P : WC 4-6-2 (1945)												
34100	7P : WC 4-6-2 (1945)												
30911	5P : V 4-4-0 (1930)								To St L.	X	X	X	X
30912	5P : V 4-4-0 (1930)								To St L.	X	X	X	X
30913	5P : V 4-4-0 (1930)												
30914	5P : V 4-4-0 (1930)												
30915	5P : V 4-4-0 (1930)												
30916	5P : V 4-4-0 (1930)												
30917	5P : V 4-4-0 (1930)												
30918	5P : V 4-4-0 (1930)												
30921	5P : V 4-4-0 (1930)	X	X	X	X	X	X	X	Ex B. Arms				
30795	5P : N15 4-6-0 (1926)	X	X	X	Ex B. Arms	To S. Lane	X	X	X	X	X	X	X
31859	5F : N 2-6-0 (1917)	X	X	X	Ex S. Lane								To H. Green
42066	4MT 2-6-4T (1948)	X	X	NEW									
42067	4MT 2-6-4T (1948)	X	X	NEW									
42068	4MT 2-6-4T (1948)	X	X	X	NEW								
42069	4MT 2-6-4T (1948)	X	X	X	NEW								
42070	4MT 2-6-4T (1948)	X	X	X	X	Ex S. Lane							
42094	4MT 2-6-4T (1948)	X	X	X	X	X	X	X	X	X	X	NEW	
42106	4MT 2-6-4T (1948)	X	X	NEW	To T. Wells	X	X	X	X	X	X	X	X
31788	3P : L1 4-4-0 (1926)	X	X	Ex B. Arms	To B. Arms	X	X	X	X	X	X	X	X
31789	3P : L1 4-4-0 (1926)	X	X	Ex B. Arms	To B. Arms	X	X	X	X	X	X	X	X
31776	3P : L 4-4-0 (1914)												
31777	3P : L 4-4-0 (1914)				To Ashford	X	X	X	X	X	X	X	X
31778	3P : L 4-4-0 (1914)	X	X	X	X	Ex Ton							
31779	3P : L 4-4-0 (1914)	X	X	X	X	Ex Ton							
31780	3P : L 4-4-0 (1914)												
31781	3P : L 4-4-0 (1914)												
31748	2P : D 4-4-0 (1901)	X	X	X	Ex Ashford	To Fav	X	X	X	X	X	X	X
31004	2F : C 0-6-0 (1900)												
31252	2F : C 0-6-0 (1900)												
31298	2F : C 0-6-0 (1900)												
31592	2F : C 0-6-0 (1900)												
31690	2F : C 0-6-0 (1900)												
31065	2F : O1 0-6-0 (1903)												To Ashford
31093	2F : O1 0-6-0 (1903)								W/D	X	X	X	
31390	2F : O1 0-6-0 (1903)								W/D	X	X	X	
31259	1P : H 0-4-4T (1904)			To Fav	X	X	X	X	X	X	X	X	X
31265	1P : H 0-4-4T (1904)				To S. Lane	X	X	X	X	X	X	X	X
31519	1P : H 0-4-4T (1904)												
31521	1P : H 0-4-4T (1904)												
31522	1P : H 0-4-4T (1904)												
31532	1P : H 0-4-4T (1904)			To Fav	X	X	X	X	X	X	X	X	X
31543	1P : H 0-4-4T (1904)			To B. Arms	X	X	X	X	X	X	X	X	X

Pacifics. To the regret of many, the Schools did not play much of a role in the working of the morning business trains and the only regular such booking was with the 08.20 Herne Bay (06.35 empty stock from Ramsgate) to Cannon Street. Other principal Ramsgate Schools' duties included the 08.56 Ramsgate to Birkenhead (via Deal) as far as Redhill and the 13.55 Ramsgate - Victoria via Chatham. The first of these was an interesting working - the only regular inter-regional trains to run from Thanet - which ran in two portions as far as Ashford, the second section starting from Margate at 09.18 and running via Canterbury West behind an Ashford L 4-4-0. At Redhill the train was joined by a third portion which came up from Hastings via Eastbourne and Brighton.

With one exception all the two-hourly Charing Cross - Deal - Ramsgate/Margate expresses were booked to Light Pacifics but the odd one out, the 09.15 Charing Cross - Ramsgate, was worked by a Bricklayers Arms Schools. The use of a 4-4-0 was something of a compliment to the class given that the 09.15 loaded to eleven vehicles whereas the Pacific-hauled 11.15, 13.15 and 15.15 were formed of nine, eight and eight coaches respectively. (Heaven forbid that conclusions should be drawn but the 11.15 from Charing Cross ran to Ramsgate in exactly the same time and with the same number of stops as the 09.15 whilst the faster timing of the 13.15 was due entirely to its non-stop run between Waterloo and Ashford. It was sometimes rather difficult to see where the value for money had come from the post-war motive power order).

Secondary passenger work at

Although the largest engines on the section - the Merchant Navy Pacifics - were authorised to run from Victoria to Ramsgate via Chatham, the trains on the route did not call for class 8 power and such appearances were therefore uncommon.   The booked workings for the class were on the 09.00 and 10.00 Continental express from Victoria which diverged from the Chatham section at Bickley Junction where they crossed over to the South Eastern main line.   35030 'Elder Dempster Line' stands on Stewarts Lane loco in 1954. (M. Bentley)

Ramsgate was divided between inside-cylinder 4-4-0's - chiefly L 4-4-0's although L1's came to the shed from time to time - and new LMS 4MT 2-6-4T's which had arrived in late 1950 and taken over much of the work formerly handled by H 0-4-4T's. Most of the 4-4-0 work was done on the Chatham section with trains to and from the Medway interspersed with trips between Faversham and Dover.   Some of this work involved duties with express traffic such as that of the 4-4-0 which worked up to Chatham with the 04.34 cheap ticket train to Chatham and returned with the Dover portion of the 08.35 Vctoria - Ramsgate. The same engine later worked the Ramsgate section of the 14.35 Victoria - Dover.

Not all the 4-4-0 work was LCDR-based and one of the Ramsgate engines worked an interestingly circuitous diagram on the South Eastern which started in an orthodox manner from Margate to Ashford but then worked a series of stopping passenger trains from Ashford to Hastings, Hastings to Tonbridge and Tonbridge to Redhill, reaching the last-mentioned just as its Schools shedmate was preparing to leave with the 07.35 Birkenhead to Ramsgate.

The homeward journey was made initially with a stopping service from Redhill to Tonbridge and finally with the Canterbury West/Margate section of the 18.18 Cannon Street - Deal - Ramsgate.

The 2-6-4T workings were exclusively South Eastern and involved a pair of two-day diagrams concerned mainly with Margate - Maidstone East stopping trains

Loco	Class	Aug-51	Sep-51	Oct-51	Nov-51	Dec-51	Jan-52	Feb-52	Mar-52	Apr-52	May-52	Jun-52	Jul-52
						LOCOMOTIVE ALLOCATIONS & TRANSFERS : RAMSGATE(74B)							
34075	7P : WC 4-6-2 (1945)	X	X	X	X	X	X	X	X	X	X	Ex Dover	
34076	7P : WC 4-6-2 (1945)	X	X	X	X	X	X	X	X	X	X	Ex Stratford	
34077	7P : WC 4-6-2 (1945)												
34078	7P : WC 4-6-2 (1945)												
34079	7P : WC 4-6-2 (1945)												
34080	7P : WC 4-6-2 (1945)												
34081	7P : WC 4-6-2 (1945)												
34082	7P : WC 4-6-2 (1945)												
34083	7P : WC 4-6-2 (1945)												
34084	7P : WC 4-6-2 (1945)												
34085	7P : WC 4-6-2 (1945)												
34086	7P : WC 4-6-2 (1945)												
34089	7P : WC 4-6-2 (1945)												
34096	7P : WC 4-6-2 (1945)												
34097	7P : WC 4-6-2 (1945)												
34098	7P : WC 4-6-2 (1945)												
34099	7P : WC 4-6-2 (1945)												
34100	7P : WC 4-6-2 (1945)												
30910	5P : V 4-4-0 (1930)	X	X	X	X	Ex St L.			To St L	X	X	X	X
30911	5P : V 4-4-0 (1930)	X	X	X	X	Ex St L.			To St L	X	X	Ex St L.	
30912	5P : V 4-4-0 (1930)	X	X	X	X	Ex St L.			To St L	X	X	Ex St L.	
30913	5P : V 4-4-0 (1930)												
30914	5P : V 4-4-0 (1930)												
30915	5P : V 4-4-0 (1930)												
30916	5P : V 4-4-0 (1930)												
30917	5P : V 4-4-0 (1930)												
30918	5P : V 4-4-0 (1930)											To Dover	X
30921	5P : V 4-4-0 (1930)		To Dover	X	X	X	X	X	X	X	X	X	X
42066	4MT 2-6-4T (1948)											To T Bges	X
42067	4MT 2-6-4T (1948)												
42068	4MT 2-6-4T (1948)												
42069	4MT 2-6-4T (1948)												
42070	4MT 2-6-4T (1948)												
42071	4MT 2-6-4T (1948)	X	Ex Ashford										
42072	4MT 2-6-4T (1948)	X	Ex Ashford										
42094	4MT 2-6-4T (1948)	To Ashford	X	X	X	X	X	X	X	X	X	X	X
31782	3P : L1 4-4-0 (1926)	X	X	X	X	X	Ex B Arms					To B. Arms	X
31783	3P : L1 4-4-0 (1926)	X	X	X	X	X	Ex B Arms					To B. Arms	X
31776	3P : L 4-4-0 (1914)		To Ashford	X	X	X	X	X	X	X	X	X	X
31778	3P : L 4-4-0 (1914)		To Ashford	X	X	Ex Ashford	To E'leigh	X	X	X	X	X	X
31779	3P : L 4-4-0 (1914)						To E'leigh	X	X	X	X	Ex E'liegh	
31780	3P : L 4-4-0 (1914)												
31781	3P : L 4-4-0 (1914)		To B. Arms	X	X	X	Ex B Arms						
31004	2F : C 0-6-0 (1900)												
31245	2F : C 0-6-0 (1900)	X	X	X	X	X	X	X	X	X	X	Ex H. Green	
31252	2F : C 0-6-0 (1900)												
31271	2F : C 0-6-0 (1900)	X	X	X	X	X	X	X	X	X	X	Ex Ashford	
31298	2F : C 0-6-0 (1900)												
31592	2F : C 0-6-0 (1900)												
31690	2F : C 0-6-0 (1900)											To H. Greer	X
31276	1P : H 0-4-4T (1904)	X	X	X	X	X	X	X	Ex Dover				
31324	1F : H 0-4-4T (1904)	X	X	X	X	X	X	X	X	X	X	Ex Fav	
31326	1P : H 0-4-4T (1904)	X	X	X	X	X	X	X	X	X	X	Ex Fav	
31519	1P : H 0-4-4T (1904)											To St L.	X
31521	1P : H 0-4-4T (1904)											To Dover	X
31522	1P : H 0-4-4T (1904)								To Ashford	X	X	X	X

The final three years of steam at Ramsgate were years of considerable difficulty, most of which stemmed from the seemingly insuperable problems posed by the maintenance of the unrebuilt Light Pacifics. In 1957 half the allocation was despatched to Bricklayers Arms with the balance being replaced by rebuilt Pacifics and Schools 4-4-0's; the latter being regarded by many crews as the best engine for the route. This view was evidently reciprocated at Stewarts Lane who, on 27 May 1959, turned out 30921 'Shrewsbury' for the 09.35 Victoria to Ramsgate. The engine is pictured whilst being prepared for the return working, the 15.22 Ramsgate to Victoria. (M. Bentley)

with the unusual feature of spending the intervening night at St Leonards shed, Hastings. Although the LMS engines were powerful, reliable and well-liked, whether the investment was worthwhile given that their duties could probably have been handled quite efficiently by H class 0-4-4T's is a matter for debate but certainly nothing the 2-6-4T's were called upon to do in East Kent compared with the sort of work they performed in the suburban service of their native railway. Unfortunately for those who had a liking for the H class, their only remaining role at Ramsgate was that of the station pilot.

Goods work was not a prominent feature of operations at Ramsgate and the shed's class C 0-6-0's were primarily involved in shunting the yards at Ramsgate, Margate, Minster, Walmer and Deal whilst one of the class shuttled between Ramsgate and Margate with a handful of local goods trips. The principal goods service left in the evening behind a Stewarts Lane 4-6-0 while the remainder of the area's needs were seen to by occasional visits from foreign N 2-6-0's.

1950/1

The chief development was the replacement of the shed's seven H class 0-4-4T's by six LMS 2-6-4T's; a move that eliminated the older engines from all regular mainline work. The period also saw the removal of the shed's O1 0-6-0's. Christmas 1950 saw an interesting variety of engines arrive at the shed for seasonal work but none, apart from an N 2-6-0 which remained at work until June

LOCOMOTIVE ALLOCATIONS & TRANSFERS : RAMSGATE(74B)													
Loco	Class	Aug-52	Sep-52	Oct-52	Nov-52	Dec-52	Jan-53	Feb-53	Mar-53	Apr-53	May-53	Jun-53	Jul-53
34075	7P : WC 4-6-2 (1945)												
34076	7P : WC 4-6-2 (1945)												
34077	7P : WC 4-6-2 (1945)												
34078	7P : WC 4-6-2 (1945)												
34079	7P : WC 4-6-2 (1945)												
34080	7P : WC 4-6-2 (1945)												
34081	7P : WC 4-6-2 (1945)												
34082	7P : WC 4-6-2 (1945)												
34083	7P : WC 4-6-2 (1945)												
34084	7P : WC 4-6-2 (1945)												
34085	7P : WC 4-6-2 (1945)												
34086	7P : WC 4-6-2 (1945)												
34089	7P : WC 4-6-2 (1945)												
34096	7P : WC 4-6-2 (1945)												
34097	7P : WC 4-6-2 (1945)												
34098	7P : WC 4-6-2 (1945)												
34099	7P : WC 4-6-2 (1945)												
34100	7P : WC 4-6-2 (1945)												
30911	5P : V 4-4-0 (1930)												
30912	5P : V 4-4-0 (1930)												
30913	5P : V 4-4-0 (1930)												
30914	5P : V 4-4-0 (1930)												
30915	5P : V 4-4-0 (1930)		To S. Lane	X	X	X	X	X	X	X	X	X	X
30916	5P : V 4-4-0 (1930)												
30917	5P : V 4-4-0 (1930)												
30918	5P : V 4-4-0 (1930)	X	X	X	X	X	X	X	Ex Dover		To Dover	X	X
30922	5P : V 4-4-0 (1930)	X	Ex N'haven										
30796	5P : N15 4-6-0 (1926)	X	X	X	X	X	X	X	Ex Dover				
30772	5P : N15 4-6-0 (1925)	X	X	X	X	X	X	X	Ex S. Lane				
33018	5F : Q1 0-6-0 (1942)	X	X	X	X	X	X	X	Ex E'leigh		To Guild	X	X
33019	5F : Q1 0-6-0 (1942)	X	X	X	X	X	X	X	Ex E'leigh				To Guild
33022	5F : Q1 0-6-0 (1942)	X	X	X	X	X	X	X	Ex E'leigh				
42067	4MT 2-6-4T (1948)												
42068	4MT 2-6-4T (1948)								To Brighton	X	Ex Brighton		
42069	4MT 2-6-4T (1948)		To Ashford	X	X	X	X	X	X	X	X	X	X
42070	4MT 2-6-4T (1948)												
42071	4MT 2-6-4T (1948)												
42072	4MT 2-6-4T (1948)												
31756	3P : L1 4-4-0 (1926)	X	Ex Dover										
31757	3P : L1 4-4-0 (1926)	X	Ex Dover										
31779	3P : L 4-4-0 (1914)												
31780	3P : L 4-4-0 (1914)												
31781	3P : L 4-4-0 (1914)												
31004	2F : C 0-6-0 (1900)												
31245	2F : C 0-6-0 (1900)												
31252	2F : C 0-6-0 (1900)												
31271	2F : C 0-6-0 (1900)												
31298	2F : C 0-6-0 (1900)												
31592	2F : C 0-6-0 (1900)												
31276	1P : H 0-4-4T (1904)												
31324	1P : H 0-4-4T (1904)												
31326	1P : H 0-4-4T (1904)												

Loco	Class	Aug-53	Sep-53	Oct-53	Nov-53	Dec-53	Jan-54	Feb-54	Mar-54	Apr-54	May-54	Jun-54	Jul-54
34075	7P : WC 4-6-2 (1945)												
34076	7P : WC 4-6-2 (1945)												
34077	7P : WC 4-6-2 (1945)												
34078	7P : WC 4-6-2 (1945)												
34079	7P : WC 4-6-2 (1945)												
34080	7P : WC 4-6-2 (1945)												
34081	7P : WC 4-6-2 (1945)												
34082	7P : WC 4-6-2 (1945)												
34083	7P : WC 4-6-2 (1945)												
34084	7P : WC 4-6-2 (1945)												
34085	7P : WC 4-6-2 (1945)												
34086	7P : WC 4-6-2 (1945)												
34089	7P : WC 4-6-2 (1945)												
34096	7P : WC 4-6-2 (1945)												
34097	7P : WC 4-6-2 (1945)												
34098	7P : WC 4-6-2 (1945)												
34099	7P : WC 4-6-2 (1945)												
34100	7P : WC 4-6-2 (1945)												
30911	5P : V 4-4-0 (1930)												
30912	5P : V 4-4-0 (1930)												
30913	5P : V 4-4-0 (1930)												
30914	5P : V 4-4-0 (1930)												
30916	5P : V 4-4-0 (1930)												
30917	5P : V 4-4-0 (1930)												
30918	5P : V 4-4-0 (1930)	X	X	X	X	X	X	X	X	X	X	Ex Dover	
30922	5P : V 4-4-0 (1930)												
30796	5P : N15 4-6-0 (1926)										To Dover	X	X
30772	5P : N15 4-6-0 (1925)												
33022	5F : Q1 0-6-0 (1942)		To Guild	X	X	X	X	X	X	X	X	X	X
42067	4MT 2-6-4T (1948)												
42068	4MT 2-6-4T (1948)				To Redhill	X	Ex Redhill						
42070	4MT 2-6-4T (1948)												
42071	4MT 2-6-4T (1948)												
42072	4MT 2-6-4T (1948)												
31756	3P : L1 4-4-0 (1926)		To Ashford	X	X	X	X	X	X	X	X	X	X
31757	3P : L1 4-4-0 (1926)		To Ashford	X	X	X	X	X	X	X	X	X	X
31779	3P : L 4-4-0 (1914)												
31780	3P : L 4-4-0 (1914)												
31781	3P : L 4-4-0 (1914)												
31004	2F : C 0-6-0 (1900)												
31245	2F : C 0-6-0 (1900)												
31252	2F : C 0-6-0 (1900)												
31271	2F : C 0-6-0 (1900)												
31298	2F : C 0-6-0 (1900)												
31592	2F : C 0-6-0 (1900)												
31276	1P : H 0-4-4T (1904)		To Ashford	X	X	X	X	X	X	X	X	X	X
31324	1P : H 0-4-4T (1904)												
31326	1P : H 0-4-4T (1904)												

LOCOMOTIVE ALLOCATIONS & TRANSFERS : RAMSGATE(74B)

Loco	Class	Aug-54	Sep-54	Oct-54	Nov-54	Dec-54	Jan-55	Feb-55	Mar-55	Apr-55	May-55	Jun-55	Jul-55
34075	7P : WC 4-6-2 (1945)												
34076	7P : WC 4-6-2 (1945)												
34077	7P : WC 4-6-2 (1945)												
34078	7P : WC 4-6-2 (1945)												
34079	7P : WC 4-6-2 (1945)												
34080	7P : WC 4-6-2 (1945)												
34081	7P : WC 4-6-2 (1945)												
34082	7P : WC 4-6-2 (1945)												
34083	7P : WC 4-6-2 (1945)												
34084	7P : WC 4-6-2 (1945)												
34085	7P : WC 4-6-2 (1945)												
34086	7P : WC 4-6-2 (1945)												
34089	7P : WC 4-6-2 (1945)			To S. Lane	X	X	X	X	X	X	X	X	X
34096	7P : WC 4-6-2 (1945)												
34097	7P : WC 4-6-2 (1945)												
34098	7P : WC 4-6-2 (1945)												
34099	7P : WC 4-6-2 (1945)												
34100	7P : WC 4-6-2 (1945)												
30911	5P : V 4-4-0 (1930)												
30912	5P : V 4-4-0 (1930)												
30913	5P : V 4-4-0 (1930)												
30914	5P : V 4-4-0 (1930)												
30916	5P : V 4-4-0 (1930)												
30917	5P : V 4-4-0 (1930)												
30918	5P : V 4-4-0 (1930)												
30922	5P : V 4-4-0 (1930)												
30772	5P : N15 4-6-0 (1925)	To H. Green	X	X	X	X	X	X	X	X	X	X	X
42067	4MT 2-6-4T (1948)											To Brighton	X
42068	4MT 2-6-4T (1948)												
42070	4MT 2-6-4T (1948)												
42071	4MT 2-6-4T (1948)												
42072	4MT 2-6-4T (1948)			To G'head	X	X	X	X	X	X	X	X	X
31779	3P : L 4-4-0 (1914)												
31780	3P : L 4-4-0 (1914)												
31781	3P : L 4-4-0 (1914)												
31004	2F : C 0-6-0 (1900)												
31245	2F : C 0-6-0 (1900)												
31252	2F : C 0-6-0 (1900)												
31271	2F : C 0-6-0 (1900)												
31298	2F : C 0-6-0 (1900)												
31592	2F : C 0-6-0 (1900)												
31310	1P : H 0-4-4T (1904)	X	X	X	X	X	X	X	X	X	X	Ex Brighton	
31324	1P : H 0-4-4T (1904)												
31326	1P : H 0-4-4T (1904)												

1951, stayed for long. One of the visitors was King Arthur 30795 'Sir Dinadan', the last of the class to sport a Malachite Green livery.

1951/2

The loss of three L 4-4-0's in the Autumn brought fears of LMS 2-6-4T's with their limited water supply having to work the Birkenhead service in the event of a shortage of Schools; a threat that was not lifted until December when one of the 4-4-0's was returned from Ashford. Immediately afterwards it was decided that better use of the L class could be made by the LSWR and two of Ramsgate's allocation (including the engine lately returned from Ashford) were sent to Eastleigh in January 1952. Their place was taken by a pair of L1 4-4-0's from Bricklayers Arms although the status quo was regained by the summer following the South Western's rejection of the L 4-4-0's. Shortly before the commencement of the Summer 1952 workings, the allocation of Light Pacifics was increased from sixteen to eighteen. One of the arrivals was 34076 '41 Squadron' which had been on loan to the Great Eastern.

1952/3

L1 4-4-0's returned to Ramsgate at the end of the 1952 summer workings and remained for twelve months although the three L 4-4-0's and five 2-6-4T's left little work for them. In early 1953 the Victoria services were thrown into chaos with several miles of track being washed away near Reculver and for some time services operated between Birchington and Victoria via Ramsgate, Minster, the wartime Canterbury connection and Faversham. Herne Bay, Chestfield and Whitstable were served by connecting push and pull trains from Faversham. To assist with the altered arrangements, a number of engines were hurriedly drafted into the area and these included a pair of King Arthur 4-6-0's and, to deal with the ballast trains, a trio of Q1 0-6-0's. Hopes that the arrival of 30796 'Sir Dodinas le Savage' and 30772 'Sir Percivale' signalled a revival of the class in Thanet were ill-founded and events dictated that the pair would in fact be the last examples of the class to be based at Ramsgate. For the moment, the absence of local N15's had not been much of an issue since the class continued to enjoyed a near-monopoly of the Victoria services and few were prepared to forecast the speed of their demise, a couple of years hence.

1953-55

While considerable change was effected towards the end of the period at the London end of the line with the replacement of King Arthur 4-6-0's by BR Standard 5MT's on the Victoria service, very few alterations were made to the allocation at Ramsgate and the time was probably one of the most stable in the shed's postwar history. The last of the Q1 0-6-0's drifted back to Guildford - the Herne Bay crisis over - whilst the shed also parted with its two L1 4-4-0's and an H 0-4-4T. In the Spring of 1954 one of the N15 4-6-0's was sent to Dover in exchange for a Schools 4-4-0, its companion leaving at the cessation of the summer when it was reallocated to Hither Green for working the 17.40 Cannon Street to Dover. In return Ramsgate received its eighteenth Light Pacific. An unprecedented transfer took place in October 1954 when one of the LMS 2-6-4T's was ordered to far-off Gateshead for duties on the Newcastle to Middlesbrough service. A few months later, in mid-1955, another 2-6-4T was lost when 42067 was exchanged for an H 0-4-4T.

1956-59

After six years in traffic it finally dawned upon the Motive Power authorities that the LMS 2-6-4T's were to a great extent wasted on the rural trains of East Kent and in May 1956 replaced the remaining three engines with a trio of LMS 2MT 2-6-2T's. The latter hardly had time to acclimatise themselves to the area for a year after their arrival they were replaced by a new batch of five Standard 2MT 2-6-2T's; virtually indistinguishable from the LMS engines except for the possession of steam attachments for snow clearing devices which had some potential for the Canterbury area which was prone to heavy falls of snow.

By the end of 1957 the problems that Ramsgate had always had with the maintenance of its Pacifics - which formed nearly 40% of the shed's complement - deepened and while on paper the depot had seventeen engines for eleven diagrams (ie six spare for maintenance, repairs and special workings), the availability of the engines had fallen to such a low level that the number of Schools 4-4-0's had to be increased from seven to twelve in order to ensure that power could be guaranteed for all trains. Fortunately the partial dieselisation of the Charing Cross - Hastings service released a number of 4-4-0's for other duties although it was interesting to note that from late 1957 the 17.05 Cannon Street to Hastings and the 20.35 Hastings to Ashford became Ramsgate Schools' workings. At the same time a Schools was also diagrammed for the 08.25 Ramsgate to Victoria and the 19.35 Victoria - Ramsgate in lieu of a Pacific.

Excellent engines though the Schools 4-4-0's were, the use of class 5 engines on class 7 duties could not be regarded as anything but a stop-gap and although the rebuilding of the Light Pacifics had commenced, it seemed unlikely that this alone would have an impact of Ramsgate's problems in the foreseeable future.

The complaints of poor running grew in volume and in early 1958 a drastic plan to resolve matters was embarked upon. All but one of Ramsgate's unrebuilt Pacifics - sixteen engines in all - were transferred away and were replaced by eight rebuilt Pacifics to cover six workings of which only two (06.29 and 07.19 Ramsgate to Cannon Street) were LCDR workings. The

LOCOMOTIVE ALLOCATIONS & TRANSFERS : RAMSGATE(74B)

Loco	Class	Aug-55	Sep-55	Oct-55	Nov-55	Dec-55	Jan-56	Feb-56	Mar-56	Apr-56	May-56	Jun-56	Jul-56
34075	7P : WC 4-6-2 (1945)												
34076	7P : WC 4-6-2 (1945)												
34077	7P : WC 4-6-2 (1945)												
34078	7P : WC 4-6-2 (1945)												
34079	7P : WC 4-6-2 (1945)												
34080	7P : WC 4-6-2 (1945)												
34081	7P : WC 4-6-2 (1945)												
34082	7P : WC 4-6-2 (1945)												
34083	7P : WC 4-6-2 (1945)												
34084	7P : WC 4-6-2 (1945)												
34085	7P : WC 4-6-2 (1945)												
34086	7P : WC 4-6-2 (1945)												
34096	7P : WC 4-6-2 (1945)												
34097	7P : WC 4-6-2 (1945)												
34098	7P : WC 4-6-2 (1945)												
34099	7P : WC 4-6-2 (1945)												
34100	7P : WC 4-6-2 (1945)												
30911	5P : V 4-4-0 (1930)												
30912	5P : V 4-4-0 (1930)		To Ashford	X	X	X	X	X	X	X	Ex Ashford		
30913	5P : V 4-4-0 (1930)												
30914	5P : V 4-4-0 (1930)												
30916	5P : V 4-4-0 (1930)												
30917	5P : V 4-4-0 (1930)												
30918	5P : V 4-4-0 (1930)												
30922	5P : V 4-4-0 (1930)												
42068	4MT 2-6-4T (1948)										To Brighton	X	X
42070	4MT 2-6-4T (1948)										To Brighton	X	X
42071	4MT 2-6-4T (1948)										To Brighton	X	X
31764	3P : L 4-4-0 (1914)	X	Ex St.L										
31769	3P : L 4-4-0 (1914)	X	Ex St.L								W/D	X	X
31779	3P : L 4-4-0 (1914)												
31780	3P : L 4-4-0 (1914)												
31781	3P : L 4-4-0 (1914)												
41301	2MT 2-6-2T (1946)	X	X	X	X	X	X	X	X	X	Ex B. Arms		
41318	2MT 2-6-2T (1946)	X	X	X	X	X	X	X	X	X	Ex T. Wells		
41319	2MT 2-6-2T (1946)	X	X	X	X	X	X	X	X	X	Ex T. Wells		
31004	2F : C 0-6-0 (1900)												
31245	2F : C 0-6-0 (1900)												
31252	2F : C 0-6-0 (1900)												
31271	2F : C 0-6-0 (1900)												
31298	2F : C 0-6-0 (1900)												
31592	2F : C 0-6-0 (1900)												
31310	1P : H 0-4-4T (1904)		To Ashford	X	X	X	X	X	X	X	X	X	X
31324	1P : H 0-4-4T (1904)												
31326	1P : H 0-4-4T (1904)												
31500	1P : H 0-4-4T (1904)	X	Ex Ashford										

LOCOMOTIVE ALLOCATIONS & TRANSFERS : RAMSGATE(74B)

Loco	Class	Aug-56	Sep-56	Oct-56	Nov-56	Dec-56	Jan-57	Feb-57	Mar-57	Apr-57	May-57	Jun-57	Jul-57
34075	7P : WC 4-6-2 (1945)												
34076	7P : WC 4-6-2 (1945)												
34077	7P : WC 4-6-2 (1945)												
34078	7P : WC 4-6-2 (1945)												
34079	7P : WC 4-6-2 (1945)												
34080	7P : WC 4-6-2 (1945)												
34081	7P : WC 4-6-2 (1945)												
34082	7P : WC 4-6-2 (1945)												
34083	7P : WC 4-6-2 (1945)												
34084	7P : WC 4-6-2 (1945)												
34085	7P : WC 4-6-2 (1945)												
34086	7P : WC 4-6-2 (1945)												
34096	7P : WC 4-6-2 (1945)												
34097	7P : WC 4-6-2 (1945)												
34098	7P : WC 4-6-2 (1945)												
34099	7P : WC 4-6-2 (1945)												
34100	7P : WC 4-6-2 (1945)												
30910	5P : V 4-4-0 (1930)	X	X	X	X	X	X	X	X	X	X	Ex St L	
30911	5P : V 4-4-0 (1930)												
30912	5P : V 4-4-0 (1930)												
30913	5P : V 4-4-0 (1930)												
30914	5P : V 4-4-0 (1930)												
30915	5P : V 4-4-0 (1930)	X	X	X	Ex S. Lane				To S. Lane	X	X	X	X
30916	5P : V 4-4-0 (1930)												
30917	5P : V 4-4-0 (1930)												
30918	5P : V 4-4-0 (1930)												
30919	5P : V 4-4-0 (1930)	X	X	X	X	X	X	X	X	X	X	Ex Dover	
30920	5P : V 4-4-0 (1930)	X	X	X	X	X	X	X	X	X	X	Ex St L	
30921	5P : V 4-4-0 (1930)	X	X	X	X	X	X	X	X	X	X	Ex Dover	
30922	5P : V 4-4-0 (1930)												
42074	4MT 2-6-4T (1948)	X	X	X	Ex T. Wells							To S. Lane	X
31764	3P : L 4-4-0 (1914)												
31779	3P : L 4-4-0 (1914)												
31780	3P : L 4-4-0 (1914)												
31781	3P : L 4-4-0 (1914)												
84025	2MT 2-6-2T (1953)	X	X	X	X	X	X	X	X	X	X	NEW	
84026	2MT 2-6-2T (1953)	X	X	X	X	X	X	X	X	X	X	NEW	
84027	2MT 2-6-2T (1953)	X	X	X	X	X	X	X	X	X	X	NEW	
84028	2MT 2-6-2T (1953)	X	X	X	X	X	X	X	X	X	X	NEW	
84029	2MT 2-6-2T (1953)	X	X	X	X	X	X	X	X	X	X	NEW	
41301	2MT 2-6-2T (1946)											To B. Arms	X
41318	2MT 2-6-2T (1946)											To Ex Jcn	X
41319	2MT 2-6-2T (1946)											To T Bges	X
31004	2F : C 0-6-0 (1900)												
31245	2F : C 0-6-0 (1900)												
31252	2F : C 0-6-0 (1900)												
31271	2F : C 0-6-0 (1900)												
31298	2F : C 0-6-0 (1900)											To Fav	X
31592	2F : C 0-6-0 (1900)												
31324	1P : H 0-4-4T (1904)												
31326	1P : H 0-4-4T (1904)												
31500	1P : H 0-4-4T (1904)												

Loco	Class	Aug-57	Sep-57	Oct-57	Nov-57	Dec-57	Jan-58	Feb-58	Mar-58	Apr-58	May-58	Jun-58	Jul-58
34016	7P : WC/R (1957)	X	X	X	X	X	X	X	X	X	NEW		
34017	7P : WC/R (1957)	X	X	X	X	X	X	X	Ex B. Arms				
34021	7P : WC/R (1957)	X	X	X	X	X	NEW						
34022	7P : WC/R (1957)	X	X	X	X	X	NEW						
34025	7P : WC/R (1957)	X	X	X	X	X	X	X	Ex B. Arms				
34026	7P : WC/R (1957)	X	X	X	X	X	X	X	NEW				
34027	7P : WC/R (1957)	X	X	X	X	X	X	X	Ex B. Arms				
34037	7P : WC/R (1957)	X	X	X	X	X	X	X	X	NEW			
34016	7P : WC 4-6-2 (1945)	X	X	X	X	X	X	X	Ex Ex Jn		R/B	X	X
34037	7P : WC 4-6-2 (1945)	X	X	X				Ex Ex Jn	R/B	X	X	X	X
34075	7P : WC 4-6-2 (1945)			To Ex Jcn	X	X	X	X	X	X	X	X	X
34076	7P : WC 4-6-2 (1945)			To Ex Jcn	X	X	X	X	X	X	X	X	X
34077	7P : WC 4-6-2 (1945)						To S. Lane	X	X	X	X	X	X
34078	7P : WC 4-6-2 (1945)												
34079	7P : WC 4-6-2 (1945)							To Ex Jcn	X	X	X	X	X
34080	7P : WC 4-6-2 (1945)						To Ex Jcn	X	X	X	X	X	X
34081	7P : WC 4-6-2 (1945)			To Ex Jcn	X	X	X	X	X	X	X	X	X
34082	7P : WC 4-6-2 (1945)						To S. Lane	X	X	X	X	X	X
34083	7P : WC 4-6-2 (1945)								To Dover	X	X	X	X
34084	7P : WC 4-6-2 (1945)									To Dover	X	X	X
34085	7P : WC 4-6-2 (1945)								To Dover	X	X	X	X
34086	7P : WC 4-6-2 (1945)			To Ex Jcn	X	X	X	X	X	X	X	X	X
34096	7P : WC 4-6-2 (1945)						To Ex Jcn	X	X	X	X	X	X
34097	7P : WC 4-6-2 (1945)								To B'mouth	X	X	X	X
34098	7P : WC 4-6-2 (1945)								To B'mouth	X	X	X	X
34099	7P : WC 4-6-2 (1945)								To B'mouth	X	X	X	X
34100	7P : WC 4-6-2 (1945)								To S. Lane	X	X	X	X
30910	5P : V 4-4-0 (1930)												
30911	5P : V 4-4-0 (1930)												
30912	5P : V 4-4-0 (1930)												
30913	5P : V 4-4-0 (1930)												
30914	5P : V 4-4-0 (1930)												
30916	5P : V 4-4-0 (1930)												
30917	5P : V 4-4-0 (1930)												
30918	5P : V 4-4-0 (1930)												
30919	5P : V 4-4-0 (1930)												
30920	5P : V 4-4-0 (1930)												
30921	5P : V 4-4-0 (1930)												
30922	5P : V 4-4-0 (1930)												
31764	3P : L 4-4-0 (1914)												
31775	3P : L 4-4-0 (1914)	X	X	X	X	X	X	X	X	X	Ex St L.		
31779	3P : L 4-4-0 (1914)												
31780	3P : L 4-4-0 (1914)												
31781	3P : L 4-4-0 (1914)												
84025	2MT 2-6-2T (1953)												
84026	2MT 2-6-2T (1953)												
84027	2MT 2-6-2T (1953)												
84028	2MT 2-6-2T (1953)												
84029	2MT 2-6-2T (1953)												
31004	2F : C 0-6-0 (1900)												
31245	2F : C 0-6-0 (1900)												
31252	2F : C 0-6-0 (1900)												
31271	2F : C 0-6-0 (1900)												
31592	2F : C 0-6-0 (1900)												
31324	1P : H 0-4-4T (1904)												
31326	1P : H 0-4-4T (1904)												
31500	1P : H 0-4-4T (1904)												

LOCOMOTIVE ALLOCATIONS & TRANSFERS : RAMSGATE(74B)

Loco	Class	Aug-58	Sep-58	Oct-58	Nov-58	Dec-58	Jan-59	Feb-59	Mar-59	Apr-59	May-59	Jun-59	Jul-59
34016	7P : WC/R (1957)											To B. Arms	X
34017	7P : WC/R (1957)											To B. Arms	X
34021	7P : WC/R (1957)											To B. Arms	X
34022	7P : WC/R (1957)											To B. Arms	X
34025	7P : WC/R (1957)											To B. Arms	X
34026	7P : WC/R (1957)											To B. Arms	X
34027	7P : WC/R (1957)											To B. Arms	X
34037	7P : WC/R (1957)											To B. Arms	X
34078	7P : WC 4-6-2 (1945)											To B. Arms	X
30910	5P : V 4-4-0 (1930)											To N. Elms	X
30911	5P : V 4-4-0 (1930)											To N. Elms	X
30912	5P : V 4-4-0 (1930)											To N. Elms	X
30913	5P : V 4-4-0 (1930)											To N. Elms	X
30914	5P : V 4-4-0 (1930)											To Brighton	X
30916	5P : V 4-4-0 (1930)											To N. Elms	X
30917	5P : V 4-4-0 (1930)											To N. Elms	X
30918	5P : V 4-4-0 (1930)											To N. Elms	X
30919	5P : V 4-4-0 (1930)											To N. Elms	X
30920	5P : V 4-4-0 (1930)											To S. Lane	X
30921	5P : V 4-4-0 (1930)											To S. Lane	X
30922	5P : V 4-4-0 (1930)											To S. Lane	X
31764	3P : L 4-4-0 (1914)											To N. Elms	X
31775	3P : L 4-4-0 (1914)											To N. Elms	X
31779	3P : L 4-4-0 (1914)											To N. Elms	X
31780	3P : L 4-4-0 (1914)											To N. Elms	X
31781	3P : L 4-4-0 (1914)											W/D	X
84025	2MT 2-6-2T (1953)											To Ashford	X
84026	2MT 2-6-2T (1953)											To Ashford	X
84027	2MT 2-6-2T (1953)											To Ashford	X
84028	2MT 2-6-2T (1953)											To Ashford	X
84029	2MT 2-6-2T (1953)											To Ashford	X
31004	2F : C 0-6-0 (1900)											To N. Elms	X
31245	2F : C 0-6-0 (1900)											To N. Elms	X
31252	2F : C 0-6-0 (1900)											To N. Elms	X
31271	2F : C 0-6-0 (1900)											To N. Elms	X
31592	2F : C 0-6-0 (1900)											To N. Elms	X
31324	1P : H 0-4-4T (1904)											To N. Elms	X
31326	1P : H 0-4-4T (1904)											To N. Elms	X
31500	1P : H 0-4-4T (1904)											To N. Elms	X

remainder worked to Charing Cross via Deal and Dover and included one two-day cycle which permitted overnight maintenance to be carried out at Bricklayers Arms. In addition and for the first time, Bricklayers Arms shed was given an allocation of seven light Pacifics - all rebuilds - which were used to work down to Ramsgate in the evenings, returning the following morning with an up business express. The fact that Bricklayers Arms, one of the most cramped and overworked depots in the London area, had to be called upon to assist testified to the gravity of the situation and it was fortuitous that the introduction of diesels on the Hastings route provided capacity just when it was most needed.

Post- 1960

Whether the scheme would have eventually restored the Southern's former reputation for timekeeping will never be known and the last year of steam operation was further bedevilled by electrification works until in June 1959 all LCDR services were handed over to electric multiple units with Ramsgate's stud of thirty-nine engines being transferred away; steam workings over the SER being worked by engines from Dover, Ashford and Bricklayers Arms.

For a year or two a little steam activity was provided by services from the Minster direction - although there was a tendency to use double-headed Type 2 diesels - but once the entire Kent electrification had been completed in 1962 almost every aspect of operational and motive power interest evaporated with daily locomotive visits contracting to six E5xxx locomotives and one type 3 diesel most of which were in connection with the parcels and newspaper trains that arrived in the early morning. Within a dozen years most of these movements had withered away as traffic evaporated from the railway and by the late 1970's the only regular appearance by a locomotive of any type was on the 03.00 newspapers ex Victoria and its return working in the evening. It made a sorry comparison with what had once been one of the most interesting sections of British Railways.

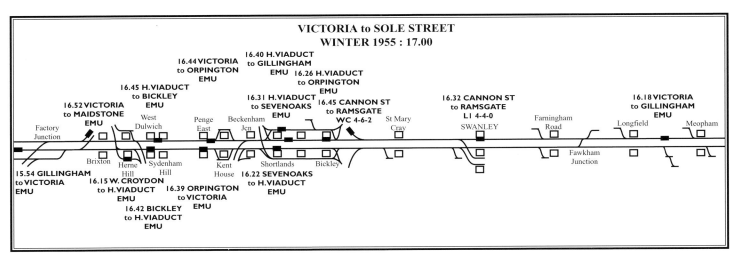

VICTORIA to SOLE STREET
WINTER 1955 : 17.00

16.44 VICTORIA to ORPINGTON EMU
16.40 H. VIADUCT to GILLINGHAM EMU
16.26 H. VIADUCT to ORPINGTON EMU
16.45 H. VIADUCT to BICKLEY EMU
16.31 H. VIADUCT to SEVENOAKS EMU
16.45 CANNON ST to RAMSGATE WC 4-6-2
16.32 CANNON ST to RAMSGATE L1 4-4-0
16.52 VICTORIA to MAIDSTONE EMU
16.18 VICTORIA to GILLINGHAM EMU

Factory Junction • West Dulwich • Penge East • Beckenham Jcn • St Mary Cray • SWANLEY • Farningham Road • Longfield • Meopham

Brixton • Herne Hill • Sydenham Hill • Kent House • Shortlands • Bickley • Fawkham Junction

15.54 GILLINGHAM to VICTORIA EMU
16.15 W. CROYDON to H. VIADUCT EMU
16.42 BICKLEY to H. VIADUCT EMU
16.39 ORPINGTON to VICTORIA EMU
16.22 SEVENOAKS to H. VIADUCT EMU

CONTROLLER'S LOG: To most intents and purposes Victoria is temporarily an all-electric station and it is interesting to see how the suburban district is nicely divided into two parts. The inner suburban area between Victoria and Bickley Junction with its high proportion of services operating to and from Orpington forms one part whilst the section beyond St Mary Cray Junction where the steam-worked business expresses from Cannon Street join, makes another. There is some overlapping by the longer-distance electrics but most leave the main line at Swanley for Sevenoaks and Maidstone whilst stopping trains from London to Gillingham are relatively infrequent.

The first of the Cannon Street trains can be seen getting into their stride: one taking a run at the bank through Swanley whilst the other eases its train over the connection between the two main lines. Unlike the morning service into Cannon Street where light Pacifics have a near-monopoly of the trade, the evening trains contain one or two surprises not the least of which is the sight of an L1 4-4-0 leading the pack with the 16.32. The novelty of the sight is leavened somewhat by the realisation that although the inside-cylinder 4-4-0's have for some years been generally confined to stopping trains east of the Medway, the L1's were the latest (1926) variants of the type and are considerably more powerful than the earlier D and E 4-4-0's. For all that, the 16.32 remains something of a swan-song. The following Cannon Street train is Pacific-hauled and it is a point of interest to see how the margin between the two alters between Swanley and Rochester.

Inter-regional trains are not writ large in the list of trains serving Kent and the sole instance - the through train from Birkenhead - is waiting to shunt its four coach dining set at Margate. A second section (two-coaches worked by an L 4-4-0) of the train, detached at Ashford to run via Dover and Deal will terminate at Ramsgate at 17.10. Earlier in the journey the train also included a three-coach portion for Hastings which ran from Redhill via Brighton and Eastbourne - a trip of many reversals!

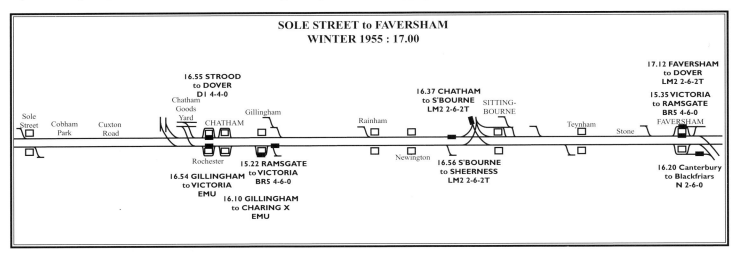

SOLE STREET to FAVERSHAM
WINTER 1955 : 17.00

16.55 STROOD to DOVER D1 4-4-0
16.37 CHATHAM to S'BOURNE LM2 2-6-2T
17.12 FAVERSHAM to DOVER LM2 2-6-2T
15.35 VICTORIA to RAMSGATE BR5 4-6-0

Sole Street • Cobham Park • Cuxton Road • Chatham Goods Yard • CHATHAM • Gillingham • Rainham • SITTINGBOURNE • Teynham • Stone • FAVERSHAM

Rochester • Newington

16.54 GILLINGHAM to VICTORIA EMU
15.22 RAMSGATE to VICTORIA BR5 4-6-0
16.10 GILLINGHAM to CHARING X EMU
16.56 S'BOURNE to SHEERNESS LM2 2-6-2T
16.20 Canterbury to Blackfriars N 2-6-0

Glancing back at the inner suburban, one can see a piece of timetabling ingenuity which prevents the 16.52 Victoria - Maidstone express from being delayed between Herne Hill and Shortlands by a pair of all-stations electrics. Finding a gap in departures from Holborn Viaduct, the Maidstone train is diverted at Brixton to the Catford route in order to overtake both of the slow trains. The gaps which allow this move are, alas, rather rare.

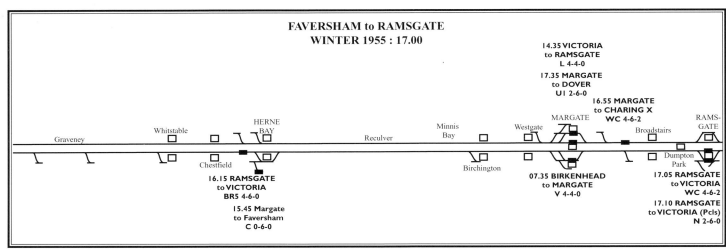

FAVERSHAM to RAMSGATE
WINTER 1955 : 17.00

14.35 VICTORIA to RAMSGATE L 4-4-0
17.35 MARGATE to DOVER U1 2-6-0
16.55 MARGATE to CHARING X WC 4-6-2

Graveney • Whitstable • HERNE BAY • Reculver • Minnis Bay • Westgate • MARGATE • Broadstairs • RAMSGATE

Chestfield • Birchington • Dumpton Park

16.15 RAMSGATE to VICTORIA BR5 4-6-0
15.45 Margate to Faversham C 0-6-0
07.35 BIRKENHEAD to MARGATE V 4-4-0
17.05 RAMSGATE to VICTORIA WC 4-6-2
17.10 RAMSGATE to VICTORIA (Pcls) N 2-6-0

124

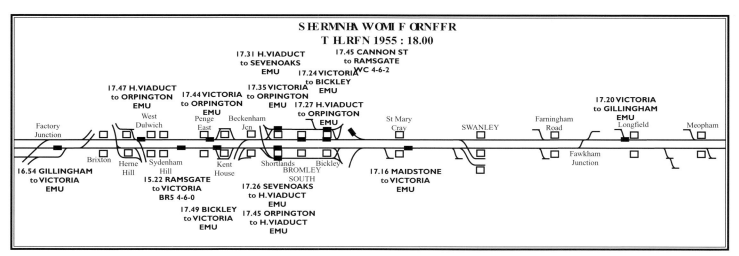

CONTROLLER'S LOG: There is now quite a rash of business expresses steaming across North Kent, most - but not all - worked by light Pacifics. The 16.32 and its L1 4-4-0 has been overtaken by the 16.45 from Cannon Street and will pause shortly for thirteen minutes at Faversham in order to make way for the 17.15. Running behind the latter is the only

direction since the up Thanet Belle is passing Stone Crossing on its non-stop run between Whitstable and Victoria. This is the fastest up train of the day, as indeed it might be during the winter when the load consists of no more than a pair of Pullman cars and four BR standard coaches. During the summer the load is increased to eight Pullmans when the case

a LM 2-6-2T share the 17.21 ex Cannon Street between them will be a fairly dramatic location in about ten minute's time.

The inner suburban service is now at its peak and no great powers of prescience are needed to gauge where the majority of season-ticket holders live since of the six services on the down road between Victoria and Bickley Junction, no less

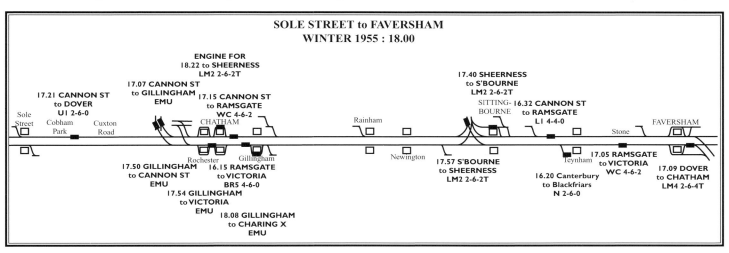

booked instance - the 17.21 ex Cannon Street - of a 2-6-0 working a London express although the appearance of the booked U1 cannot be guaranteed since it is booked to run up light from Gillingham and if an unbalanced engine happens to be available in London, the latter is likely to be put into the working instead. The 17.21 will divide at Chatham where an LMS 2-6-2 tank is standing by to take the rear portion forward to Sheerness.

Not all the express working is in the down

for Pacific haulage is strengthened somewhat. Special attention has to be given to the path the Pullman receives through the Medway towns since in addition to the usual gaggle of North Kent electrics, the 16.15 Ramsgate to Victoria - the slowest service of the day - is booked to stand for seventeen minutes in the loop platform to allow the Pullman to overtake. Needless to say, Chatham and the tight chasm in which the station sits can, with the Pullman overtaking the 16.15 Ramsgate on one side whilst the U1 and

than four terminate at Orpington whilst a fifth stops short - the platform capacity at Orpington is finite! - at Bickley. The odd-man out is a Holborn Viaduct to Sevenoaks all-stations train which has run via Catford to Shortlands and is running down the local line to overtake the 17.35 ex Victoria before reaching Bickley Junction. The operating discipline called for by the LCDR - as it is still known - can be assessed from the fact this perfectly routine crossing of paths is allowed no more than sixty seconds.

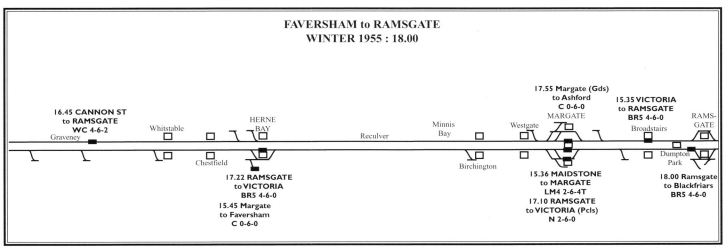

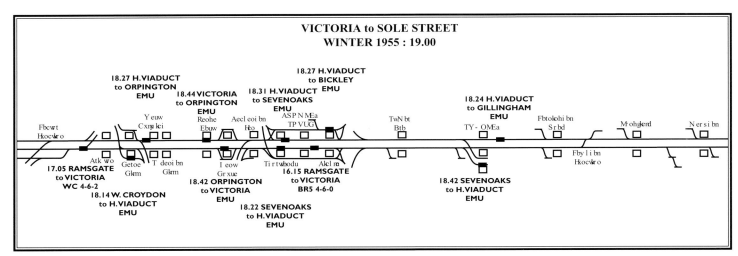

VICTORIA to SOLE STREET
WINTER 1955 : 19.00

18.27 H.VIADUCT to ORPINGTON EMU
18.44 VICTORIA to ORPINGTON EMU
18.31 H.VIADUCT to SEVENOAKS EMU
18.27 H.VIADUCT to BICKLEY EMU
18.24 H.VIADUCT to GILLINGHAM EMU

17.05 RAMSGATE to VICTORIA WC 4-6-2
18.14 W. CROYDON to H.VIADUCT EMU
18.42 ORPINGTON to VICTORIA EMU
18.22 SEVENOAKS to H.VIADUCT EMU
16.15 RAMSGATE to VICTORIA BR5 4-6-0
18.42 SEVENOAKS to H.VIADUCT EMU

CONTROLLER'S LOG: Although Victoria is still heavily thronged with outgoing passengers, the worst of the rush has passed and the train service is gradually reverting back to its basic hourly pattern of three Orpington trains plus a combined Maidstone/Gillingham departure. Similarly Holborn Viaduct is winding itself down to three Sevenoaks via Catford trains per hour and a half-hourly service to West Croydon via Herne Hill. At Victoria suburban service at its most critical time, the nine coaches of the 19.35 have been serviced in the station where they arrived at 18.12 in the 15.22 from Ramsgate. As though in reflection of its status, the empty stock of the Thanet Belle is not hauled to Stewarts Lane sidings by anything so ordinary as the usual H 0-4-4T or E2 0-6-0T but has nothing less than the N 2-6-0 which has been shunting at Eardley carriage sidings for much of the day and will later work the 01.35 which serves all stations to Rainham before running fast to Blackfriars calling only at Hoo Junction en route. This is followed by the 19.17 from Teynham which clears any goods left by the 16.20 ex Canterbury together with any traffic of a more general nature. The operational interest of this train lies in the engine-change that takes place at Sittingbourne where the LMS tank is replaced by a C 0-6-0.

Another 0-6-0 is arriving in Faversham

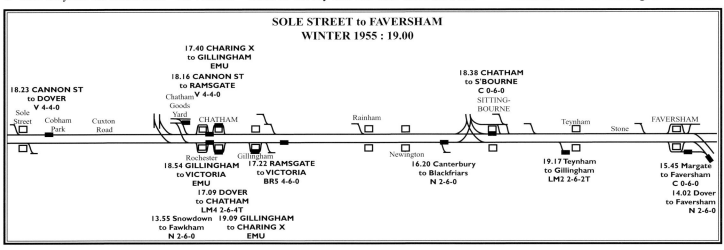

SOLE STREET to FAVERSHAM
WINTER 1955 : 19.00

17.40 CHARING X to GILLINGHAM EMU
18.16 CANNON ST to RAMSGATE Chatham V 4-4-0
18.23 CANNON ST to DOVER V 4-4-0
18.38 CHATHAM to S'BOURNE C 0-6-0

Sole Street — Cobham Park — Cuxton Road — CHATHAM — Rainham — SITTINGBOURNE — Teynham — Stone — FAVERSHAM

18.54 GILLINGHAM to VICTORIA EMU
17.22 RAMSGATE to VICTORIA BR5 4-6-0
17.09 DOVER to CHATHAM LM4 2-6-4T
13.55 Snowdown to Fawkham N 2-6-0
19.09 GILLINGHAM to CHARING X EMU
16.20 Canterbury to Blackfriars N 2-6-0
19.17 Teynham to Gillingham LM2 2-6-2T
15.45 Margate to Faversham C 0-6-0
14.02 Dover to Faversham N 2-6-0

it takes time for one to realise that matters are quietening down since steam services are in the increase: The Thanet Belle has passed Brixton and will arrive in a few minutes time whilst the 16.15 from Ramsgate is approaching Bromley South. In addition a West Country Pacific is due to back down from Stewarts Lane to work the 19.35 express to Ramsgate. In order not to interfere with the smooth running of the Herne Hill to Faversham goods. Moguls are by no means unknown at Victoria but, during the day especially, they are uncommon enough to warrant attention.

With the easing of the peak, goods services have started to reappear, most of the trains at this time of night being arranged for the heavy fruit traffic that originates east of the Medway.

The first of these is the 16.20 ex Canterbury yard with fruit and goods from the Margate line which will be picked up by the 18.00 Ramsgate - Blackfriars which is now approaching Margate.

The last of the Cannon Street expresses are at Chatham and Cobham Park respectively, both worked by Schools 4-4-0's which may not have the brute force of a Pacific but are certainly more dependable. The description of them being a 4-6-0 in 4-4-0 clothing is not wide of the mark.

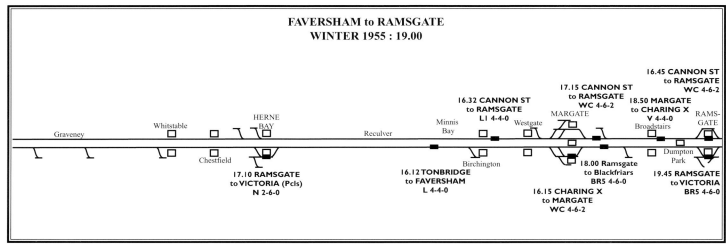

FAVERSHAM to RAMSGATE
WINTER 1955 : 19.00

16.45 CANNON ST to RAMSGATE WC 4-6-2
17.15 CANNON ST to RAMSGATE WC 4-6-2
16.32 CANNON ST to RAMSGATE L1 4-4-0
18.50 MARGATE to CHARING X V 4-4-0

Graveney — Whitstable — HERNE BAY — Reculver — Minnis Bay — Westgate — MARGATE — Broadstairs — RAMSGATE

Chestfield
17.10 RAMSGATE to VICTORIA (Pcls) N 2-6-0
Birchington
16.12 TONBRIDGE to FAVERSHAM L 4-4-0
18.00 Ramsgate to Blackfriars BR5 4-6-0
16.15 CHARING X to MARGATE WC 4-6-2
Dumpton Park
19.45 RAMSGATE to VICTORIA BR5 4-6-0

DOVER PRIORY

DOVER PRIORY

STATION WORKING (1954/5)

Train	Arrive	Engine	Shed	Dep	Destination
03.00 Light ex Dover Marine	03.05	BR4 4-6-0	Dover 429		(To Work 03.30 Vans)
23.50 London Bge via Redhill	03.08	N15 4-6-0	Ash 340	03.28	Deal
		BR4 4-6-0	Dover 429	03.30	Dover Marine (Pcls)
01.10 Ashford (Goods)				04/05	Betteshanger
Light ex Dover loco	04.15	LM4 2-6-4T	Ash 354		(To work 04.42 Faversham)
Light ex Deal	04.40	N15 4-6-0	Ash 340		(To work 04.55 Ashford)
		LM4 2-6-4T	Ash 354	04.42	Faversham
		N15 4-6-0	Ash 340	04.55	Ashford
Light ex Dover loco		O1 0-6-0	Dover 459	05/05	Light to Shepherdswell
22.00 Hither Green via Chatham		N 2-6-0	HG 176	05/15	Dover Town
04.50 Folkestone (Staff)	05.14	LM4 2-6-4T	Dover 448	05.32	Canterbury E
Light ex Dover loco	05.50	D1 4-4-0	Dover 444		(To work 06.10 Gillingham)
Light ex Dover loco		LM4 2-6-4T	Dover 449	05/58	Light to Deal
05.05 Faversham	06.00	U1 2-6-0	Fav 260		(Turn and work 07.42 Faversham)
		D1 4-4-0	Dover 444	06.10	Gillingham
05.31 Ramsgate	06.17	WC 4-6-2	Ram 456	06.20	Charing Cross
06.15 Dover Town		O1 0-6-0	Dover 461	06/25	Shepherdswell
Light ex Dover loco	06.29	L1 4-4-0	Dover 438		(To work 06.55 Maidstone)
03.40 London Bridge	06.36	BR4 2-6-0	Red 628	06.45	Ramsgate
		L1 4-4-0	Dover 438	06.55	Maidstone
06.20 Canterbury East	06.58	LM4 2-6-4T	Dover 448	07.05	Folkestone Jcn
07.00 Dover Marine ECS	07.05	LM4 2-6-4T	Dover 450	07.08	Margate
06.14 Faversham	07.20	N 2-6-0	BLA 121		(Turn and work 08.17 Faversham)
23.15 Hither Green (Goods)	07.20	N 2-6-0	HG 171		
06.44 Ramsgate	07.36	WC 4-6-2	Ram 468	07.39	Cannon Street
		U1 2-6-0	Fav 260	07.42	Chatham
07.35 Dover (Bulwark St)	07.45	N 2-6-0	HG 172		
07.30 Shorncliffe	07.52	L 4-4-0	Ash 347	07.54	Minster
		N 2-6-0	BLA 121	08.17	Faversham
07.28 Minster	08.21	LM4 2-6-4T	Dover 449	08.24	Maidstone
		N 2-6-0	HG 172	08.30	Dover Marine (Pcls)
Light ex Dover loco	08.30	WC 4-6-2	Dover 433		(To work 08.59 Charing X)
07.36 Margate	08.40	WC 4-6-2	Ram 469	08.42	Charing Cross
07.51 Ashford	08.40	LM2 2-6-2T	Ash 360	08.46	Faversham
07.37 Faversham	08.47	LM4 2-6-4T	Ash 354		
		LM4 2-6-4T	Ash 354	08.50	Light to Dover Loco)
		WC 4-6-2	Dover 433	08.59	Charing Cross
05.50 Cannon St via Chatham	09.11	E1 4-4-0	S. Lane 46		
09.10 Dover Marine (ECS)	09.14	WC 4-6-2	Dover 431		(Works 09.20)
		E1 4-4-0	S. Lane 46	09.16	Light to Dover Marine
		WC 4-6-2	Dover 431	09.20	Victoria
06.22 Cannon Street	09.26	N15 4-6-0	Dover 432		
		N15 4-6-0	Dover 432	09.30	Light to Dover Loco
07.12 Cannon Street	09.39	E1 4-4-0	BLA 90	09.45	Margate
08.56 Ramsgate	09.44	V 4-4-0	Ram 485	09.47	Birkenhead
10.00 Dover Town		N 2-6-0	HG 176	10/05	Hoo Junction
09.18 Faversham	10.15	D1 4-4-0	Fav 262		(Stock forms 11.06 CX)
		D1 4-4-0	Fav 262	10.20	Dover Marine Pcls
06.05 Reading South	10.21	L 4-4-0	Ton 290	10.30	Margate
Light ex Dover Marine	10.40	D1 4-4-0	Fav 262		(To work 11.19 Faversham)
09.40 Margate	10.46	WC 4-6-2	Ram 472	10.50	Charing Cross
Light ex Dover loco	10.55	WC 4-6-2	Dover 434		(To work 11.06 CX)
		WC 4-6-2	Dover 434	11.06	Charing Cross
08.35 Victoria	11.11	L 4-4-0	Ram 489		
		L 4-4-0	Ram 489	11.15	Light to Dover Marine
		D1 4-4-0	Fav 262	11.19	Faversham
09.15 Charing Cross	11.21	V 4-4-0	BLA 83	11.26	Ramsgate
Light ex Dover loco	11.29	LM4 2-6-4T	Ash 354		(To work 11.45 Ashford)
		LM4 2-6-4T	Ash 354	11.45	Ashford
06.40 Faversham (Goods)		N 2-6-0	Dover 452	11/55	Dover Town
10.34 Maidstone	12.02	LM4 2-6-4T	Dover 449		
		LM4 2-6-4T	Dover 449	12.12	Light to Dover Marine
Light ex Dover loco	12.14	E1 4-4-0	S. Lane 46		(To work 12.37 Gillingham)
Light ex Dover Marine	12.15	L 4-4-0	Ram 489		(To work 13.05 Faversham)
11.30 Ramsgate	12.19	L 4-4-0	Ash 347	12.23	Charing Cross
12.20 Dover Town (Goods)		BR4 4-6-0	Dover 422	12/25	Sandwich
		E1 4-4-0	S. Lane 46	12.37	Gillingham
12.30 Shorncliffe	12.56	LM4 2-6-4T	Dover 448	12.59	Minster
		L 4-4-0	Ram 489	13.05	Faversham
12.06 Faversham	13.07	LM2 2-6-2T	Ash 360		(Works station pilot until 15.28)
12.35 Minster	13.15	LM4 2-6-4T	Dover 450		
		LM4 2-6-4T	Dover 450	13.17	Light to Dover loco
11.15 Charing Cross	13.22	WC 4-6-2	Ram 470	13.25	Margate
12.36 Margate	13.40	V 4-4-0	BLA 81	13.44	Charing Cross

Train	Arrive	Engine	Shed	Dep	Destination
05.23 Herne Hill via Chatham		N 2-6-0	S. Lane 62	13/55	Dover Town
14.02 Dover Town		N 2-6-0	Dover 451	14/10	Faversham (Goods)
13.13 Faversham	14.10	L 4-4-0	Ram 490		
		L 4-4-0	Ram 490	14.14	Light to Dover loco
Light ex Dover loco	14.30	LM4 2-6-4T	Dover 450		
		LM4 2-6-4T	Dover 450	14.40	Canterbury E
13.50 Margate	14.55	BR4 2-6-0	Red 628	14.58	Maidstone
14.42 Shepherdswell		O1 0-6-0	Dover 461	15/02	Dover Town
14.20 Faversham	15.19	D1 4-4-0	Fav 262		(Forms 15.34 ECS)
(Ex Station Pilot)		LM2 2-6-2T	Ash 360	15.28	Faversham
13.51 Maidstone	15.31	E1 4-4-0	BLA 90		(Turn and work 17.00 Ashford)
		D1 4-4-0	Fav 262	15.34	Folkestone Jcn ECS
14.45 Sandwich (Goods)		BR4 4-6-0	Dover 422	15/40	Dover Town
Light ex Dover loco	15.40	L 4-4-0	Ram 490		(Works 16.18 Faversham)
14.45 Margate	15.52	V 4-4-0	BLA 83	15.57	Cannon Street
08.40 Hoo Junction		N & O1	Fav 277/Dvr 459	16/08	Dover Town
		L 4-4-0	Ram 490	16.18	Faversham
15.43 Canterbury East	16.20	LM4 2-6-4T	Dover 450	16.22	Dover Marine ECS
07.35 Birkenhead	16.22	L 4-4-0	Ash 345	16.25	Ramsgate
15.25 Margate	16.27	WC 4-6-2	Ram 474	16.30	Charing Cross
16.17 Shorncliffe	16.39	LM4 2-6-4T	Dover 449	16.43	Minster
16.40 Dover Marine ECS	16.44	LM4 2-6-4T	Dover 450		(Works 17.09 Chatham)
		E1 4-4-0	BLA 90	17.00	Tonbridge
14.35 Victoria	17.06	WC 4-6-2	Dover 431		
		WC 4-6-2	Dover 431	17.08	Light to Dover Loco
		LM4 2-6-4T	Dover 450	17.09	Chatham
Light ex Dover loco	15.40	D1 4-4-0	Fav 262		(To work 17.40 Victoria)
15.15 Charing Cross	17.25	WC 4-6-2	Ram 472	17.30	Ramsgate
16.50 Minster	17.35	LM4 2-6-4T	Dover 448	17.38	Shorncliffe
		D1 4-4-0	Fav 262	17.40	Victoria
16.15 Charing Cross	17.49	WC 4-6-2	Dover 434	17.52	Margate
16.55 Margate	18.08	N15 4-6-0	Ash 340	18.14	Charing Cross
17.12 Faversham	18.17	LM2 2-6-2T	Ash 360		(Forms 18.36 Shorncliffe)
		N 2-6-0	Dover 452	18/20	Dover Town (Goods)
17.32 Ashford	18.18	LM4 2-6-4T	Ash 355	18.30	Faversham
		LM2 2-6-2T	Ash 360	18.36	Shorncliffe via Dover Marine
17.00 Cannon Street	18.46	WC 4-6-2	Ram 465	18.49	Ramsgate
17.35 Margate	18.53	U1 276	Fav 276		(Turn and work 19.48 Faversham)
18.50 Dover Town (Goods)		N 2-6-0	Dover 452	18/55	Hoo Junction
18.40 Shorncliffe	19.00	LM4 2-6-4T	Dover 448		
16.55 Strood	19.01	D1 4-4-0	Dover 444	19.05	Dover Marine ECS
		LM4 2-6-4T	Dover 448	19.08	Light to Dover Loco
Light ex Dover Marine	19.09	LM2 2-6-2T	Ash 360		(To work 19.16 Maidstone)
		LM2 2-6-2T	Ash 360	19.16	Maidstone
18.14 Ashford via Deal	19.42	N 2-6-0	Dover 453	19.45	Dover Marine ECS
17.40 Cannon Street	19.46	N15 4-6-0	HG 182		(Shunt carriage stock to 20.15)
		U1 2-6-0	Fav 276	19.48	Faversham
18.50 Margate	19.59	V 4-4-0	Ram 485	20.02	Charing Cross
17.21 Cannon St via Chatham	20.06	U1 2-6-0	Fav 260		
		U1 2-6-0	Fav 260	20.08	Light to Dover Loco
20.00 Dover Town		N 2-6-0	S. Lane 62	20/10	Hither Green via Chatham
		N15 4-6-0	HG 182	20.15	Light to Dover Loco
18.18 Cannon Street	20.18	V 4-4-0	Ram 477	20.22	Ramsgate
20.20 Dover Marine Pcls	20.24	LM4 2-6-4T	Dover 448		(Works 21.13 Faversham)
19.35 Ramsgate	20.33	E1 4-4-0	BLA 91	20.36	H. Viaduct via Maidstone
18.23 Cannon St via Chatham	20.53	V 4-4-0	BLA 81		
		V 4-4-0	BLA 81	21.00	Light to Dover Loco
19.15 Charing Cross	20.58	WC 4-6-2	Ram 468	21.01	Margate
		LM4 2-6-4T	Dover 448	21.13	Faversham
21.40 Dover Town		N 2-6-0	Fav 277	21/50	Faversham (Goods)
21.50 Dover Marine ECS	21.55	U1 2-6-0	Fav 260		(Forms 22.40 attachment)
21.01 Faversham	22.00	LM4 2-6-4T	Ash 355		(Steam heat 22.40 stock)
21.17 Ramsgate	22.17	LM4 2-6-4T	Dover 449	22.21	Folkestone Central
19.34 Charing Cross	22.23	V 4-4-0	Ram 485	22.26	Ramsgate
Light ex Dover loco	22.30	V 4-4-0	BLA 81		(To re-engine 21.28 ex Margate)
21.28 Margate	22.31	WC 4-6-2	Dover 434		(Change engines)
		WC 4-6-2	Dover 434	22.32	Light to Dover Loco
(21.28 Margate)		V 4-4-0	BLA 81	22.40	Cannon Street via Redhill
		LM4 2-6-4T	Ash 355	22.45	Light to Dover Loco
		U1 2-6-0	Fav 260	22.47	Faversham
21.15 Charing Cross	23.31	WC 4-6-2	Ram 474	23.34	Ramsgate
22.57 Faversham	23.55	LM4 2-6-4T	Dover 448	00.20	Folkestone Jcn ECS
22.50 Charing Cross	00.58	L1 4-4-0	Dover 438		
		L1 4-4-0	Dover 438	01.05	Light to Dover Loco

Served by the Charing Cross - Deal - Ramsgate route, Dover was primarily a South Eastern location and will be dealt with more fully in the forthcoming title which will deal with the SER. While the main London service was routed via Ashford, the LCDR route to Victoria provided a stopping service via Canterbury East which although slower must have broken records for motive power variety with pregrouping 4-4-0's alternating with LMS 2-6-2 and 2-6-4 tanks. On most services a change of train was required at Faversham although a handful of services ran beyond to the Medway towns. One train, the 09.20 from Priory, ran through to London and was the route's only express other than the odd seasons when the Night Ferry was diverted away from the Tonbridge route.

Passenger traffic however was not the primary interest between Dover and Faversham and much of the operating activity centred on the collieries at Tilmanstone and Snowdown. The former was especially interesting as the branch that connected the colliery with the main line at Shepherdswell was both steeply graded and heavily restricted, so much so that the only engines permitted to use it were the superannuated 01 0-6-0's and the A1X Terrier 0-6-0T's. Since the latter were hardly suited to the rigours of heavy mineral work, those who paid a visit to the area were treated to the sound and fury of an 01 battling heartily against the forces of gravity and old age, long after they had finished on the rest of the system. Two of the class were in daily use on the branch - one making five return trips, the other two - with three others being retained at Dover to cover for repairs and maintenance.

The gradients on the line were severe by Southern standards - 1/153 from Faversham to MP 57, a fall at 1/154 to Canterbury, a rise at 1/243 to Shepherdswell followed by a drop of 1/129 to Dover Priory - and because of this all main line goods services were booked to N 2-6-0 locomotives.

Fruit and the hops for which Kent was famous were also important traffics and were catered for by an afternoon express service which ran direct from Canterbury to Blackfriars and connected at Hoo Junction with direct services to Redhill and Eastleigh. This too was an N 2-6-0 working.

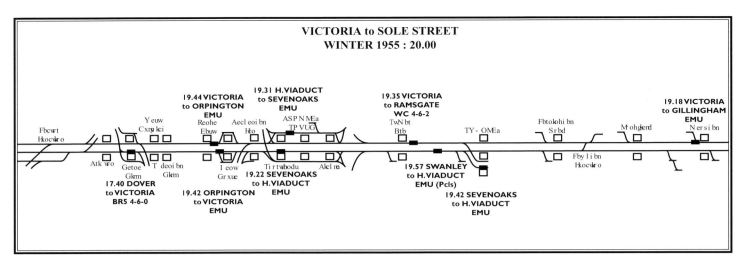

VICTORIA to SOLE STREET
WINTER 1955 : 20.00

19.44 VICTORIA to ORPINGTON EMU

19.31 H.VIADUCT to SEVENOAKS EMU

19.35 VICTORIA to RAMSGATE WC 4-6-2

19.18 VICTORIA to GILLINGHAM EMU

17.40 DOVER to VICTORIA BR5 4-6-0

19.42 ORPINGTON to VICTORIA EMU

19.22 SEVENOAKS to H.VIADUCT EMU

19.57 SWANLEY to H.VIADUCT EMU (Pcls)

19.42 SEVENOAKS to H.VIADUCT EMU

CONTROLLER'S LOG: The inner suburban area has returned to its off-peak pattern of service and steam is once again operating in the usual way from Victoria. The 19.35 to Ramsgate - one of the few expresses not to call at Bromley South - has just swept its nine-coach buffet set through St Mary Cray; its Ramsgate crew getting ready, no doubt, to take advantage the Ramsgate coaches that went down in the 05.10. The latter were attached to the Dover section at Faversham.

If any observers remain at Victoria so late in the evening, few will spare a tired and begrimed 4-6-0 more than a brief glance since all attention will be focused on the thirteen coaches - including six wagon-lit - of the Night one of the Southern's most arduous diagrams.

The Night Ferry is not the only double-headed train on the system at the moment as a C 0-6-0 and an LMS 2-6-2T have recently arrived in Chatham with the 19.30 ex Sittingbourne. Not, perhaps, in quite the same league as the Ferry, the Sittingbourne train is only double-headed for the sake of convenience - the 2-6-

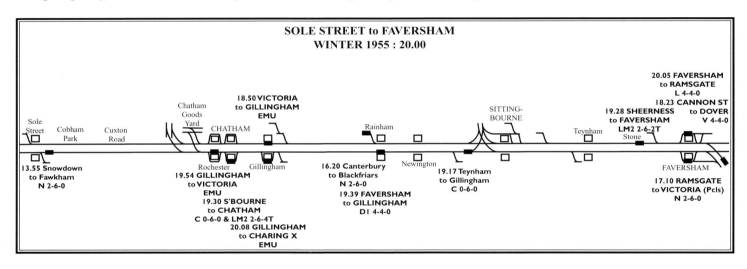

SOLE STREET to FAVERSHAM
WINTER 1955 : 20.00

20.05 FAVERSHAM to RAMSGATE L 4-4-0

18.50 VICTORIA to GILLINGHAM EMU

19.28 SHEERNESS to FAVERSHAM LM2 2-6-2T

18.23 CANNON ST to DOVER V 4-4-0

13.55 Snowdown to Fawkham N 2-6-0

19.54 GILLINGHAM to VICTORIA EMU

19.30 S'BOURNE to CHATHAM C 0-6-0 & LM2 2-6-4T

20.08 GILLINGHAM to CHARING X EMU

16.20 Canterbury to Blackfriars N 2-6-0

19.39 FAVERSHAM to GILLINGHAM D1 4-4-0

19.17 Teynham to Gillingham C 0-6-0

17.10 RAMSGATE to VICTORIA (Pcls) N 2-6-0

of the three mile fall at 1 in 139 after Swanley in order to get up Sole Street bank with too much bother. The light Pacific concerned has not had an especially busy day and has been sitting on Stewarts Lane loco since arriving in Victoria nine hours ago with the 08.25 from Ramsgate. In the other direction the ten-coach 17.40 ex Dover is passing Herne Hill; a mongrel of a train consisting of the engine off the 11.35 Pullman, the Dover portion of the 14.35 ex Victoria and

Ferry which is running into platform 1 behind an E1 4-4-0. Musing as to why the train-ferry idea has not been extended to the day trains is interrupted by the sight of the Night Ferry's motive power - a light Pacific double-headed with an L1 4-4-0. The pair worked into London with the up Ferry this morning but whilst the 4-4-0 has spent the day in London - most of it on Stewarts Lane loco - the Pacific worked the 12.30 boat train to Dover and the 17.15 return:

2T is quite equal to the six birdcage coaches - and not infrequently the 0-6-0, which arrives in Sittingbourne with the 18.38 from Chatham, runs light to Chatham Sidings to pick up its next working, the 20.55 goods to Hoo Junction. When this happens one must ensure that the Gillingham men who relieve the 0-6-0 at Chatham know where to find their engine. The 2-6-2T stays with the stock and works it back to Faversham at 20.38.

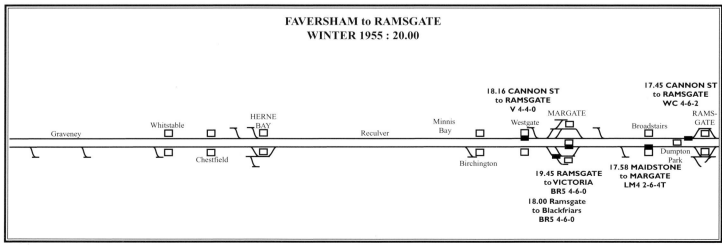

FAVERSHAM to RAMSGATE
WINTER 1955 : 20.00

18.16 CANNON ST to RAMSGATE V 4-4-0

17.45 CANNON ST to RAMSGATE WC 4-6-2

19.45 RAMSGATE to VICTORIA BR5 4-6-0

18.00 Ramsgate to Blackfriars BR5 4-6-0

17.58 MAIDSTONE to MARGATE LM4 2-6-4T

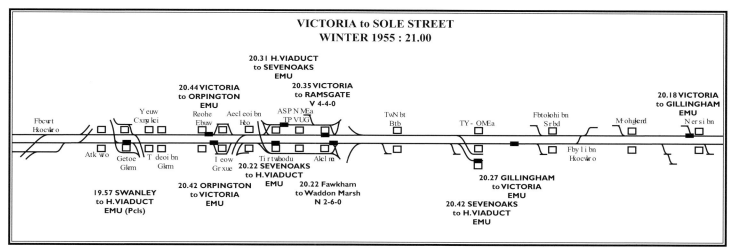

CONTROLLER'S LOG: For obvious reasons the inner-suburban area does not see much in the way of goods traffic and the train now approaching Bickley, the 20.22 Fawkham to Waddon Marsh, is the first of its type for about fifteen hours. In spite of its title the train is actually the 13.55 from Snowdown Colliery which sets down and collects Gravesend traffic at Fawkham before going forward as a through train to Waddon Marsh, a power station and a large industrial estate near Croydon. The route taken is unusual since the service leaves the LCDR at Beckenham Junction where it transfers to the LBSCR branch to run via Norwood Junction and West Croydon. The engine is a Stewarts Lane N 2-6-0 and left London in the early hours of the morning with the 01.35 Herne Hill to Faversham Goods. Upon reaching Waddon Marsh the engine will be serviced by Norwood Junction loco and will spend most of tomorrow as the carriage pilot at Eardley. Its next LCDR appearance will be the working of the Pullman empty stock from Victoria to Stewarts Lane tomorrow night.

The last Ramsgate - Victoria express of the day is running into Sittingbourne and any subsequent travel will have to be made in one of the several parcels services in which limited passenger accommodation is provided. Most of these services are rather tedious and decant their passengers in London at an awkward time although this does not - so far as the enthusiast is concerned - diminish their interest. The 19.35 Ramsgate to Holborn Viaduct, for example, is the only through train run via Maidstone East and does so after running to Ashford 'the long way round' via Deal and Dover. On top of this, the service is worked throughout by an E1 4-4-0. The 21.10 Ramsgate to Charing Cross is a less interesting alternative although it does provide the uncommon experience of running through Dartford and Woolwich behind a steam engine - an L1 4-4-0 in this case.

A third choice is the 21.28 Margate to Cannon Street which takes the SER route via Deal and Dover to Ashford but then goes on via Redhill and East Croydon. The Pacific which starts the train from Margate goes only as far as Dover where it is replaced by a Schools 4-4-0.

Not every parcels train conveys passengers and one feels some sympathy for those en route to the North Kent area who look wistfully at the 20.59 ex Gillingham and its E1 4-4-0 before boarding the 21.10 electric.

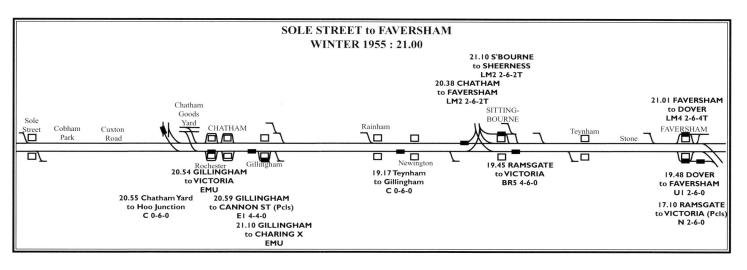

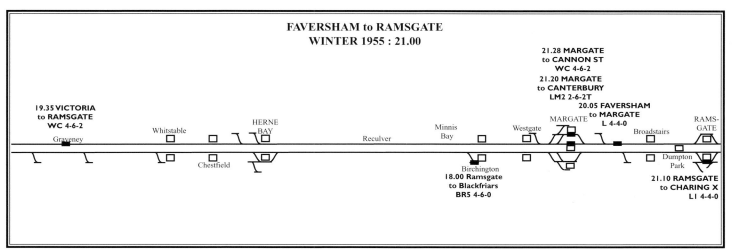

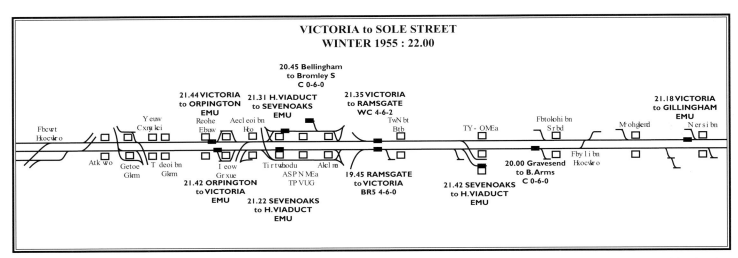

VICTORIA to SOLE STREET
WINTER 1955 : 22.00

20.45 Bellingham
to Bromley S
C 0-6-0

21.44 VICTORIA
to ORPINGTON
EMU

21.31 H.VIADUCT
to SEVENOAKS
EMU

21.35 VICTORIA
to RAMSGATE
WC 4-6-2

21.18 VICTORIA
to GILLINGHAM
EMU

Fbcwt
Hxocvkro

Y euw
Cxrgu kci

Reohe
Ebuw

Aecl eoi bn
Hxo

TwN bt
Btb

TY - OMEa

Fbtolohi bn
Sr bd

M'ohgkerd

N er si bn

Atk wo
Getoe
Gkm

T deoi bn
Gkm

I eow
Gr xue

Ti r twbodu
ASP N MEa
TP VUG

Akcl m

Fby l i bn
Hxocvkro

21.42 ORPINGTON
to VICTORIA
EMU

21.22 SEVENOAKS
to H.VIADUCT
EMU

19.45 RAMSGATE
to VICTORIA
BR5 4-6-0

21.42 SEVENOAKS
to H.VIADUCT
EMU

20.00 Gravesend
to B.Arms
C 0-6-0

CONTROLLER'S LOG: The last of the day's Ramsgate expresses mark the transition from evening to night as they pass each other near St Mary Cray. Both engines are travel-stained since both have achieved the unusual distinction of completing two return trip between London and Ramsgate in the same day. The

by express engines on other parts of BR.

Apart from the 18.00 Ramsgate to Blackfriars which is making up a full load at Faversham, the important fruit trains mentioned earlier have disappeared from view leaving the remaining goods traffic to a pair of C 0-6-0's. One has just passed Farningham Road with the

this is the one Ramsgate express of the day that does not have a Dover connection. The next leaves at 22.57 and runs in connection with the 21.35 ex Victoria which is only just leaving the London area.

The train standing in No.4 platform at Margate is ostensibly a stopping service from

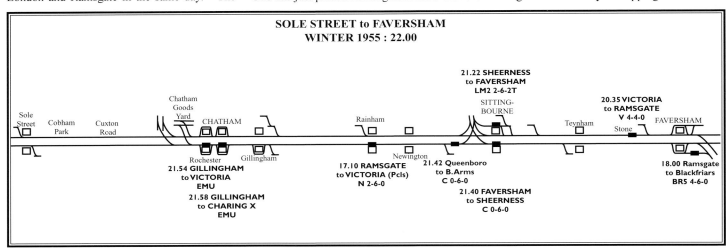

SOLE STREET to FAVERSHAM
WINTER 1955 : 22.00

21.22 SHEERNESS
to FAVERSHAM
LM2 2-6-2T

SITTING-
BOURNE

20.35 VICTORIA
to RAMSGATE
V 4-4-0

Sole
Street

Cobham
Park

Cuxton
Road

Chatham
Goods
Yard

CHATHAM

Rainham

Teynham

Stone

FAVERSHAM

Rochester

Gillingham

Newington

21.54 GILLINGHAM
to VICTORIA
EMU

17.10 RAMSGATE
to VICTORIA (Pcls)
N 2-6-0

21.42 Queenboro
to B.Arms
C 0-6-0

18.00 Ramsgate
to Blackfriars
BR5 4-6-0

21.58 GILLINGHAM
to CHARING X
EMU

21.40 FAVERSHAM
to SHEERNESS
C 0-6-0

Pacific of the down train has been on the move for something like fifteen hours during which time it has worked the 11.15 Charing Cross to Ramsgate via Dover and Deal as well as the 21.35 from Victoria whilst the 4-6-0 was the engine that worked both the 03.30 Newspapers and the 15.35 'Granville'. Long hours rather than high mileages is the totem of most South Eastern engines and the relatively long distances - about 300 miles - covered by these engines are just about the nearest the division comes to matching the daily mileages routinely covered

evening Gravesend - Bricklayers Arms goods whilst a Hither Green-based member of the same class prepares the 23.45 to Herne Hill in the Gas Siding at Bromley South. Another C joins the main line near Sittingbourne with the night goods from Queenborough to Bricklayers Arms although in this case the 0-6-0 will hand over to an N 2-6-0 in Chatham Goods.

On the passenger side a Schools 4-4-0 shuts off for the Faversham stop of the 20.35 Victoria - Ramsgate and one hopes there are no Canterbury or Dover passengers aboard since

Tonbridge via Ashford and Canterbury although in fact it is a through service from London, being formed at Tonbridge from the rear four coaches of the 18.18 Cannon Street to Ramsgate via Dover. Not only is it one of the few trains to run through from London to Canterbury West but it offers the enthusiast an opportunity to cover much of the London - Thanet distance behind an inside cylinder 4-4-0. (It might be added that haulage between London and Tonbridge is also four-coupled albeit by one of the more modern Schools engines).

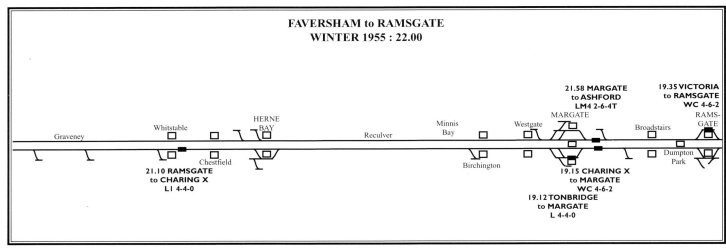

FAVERSHAM to RAMSGATE
WINTER 1955 : 22.00

21.58 MARGATE
to ASHFORD
LM4 2-6-4T

19.35 VICTORIA
to RAMSGATE
WC 4-6-2

MARGATE

Graveney

Whitstable

HERNE
BAY

Reculver

Minnis
Bay

Westgate

Broadstairs

RAMS-
GATE

Chestfield

Birchington

Dumpton
Park

21.10 RAMSGATE
to CHARING X
L1 4-4-0

19.15 CHARING X
to MARGATE
WC 4-6-2

19.12 TONBRIDGE
to MARGATE
L 4-4-0

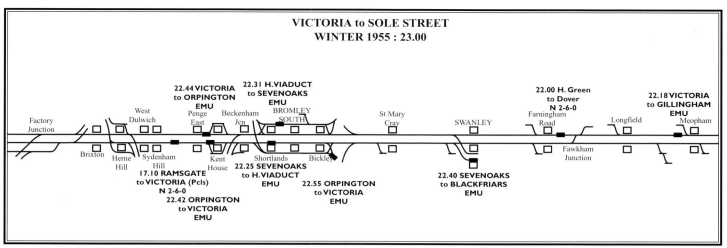

VICTORIA to SOLE STREET
WINTER 1955 : 23.00

CONTROLLER'S LOG: While other parts of British Railways are heavily involved with sleeping car services, TPO's and the like, the LCDR has the reputation of switching off for the night and being a two-shift railway. It is certainly true that the contrast between day and night is marked but it is far from true to say the line sleeps and the line position now shows

Chatham a D1 4-4-0 waits to connect with the 22.18 from Victoria and provides the last service of the day to stations beyond Gillingham. With 4-4-0's standing on the up and down sides, the atmosphere at Chatham has, in spite of the third rail, a distinctly pregrouping taste.

Quite a number of goods trains are taking advantage of the cessation in passenger activities

although the 20.00 ex Dover is relieved again at Gillingham. Frequent changes of crews makes train operating extremely difficult when the service is running awry but the train that takes the biscuit is the 22.00 Hither Green to Dover which is now passing Fawkham Junction. This service is worked by Stewarts Lane men to Chatham where they are relieved by a

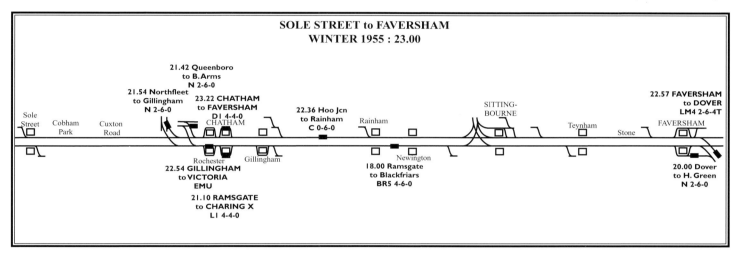

SOLE STREET to FAVERSHAM
WINTER 1955 : 23.00

far more activity than many people would give credit for.

The standard Ramsgate - Victoria service has finished for the day but the 21.10 Ramsgate to Charing Cross exists for the benefit of stragglers plus those who want to be reminded of what the North Kent line was like prior to electrification. Those prosaic souls who merely want to get to London as quickly as possible can leave the 21.10 at Gillingham and transfer to the 22.54 electric to Victoria via Sole Street. On the other side of

and chief amongst these is the 18.00 Ramsgate - Blackfriars express goods which is powered not by the usual N 2-6-0 but by the BR 5MT 4-6-0 which worked down to the coast with the 12.35 Victoria - Ramsgate express. Behind it is the 20.00 Dover to Hither Green which is attaching at Faversham and will leave shortly after the arrival of the 18.50 Dover to Hoo Junction, the latter running via Deal in order to collect trafffic at Betteshanger colliery. All three of these services are worked by Faversham men

Gillingham set who work the train the two and a half miles to Gillingham where they hand over to a Faversham crew. Finally a set of Dover men take over at Faversham and work the train to its destination. The chances of these crews being in the right place at the booked time on a foggy night when trains are all over the place are incalculable!

Good days and bad, the one element that cannot be abstracted from the Kent coast is its operating fascination - surely it has no parallel!

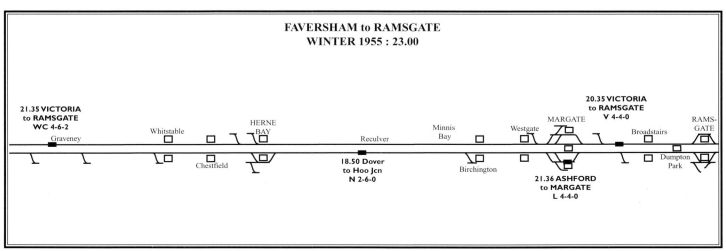

FAVERSHAM to RAMSGATE
WINTER 1955 : 23.00

PRINCIPAL LCDR ENGINE DIAGRAMS : 1955

Loco	Class	Diagram	Outward	Return
MN 4-6-2	8P	SL 2/1	09.00 Victoria - Dover Marine (10.40)	11.55 ECS Dover Marine - Folkestone. (12.10)
MN 4-6-2	8P	SL 2/2	15.50 Folkestone Jcn - Dover Marine (16.05)	18.10 Dover Marine - Victoria (19.50)
MN 4-6-2	8P	SL3	10.00 Victoria - Dover Marine (11.32)	13.05 Dover Marine - Victoria (15.05)
BR7 4-6-2	7P	SL 4	13.00 Victoria - Folkestone Jcn (14.26)	15.27 ECS Folkestone Jcn - Dover Marine (15.42)
BR7 4-6-2	7P	SL 4/2		16.58 Dover Marine - Victoria (18.30)
WC 4-6-2	7P	DVR 430/1	07.10 Dover Marine - Victoria (09.10)	12.30 Victoria - Dover Marine (14.21)
WC 4-6-2	7P	DVR 430/2	17.15 Dover Marine - Victoria (18.50)	21.00 Victoria - Dover Marine (22.40)
WC 4-6-2	7P	DVR 431	09.20 Dover P - Victoria (11.28)	14.35 Victoria - Dover P (17.06)
WC 4-6-2	7P	RAM 466	06.06 Ramsgate - Cannon St (08.28)	17.45 Cannon St - Ramsgate (20.02)
WC 4-6-2	7P	RAM 467	06.29 Ramsgate - Cannon St (08.54)	17.15 Cannon St - Ramsgate (19.12)
WC 4-6-2	7P	RAM 470/1	07.20 Ramsgate - Cannon St (09.19)	11.15 Charing X - Deal - Ramsgate (14.12)
WC 4-6-2	7P	RAM 470/2	17.05 Ramsgate - Victoria (19.05)	21.35 Victoria - Ramsgate (00.00)
WC 4-6-2	7P	RAM 471	07.35 Ramsgate - Cannon St (09.36)	16.45 Cannon St - Ramsgate (18.55)
WC 4-6-2	7P	RAM 473	08.25 Ramsgate - Victoria (10.27)	19.35 Victoria - Ramsgate (22.00)
V 4-4-0	5P	BLA 81/1	04.50 London Bge - Redhill - Margate (09.07)	12.40 Margate - Deal - Charing Cross (15.46)
V 4-4-0	5P	BLA 81/2	18.23 Cannon St - Dover P (20.53)	22.40 Dover P - Redhill - Cannon St (01.26)
V 4-4-0	5P	RAM 478	08.20 Herne Bay - Cannon St (09.56)	18.16 Cannon St - Ramsgate (20.22)
V 4-4-0	5P	RAM 481	13.55 Ramsgate - Victoria (16.20)	20.35 Victoria - Ramsgate (23.12)
BR5 4-6-0	5MT	SL 10	10.35 Victoria - Ramsgate (13.10)	16.15 Ramsgate - Victoria (19.22)
BR5 4-6-0	5MT	SL 11	11.35 Victoria - Ramsgate (14.14)	17.22 Ramsgate - Victoria (20.07)
BR5 4-6-0	5MT	SL 12	05.10 Victoria - Ramsgate (08.42)	11.15 Ramsgate - Victoria (14.10)
BR5 4-6-0	5MT	SL 13	08.35 Victoria - Ramsgate (10.56)	13.10 Ramsgate - Victoria (15.48)
BR5 4-6-0	5MT	SL 14	09.35 Victoria - Ramsgate (12.06)	15.22 Ramsgate - Victoria (18.12)
BR5 4-6-0	5MT	SL 15	12.35 Victoria - Ramsgate (15.22)	*18.00 Ramsgate - Herne Hill (00.58)*
BR5 4-6-0	5MT	SL 16	03.30 (News) Victoria - Ramsgate (07.31)	09.25 Ramsgate - Victoria (11.49)
BR5 4-6-0	5MT	SL 16	15.35 Victoria - Ramsgate (18.08)	19.45 Ramsgate - Victoria (22.26)
N 2-6-0	5F	BLA 121/1	*01.10 B. Arms - Faversham (03.59)*	*11.40 Faversham - Whitstable (11.57)*
N 2-6-0	5F	BLA 121/2	*13.20 Whitstable - Faversham (13.50)*	*16.20 Canterbury E - Blackfriars (22.30)*
N 2-6-0	5F	BLA 125/1	*01.00 B. Arms - Chatham (02.21)*	*04.22 Hoo Jcn - Hither Green (05.30)*
N 2-6-0	5F	BLA 125/2	*10.50 H. Green - Chatham (12.45)*	*23.15 Gillingham - B. Arms (02.15)*
N 2-6-0	5F	DVR 451	*14.02 Dover T - Faversham (19.18)*	*23.55 Sittingbourne - Shepherdswell (01.58)*
N 2-6-0	5F	DVR 452	*18.50 Dover T - Gillingham (02.02)*	*03.58 Chatham - Deal (09.41)*
N 2-6-0	5F	DVR 453	*03.30 Shepherdswell - Faversham (05.00)*	*06.40 Faversham - Dover T (12.05)*
N 2-6-0	5F	FV 277/1	*02.30 Faversham - Hoo Jcn (05.43)*	*08.40 Hoo Jcn - Chatham (09.02)*
N 2-6-0	5F	FV 277/2	*13.00 Sittingbourne - Dover T (16.18)*	*19.35 Shorncliffe - Faversham (00.50)*
N 2-6-0	5F	Gill 236/1	*02.15 Gillingham - Hoo Jcn (03.25)*	*03.45 Hoo Jcn - Northfleet (04.00)*
N 2-6-0	5F	Gill 236/2	*11.24 Chatham - Hoo Jcn (11.42)*	*12.50 Hoo Jcn - Grain (14.35)*
N 2-6-0	5F	Gill 236/3	*15.50 Grain - Hoo Jcn (19.38)*	*21.54 Northfleet - Chatham (23.05)*
N 2-6-0	5F	HG 172	*23.20 Hither Green - Dover T (05.35) via SER*	*11.00 Shepherdswell - Hoo Jcn (13.10)*
N 2-6-0	5F	HG 176	*22.00 H. Green - Dover T (05.25)*	*10.00 Dover T - Hoo Jcn (13.45)*
N 2-6-0	5F	SL 61/1	*01.35 Herne Hill - Faversham (04.45)*	*06.25 Faversham - Snowdown (07.25)*
N 2-6-0	5F	SL 61/2	*13.55 Snowdown - Fawkham (20.10)*	*20.22 Fawkham - Waddon Marsh (21.54)*
N 2-6-0	5F	SL 62	*05.23 Herne Hill - Dover T (02.05)*	*20.00 Dover T - Hither Green (02.42)*
N 2-6-0	5F	SL 63	07.00 Cannon St - Ramsgate (10.18)	*17.10 Ramsgate - Victoria (23.26)*
U1 2-6-0	4P	FV 260	07.42 Dover P - Chatham (09.29)	17.21 Cannon St - Dover P (20.06)
LM4 2-6-4T	4MT	DVR 450	17.09 Dover P - Chatham (18.42)	*02.28 Strood - Snowdown (04.50)*
D1 4-4-0	3P	DVR 444	06.10 Dover P - Gillingham (07.53)	16.55 Strood - Dover P. (19.01)
E1 4-4-0	3P	BLA 91	11.00 (Pcls) H. Via - Ramsgate (16.06)	19.35 Ramsgate - H. Via (23.58)
E1 4-4-0	3P	SL 45	03.00 H. Via - Ramsgate (06.10)	08.44 Ramsgate - Chatham (10.22)
E1 4-4-0	3P	SL 46/1	05.50 Cannon St - Dover P (09.11)	12.37 Dover P - Gillingham (14.06)
E1 4-4-0	3P	SL 46/2	*01.05 Sittingbourne - Herne Hill (04.08)*	
L 4-4-0	3P	RAM 489/1	04.34 Ramsgate - Chatham (06.22)	09.38 Chatham - Dover P (11.11)
L 4-4-0	3P	RAM 489/2	13.05 Dover P - Faversham (14.02)	16.11 Faversham - Ramsgate (17.19)
L 4-4-0	3P	RAM 489/3	17.36 Ramsgate - Ashford (18.47)	21.36 Ashford - Margate (22.55)
L 4-4-0	3P	RAM 490/1	07.07 Ramsgate - Gillingham (08.41)	10.46 Chatham - Faversham (11.19)
L 4-4-0	3P	RAM 490/2	13.13 Faversham - Dover P (14.10)	16.18 Dover P - Faversham (17.16)
L 4-4-0	3P	RAM 490/3		20.05 Faversham - Ramsgate (21.10)
L1 4-4-0	3P	BLA 88	16.32 Cannon St - Ramsgate (19.27)	21.10 Ramsgate - Charing X (00.29)
L1 4-4-0	3P	DVR 437	07.10 (Pilot) Dover Marine - Victoria (09.10)	21.00 (Pilot) Victoria - Dover Marine (22.40)
C 0-6-0	2F	FV 279	*12.13 Faversham - Margate (14.55)*	*15.45 Margate - Faversham (18.45)*
C 0-6-0	2F	Gill 240	*04.38 Hoo Jcn - Allhallows (06.55)*	*23.40 Herne Hill - Chatham (01.55)*

The above workings are a precis of the actual diagrams the full details of which are given in the body of the book.   Goods services are shown in italics